The No-Garden Gardener

The No-Garden GARDENER

Creating gardens on patios, balconies, terraces, and in other small spaces

JANE COURTIER

SYDNEY • AUCKLAND • CAPE TOWN

A READER'S DIGEST BOOK

Published by The Reader's Digest Association South Africa (Pty) Ltd
130 Strand Street, Cape Town 8000, South Africa

Conceived, edited and designed by
Marshall Editions Ltd
The Orangery
161 New Bond Street
London W1Y 9PA

Copyright © 1999 Marshall Editions Developments Ltd

All rights reserved. Unauthorized reproduction, whether in whole or in part, or in any manner, whether mechanical, electronic or otherwise, except as permitted under the Copyright Act or by written permission of the publisher, is prohibited.

ISBN 1-874912-97-1

Project editor	Gwen Rigby
Designer	Gary Ottewill
Picture editor	Zilda Tandy
DTP editors	Lesley Gilbert, Keith Bambury
Production	Nikki Ingram
Managing editor	Clare Currie
Art director	Sean Keogh
Editorial director	Sophie Collins
Editorial coordinator	Rebecca Clunes
Editorial assistant	Sophie Sandy

® Reader's Digest, The Digest and the Pegasus logo are registered trademarks of The Reader's Digest Association, Inc., of Pleasantville, New York, USA.

Originated in Italy by Articolor
Printed and bound in Italy by LEGO Spa

Contents

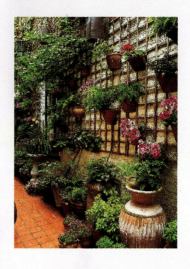

Introduction	6
About this book	9

CHAPTER ONE
Homes without gardens — 10

Examining the possibilities	12
"No-garden" situations	16
Walls, fences, alleys and walkways	20
Paths, entrances and steps	22
Balconies	24
Roof gardens	26
Enclosed gardens	28
Conservatories and garden rooms	32
Assessing your own situation	34
Urban situations	42
Special needs gardening	44

CHAPTER TWO
Design and planning — 48

The importance of design	50
Creating the illusion of space	52
Maintaining year-round interest	54
Grouping containers	56
Alpine gardens	58
Vertical gardening	60
Water gardens	67
Water features	70
Food from small areas	72
Raised beds	78
Choosing containers	82
Plant partners	86
Containers for all situations	88

CHAPTER THREE
Basic gardening — 94

How plants grow	96
Types of plant	102
Choosing plants	106
Tools and equipment	110
Growing in the ground	112
Planting techniques	114
Growing in containers	116
Plant supports	126
Training plants	130
Plant maintenance	134
Winter care	140
Propagation	142
Keeping plants healthy	150

CHAPTER FOUR
Plant directory — 156

Plants for special places	158
About the plants	168
Index	220
Acknowledgments	224

Introduction

We live in a crowded world. As populations continue to grow, our lifestyles have changed accordingly. Although commerce, business and industry have taken over from agriculture, many of us still have a desire to see things flourish that we have grown ourselves. The fact that we have chosen the benefit of living in a city or on a housing development does not mean we have lost the desire to see things grow. There is no reason at all why we cannot combine the two and provide ourselves with a very pleasant environment.

Where building land is at a premium, and city living is increasingly the norm, the maximum number of dwellings must fit into the minimum amount of space. That often means blocks of high-rise apartments and streets of close-set terrace houses where garden space may have been reduced to small yards, balconies or roof gardens.

The more crowded our living conditions become, the greater is our desire for our own space to breathe in, and to keep in touch in some small way with the natural world. Growing plants fulfils a basic, instinctive need, and it can help relieve stress by providing a calm, refreshing oasis in our busy lives.

Houseplants have rarely been more popular, but they are obviously not the whole answer for a homeowner who craves a garden to tend. While they provide welcome greenery and flowers to enhance our living space, outdoor plants give us something extra. Rather than thriving in an artificial and protected environment, they speak to us of fresh air and open spaces, sunlight and sweet summer scents. They attract birds, butterflies and a host of other small creatures, and as they flourish can give a sense of satisfaction disproportionate to their size. As they transform themselves with the changing seasons, outdoor plants remind us of the patterns of nature.

If you think all this is denied you because you don't have a garden, think again. The pleasures of growing plants are available to everyone who cares to enjoy them, no matter how restricted the available space. Even those would-be gardeners who have chosen life in upper-storey apartments, with no ground space, may be able to use window boxes, hanging baskets and wall pots to make all the difference to their outlook. House walls and boundary fences can support prolific climbers and wall plants, and the variety of containers available means that paths, patios, steps, porches, balconies and basements can become green havens.

All you need is to understand the requirements of your situation, and second to be aware of the various options open to you – which is just what this book will help you to do. In this way, you can enter into partnership with your environment, and achieve results that will not only give you great satisfaction but may also benefit the whole neighbourhood.

Gardening in a small space is both challenging and rewarding. Each plant assumes greater importance, and a true sense of achievement is gained as you raise each one to maturity. Make the most of the space you have and you'll be surprised at just how much pleasure you can get from gardening without a garden!

About this book

To help you get started, Chapters 1 and 2 discuss the basics of design and planning and suggest practical ways of making your own garden space work for you, be it a window box, a balcony or a roof garden. There are inspiring examples of "no-garden" situations, and planting plans to help you create the particular style that appeals to you.

Once you have decided how you want your garden to look, Chapter 3 provides the practical information you need to put your ideas into practice. There are step-by-step guides to all the main techniques, and a wealth of tips on propagation, plant maintainance, pests and diseases, tools, soil and buying plants.

An invaluable section called "Plants for Special Places" provides an alphabetical list of plants for special purposes. Whether you are looking for a conifer to grow in a container, some hardy groundcover, scented plants, or plants that provide year-round interest, you are sure to find something here to suit your needs.

The directory of plants lists them alphabetically by their botanical names and also gives their family and common names. Each plant's main features are described, and the species and cultivars most appropriate for growing in confined spaces are highlighted, along with information on cultivation, care and propagation.

Chapter One

Homes *without* gardens

The first step in turning your currently bare area into a special space filled with plants is to take a good, hard look at exactly what you have to work with. In this chapter we define precisely what we mean by homes without gardens and then look at the possibilities – and the resulting benefits – each situation offers. Once we have surveyed the many types of "no-garden" that can successfully be turned into plant havens (with some inspiring examples to show just what can be done), it will be time to get down to a thorough assessment of your own situation and decide what you can achieve.

There are many points to bear in mind, but this chapter will guide you through them so that you have a clearer idea of what is feasible in your position.

The wonderful examples of "no-garden" gardens shown in this book, such as this tiny flower-filled balcony, will inspire and encourage you to see the promise rather than the limitations of your situation and to create your own oasis.

Homes without gardens

Examining the possibilities

Garden: A piece of ground on which flowers etc. are cultivated; a pleasant spot; a fertile region.

(Chambers Everyday Dictionary)

For most people, the very word "garden" conjures up an image of colourful flowers, leafy trees, spreading lawns – a green and beautiful place of peace and tranquillity. In reality, very few people – particularly those living in cities – have the luxury of an expanse of land available to them. At the same time, most people don't have the time or resources to tend a large garden and are satisfied with a more modest challenge. Many gardens of restricted size present common problems – poor air and soil quality and seemingly unpromising shapes and outlooks. But it should also be realised that there is no area in which a "garden" cannot be made. The only limits are the gardener's imagination and ambition, and with ideas and some practical know-how obtained from this book, these can be unbounded.

Even in more rural areas, modern housing estates allow litttle space for gardens, and if there are communal playgrounds for children, any planting may be restricted by the need to be safe, vandal proof and low maintenance. The planting ideas that work in the inner suburbs can also be used to improve the landscape in these closely settled areas.

Where developers have been more generous with the land allotted to each home, surfaces are often paved over to avoid problems with weeds and wet-weather mud. This applies especially to apartment and townhouse developments, but increasingly front gardens in older properties, too, have vanished under tarmac to allow for off-street parking.

For the purposes of this book, homes without gardens include the obvious candidates, such as upper-storey flats that have no ground space at all, and those homes with small, hard-surfaced yards and patios, steps, porches and paths that have a little ground space but no growing space. A garden, by our definition, needs to have a reasonable area of fertile soil into which plants can be set directly, and the soil must be sufficiently deep to provide the plants with most of the water and nutrients they need to develop. If you do not possess

Limited space does not mean that you cannot grow plants. With imagination, a small flat roof can be turned into a garden; a walkway bounded by a high brick wall can be made to seem wider by the repeated use of shaped trellises and regular planting.

Examining the possibilities

such a growing area, you qualify for full membership of our club – the "no-garden" gardeners.

Having assessed that you have no garden, you may also be under the illusion that you are, therefore, unable to enjoy growing garden plants. You have probably decorated the interior of your home with an array of well-cultivated, expensive houseplants, which bring you pleasure with their lush foliage and bright flowers; these are your garden substitutes, and you may think that you will have to be satisfied with them.

But, as we will show, it is possible to garden without a garden. Situations not traditionally used for planting and growing can be made to bloom with only a small amount of skill and dedication. The rewards will certainly be worth the time spent.

Why grow plants?

There are many advantages in growing plants, even in the most challenging positions. First and foremost, there is the sheer satisfaction of raising a plant and seeing it develop and mature; this satisfaction is evident in any situation, but particularly so when the odds are stacked against you. In a "no-garden" situation you know that the plants are almost entirely dependent on you for their needs, from the soil they grow in to the last drop of water. So you can take all the credit when things go right!

In inhospitable surroundings, plants provide a contrast which makes them an even greater joy. They can offer ever-changing colour and form; the gradual development of their shape, the formation and unfolding of flower buds, the autumnal colour changes of their foliage – no non-living decoration can ever compete with these things. Many plants also have the bonus of fragrance, either from their foliage or flowers, which is even better appreciated at close quarters. And in an area of closely set housing, plants provide an easy way to give your home individuality and set it apart from its neighbours. Plants soften harsh outlines and mellow uncompromising building materials; they can also disguise flaws and imperfections and give a rapid face-lift to almost any building.

Vegetables can be grown in a hanging basket – and very decorative they are, too. And even in a tiny area, there is sometimes room for a small pond surrounded by a few flowering shrubs in containers.

A living screen

A major problem of living in densely populated areas is that of being overlooked by neighbouring dwellings. Plants can provide a perfect screen, helping to provide you with some breathing space and also privacy from your neighbours. This is probably most valuable in warm weather, when you want to open your windows and make the most of the little outdoor space you have, but evergreens will provide you with a screen all year round.

There is often a particular pleasure to be had in the seasonal changes your plants undergo, and in the challenge of keeping the display looking good at all times. Plants can also be used to hide anything you may find unsightly, allowing you to mould the scene from your windows.

The colours and perfumes of flowers are always a delight, but if you long to harvest your own home-grown food, don't

Examining the possibilities

Gardening in containers (above) means that you can grow unexpected plants side by side – here arum lilies and calamondin – and gives you the chance to add extra plants in any space that is attractive architecturally (left), but has little soil.

let lack of space deter you. Fruit and vegetables can be grown in containers with great success, and while you are not likely to produce large crops, they will give you great satisfaction. If you choose varieties carefully, you will be able to sample delicacies that are not often not available in the supermarket, and they will certainly be much fresher than anything else you are likely to eat.

Encouraging wildlife

Plants growing outside will be visited by a range of wildlife, some of which you will be more pleased to see than others. There will be pests, of course, but there will also be more welcome creatures. Bees will visit flowers for both pollen and nectar; hover flies, ladybirds, lacewings and a variety of other insects – beneficial or otherwise – will be seen. Miniature water gardens may be graced by dragonflies, and nectar-rich blooms will attract butterflies. Where plants provide cover, perching positions and a food supply in the form of berries, seeds, nectar or insects, birds will often be attracted.

It is, perhaps, especially important that children be given the chance to find out at first hand about living things, and some will enjoy the responsibility of nurturing their own pots of plants. Gardening on such a small scale will be very appealing to them, and they will not be overwhelmed as they could be by a larger area.

Elderly people, too, may find their "no-garden" easier to enjoy and much more practical when they no longer have the strength, stamina or dexterity to maintain a larger garden. This applies equally to younger people with physical limitations on their abilities.

There are few environments that cannot be improved by plants. Boost your confidence by starting with something cheap and cheerful from seed, such as nasturtiums, or a few pots of bright annuals. In this book you will find all the guidance you need on choosing plants to suit your situation and on techniques, but be prepared to experiment. No one can say exactly how a plant will react to a particular set of conditions, and you could be in for some pleasant surprises. At the very least, it will make life more interesting.

Homes without gardens

"No-garden" situations

We have broadly defined "no-gardens" as areas where there is little or no soil in which to plant. However, that still leaves a number of widely differing situations. What they all have in common is the need to overcome a restriction on space and planting possibilities. The types of situation fall conveniently into three main categories: no ground space (pp.16–19); little ground space, such as walkways and balconies (pp.20–25); and slightly larger ground space, such as roof gardens and patios (pp.26–33).

No ground space

There can be no argument that this fits the description of having no garden. It is a situation probably most typical of an upper-floor apartment, where the dwelling has no horizontal surfaces outside, apart, perhaps, from window ledges. Vertical walls have to provide all the growing space for plants.

Restricted as it is, this situation can still support an attractive plant display. Obviously, containers are essential,

Begonias, petunias and lobelia (above) have been used for this brilliantly colourful window box outside a country cottage. A similar grouping (right), but with a different colour scheme, helps to mask an unattractive outlook from a town house.

and they will have to be fairly small containers, too, which means that extra attention will need to be paid to feeding and watering. The containers must be secured firmly to the wall, not balanced on window ledges. While they may appear quite safe when the plants in them are small, they will become increasingly top-heavy as the plants grow. In hot weather compost dries out quickly and the rootball and pot become much lighter as the day goes on, so the slightest breeze or movement nearby may cause a pot to topple over. Apart from ruining your plants, this could cause injury and damage to people or property below.

A large variety of wall pots and troughs is available (*see* pp.84–85), many of which have fixing holes so that they

"No-garden" situations

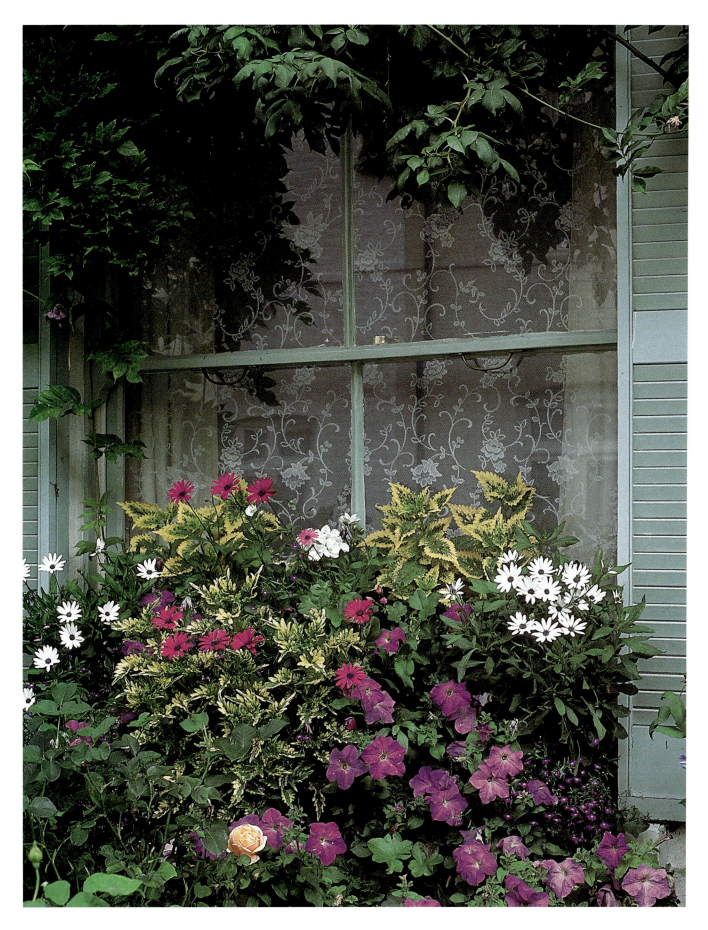

Homes without gardens

"No-garden" situations

can be screwed to the wall, but the number and position of these holes is sometimes inadequate for good support. Only small, lightweight containers are suitable for fixing directly to the wall without additional support, and adding a metal bracket beneath the container gives extra security and peace of mind. If there is a suitable drainpipe, special rings that hold small pots can usually be clipped around it.

Window boxes and hanging baskets

These often give some of the most eye-catching displays, and with careful planting can be attractive all year round. The type of window ledge and window opening needs to be taken into account when deciding on the style of window box (*see* pp.84-85) and the way it is fixed. Brackets are essential; a fully planted window box is heavy, even when lightweight materials and composts are used.

Hanging baskets are always popular, and again there are many styles available (*see* p.84–85). Because the basket is viewed in the round, it is held away from the wall on a bracket or hung from an overhead support. Don't underestimate the weight of a basket filled with compost and plants, especially when it is freshly watered. Because the security of the baskets is so important, carefully examine the wall on which they are to be fixed. Old crumbling brickwork or loose plaster will not provide good anchor points, and special equipment may be needed for cavity walls. A good DIY centre or ironmonger will be able to advise you.

Where possible, use a ladder outside the building to gain access to the wall, rather than leaning out of a window. But remember that you will need access to the containers for watering, feeding, deadheading and replanting, so you must be able to reach them easily and safely from inside – it may be safer and simpler to pay a builder to fix the brackets in place. Consider also whether you want to decorate the outside of the building for the benefit of passers-by, or whether you want to be able to see the display from inside. Remember, if you hang pots and baskets where they can be enjoyed from indoors they will cut down the amount of light entering rooms through the windows.

Walls reflect a great deal of heat, and in sunny positions plants will dry out rapidly, especially if it is windy. Little rain is likely to reach the containers, and they may need watering several times a day in hot weather. Surplus water must be free to drain away without causing a problem for people and

These large, well-grown baskets show how varied planting can be while still following the scheme of bedding plants. They use pelargoniums, busy lizzies, petunias and lobelia in hot or pale tones, taller fuchsias, and trailers like glechoma.

Hardly visible from inside the building, the hanging baskets above, uniformly massed with summer annuals, are a treat for people walking past in the street below. Watering such hanging baskets can be a problem, best solved by using a pulley to raise and lower them, or a hose lance – a rigid extension to a hose.

Troughs set on the retaining wall of this balcony and well filled with pelargoniums and petunias provide brilliant colour and extra privacy, while cascades of virginia creeper break the starkness of the white walls.

properties below, so choose containers with capacious drip trays or self-watering troughs, or hanging baskets on a pulley system that makes watering easier.

Choosing your plants

The most popular plants for wall pots, hanging baskets and window boxes are free-flowering bedding plants, with some upright specimens and trailers. You can also grow climbers, either self-clinging or supported on a trellis, but because there is relatively little soil in a container perennial climbers are likely to be short-lived, and annuals are probably better.

An advantage of smaller containers is that the plants can be replaced quite cheaply as they pass their best. Individual plants can also be removed easily if they are kept in their own pots inside a window box. Keeping wall containers attractive during a cold winter can be a challenge. The small, exposed volume of compost means plant roots are subject to damage by cold, but their sheltered position and the warmth coming through the walls should help to protect them.

AVOIDING STRUCTURAL DAMAGE

When drilling fixing holes in outside walls, use a power drill fitted with the correct size masonry bit. With brick walls, it may be safer to drill into the brickwork than into the mortar if the mortar is soft or crumbling, but if the container is going to be removed later, you will be left with a permanent hole in the brick. Making the hole in the mortar means it can be easily filled in again later.

The best fixing to use in walls is a wall plug, a type of bolt that opens up to grip the masonry as the screw is tightened. Another method is to drill holes, insert pieces of wooden doweling, then screw directly into the doweling. For extra security, fix a flat piece of wood to the wall using wall plugs and screw the bracket to the wood – this helps to spread the load. Always put any extra screws into the top of a bracket rather than the base, since it is the top that has to bear the maximum load.

Homes without gardens

Walls, fences, alleys and walkways

There is a world of difference between having only a vertical wall on which to grow your plants and having even the tiniest area of horizontal space in which to place a few containers. Even unlikely corners can be brightened up with a little imagination and some well-chosen plants.

Walls and fences

These have an important role to play in supporting wall pots and hanging baskets, but if it is possible to use the ground at the base of the wall, many more opportunities are opened up. It may be feasible to make planting holes by lifting paving slabs or breaking up small areas of concrete so that plants can be set directly into the soil at the base of the wall. This makes growing perennial plants and shrubs possible. With room for roots to spread under the hard surface, plants should have better access to nutrients and moisture and so grow larger and be easier to care for. It is often the case, however, that there is no soil to speak of under the surface, but even if you cannot import suitable soil to make a planting pocket, climbers can still be grown in containers placed against the wall. The size and weight of containers is less restricted when they are set on the ground, which allows for more ambitious planting. Shrubby wall

A narrow bed against the house wall, filled with climbing roses, bedding plants and a few plants in pots, enlivens this walkway.

plants such as pyracantha or cotoneaster and climbers like clematis, roses, parthenocissus and honeysuckle are all possibilities. Make sure that the damp-proof course is not bridged nor air vents obstructed when positioning containers.

As well as your own house wall, there may be garden walls, boundary walls, sheds and adjoining property walls which you can use to support plants. But where the structures do not belong to you, make sure you have the permission of their owners before attaching any fixings such as bolts, nails, trelliswork and so on to any wall or fence, since this could be viewed as having damaged the structure.

Alleys and walkways

Such areas are commonly found between blocks of apartments and pairs of semi-detached houses, as well as at the ends of terraces and between houses and their garages. They are designed to allow access to the rear of the properties, generally with the minimum waste of space, so they are nearly always narrow and often shaded. A through-draught is common in narrow passageways, and they tend to form wind tunnels, which can make them less than ideal places for growing plants, but this effect can be prevented or decreased by fitting a gate at one or both ends.

Where space allows, set plants in containers along the walkways, and use the walls to support climbers and wall plants: shade-lovers and foliage plants are probably the best choice. Sometimes it is possible to span the top of the walkway with timbers supported on sturdy uprights or attached to the walls to make a sort of pergola on which climbers can be trained to form a green roof. They are likely to grow more vigorously in the better light there, but they will cut down the amount of light that filters through to plants below. In sunny aspects, the shade they give may be welcome, for enclosed spaces in full sun can become uncomfortably warm as the heat is bounced off the adjoining walls.

Don't forget that the purpose of the walkway is to allow access, often for bulky loads, and it is easy to obstruct it with too many containers or overgrown plants.

Massed hydrangeas (above) fill beds at the base of the wall on each side of a door that opens straight on to the street.

Climbers and plants in a variety of pots, on the trellis and on the ground, turn an alleyway (right) into a lush, inviting garden.

Paths, entrances and steps

A path – usually leading to the front door of a house, but also sometimes to the back – is frequently flanked by railings, walls or hard-surfaced areas unsuitable for planting. Its individual shape, design and material need to be considered when deciding on how to plant it up.

The path should look pleasing, and it may be worth re-laying one that is old, damaged or simply unattractive. Depending on its width, containers of plants can line each side or be staggered along it. Spreading groundcover plants can be set at the sides if space allows, but remember that the path's primary purpose is to give access and impeding it with hummocks of creeping plants can be a hazard. If there are walls or railings beside the path, you can train climbing plants up them, but avoid prickly types whose stems may catch at passers-by, or rampant growers, which will restrict room on the path.

Clothed with creeping foliage plants, steps up to an entrance (above) blend in with their surroundings. The soft colour of the brick path, the pink geraniums and flowering shrub (left) echo the shade of the walls, creating an inviting entrance, while an eclectic selection of plant pots (right), ranged on some wooden porch steps, make an instantly appealing impression.

Entrances

Front paths and entrances are particularly important because they give visitors their first impression of your home. Typically, a front path runs straight from the pavement a relatively short distance to the front door; in this instance, the door will naturally form the focal point to which the eye is led. Planting along the path should usually reinforce this. A short path can be made to look longer by planting larger specimens near the road and decreasing the size of plants and their containers as they approach the door, while smaller plants at the front and larger plants closest to the door will make the entrance appear more imposing and give it extra emphasis. Formality is often favoured in this situation, with symmetrical planting either side of the doorway and path; a pair of identical standard plants, such as bay, are favourite subjects to stand guard at each side of the entrance.

Steps

The entrance to a house sometimes consists of a flight of steps, whether it is going up to the front door or down to a lower level or basement. The tiered arrangement is ideal for displaying plants, and groups of containers placed here are attractive. Keep them well to the sides of the steps and take care that they do not make access to the handrail difficult.

Back paths and porches

At the back of the house, the path will usually be viewed from the building. There is unlikely to be an obvious focal point at the far end, so interest will be centred on the path itself, and since this area is more frequently viewed by the homeowner than the passer-by, a less formal approach is often better. Although the main object with small spaces is normally to make them appear larger, a long narrow area may benefit from some foreshortening by placing staggered groups of plants on the path, rather than emphasizing its narrowness by setting plants along each side.

By framing the door with greenery and flowers, planting can be used to emphasize the path's arrival at the house. There is usually the opportunity to spread upwards, using the house walls, and there may be a porch that climbers can scramble over. If this is simply a roof attached to the doorway by brackets, it will bear less weight than if it is supported by uprights, so choose the plants carefully, avoiding very dense, vigorous specimens. Plants with scented flowers or aromatic foliage are ideal here, and they will also make it a pleasant place to sit on a mild evening.

Paths, entrances and steps

Homes without gardens

Balconies

The ornate woodwork forms an attractive frame for the troughs and hanging baskets on this balcony. Although it is too small to sit on, chairs set just inside the double doors would be almost as good.

Although balconies are most often a feature of apartments, houses may also have balconies on upper storeys, especially if there is a good view to be enjoyed. Some balconies are constructed primarily to afford access to the outside of the building for maintenance; these are usually narrow, with just enough room to step out on to them. Others feature as an extra room, with enough space for several people to sit outside comfortably.

The construction of the balcony must be taken into account when deciding what plants you can grow there; the most important aspect is its load-bearing capacity. It may be of a cantilevered design, jutting out from the building with no visible means of support; it may be supported by pillars or posts from ground level, or be built as a flat roof to a room below. A supported balcony usually looks safer to the unqualified eye, but this is not necessarily the case, and if you have any doubts about a balcony's load-bearing capacity you should arrange for a structural engineer to inspect it.

Although perhaps not as attractive as terracotta or glazed pottery containers, plastic pots are much lighter and so are more suitable for use on a balcony garden.

The floor of the balcony should be waterproof, particularly if there is living space immediately below. And since there is likely to be considerably more run-off where regular watering is taking place than from a balcony on which there are no plants, you should check that provision for drainage is adequate. Take particular care if the living space below does not belong to you, since you will be held responsible for any damage to the property caused by your activities. Third-party insurance cover should be arranged, and you should check that your balcony garden is covered by your own house and contents insurance. If the property is rented, it is always a good policy to obtain the landlord's agreement to your proposals first.

If the balcony of a reasonably modern dwelling is large enough to be used as a living area, with access through full-length doors, it is fairly safe to assume that it has been constructed to a sufficiently high standard to be used as a container garden. On older properties, however, this may not be the case; building standards were lower, and wear and tear may have weakened the structure further.

Lightweight materials

However sturdy the balcony, it makes sense to keep the load to a minimum by using lightweight plastic containers rather than terracotta, and soilless composts rather than soil-based types. But these have their drawbacks; soilless composts require more frequent watering, and you may need to secure the containers to the floor or walls to prevent them being blown over. Remember that freshly watered compost weighs considerably more than that which is just moist, and that as plants grow they will not only weigh more themselves but will demand increasing amounts of water. It may be tempting to construct soil beds on the balcony rather than to use containers, but the extra weight, plus drainage problems and the risk of damage to the property through penetrating damp, make this a less desirable option.

The more attractive you make the balcony, the more use it is likely to get and the greater the potential for accidents. Before using any balcony as a mini-garden, check the surrounds. These may be solid walls, but railings are common; on older properties particularly, they may not be safe – make sure the space between them is not wide enough for a child to squeeze through. Toughened glass can be used as a safety barrier that will not cut out light or detract from the view.

As with any situation in which ground space is limited, climbing plants are valuable, but because many balconies are exposed to strong winds, supports for climbers need to be well secured. Keep the plant growth thinned so that wind can filter through; if wind meets a solid wall of foliage the plants and their supports are likely to be blown down.

Tempting though it may be to fill your entire balcony area with plants, try to leave enough space for a couple of chairs and a table so that you can sit out and enjoy your surroundings.

Make sure that containers can be moved fairly easily so that access to the outside of the building is still possible, and resist the temptation to balance pots on the edges of surrounding walls or railings. Sooner or later they will fall off, and they are almost bound to do some damage in the process.

Homes without gardens

Roof gardens

Skilfully sited supports and planting help to mask unattractive features without obstructing the fine view from this roof garden.

Some city dwellers are lucky enough to have a slightly larger ground space to cultivate. A flat roof, for instance, offers a tempting prospect for making a garden, and roof gardens can be spectacularly successful, often offering a degree of privacy difficult to find elsewhere in a densely populated urban location. The sheer unexpectedness of a plant haven so far from the ground gives it the feeling of an oasis, a truly secret garden.

Who does the roof belong to?

A flat roof often tops a block of apartments, and the first step is to find out who owns the roof and/or is responsible for its maintenance. Before going further you will need to come to an arrangement with all the interested parties. The other occupants of the block may be more than happy to allow you sole use of the roof in return for taking the responsibility for its upkeep, or they may wish to share the roof garden, with everyone contributing to the expenses. Either way, you will need to take legal advice and arrange suitable insurance cover for both yourself and third parties.

Much of what has already been said about balconies also applies to roof gardens. The roof may have been constructed with a garden in mind, but it is more likely that you will want to convert a currently unused roof.

Gaining access

Take a good look at the access. It may be fairly simple to clamber out on to the roof, but will you be able to carry equipment and plants up to it? And how about a watering containers? The expense of installing a tap and water supply to the roof is probably a wise investment, and you should also consider installing a power supply if you want to use the roof garden in the evening.

The roof surface must be waterproof and in good repair. Under a roof garden it will probably have to stand up to more

A feeling of space, of two "rooms", is created here by the contrast between the shadowy wall and the sunny seating area.

Roof gardens

On this roof garden, shaped trelliswork and raised beds filled with shrubs and climbing plants help to hide an unsightly wall and drainpipe.

wear and tear than was envisaged when it was laid. Check the drainage, and ensure that nothing you do will impede it. Options for suitable flooring material range from conventional or lightweight paving slabs to gravel, shredded bark, artificial turf and attractive timber decking.

Windbreaks

Because the garden will be relatively high up, strong winds are likely to damage plants and fittings, and accelerate moisture loss. Some form of windbreak will improve this, often in combination with a wall extension, which for safety reasons should reach at least waist height. The barrier can take the form of brickwork, screenwalling or railings; above this height, trelliswork to support climbing plants, or wind-resistant hedging plants can provide shelter. Toughened glass panels, professionally installed, are also excellent, or you can use small-mesh screening on the windward side only.

Weight distribution

Raised beds of soil are possible on a roof garden, but, as with balconies, weight distribution and drainage problems usually make containers a better option. Wooden pallets help to spread the load of large and heavy containers. It is always a good idea to raise containers off the ground, both for good drainage and to prevent root growth emerging unnoticed through the base of the pot and damaging the roof surface. Ask a structural engineer to advise you on load bearing, and also to identify, if possible, where the load-bearing supports are so that you can set the heaviest items in the safest place.

The patterned paved floor is in itself an attractive feature of this sunny roof garden, which leads down to the one shown above.

Homes without gardens

Enclosed gardens

An enclosed patio can be crowded with plants, as if it were an outdoor conservatory, to be viewed from inside the house.

Alternatively, it can be a secluded corner in which to sit in the sun and enjoy a few plants specially chosen for their scent and colour.

A paved area, usually adjoining the house, a patio is a place for relaxation and enjoyment. It may form a small part of a larger garden, but often the patio is all there is – a self-contained area which becomes a "patio garden".

Patio gardens

Especially where boundary walls provide shelter from the wind, enclosed patios can often be suntraps. The paved surface reflects the sun's warmth and the temperature inside the patio garden can be much higher than that outside. This can present difficult conditions for plants, which may suffer from moisture stress and sun scorch, and in warm, sunny climates some form of shade is essential. Pergolas or similar structures over which vines, roses or wisteria can climb offer both shelter from wind and pleasant dappled shade below. Where a patio garden is not on the sunny side of the house, high walls can cast permanent shade and it can be a delightful cool retreat in which to relax at the end of a busy day in the city. Although the choice of plants is more restricted, some choice specimens need shade to grow well.

Enclosed gardens

The formal design of this courtyard is emphasised by the central fountain and pool, clipped evergreens and palms in pots.

Courtyard gardens

The distinction between a courtyard and a patio is rather blurred. Originally a courtyard was a square or rectangular open space entirely surrounded by buildings; modern "courtyard developments" are based on the same principle. A courtyard is always regular in shape and often has a central feature. It usually has a hard surface, such as paving or gravel, and is always surrounded by walls.

Formality is the keynote; symmetrical planting schemes, traditional-style containers and ornaments, standard plants, clipped topiary and regulated colour schemes all help to give the right effect. A small pool, fountain or tree makes an excellent central focal point; a sundial, birdbath, striking ornament or well-planted container would also look good.

This traditional courtyard garden at the centre of a house is complete with trees, classical ornaments and a stone birdbath.

Homes without gardens

Enclosed gardens

Basements

An area that lies below the level of its surroundings, a basement is generally found where a house is built on sloping ground: part of the higher side of the slope is dug out to enable full use to be made of the lower floor. The size of the basement area can vary considerably but it is rarely large; it may be big enough for access down a flight of steps, or it may simply allow light through a single window.

Basements are usually a feature of older houses or possibly apartment blocks, and are inclined to be depressing and gloomy if the aspect is sunless, dank and damp. If family living rooms or the kitchen look out on a basement, then it certainly needs to be given a cheerful outlook. Because it is a sunken area, there is bound to be less light than at ground level, and what light there is decreases as the depth of the basement increases.

Plants grown in such a position are likely always to be reaching upward for light, and many sun-loving plants will probably fail entirely, but there are plenty of attractive shade-tolerant subjects to choose from. Lacy ferns and dramatic foliage plants enjoy the shade and will give the area a lush beauty. The low light levels can often be greatly improved by painting the walls white or a light colour; the floor can also be painted with floor paint, covered with light-coloured stone chippings or gravel, or resurfaced with suitable paving slabs.

Add colour each season by bringing in pots of flowers in full bloom. If there is a brighter outside area, container plants can be rotated, giving them a fairly short spell to cheer up the basement before bringing them back up to better conditions to recuperate. It may also be possible to supplement the natural light with some form of artificial lighting.

Small spreading plants set in holes in the paving give a charming chequerboard effect to this yard. The white-painted fence and cheerful planting have transformed an otherwise dreary area into a bright, airy space in which to relax.

SHARED GARDENS

Communal open spaces are increasingly becoming a feature of some housing estates. Attractively planted areas make the houses more desirable, but they can often be frustrating for would-be gardeners. Usually contractors are employed to maintain the gardens, and because the landscape has been carefully planned, owners are often prevented from taking any part in the planting schemes. Sometimes they are allowed to tend their immediate "gardens", but with strict limitations on the size and type of plants that may be used, or the structures that may be erected.

Before buying such a property, check any limitations on your gardening activities. It is intensely disappointing to discover, too late, that you can play no part in maintaining or improving your surroundings when they may be what attracted you initially.

Enclosed gardens

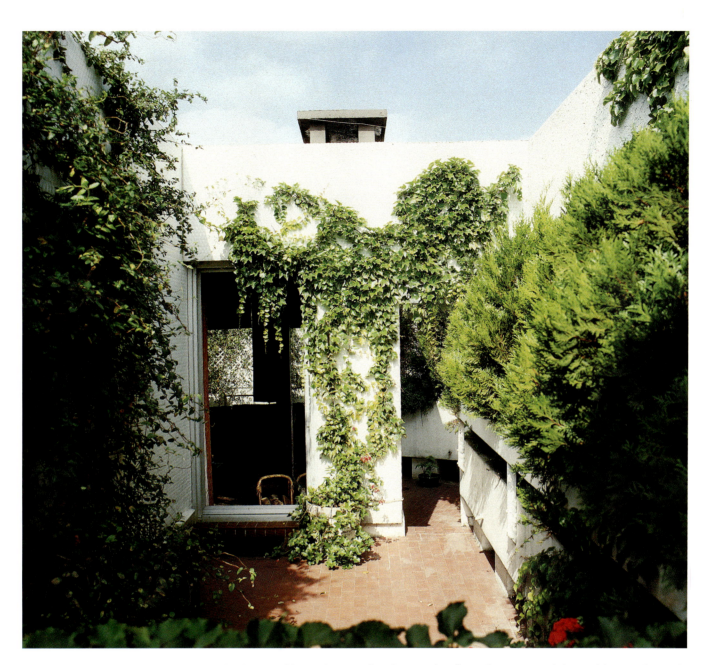

In a warm climate, a basement area such as this, with creeper-clad walls and overhanging bushes, makes a safe, cool place for children to play.

Water can also be a problem. The proximity of the building to the growing area may prevent useful amounts of rain reaching plants, and yet the basement could receive sufficient run-off to cause flooding. Flooding can also be caused by over-enthusiastic watering. Efficient drainage is, therefore, essential to prevent damp from penetrating the house. In addition, drain holes must not be blocked by dead leaves, soil or containers full of plants.

On the plus side, basements have ready-made supports for plants in the form of walls which can be covered in climbers, and they are sheltered from wind, forming true "sunken gardens". But bear in mind that cold air sinks, and will tend to settle in low-level areas, making them unsuitable for tender plants in regions with cold winters.

Yards

Sometimes concreted and surrounded by walls or fencing, a city backyard is often no more than a place for dustbins and a washing line. As with a basement, simply painting the walls in light colours and breaking up a concrete floor and, if the yard is small, replacing it with paving can make a tremendous improvement. Climbing plants and shrubs in containers can be trained on the walls, plants on trelliswork can screen sheds and bins, and a timber pergola covered with climbers will provide privacy and a pleasant spot in which to sit.

Homes without gardens

Conservatories and garden rooms

An increasingly popular feature of homes today is the "conservatory", often simply a light, airy, extra room for family use, complete with carpets and soft furnishings. This is a long way from the conservatory's original purpose as a type of ornate greenhouse attached to the home primarily for growing plants, usually exotic species that required warmth and shelter, and a lot of expert care.

A conservatory may be made from plastic, wood or metal, and has glass walls, usually to ground level, and generally a transparent roof as well. Because the conservatory is in frequent use by people, the glass should be reinforced for safety. In very sunny climates, the roof may be solid. As a general rule, conservatories are "add-ons". Their position is often dictated by aspect – a sunny site is preferable – but they tend to be more common at the back of a house than the front.

Converting an indoor room

If you inherit a conservatory, you may need to convert it from an indoor room to a garden room. A suitable floor is essential; paving slabs, stonework, bricks or gravel will give the strongest garden feel, while quarry or ceramic tiles give a "halfway house" effect. Make sure that the flooring will stand up to reasonable amounts of water and that there is efficient drainage. You can rely entirely on groups of container plants, or if the room is designed more as a greenhouse, planting beds can be made in the floor or raised beds can be constructed.

The good light, warmth from the sun and shelter from wind make a conservatory the perfect place for growing plants. Nearly all plants – not just exotic or tender species – will flourish in such conditions. As in all confined spaces, care must be taken to choose suitable plants, and to keep them under control. When choosing plants, don't be too ambitious. Trees and vigorous shrubs are best confined to containers. Small shrubs, perennials and bedding plants can safely be grown in beds around the edge, but remember that they are likely to make much larger, faster-growing plants than they would in the open garden. Take advantage of the protected position to try some choice, slower-growing and dwarf varieties. In cold areas it is tempting to use the conservatory to grow tender plants, but you will usually need heating to bring them safely through the winter.

Shade and ventilation

While the warmth of the conservatory will be appreciated in the winter and at each end of the growing season, in summer the problem will be too much heat. Shading is essential; roller blinds for the roof and walls are the easiest method, but can be expensive. Paint-on shading materials are cheap but unattractive. Climbers on trelliswork can be effective, since as the season progresses they will grow to provide increasing shade when it is needed.

Good ventilation is essential, too. There should be opening vents in the roof as well as in the side walls; have them fitted as extras if necessary. Doors opening to the outside are also useful for ventilation, even if there is virtually nowhere to step out to. Fresh air is needed to prevent overheating, and it will maintain the buoyant atmosphere required for healthy plant growth. It will also enable you to feel that you are sitting in a protected garden rather than an exotic hothouse.

Screen houses

A screen or shade house – a treated timber structure to which wire screening is stapled – is generally a feature of warmer climates. It is like a conservatory, with light-filtering shadecloth replacing the glass, and can vary from a small porch to a sizeable room. The mesh affords minimal protection from the weather, but it does cut down wind and offer shade from strong sun, making a protected spot for growing and enjoying plants – and it will keep out insects. The floor, often made from timber as well, should slope so that water will drain away from the house.

The wooden slatted walls and roof of this garden room (right) are made of removable sections and provide welcome shade, creating a haven in which you could even grow tender, exotic plants for cut flowers, such as these strelitzias (also known as bird of paradise or crane flowers).

Homes without gardens

Assessing your own situation

Once you have decided that you are going to make the best of the space you have for growing plants, you need to think carefully about exactly how you are going to do it. No two situations are exactly the same; even if your circumstances are very similar to those of your neighbour, you will probably have quite different ideas and capabilities. It helps to sit down with a notebook and work your way through a list of exactly what you have, and what you would like (or feel you are able) to do with it. The smaller the space, the more precious it becomes, and the less tolerant you are likely to be of mistakes and wasted effort.

First, outline the basic facilities you have, then make a note of what you would like to achieve. Go on to make more detailed notes about your own situation – on the following pages we will go through several of the points you need to bear in mind, some of which may not immediately occur to you. When you have done this, go back to your original objectives and see if you need to adjust them or would like to add to them in light of the information you have gathered. It's well worth spending quite a bit of time on this, since it is often the case that the smaller the space, the more planning is needed.

What space do you have?

Which of the three main categories we have covered fits your "no-garden" best – no ground space, a small amount of ground space, or slightly larger ground space? Make a note of exactly what it is – balcony, patio garden, roof garden and so on – and its overall size. If applicable, look into its load-bearing capacity and structural details, getting expert advice where necessary. (It helps to have a good idea of what you would like to do with the area so that you can discuss all the possibilities with the structural engineer.)

How much time do you have?

You may be able to do "little and often" on a daily basis, or have only a few hours at weekends. How much interest do you have in gardening? Do you want to spend a lot of time on challenging plants and situations, or are you more concerned with getting the maximum results for the minimum of effort?

You may lack confidence in your horticultural skills and want to start with something quick and simple, moving on to more "difficult" subjects as your experience increases, or you may already be a skilled gardener who has had to give up a larger garden and wants to make the most of the possibilities now available.

What do you want?

There are many good reasons for growing plants around your home. You may agree with some or all of those that have been mentioned, or you may have a different set of requirements. It will help to avoid mistakes if you have a clear idea of your aims and your likes and dislikes; to help you think it through, the main points to consider are set out below.

POINTS YOU SHOULD CONSIDER

COLOUR In a small space it is usually far more telling to decide on a colour theme than to mix plants at random. If you want somewhere to relax, flowers in soft pastel shades may suit you, or even the ultimate in calming colour schemes, a white garden. Pure white flowers gleaming against soft green foliage are particularly effective in the evening light. Hot colours – brilliant scarlets, oranges and yellows – give a quite different effect to cool blues, purples, greens and white.

FOLIAGE Flowers are not the only decorative feature of plants. Apart from the many shades of green, grey, cream, blue, purple, red, yellow and orange that exist in foliage, there are the shapes and textures of the leaves to take into account – the large, bold hand-shapes of fatsia; cool, frilly ferns; spiky phormiums; succulent sedum; the delicate filigree of steely blue rue. Some leaves, such as those of soft, velvety lamb's ears, *Stachys byzantina*, beg to be touched; others, like prickly hollies and tooth-edged agaves, warn you off.

SCENT In a small area this is even more enjoyable than in a large garden. Jasmine, honey-scented petunias, philadelphus and butterfly-attracting buddleja are some of the scents of summer. Shrubby honeysuckles, witch hazel, daphne, violets, viburnum and chimonanthus give off amazingly powerful fragrances on cold winter days. Foliage can be strongly aromatic, especially when bruised or rubbed;

Assessing your own situation

Create your "no-garden" to suit your lifestyle, but remember to leave enough space among the plants so that you can sit out and enjoy it.

choisya, perovskia, myrtle, rosemary, pelagonium, artemisia and many others have fascinating spicy scents.

TIME OF DAY The hours when your "no-garden" is most often used may influence you. Perhaps bright morning sun makes it the ideal place to have breakfast, or maybe you want a place in which to sit out in the evening, when you come home from work. If evenings are important, fragrant, night-opening flowers such as ornamental tobacco (*Nicotiana*) and Virginian stock (*Malcomia maritima*), are more appropriate than those that fold their petals as soon as the sun leaves them. Some form of soft artificial lighting will greatly extend your use of the area.

SEASONAL INTEREST Although summer is the most obvious time to enjoy plants, you may also want to plan your scheme so that it is pleasing all year round. Once the summer-flowering plants have faded, do you put the gardening tools away until next spring? Or do you want to extend your gardening into autumn and winter, with containers of shrubs for autumn leaf colour, autumn-flowering plants, evergreens with bold foliage for pleasure throughout the year, and winter-flowering bulbs?

SCREENING Protection from neighbours or overlooking windows may be valuable to you, and the positioning of tall plants and climbers can help greatly. If your "no-garden" area is in full sun, plants or a pergola to provide shade in the warmest weather will be important. And will your plants be viewed mainly from inside or outside the house? It will make all the difference to the way you arrange them.

Homes without gardens

Assessing your own situation

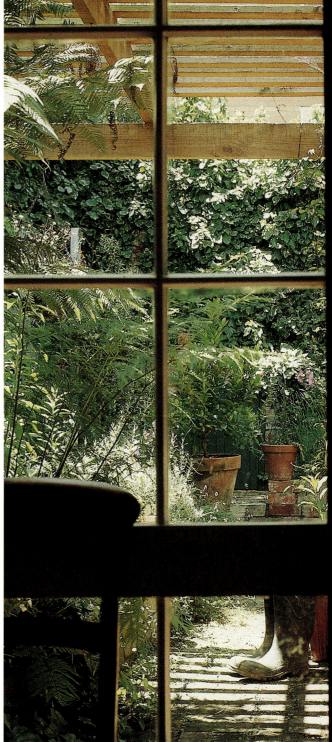

Aspect and light

All plants need light to grow. If deprived of light entirely, the plant will lose its chlorophyll and the leaves and stems will become creamy white instead of green. More importantly, this will prevent the plant from manufacturing food, and it will eventually die.

In a narrow passageway, set flowering plants where they will benefit from whatever sun shines into the area. Climbing plants will reach upwards for the light they need to thrive.

Few plants are faced with complete darkness, but the amount, duration and quality of light does vary greatly from one position to another, and the growth of plants will suffer progressively if the light they receive is not adequate. Small areas are more likely to suffer from lack of light than larger ones because the surrounding objects that block out light remain the same height and cast the same amount of shade regardless of the size of the plot. So the smaller plot receives a far greater proportion of shade than a large plot in a similar situation.

If your "no-garden" is shaded or partially shaded, you will need to know the extent of the problem. Draw a rough scale-diagram and note the direction in which the plot faces. Sketch the position and extent of the shade at different times of the day, say 9am, noon, 3pm and 6pm. (If possible, carry this out in all four seasons, but the main growing season is obviously the most important time.) You may find that some areas are in constant shadow, whereas others receive several hours of sun at different times of the day.

Density of shade

Even in an area which receives no direct sun, the depth of shade can be quite variable. Density of shade is difficult for the human eye to judge accurately, and a photographic light meter is useful for discovering just how gloomy the different parts of your growing space are. A plot which appears to be

Assessing your own situation

An area that gets too much sun can be turned into a cool green retreat during hot weather with a slatted roof built over part of it and a large tilting garden umbrella to provide shade all day.

more or less evenly shaded can, in fact, have much lighter and darker areas within it and this can be important when it comes to positioning the plants.

Shade can be cast by surrounding buildings, fences and walls, shrubs, hedges and trees. It may be possible to remove some obstacles to allow more light through; even if they don't belong to you, you may find the owners happy to cooperate if approached in the right way. Trees can be lopped or thinned; hedges and fences can be lowered. Buildings and high walls are obviously permanent features, but painting walls white or in light colours, or even fixing a mirror in a suitable position, can improve the overall brightness.

Plants vary considerably in the amount of light they need to remain healthy; as a general rule, those with silver, blue or variegated foliage need bright, sunny conditions and will not thrive in a gloomy situation. Silver plants tend to be covered in fine hairs that are meant to protect them from too much sun in their native climates; variegated plants may grow satisfactorily in shade but they tend to lose their leaf markings and become plain green. Other plants are well adapted to low light levels, and these are the ones to choose (*see* p.162).

Light from one side

Many small areas, and balconies in particular, suffer from a one-sided light source. Plants grow towards the light, and you will soon find your plants leaning in that direction. This spoils their appearance and makes plants in containers more likely to topple over. To keep the plants upright and bushy, turn the containers a quarter-turn every few days. Those plants that are in the ground or in raised beds can sometimes be evened-up by careful pruning, but a strongly one-sided light source will always produce plants that grow towards it.

Too much sun

The suntrap patio or balcony can be an inhospitable place. Constant, bright sun can be almost as much of a problem as excessive shade, causing delicate foliage to become scorched and compost and plants to dry out rapidly. Fortunately, the problem is usually more easily solved than that of too much shade and it may only be temporary – when seedlings require protection at the beginning of the season, for example.

Once again, note the direction the area faces and the times when it receives the strongest, hottest sun. You can then fix shading to give some relief to the plants when they most need it. A trellis covered with climbers, bamboo fencing, wattle hurdles, awnings or some type of shadecloth could all be used.

As with shady areas, the choice of plants is important (*see* p.163). In a sun-baked plot you can grow sun lovers that are well protected against drying out and scorch, and these often have the bonus of brilliantly coloured flowers. Don't be misled, however, into thinking that you can automatically grow exotic, tender subjects; you may have sufficient sun, but bear in mind the plants' minimum temperature requirements as well. Just because the area is hot on sunny summer days doesn't necessarily mean it is mild enough for tender plants during the colder seasons.

Assessing your own situation

The brilliant scarlet berries of hardy, evergreen skimmia persist throughout the winter, and even the white spring flowers will endure sharp frost.

Climate

There are two ways in which to consider the climate of your gardening space – the macroclimate, or the prevailing weather conditions in the part of the world in which you live, and the microclimate, the climate of your immediate surroundings.

The big picture

When you are growing plants in a very small space, a lot of human intervention is needed to ensure that they survive, and this reduces the effect that the natural climate has upon their growth. For example, few small-space gardeners would rely on rainfall to supply all their plants' water requirements. However, one natural element that retains its importance is temperature, particularly when there is a likelihood of the plants being exposed to frost. Each plant species has its own optimum temperature range for growth; outside this range growth will slow down or even stop, although the plant remains alive. There are degrees of susceptibility to frost damage.

HARDY PLANTS These will survive frosts, generally in a dormant state; their branches, and sometimes their foliage, have natural protection against cold weather. Other plants may have their topgrowth killed, but the roots will survive underground to produce new shoots the following spring. Some species will survive short spells of temperatures just below freezing but may be killed by repeated or prolonged frosts, or by temperatures that dip more sharply. You will occasionally see plants described as "dubiously hardy", meaning that sometimes they survive low temperatures, sometimes they don't – it's a matter of luck.

There are hardy plants which will not themselves be harmed by frosts but which nevertheless can have their display spoiled. The waxy, pink-white chalices of magnolia blossoms are reduced to an unappealing brown mush by late spring frosts, and if one cold night turns the centres of strawberry blossoms black you can wave goodbye to fruit in the summer.

TENDER PLANTS For certain plants, temperatures that drop to freezing or below spell death; water in the cells expands as it freezes, rupturing the cell walls, and the plant tissue collapses. Such plants are known as tender, frost-tender or non-hardy. In an area which is subject to frosts, tender plants can be grown later in the season, once the risk is over. The average date of the last frost for your area can usually be obtained from the local weather centre, but this will vary quite widely from one year to another, and you should allow plenty of leeway before putting tender plants outdoors. Most tender bedding plants you buy will have been raised in a greenhouse, where conditions are warmer and more protected than those outside. Putting them straight outdoors can check their growth severely or even kill them, and they must be gradually acclimatized. This usually means putting them, in their containers, first in a sheltered spot outside (bringing

Plants that would usually be grown as houseplants, such as Swiss cheese plant, Monstera deliciosa and Fatsia japonica, can flourish in a small sheltered patio, which may be several degrees warmer than an adjoining open garden.

Assessing your own situation

A narrow basement area, filled with plants in hanging baskets, shows how an unpromising space can be clothed in green. The large mirror in the bathroom cleverly doubles the impact.

artificial heat leaks from even well-insulated buildings during winter; and brick and stone buildings absorb the sun's warmth during the day and give it out at night like giant storage heaters. Town plots tend to be surrounded by walls and buildings which protect them from wind and give them shelter. This may well extend the growing season at both ends, and, if you have a particularly sheltered place, your microclimate may allow you to coax some of the more exotic plants into a good display.

A basement or patio that is in constant shade will be much cooler than one receiving at least some direct sun. Ironically, the most sheltered gardens are also sometimes the most prone to frost damage. Cold air behaves like water, flowing down hills and sinking to lower levels. If it cannot escape from the area – if it is stopped in its downwards movement by a brick wall, say – the cold air is trapped and the site becomes a frost pocket, making plants within it more prone to damage than in neighbouring areas.

BALCONIES, ROOF GARDENS AND HANGING BASKETS
On upper storeys these can be very exposed; temperatures may be lower overall and the wind will dry plants out and damage foliage and flowers.

them indoors at night if possible), then leaving them out night and day, and finally moving them to their more exposed final growing positions. The process is called hardening-off, and usually takes about a week or 10 days.

In temperate zones, some warmth-loving plants will survive the summer outdoors, but never achieve their full potential because the temperatures are not high enough or the season is too short. Usually they fail to flower or fruit, but this may not be important if their foliage or habit of growth is sufficiently attractive on its own.

Your own microclimate:

There is no substitute for personal experience when it comes to microclimates and it is worth buying a maximum/minimum thermometer and keeping a year-round record of temperatures, weather conditions and other information on plant performance in your plot.

SMALL YARDS, BASEMENTS AND PATIOS Especially in built-up areas, these often have a distinct microclimate. Cities and towns tend to be several degrees warmer than the surrounding countryside for several reasons: industrial and commercial processes release waste heat into the atmosphere;

The spring-flowering Japanese quince, **Chaenomeles japonica**, *and Dutch hyacinths, grown here against a wall, will benefit from the microclimate created by the protection afforded by the wall and the warmth radiating from it.*

Assessing your own situation

The water supply

All plants need water to grow. In the wild, this is supplied by rain, but in "no-garden" situations natural rainfall is unlikely to be sufficient. Plants grown in small areas or against walls are usually sheltered from rain and the water doesn't reach their roots. Plants are also more likely to be in containers, which hold only a small volume of soil and so have a limited capacity for water storage. Vigorously growing plants will soon fill their containers with roots, decreasing the space for water while at the same time increasing the demand.

Hand in hand with water goes humidity – the amount of water vapour in the air. Most plants grow better in relatively humid conditions than in dry air, and even when sufficient water is available to the roots through the compost, the atmosphere can remain uncomfortably dry for them.

When to water

Water is becoming an increasingly valuable resource and you should try to ensure it is not wasted. The best times to water are in the early morning and the evening. Watering plants in full sun can lead to leaf scorch, since water droplets on foliage act like magnifying lenses, intensifying the sun's rays; the water will also evaporate more quickly and be wasted. But if plants show signs of wilting, they should be watered as quickly as possible, even if they are in the sunshine.

Many containers will need watering three times a day in hot, sunny weather. The "no-garden" gardener will, therefore, find watering a constant task, and the easier it can be made, the better. If daily watering entails frequent trips from the plants through the living room to the kitchen in order to refill watering cans, it will soon become a hated chore. And many kitchen and bathroom sinks are simply not designed for filling large containers. Wherever possible a tap should be installed close to the plants; this is particularly relevant for roof gardens, where the water must be carried upwards.

Watering can be carried out by means of cans, hoses or a permanent watering system. For a fairly small number of plants, a watering can is sufficient. Choose one that is well balanced and not too heavy when full. Check that it will fit easily under your tap. A long curved spout makes it simpler to get the water where you want it and a rose will be useful for watering some plants. Hoses make watering quicker and easier, but it can be difficult to control the supply. Fitting a watering gun that allows you to switch off the supply will help, but make sure you buy a good-quality hose and use well-designed fittings to connect the hose to the tap and the gun to the hose, or the pressure could burst the hose or blow it off the tap. The ultimate in labour-saving devices is an automated watering system.

Computer-controlled systems are available to carry out watering in your absence – a boon if you are often away. Simpler seep-hose or sprinkler systems can be set up permanently among the plants, ready to be attached to a tap and turned on as required, or used with a timer. There are also "self-watering" containers, which generally incorporate a reservoir of water and a wick system to keep the compost moist.

You can help to minimize water use by growing plants that need little water, such as hardy daisies, geraniums and echeveria (right), and by mixing water-retaining granules with the compost.

Drainage

Although drying out is a major problem with plants in containers, the compost must not remain saturated – efficient drainage is necessary to enable air to penetrate to the roots. Moisten the compost thoroughly, right to the base of the pot, then allow the excess water to drain away. Think about where this water will go, and whether it is likely to cause inconvenience or damage to your own or neighbouring properties; drips from hanging baskets and wall pots can be particularly troublesome. You may need to consider some form of drainage system.

Subsidence

Plants growing too close to buildings can cause all sorts of problems in small gardens, but the main ones occur where trees are grown directly in garden soil. If this is a certain type of clay, the large volume of moisture removed from it by a tree or large bush can cause the soil to shrink, leading to subsidence and cracking of nearby buildings. Removing the offending tree does not necessarily help; the sudden increase in the amount of soil water can cause the soil to heave, which will have to more or less the same effect on the buildings.

Plants grown in containers are safe unless the roots penetrate the soil beneath the container; raising containers off the ground slightly makes this less likely and also improves drainage. Wall plants and climbers set into soil at the base of walls are unlikely to cause damage because neither their root systems nor leaf area are extensive enough to make sufficient difference to the moisture levels of the soil.

Homes without gardens

Urban situations

Many "no-gardens" are likely to be in densely populated areas, and this brings its own problems. Our territorial instinct becomes intensified when we don't have all that much territory of our own, and our defence of it often leads to surprisingly aggressive behaviour. Trouble arises both when we feel our territory is being encroached upon, and when our neighbours feel that we are encroaching upon them.

Avoiding trouble

Boundaries are a common cause of contention. Where possible, check the legal ownership of boundary walls and fences; this should appear on your property deeds. If ownership is not clear, it is a good idea to ask neighbours whether they object to your attaching plant supports or other fixtures to your side of a party wall. Remember that if your plants cause damage to property that is not your own, you could be liable to pay compensation; climbing plants have been known to damage woodwork, rendering and mortar.

Always check that your household insurance covers you and third parties against accidents that could occur because of your plants. A hose left running could flood your own and neighbouring premises; badly positioned and over-heavy containers may cause the collapse of a roof; an insecure pot or window box falling from an upper storey may damage cars parked below or injure passers-by. It is up to you to take all possible steps to ensure that accidents don't happen, but there is a limit to the number of problems you are able to foresee.

There is a lot of potential for more minor annoyances, too. Your lush screen of climbing plants may provide you with privacy, but deprive the adjoining property of sunlight. Leaves and petals fall not just on your own plot but may cause a

A flourishing vine makes a "ceiling" for an outdoor room – neighbours are unlikely to object to a solution which guards the owner's privacy and simultaneously enhances their outlook.

nuisance to neighbours. Plants have no regard for boundaries, and branches, roots and suckers can spread well beyond their own territory. In most instances, owners are within their rights to remove any part of a plant which impinges on their property, even if their actions damage or kill the plant; it is up to gardeners to make sure they keep their plants within bounds.

Many disputes needlessly end up as costly, protracted legal cases; the only people who gain from these are the lawyers. Common sense, thoughtfulness and, above all, good communication should prevent things getting as far as this. Consider what impact your activities may have upon other people at the planning stage, and try to forestall possible difficulties by talking to the people concerned at the start.

Protecting yourself

In some situations you are far more likely to find yourself on the receiving end of a nuisance than to be the cause of it. If your land, or parts of it, are accessible to the public, it is a sad fact that you may find it subject to theft, vandalism or simple carelessness that causes a great deal of damage.

Wooden trelliswork, lightly covered in creeper, and tall tripods with sweet peas and runner beans help to provide some privacy on this roof garden and to disguise the bleak surrounding walls.

Urban situations

An airy trellis supporting shrubby foliage provides seclusion for this alfresco sitting and dining space, but is unlikely to rob neighbouring apartments of light.

The theft of plants, ornaments and garden equipment is becoming increasingly common. Plants in containers are prime targets because they are relatively quick and easy to move; it has been known for the hanging baskets and window boxes of an entire street to be removed overnight, presumably to reappear within a few days at a car boot sale or on a market stall.

Several anti-theft devices are possible – hanging basket brackets that incorporate padlocks, chains and locks to secure ornaments or tubs to brackets set in concrete, intruder alarms and so on. Outdoor lighting is also a useful deterrent, but the types that are operated by sensing body heat or movement are not appropriate where legitimate passers-by would trigger them frequently. Permanent, low-level lighting in such a situation is less irritating than the continual "on-off" operation of high-intensity security lights.

Vandalism is another common concern, and is often particularly prevalent where a house with an attractive display of plants is unusual. Whether it is through boredom, or perhaps, resentment or simply the distrust of anything that does not conform to the norm, such plant displays are sometimes the target of destructive attacks, which can be heartbreaking, as well as costly. Taking the same precautions as you would against theft can help prevent damage, but vandalism is more difficult to guard against. Special insurance policies for garden plants and equipment are available if such items are not covered by your household policy.

If your plants adjoin a public thoroughfare, they may be damaged unintentionally by people brushing past them or taking a short cut across a corner of your property. The remedy lies in planting those species that offer natural resistance to both theft and damage.

Homes without gardens

Special needs gardening

A gardener confined to a wheelchair can enjoy preparing the soil and tending plants in a raised bed without assistance.

There are many groups of people who require something a little different from their plants and gardening activities. They may be physically disabled in a number of ways, limiting the tasks they can do or the stimuli they can enjoy; they may have emotional or mental needs that can be at least partly fulfilled or helped by growing and appreciating plants. Among gardeners who could be classed as having special needs are those with chronic back trouble, blind people, those with arthritis, wheelchair users, and people with learning difficulties.

"No-garden" situations are often particularly appropriate for special needs gardeners. The areas involved are small, requiring less work to keep them looking good, and making it easier to plan the entire plot around the requirements of the gardener. Close contact with the plants is possible – indeed, often unavoidable – so their finer details can be appreciated and their needs and problems more easily and quickly noticed.

The requirements and capabilities of different people are so varied that individual planning is necessary and should always closely involve the gardeners themselves, or at least those who have a good knowledge of their condition and limitations. Don't forget that in many instances the person involved may become increasingly less able over time. If this is the case – when the person is elderly, for example – build in features that can easily be adapted to something less labour intensive at a later stage. A raised bed could be used initially for growing vegetables from seed; if this becomes too difficult it is simple to plant it up with permanent groundcover subjects. But bear in mind that most gardeners find it more rewarding to work to the limit of their capabilities. If people are keen and reasonably able gardeners, a totally labour-free plot will be frustrating and disappointing, no matter how attractive it might look. To provide a sense of achievement, the growing of plants needs to present some sort of challenge, no matter how small. Overcoming obstacles and difficulties gives the grower a real sense of pride, so don't underestimate the capabilities of the gardener.

Many accidents and injuries involve gardening activities, and special needs gardeners are likely to be particularly at risk. Safety is of primary importance, and while many aspects of safety are common sense, different groups may have their own particular problems that would never occur to someone else. Help and guidance can often be obtained from specialist associations.

Independence is valuable to all of us, and it becomes particularly precious when threatened. Maintaining or increasing the independence and self-confidence of those with special needs through plants and gardening is important, and it is certainly worth spending time and thought on it in the initial planning stages.

Infirm and elderly gardeners

Into this rather "catch-all" category come those who lack strength and dexterity to a degree that interferes with normal gardening activities. This may be due to one or more reasons, from a simple "bad back", to old age or severe physical disability, including the use of a wheelchair. Lifting, bending and stretching are likely to be restricted, and some people may lack the stamina to continue working for more than a short spell at a time.

Plots for such gardeners need to be safe and plants easily accessible. Paving should be firm and level,

Special easy-grip hand tools, with extensions that fit over the forearm, are particularly useful for people with arthritis.

The visual liveliness, the subtle and attractive water features and the broad, paved path in this professionally planned area for gardeners and garden users with special needs could inspire use on a more modest scale in a smaller space.

without the hazards of creeping plants, slippery dead leaves or algal growth. There should be clear areas about 1m (3ft) wide so that wheelchair users or people with walking frames or sticks are able to get about comfortably; changes in level should be dealt with by ramps or very wide, shallow steps. Hand rails may also be useful.

Raised beds are an excellent way of bringing plants up to an easy working level. They are not only good for wheelchair users and those who have problems bending, but make gardening far less tiring for anyone who is not physically strong. The ideal height is usually about 60cm (24in); top the walls with broad, flat coping stones to make them suitable for sitting on while working with the plants. The width of the bed should be limited to suit the reach of the gardener – about 1.2m (4ft) if it is accessible from all sides.

If space allows, a potting bench, with compost stored in a raised hopper below, will make it easier to pot up seedlings or young plants or to plant up small containers when working from a chair or wheelchair. Larger plant containers can be moved about more easily if they are placed on metal or wooden stands with castors, and hanging baskets with a

Special needs gardening

pulley system allow the basket to be lowered for watering and maintenance. Watering is often a problem, since water is heavy to carry and cans may be difficult to control.

The best method of watering is with a hose, preferably on a reel that permits water to flow through the hose while it is not fully unwound from the reel. Fit a gun to the hose so that the water flow can be turned on and off easily. Sprinkler or drip systems will automate watering to a large extent, or a computerised system can be set up to automate it completely. This is easier and less expensive to install in a small growing space than in a larger garden.

Garden tools can often be adapted to make them easier to use, and specialist tools are sometimes available. Fitting a hand grip half-way up the shaft of a normal spade or fork gives better control, and fitting a long handle to hand tools such as trowels and forks means they can be used without bending. Long-handled soil millers, seed sowers and bulb planters are also available, and ratchet action pruners help those who have a weak grip.

Blind and partially-sighted gardeners

Sight is often the most important sense as far as many gardeners are concerned, but if we considered our other senses a little more when growing plants, we should all find the end result so much more rewarding.

Those people who have some limited vision may be able to appreciate strong colours and distinctive shapes. Blocks of single colours, rather than mixed plantings, stand out best, and bold, repeated colour patterns work well. Choose plants whose flowers provide a sharp contrast to their leaves: white flowers, for example, show up better against dark green or red foliage than they do against pale or variegated leaves. Keep backgrounds such as paving, walls and fences simple and unpatterned to avoid confusing images.

For those without sight, the senses of smell, touch and hearing take over, but these senses can be stimulated in all gardeners, not merely those who are blind. Scent is provided not only by flowers but by foliage, and can range from the sweetly fragrant to the unexpectedly pungent. Position scented plants with care. Low-growing

The leaves of many of the common herbs, such as sage, have a pleasing texture as well as a pungent aroma.

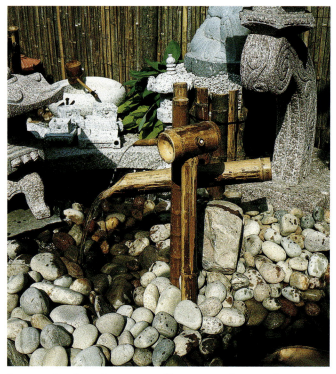

Japanese bamboo pipes operated by water make a regular, pleasant hollow ring as they knock rhythmically against stones placed in a pool beneath them.

flowers such as hyacinths should be planted in raised beds or tall containers, where their fragrance is more likely to be noticed. Flowers that give off their perfume in the evening, such as night-scented stock and ornamental tobacco, are best placed by a door or window, so the scent will drift into the house. Foliage often needs to be bruised before it will release its fragrance, so place aromatic plants where they will be brushed against or trodden on, or where their leaves can be easily stroked or pressed.

Don't just stick to sweet perfumes such as those from lilies and jasmine, lovely as these are – try the sharp citrus aromas of lemon verbena or lemon-scented geranium, the pineapple smell of Moroccan broom, or the spicy eastern aromas of the curry plant. Some plants have surprising scents – the strong, musky, fox odour of crown imperials or the pungent rancid-coconut smell of rue – which add an element of fun and variety.

Textures of plants are fascinatingly diverse, too. The smooth, velvet plush of lamb's ears (*Stachys byzantina*) just begs to be stroked, while the softly prickly needles of spreading junipers form a resilient spiky mat. Beware of planting sharply thorned or very spiky-leaved plants such as yuccas, which could cause injury. The blue grass *Festuca glauca* makes rounded hummocks of fluffy spikes, and the tall blue thistles of *Echinops ritro* are perfectly round, lightly prickly globes.

Adding sound

One of the most pleasant sounds is that of water, and a splashing fountain always has a soothing effect. It is not necessary to have a pond, but there must be some standing water to provide the splash – a fountain or wall spout falling on to pebbles is virtually silent. Some other garden ornaments, such as wind chimes, make a pleasant sound. They may be made of metal, wood, ceramic or seashells, and each produces a completely different sound.

Differing textures can be provided by ornaments and surfaces as well as plants. A change in the surface texture underfoot helps blind people to know where they are or if they are approaching a possible hazard such as steps, while pebbles, stonework and smooth wooden sculptures are all pleasant or interesting to touch.

Gardeners with learning difficulties

These are usually, though not always, young people, and as with other forms of disability, their difficulty can be mild or severe. For far too long, people with learning difficulties were guided toward an occupation in horticulture for all the wrong reasons – mainly that it was felt to be intellectually undemanding. Growing and caring for plants is certainly a suitable occupation, but because it is enjoyable, rewarding, stimulating, and encourages improved self-esteem and independence.

It is impossible to generalise about the conditions that are described as "learning difficulties" because they are so diverse, but the skills that are involved in growing plants are valuable for many young people, and adults too. Simple tasks, such as pricking out seedlings, improve dexterity, watering encourages estimating skills and planting in regular formations enhances the appreciation of patterns and helps number skills. Simply taking responsibility for plants and watching them develop and grow builds up confidence, providing a source of pleasure and pride.

Many people with learning difficulties require a great deal of stimulation, and the ideas discussed already in "Blind and partially-sighted gardeners" on page 46 can be put to good use for them. Plants and garden features should have lots of different textures, smells and sounds so that they can be touched, stroked, smelt and heard. And do not forget taste; almost everyone likes to grow things they can eat. Herbs, cherry-fruited tomatoes, sweet peppers, different varieties of lettuce with a range of leaf shapes and colours, radishes, salad onions and carrots are simple to grow and can be fitted easily into small-space gardens, window boxes or hanging baskets.

Make sure that poisonous or potentially damaging plants are excluded and that water features are safely constructed. A child or anyone with a disability who could not get back up after a fall could drown in a few centimetres of water; there is also the risk of electrocution if pumps are installed.

Laburnum seeds

Yew berries

SOME COMMON POISONOUS GARDEN PLANTS

BOTANICAL NAME	COMMON NAME	POISONOUS PART
Aconitum napellus	monkshood	leaves and seeds
Colchicum autumnale	autumn crocus	corms
Convallaria majalis	lily of the valley	red berries
Daphne spp.	daphne, mezereon	yellow or red berries
Ilex aquifolium	holly	red or yellow berries
Iris foetidissima	gladwyn iris	scarlet or yellow berries
Laburnum anagyroides	golden chain	seeds in bean-like pods
Ligustrum vulgare	privet	black berries
Lupinus spp.	lupin	seeds in bean-like pods
Nerium oleander	oleander	leaves and flowers
Phytolacca americana	pokeweed	all parts
Prunus laurocerasus	cherry laurel	black berries
Taxus baccata	yew	seeds in berry-like capsules

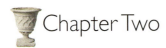

Chapter Two

Design and planning

The smaller your space, the more important good design becomes – it is crucial when you want to make the most of very little. In this chapter we look at some of the basic points to consider when planning your planting, to help you get the maximum pleasure and satisfaction from your growing space, whatever its size.

As well as general design principles, we look at a wide range of special features that can give your "no-garden" the extra something that will turn it into a special place. Being limited in space doesn't mean you need to be limited in imagination or for choice, and you will be surprised at what you can achieved in even the smallest, most unpromising area.

A limited range of plants and colours – grasses shading from yellow-green to almost blue, a natural wood deck and chair, and a russet-leafed Japanese maple and terracotta pots – are used here to create a feeling of space and unity in a small area.

48

Design and planning

The importance of design

The matching pairs of upright plants marching up the broad, straight steps to the twin conifers, and the restricted colours, are all in keeping with the formal lines of this patio garden.

Garden design is a grand-sounding term perhaps more readily associated with rolling landscapes than with our tiny plots. But as soon as you have a group of plants, you have the potential to increase or decrease their aesthetic appeal by the way you arrange them, both in relation to each other and to their surroundings. That arrangement is what design is about.

If you have followed the steps in assessing your situation on pages 34–43, you have already begun the process of designing. You know what you have and what you want from it, and the practical aspects of whether it is possible to achieve your goal, or whether you must compromise and adapt. You have the basic outline; now it's time to put some detail on the plan.

Choosing the materials

Materials for paving, walls, ornaments, containers and so on should be chosen to harmonise with each other and with the surroundings. Terracotta pots and the reddish tones in natural stone, for example, fit in more comfortably with a red-brick house than they would with one of grey stone. And a wall decorated with hanging baskets and window boxes is more pleasing if the boxes and baskets are all constructed from a similar material, such as black wrought iron, than if a mixture of plastic, wood and metal containers is used.

If you have a collection of ornaments and containers in differing materials and colours, you can often unify them by painting them with ordinary emulsion paint. A subtle variety of tones of the same colour may be more successful than painting each pot exactly the same shade. You can also paint patterns, either by eye or using stencils, or carry out special paint effects to give a "distressed" appearance – the technique is much the same as that used in home decorating.

Warm, earthy tones of green and reddish brown give a natural-looking result, but bright, bold, primary colours can

The importance of design

Informality is the keynote of this natural-looking planting, while the soft yellowy orange flowers make a pleasing contrast with the blue front door.

Pots that harmonise with the bricks and tiles, and flowers with a linking colour theme give this group unity.

GARDEN STYLES:

Most planned gardens are based on a definite style, whether it is an informal cottage garden or a modern garden with stark landscaping and striking planting. Our "no-garden" areas don't have as much scope, but you should still plan them with a particular style in mind to ensure that the end product is harmonious and not merely a jumble of assorted plants and containers. Here are a few suggestions to help you.

FORMAL Straight lines, evenly spaced plantings, planned colour schemes. Regular shapes for beds or arrangements of containers. Matched plants and containers, often in pairs or rows. Clipped shrubs.

INFORMAL Flowing lines, plants allowed to make their own shapes. A mixture of colours and textures; planting in groups of odd numbers. Rural, cottage-style gardens.

RELAXING Muted tones, white and pastel colours; soft outlines; silver and grey foliage; gentle sounds. Somewhere to sit a priority.

EYE-CATCHING Bright colours; architectural plants; exotic flowers; a striking sculpture or ornament.

PRODUCTIVE Featuring fruit, vegetables and herbs, planned to match or contrast their forms and colours so that they are appealing to the eye as well as useful.

OUTSIDE ROOM A continuation of the colour scheme of an interior room; somewhere to sit, with awnings and trellises for shelter. Containers and ornaments, such as large glazed pots, which would be equally at home indoors.

also be very effective if the right plants are chosen to complement them. But you must beware of making the containers more eye-catching than the plants you intend to put into them.

Designing with plants

The design of larger gardens is often based on overall shapes, with plants simply providing blocks of colour and variations in height. In "no-garden" situations, individual plants play a much more significant role. A limited colour range is usually the most effective. Colours can be chosen either to harmonise or to contrast: on a colour wheel, those colours adjacent to each other harmonise, while those opposite contrast. Brilliant red blooms standing out against a background of green foliage are an obvious example of the power of contrasting colours, while a mixture of silvery blue leaves, pale blue, lilac and pink flowers forms a restful combination. Colours are often divided into "hot" (yellow, orange, red) and "cool" (green, blue) shades, but the depth of the colour must also be taken into account – a pale, creamy yellow has quite a different effect to that of an intense golden yellow. If you use the full range of colours, place the strongest colours farthest away, graduating to pastels and white at the front of the display.

The shape, size and texture of flowers and foliage must also be considered; small blooms and delicate foliage are easily overpowered by robust specimens, which need careful siting.

Design and planning

Creating the illusion of space

Even simple ploys can trick the eye. This garden is made to seem bigger by the winding path, part of which is hidden from view, and the line of pots that are smaller the farther away they are.

Every garden needs storage space and, as this witty example shows, even the most mundane shed can be turned into an unusual and attractive feature that adds another dimension to the garden.

A small space can be made to look and feel bigger than it really is by the careful use of plants and features. Even on a balcony, where the boundaries are obvious, a feeling of openness can make it a much more pleasant place. In order to achieve the desired effect, we must deceive the eye in one or more of a number of ways, manipulating perspective, proportion and scale, and colour.

Using perspective

As children, perhaps we learned about perspective with the example of parallel railway lines, which appear to come closer to each other as they recede until they finally meet at the horizon. A false perspective can be created by deliberately narrowing the width of a path, for example, as it extends away from the viewpoint, making the end seem farther away than it really is. But the eye will not be deceived by this unless the proportions of the surrounding plants and objects are in keeping.

Objects in the distance appear smaller, so shrubs, plants and ornaments should decrease in size the farther away from the viewpoint they are. In a very small plot the effect can be achieved by using just two objects, such as plant pots which are identical in all but size. Place the larger one in the foreground and the smaller at the farthest point, and the distance between them will be exaggerated. If the plot is surrounded by walls, fences or hedges, the tops can be sloped so that their height decreases towards the far end of the plot.

This manipulation of perspective will, of course, work from one viewpoint only. Generally the main viewpoint is near the entrance to the house, but it may be advisable to create a slightly different sitting and "viewing" area to fit in with the shape of the plot. On a balcony, for example, the doors are likely to open midway down the long axis, and while a sitting area just outside the doors may be practical, it cuts the balcony in two, making it appear even smaller than it really is. Move the sitting area to one end of the balcony, and you can extend the view and have more scope for imaginative design.

Specially constructed trellis panels can be bought which give an altered sense of perspective, appearing as a receding tunnel round a doorway or a focal point.

Creating the illusion of space

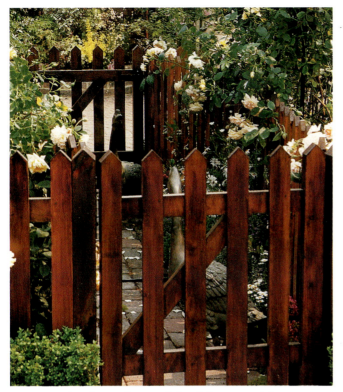

A mirror, placed some distance behind the gate and fence, creates the illusion of a path bordered by flowers running between a pair of gates, and greatly increases the feeling of space in this garden.

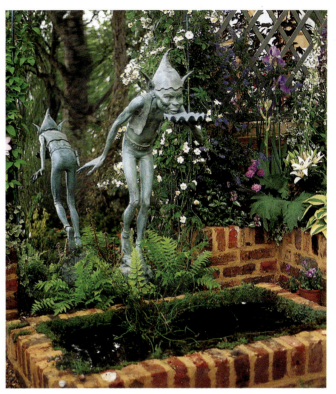

In this tiny enclosed space, the clever siting of a mirror deceives the eye and makes the garden appear much larger than it is by allowing you to see the statue in the round.

Unity of style

Use either curves, circles and flowing lines, or straight lines and sharp angles – don't mix the two. Unity is important to give an impression of space. A hotch-potch of different styles is restless and makes an area seem smaller than it is because the eye tends constantly to be moving from one object to another, rather than following a continuous line without unnecessary interruptions. Keep to one style of container and ornament, rather than using several different types.

Using colour

The eye can also be tricked by colour. The "hot" colours of the spectrum stand out more and appear closer than the "cool" colours, which tend to recede. So colours are often arranged with the hot shades farthest away and the cool ones in the foreground, an arrangement which is intended to even out this tendency and give the colours equal prominence.

But if you want to make an area appear larger, this can be achieved by placing the hot colours in the foreground, with the cool shades receding into the distance. This mimics the natural landscape, where distant objects appear as soft grey or blue shapes on the horizon. Misty pastel shades blur the edges of boundaries, giving the impression that the "garden" extends beyond the line of sight.

Trompe l'oeil

This is deception of the eye carried to extremes. Whereas the manipulation of perspective and colour is relatively subtle, a *trompe l'oeil* is a straightforward trick, creating an illusion of something that is not there at all. Some effects are simple to achieve, while others require considerable skill. Generally, a blank wall on which to create the illusion is needed.

A gateway on a wall suggests a garden beyond it, although the gate may be entirely false. An archway of artificial brick facings or trelliswork framing a wrought-iron gate on a solid wall is both easy to construct and effective. For extra realism, a mirror behind the wrought iron gate will reflect the existing planting, while the wrought iron "screen" of the gate helps to conceal the fact that it is just a reflection. Carefully placed mirrors are invaluable for giving an impression of a larger plot, or increasing the impact of a special feature, but they should be positioned so that they do not immediately reflect the viewer, so giving the game away.

If you are skilled with a paintbrush, you could paint a scene to enlarge your "garden", using a knowledge of perspective to give a realistic effect – an open gate with a glimpse of flowers and lawns beyond, pathways, climbing plants and flowers, trees, or simply blue skies and white clouds to give an impression of fresh air and open spaces.

Design and planning

Maintaining year-round interest

Although it is relatively easy to achieve an attractive blaze of colour from plants during the summer, it is less simple to make sure that there is something of interest for the rest of the year as well. In most "no-garden" situations, all the plants are on display all the time; there is rarely room to bring plants on in the background and set them out only when they have started flowering. So good planning is essential to get the most from your plants throughout the year.

If you have no ground space or only a small amount of ground space, you need to rely entirely on the plants to provide interest. There are two ways to approach the problem: either to use evergreens as the main plants, changing the flowering plants around them with the seasons, or to replace all the plants two or three times a year.

Establishing a basic framework of evergreens

Most of the plants grown in these situations are likely to be in containers. If you want to maintain a basic framework of evergreens all year round, use as large a container as is practical, preferably filled with soil-based compost, since this will keep the plants growing healthily for longer. Among the evergreens could be dwarf conifers, cordyline, euonymus, camellia or bay, planted either as single specimens or in groups, depending on the size of both the plants and the container. Fill in with trailing ivies and hebes, which remain attractive all year, leaving space for seasonal flowering plants to be added. The temporary residents should be planted in pots, sunk into the main container and covered with a thin layer of compost; this makes it easy to remove them as they pass their best.

Replacing the entire planting can pose difficulties when you are short of space. If you want winter-interest plants to become well established, you have to take out summer-flowering ones while they are still looking good in early to mid-autumn. There may be several dull weeks before the winter plants come into their own.

It is useful to have two containers, planting up one with the next season's plants in advance of the end of the current season's display, and keeping it out of the way until it is time to change them over – but this depends on your having a suitable "out of the way" place to grow them on.

If you have space to grow plants in the ground, the choice is the same as for containers – to have some permanent specimens, or replant regularly with seasonal plants?

Hanging baskets are a problem in cold winters. However, in a sheltered position you could try a basket planted entirely with hardy trailing plants such as variegated ivies. Line the basket in the usual way, then, to give extra insulation to the roots, place a piece of bubble polythene (perforated for drainage) inside the lining before filling it with compost.

Using hard landscaping

In the larger ground space provided by a patio or roof garden, you can provide year-round interest with ornaments, statues and sculptures, and even the materials for walls and paving can combine to form a pleasing scene when some plants have died back. It is important to keep an out-of-season garden area tidy. Remove dead and dying foliage, prune plants that require it, and keep the ground swept and clean.

Plants for year-round interest

Some strongly architectural shrubs such as *Cordyline australis* and *Yucca gloriosa*, or the fantastic corkscrew branches of the twisted hazel, *Corylus avellana* 'Contorta', show up even better in winter. The bright red stems of the dogwood, *Cornus alba* 'Sibirica' make a showy display in winter, camellias flower, and a wall plant such as pyracantha provides interest both in early summer, with its creamy flowers, and in winter, with bright evergreen leaves and long-lasting scarlet or orange berries. Spring can begin early and continue into summer with bulbs, daisies, forget-me-nots and polyanthus. There is no shortage of plants for summer, some flowering well into autumn, when bulbs such as colchicums and nerines take over. Japanese acers provide splendid autumn leaf colour, while winter-flowering heathers and pansies, and many conifers and evergreen shrubs with variegated and coloured leaves, will give winter colour. More ideas for year-round plantings are given on page 165.

Ornamental cabbages are unusual and hardy plants that will thrive in a pot and provide colour on bleak winter days.

Pyracantha will survive severe winter conditions, rewarding you with a glimpse of its bright berries even under a blanket of snow.

Maintaining year-round interest

Design and planning

Grouping containers

When planting a flower border, you usually take care to follow a planting scheme, bearing in mind how the plants relate to each other and considering the border as a whole. When planting a number of containers, this is often not the case. Each container tends to be regarded as a separate entity and is not considered in relation to the others. This is a pity, since, in a small area especially, the various containers look best when they are grouped together to form a pleasing and harmonious whole, giving a sense of unity and making a "garden" – rather than a jumbled collection of pots – out of the smallest space.

You will need something of a designer's eye to arrange your containers in the most pleasing manner. An arrangement works best if there is some theme to link all the parts: using all terracotta pots in varying styles, perhaps, or a variety of tubs and troughs made from wood. If the containers are in a mixture of styles they can be linked by their colour, or the planting can form the linking theme, with some of the same plants appearing in each of the different pots. Or, a similar colour scheme can run through all the containers.

Creating a satisfying composition

Your container group may be viewed from one direction only, or from several different sides – you will need to take this into account when planting it up. A roughly triangular outline is often the most successful composition. The apex of the triangle can be central or to one side, formed by a tall plant in a tall container. Try to achieve a balance between the size and shape of the container and the plant it holds. Not only does a tall specimen in a low container look uncomfortable, it is at risk of being blown over. If your container isn't tall enough, you can stand it on a brick or an upturned pot which will eventually be hidden by the plants around it. Other containers and their plants of varying shapes and sizes should be arranged to fill in the triangle. You will need to assess whether it is the pot or the plant it contains that is the more eye-catching, and position it accordingly. Sometimes a decorative empty container, perhaps lying on its side, makes a perfect addition to the group.

Making an impact

Groups of odd numbers of containers are always the most satisfying – one large pot and two medium-sized ones, for example, or one large, one medium and three small. Avoid placing the pots in straight rows; a slightly staggered outline works best. If you have raised beds, low walls or steps, use them to vary the levels of the containers. You can also add height with hanging baskets and wall pots in relatively low positions on walls or fences so that they form part of the group. Make a link between them and the containers at ground level by using similar plantings or by continuing the colour scheme upwards.

The basic rules of using odd numbers and different heights of containers are successfully demonstrated by this grouping. The link between the colours of both pots and plants helps to give the arrangement cohesion.

Grouping containers

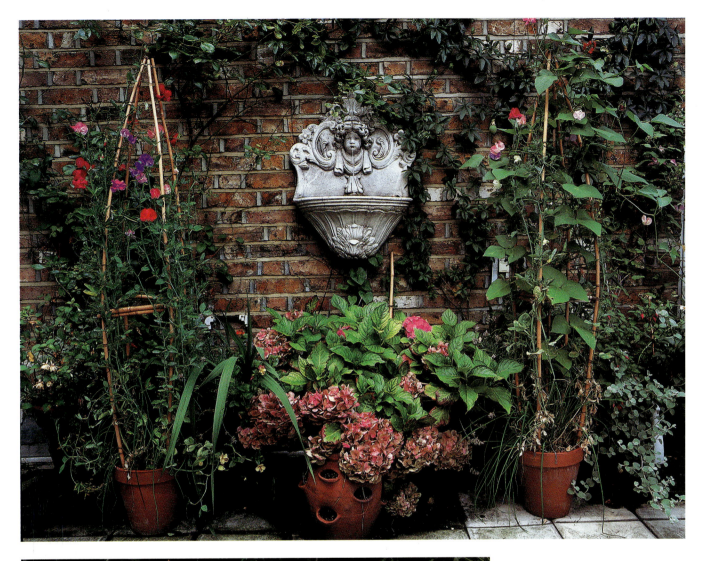

In this more complex grouping (above), the symmetrically placed pots, containing similar plants, and the triangular shapes formed by the canes all draw the eye upwards to the wall fountain.

It is not immediately obvious that the arrangement (left) is based on a triangle. The planting and colours are varied, but a feeling of unity is achieved by using the same material – gravel, pebbles and rocks – and, dominating the group, a fine raised stone trough.

Design and planning

Alpine gardens

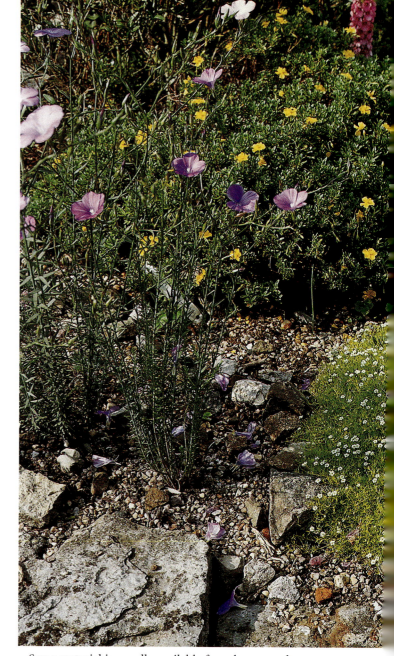

The neat forms, low growth and small, jewel-bright flowers of alpine plants need to be appreciated at close quarters, and they are perfectly in scale in confined spaces. They do, however, generally need a degree of specialised care, and there are several ways in which they can be grown.

Alpines are defined as plants which, in the wild, are found growing above the tree line. As far as most gardeners are concerned, that definition is not too strictly adhered to, and the term tends to include a fairly wide variety of similar, low-growing subjects, which will happily grow at lower altitudes and are popularly known as rock plants.

A miniature alpine garden can even be created in terracotta pots filled with free-draining compost.

In the mountains, alpines are subjected to dry, cold, windy conditions and grow in thin, stony soil or in crevices in rocks. Their low habit of growth helps them to resist the wind, and spreading root systems enable them to extract the maximum moisture and nutrients from the poor soil. They have adaptations to help them cope with high water loss, and this is possibly the most important point to bear in mind when growing them away from their natural habitat – they demand very free-draining conditions, and waterlogging, or moisture remaining in the crowns of the plants, will quickly cause them to rot and die.

Scree gardens

Natural weathering of the rocks in mountain areas produces slopes consisting of small rocky fragments and stones known as scree, which is colonised by a variety of attractive plants. In a small garden area, a scree garden can sometimes be more successful than a rock garden, which uses rocks and boulders on a larger scale. As for all alpine and rock plants, an open, sunny site is necessary.

Such a garden must be well drained, and constructing a scree bed on a slight slope improves drainage and helps to display the flowers well. If the bed is to be at ground level, the soil beneath it should be dug out and replaced by a layer of free-draining rubble before being topped with scree material; a raised bed is often more practical (*see* pp.78–81), provided you pay particular attention to good drainage.

Scree material is usually available from larger garden centres or alpine specialists, but if you live in a suitable area, a visit to a stone quarry is the ideal way to obtain it. The main area of the bed should consist of scree compost, made from one part of good-quality topsoil or soil-based potting compost, one part of peat or peat substitute, and three parts of gravel and rock fragments. Once planting is complete, the area is topdressed with a layer of scree material.

When planting in scree compost, shake or gently wash off much of the existing compost around the roots of the plants, and spread the roots out well in the scree bed. Firm plants in lightly, taking care not to damage the roots or crown, and finish with a layer of rock chippings about 25cm (10in) deep spread over the surface of the bed and tucked carefully around the neck of the plants.

The plants will need careful and regular watering for a little while after planting, but once they are established they will require watering only occasionally, if at all, depending on how

Alpine gardens

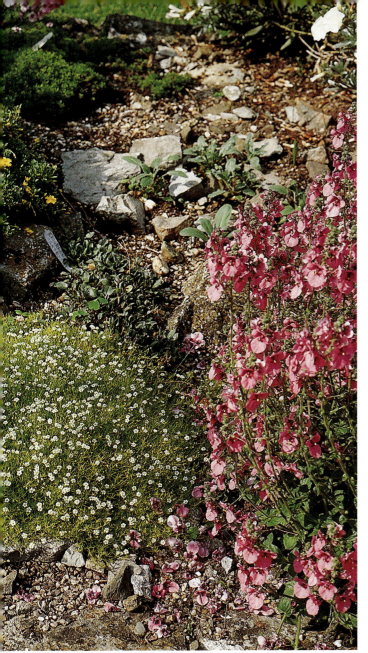

Colourful, low-growing alpines are most at home in an open, sunny bed that has been built up with rocks and has a surface covered in rock chippings and gravel to ensure good drainage.

much rain they receive. In wet weather, some individual plants may have to be protected from excess rain to prevent the crowns rotting. The easiest way to do this is to erect a pane of glass supported on sticks over the top of the plant; this protects it from the wet while allowing the free flow of air.

Rock gardens

Building a natural-looking rock garden is an art. Take your time when selecting stones, ensuring that they will fit together well. Although stone is expensive, buy reasonably large pieces, remembering that about one-third of each rock will be buried in the soil – but make sure that the pieces are not so large and heavy that you will not be able to manoeuvre them into position. To cut down on the number of stones, plan the rock garden as two or three rocky outcrops of larger stones surrounded by scree.

The "plum pudding" style of rockery is all too often seen – a large mound of soil with stones poked into the outside like decorations on a cake. Use stones and soil together to build up the slope as you go. Make a base of rubble for good drainage and cover this with good-quality topsoil. Form outcrops of rock from small groups of suitable stones, setting each one on a ledge of soil that slopes slightly backwards and building up well-trodden topsoil around and behind it to hold it firmly in place. For a natural look, the strata lines must run in the same direction on each piece of rock. Try to use some of the larger stones at the highest point of the rock garden.

Once all the stones are in place, plant your chosen plants in pockets at the base of the rocks, in fissures within the rock, and in scree areas between the stones. Then topdress with gravel or rock chippings to improve the overall appearance of the rock garden as well as the drainage around the plants.

MAKING A TUFA ROCK GARDEN

Tufa is a soft, porous limestone which plant roots will penetrate readily, and a piece of tufa planted with alpines makes an unusual feature that will take up little space. It can either stand alone or form part of a rock garden.

Choose an attractively shaped piece of rock and set it in position. Use a cold chisel to form or enlarge suitable, downwards-sloping planting holes. Wash most of the compost off the roots of the plants, then set them in the holes. Firm the plants into place with an alpine plant compost made from one part topsoil or soil-based compost, one part peat or peat substitute, and one part grit. Water regularly until the plants are established and after that only when necessary – the porous rock will soak up moisture and supply it to the plants. Tufa is not universally available.

Alpines root quickly in holes in tufa rock.

Design and planning

Vertical gardening

When ground space is limited, it is often possible to make use of house and garden walls, fences and trellises to support climbing, trailing or wall-trained plants. If you can't spread out – spread upwards.

Climbing plants are those that have a natural tendency to scramble upwards and outwards. They may be self-clinging or may need to be tied in to supports. Trailers produce long, lax stems, which hang down rather than grow upwards – although a climber with no suitable support is also likely to turn into a trailer. Wall plants are those shrubs that are easy to train against a wall or similar support, but which do not produce long, questing stems and are not self-clinging. Climbers include honeysuckle and Virginia creeper; trailers, lysimachia and ground ivy; wall plants, pyracantha and cotoneaster.

How plants climb

In nature, the shoots of climbing plants extend until they find something tall up which they can travel. They make their upwards journey in a number of ways. Truly self-clinging types produce pads of aerial roots, or tendrils which cling tightly to rough surfaces – ivy and Virginia creeper are among them. Other climbers, such as runner beans and honeysuckle, have twining stems which coil clockwise or anticlockwise according to species. Sometimes they need a little help to start them climbing, so it is important to know in which direction they twine. Start them off the wrong way and they will simply unravel themselves. Plants such as clematis have twining leaf stems; others, such as passion flowers, have slender tendrils which coil tightly as soon as they touch a suitable object. The exotic glory lily, *Gloriosa superba*, has leaves which are modified into twining tendrils at their tips. Some plants grown as climbers have long, supple, arching stems which, left to their own devices, would tend simply to sprawl over other plants. They need training and tying in if they are to climb.

Fragrant honeysuckle (above), with its trumpet-shaped blooms, is one of the most rewarding climbers to grow in a small garden area.

Self-clinging climbers have a bad reputation. While they are not likely to do serious harm to walls in good condition, they can dislodge loose mortar and plaster; their growth may block gutters and they can lift tiles if allowed to scramble over roofs. Keeping the plants trimmed back and growing them up a suitable support will avoid these problems (*see pp.128–129*).

Growing climbers in containers

Most climbing plants can be grown in containers, although this may limit the height they will reach. Generally, the larger the container, the better, particularly for perennial and shrubby species. Care is needed to ensure that the topgrowth does not overbalance the container; use sturdy terracotta or ceramic pots rather than lightweight plastic ones, and loam-based rather than soilless compost. Planting climbers in the ground at the base of walls cuts down the amount of watering needed, allows the plants a free root run, and keeps the root area cool for those species, such as clematis, that prefer to have their roots in the shade.

Choosing the plants

Careful pruning is necessary to prevent climbing plants from developing unattractive bare stems at the base. This can also be overcome by planting climbers with other climbers, or with plants that make bushy growth low down. Careful selection of the accompanying plant can also provide flowers, fruit or leaf colour when the climber is not at its best. The flowers of spring-blooming *Clematis montana*, for example, may be followed by those of a climbing rose through summer, while a variegated or plain-leafed ivy will provide a pleasing backdrop at all times.

The aspect of a wall or fence can be important. Most climbing plants prefer a sunny location, but ivies, some honeysuckles and some species of parthenocissus will put up with a sunless position, and lapageria likes part-shade.

Many climbing plants are perennial, but there are several useful annuals which are easy to control and allow access to walls and fences for maintenance in winter. Morning glory, *Ipomoea tricolor*; sweet pea, *Lathyrus odoratus*; nasturtium, *Tropaeolum* spp.; and black-eyed Susan, *Thunbergia alata*, are easy to raise from seed and make rapid growth.

Growing plants on vertical supports means you can enjoy some you would not otherwise have had room for in a shady, narrow town garden, and it allows the plants to reach upwards for light and air.

Design and planning

Vertical gardening

Walls and fences

Always make certain that any wall or fence that is to support a climbing plant is in a good state of repair before planting against it. Loose, crumbling mortar or rendering, unstable bricks, weatherboarding or tiles that can be dislodged, will only be made worse by attaching plant supports or training self-clinging climbers against them. Carry out any necessary repair work before planting.

The wall in question may be the wall of your own house, a neighbouring house, a boundary wall in a garden, or that of a shed or other outbuilding. Walls of dwelling houses are there primarily to provide insulation and protection against the weather for the house occupants, and are constructed to maximise that protection, with damp-proof courses and cavities. Uncontrolled growth of plants can compromise this function, bridging damp-proof courses, holding moisture against the wall, harbouring vermin and penetrating the brickwork, to say nothing of blocking guttering and causing damage to roofs.

Controlling climbers

Before planting a vigorous climber, ensure that you will be able to keep its growth under control; this may be even more important if the wall is that of a neighbouring dwelling, since you could find yourself liable for any damage caused. A ladder, long-arm pruners or pruning saws may be required. Sometimes the necessary pruning can be carried out – with care – from an upstairs window to prevent growth extending into gutters or on to the roof. If you own only part of the wall, you will need to be able to prevent the climber extending to the parts of the wall that do not belong to you.

Similar care should be taken to prevent damage to the walls of outbuildings, although these are usually less important, and to garden walls. They are generally all there for a purpose other than providing a home for climbing plants, and are likely to be troublesome and expensive to rebuild or repair.

While a wall is often simply a convenient surface on which to extend your plant display, sometimes you will want to grow plants over it specifically to disguise it; not all walls and buildings are things of beauty. You may also wish to extend the height of a wall or fence with trelliswork in order to screen off an unappealing view or to provide extra privacy for yourself. In addition, a house wall is often a particularly good place to grow a scented climber, such as honeysuckle, jasmine, old-fashioned roses, sweet peas and wisteria, since the fragrance will drift in through open windows.

As well as providing privacy, the high white wall, topped by a classical bust, and the rose-covered trellis, coupled with the lush flowering plants, give this city roof garden an almost tropical feel.

If the wall is to be left partly exposed, choose a plant that will blend well with the texture and colour of the materials from which the wall is made. It may be brick, concrete, stone, or white-rendered – each provides a

Vertical gardening

A vigorous climber, such as Virginia creeper, will thrive in the small amount of soil at the base of a wall.

The hollow area should be as deep as possible, since it will dry out quickly, and it should be filled with good-quality, fertile topsoil. The construction of dry-stone walls means that plants can be set in pockets of soil and compost between the stones. Use compact alpines, which will thrive in these free-draining conditions, and avoid vigorous plants with strong, penetrating roots, since they could undermine the stones and cause the wall to collapse.

Balconies and roof gardens

Climbers and trailers are especially suitable for balconies and roof gardens. They help to make the garden area three-dimensional, provide privacy, and give protection from strong winds, which can be a problem in any area raised off the ground. At the same time, trailing plants tumbling over the boundaries disguise the edges of the area and help it to merge with the more distant scenery.

In these situations, climbers and trailers will of necessity have to be grown in containers. Vigorous climbers intended to help provide a weather screen will be particularly prone to being blown over and damaged by wind. Make sure that all containers and plant supports are firmly secured; once the supports are covered by stems in full leaf they will provide a considerable amount of resistance to the wind and may easily be damaged. In exposed positions, it is probably best to grow annual or deciduous climbers, or species that may be cut down in autumn to regrow the following spring. This reduces wind resistance during the winter, when the weather is likely to be at its worst, and may prevent a great deal of damage.

completely different background for the plants. Fences, too, come in a variety of colours and styles, and you may find that it is desirable to repaint or stain them to give a more pleasing foil for your chosen plants.

Garden walls are sometimes constructed with a hollow top section which can be filled with soil in which trailing plants can be set. It may be possible to add such a planting area to an existing wall by building up a few courses (rows) of bricks.

Design and planning

Vertical gardening

A pergola covered in wisteria gives this patio the air of a much larger garden and provides a welcome sitting area in summer.

Pergolas, arches and pillars

As well as walls and fences, there are several other means of supporting plants to make use of vertical growing space.

A pergola consists of timber uprights supporting an open arrangement of crossbeams. It is often rectangular, but a round or octagonal pergola can be both attractive and practical in a small area. Any pergola gives at least an impression of providing some shelter; once clothed in plants, this impression can become reality, with more vigorous varieties allowed to grow over the top of the pergola to provide shade and a little protection from rain. Hanging baskets can be suspended from the crossbeams, but make sure that they hang sufficiently high to allow you to walk beneath them and any trailing plants in them. Pergolas are often used over walkways to link two different areas, as are arches, which can also frame a gateway or entrance.

A traditional arch has a rounded top, but rectangular, flat-topped frameworks are also known as arches. They may be made from timber, metal or wirework, and may be two-dimensional or extended to form a short tunnel. A slightly elongated archway with a seat under it becomes an arbour, a pleasant, intimate place in which to sit and enjoy the view. As with a pergola, plants may be grown up the uprights and over the top of an arch.

Pillars are simply uprights which can be clothed with plants. They may be single or grouped in rows or patterns and are most frequently sturdy wooden posts driven firmly into the ground to hold them upright. In most "no-gardens", where a hard surface makes it impossible to drive a pillar into the ground, it can be supported on a crosspiece of timber at the base, with climbing plants in containers around it.

Tripods, consisting of three pieces of timber lashed firmly together at the top to form a wigwam, give a similar impression to pillars. Plants may be set either in soil at the base of each upright, or in a large container in the centre of the tripod, the shoots being trained around the uprights and eventually forming a complete screen. A sturdy tripod may be free-standing on a hard surface as long as it is firmly secured at the top and is strong enough to support the plants' weight.

Outbuildings and porches

Garden sheds, garages and porches also provide an opportunity for growing plants; sometimes, indeed, climbers may be necessary to disguise an unattractive outbuilding. But take care: very vigorous growers, such as Russian vine, *Polygonum baldschuanicum*, will rapidly cover an entire building, but can be invasive and difficult to control and the heavy growth can easily cause the roof of a decrepit or old building to collapse.

Ivy is another rapid grower, but when it reaches the top of its climb it produces shrubby and woody shoots. These bear differently shaped leaves and clusters of flowers and fruits, and their growth is very dense.

A porch may provide both uprights and a roof for plants to grow over, but a porch roof which is attached directly to the house wall, rather than being supported by uprights, is not likely to be able to bear much weight. Where the structure is sturdy enough to support dense plant growth, this can form a welcome screen and weather protection by a door.

Plants as supports

Climbing and scrambling plants can also be grown through other plants, in imitation of their natural growing conditions. Take care that the climber does not overpower or damage the supporting plant, which may be a tree, shrub or another climber. Choose plants that complement each other or extend the season of interest of the partner plant. A *jackmannii* hybrid clematis twining through a spring-flowering shrub, for example, will produce flowers ready to take over for the summer once those of the shrub have faded.

Climbers around the door to a courtyard garden emphasise its rustic nature and soften the starkness of the high walls.

Water gardens

There is something intrinsically fascinating about water, and certainly it adds a new dimension to a garden. Fountains and waterfalls add life to a still garden scene; their gentle splashing sounds are soothing and relaxing and bring a welcome touch of coolness on a hot summer day. Many types of wildlife are attracted to water, even in inner cities, and birds, insects and amphibians may become regular visitors.

Will a water feature work?

A pond or water feature is often considered suitable only for a large garden – something that demands plenty of space and is time-consuming and difficult both to construct and maintain. This is far from the case; if you have sufficient ground space in which to stand a large tub, you have enough room for a minipond, and setting it up is hardly more difficult than planting up the tub in the normal way.

Points to consider

If your garden space is a roof garden or balcony, the weight of the water must be taken into account; it is remarkably heavy, and you must be confident that the structure will be able to support the volume of water that you have in mind. You must also be quite sure that your feature is watertight, and not likely to spring a leak.

A pond of any sort needs full sun to thrive; a shady position is not ideal for water plants, and overhanging trees or shrubs should be avoided, since their falling leaves will pollute the water. However, all is not lost if your garden space is in the shade, for a water feature that does not involve water plants is still a possibility.

Any water feature requires a convenient supply of water. Pools need regular topping up and occasionally a complete change of water (although this should be avoided if possible). However, it is unavoidable that some water will be lost through evaporation, and this will need to be replaced.

An informal pond, with water spilling from a terracotta urn over stones, provides ideal conditions for moisture-loving plants and will add interest to your garden by attracting birds, insects and, if you are lucky, even a frog or two.

If your aim is to have moving water, there must be a convenient electricity supply to operate a pump that will recirculate the water from a reservoir.

Fish not only add to the attraction and interest of a pool, they make short work of mosquitoes and other troublesome insect larvae that hatch out in still, open water. In small pools in cold climates, fish may be a problem to care for during the winter, and they are likely to need feeding during spring and summer, too. If you don't want the responsibility of fish, you will need to control breeding mosquitoes chemically.

Young children, even more than adults, are fascinated by water, but a small pond can be a dangerous place for a toddler. A child can drown in water that is less than 15cm (6in) deep. However, the very small garden spaces we are considering are likely to be safer than larger gardens, simply because it should be easier to keep a young child in sight.

The amount of space you have will dictate whether you opt for a mini-pond in a container, a larger pool, either raised or at ground level, or a water feature, which can make better use of vertical space. Then you must choose between formal and informal styles, taking your surroundings into consideration. Formal styles usually integrate better into small spaces.

You do not need too much specialised equipment to construct a water garden, and most large garden centres stock a sufficient range of items. For a wider choice, it is worth visiting a specialist aquatic garden centre, many of which may also operate a mail-order business and have a helpful catalogue.

Ponds

Where there is space for something a little larger than a mini-pond, you must choose between a sunken pond, in which the surface of the water is level with the surrounding ground, or a pool constructed above ground level. In many "no-garden" situations, the excavation necessary for a sunken pond may be impossible, although you may be able to compromise with a shallow excavation and a low retaining wall so that part of the structure is below ground level and part above.

The most popular materials for pools are fibreglass moulds, or liners of laminated PVC or butyl rubber. Fibreglass moulds are inflexible and available in only a limited range of shapes and sizes. They must be installed below ground or only partially above ground. The above-ground portions must be surrounded by packed soil and a retaining wall, since they are not strong enough to support the weight of the water by themselves.

Liners are much more flexible and can be cut to suit whatever shape is desired; they are particularly useful for raised ponds.

Design and planning

Water gardens

Butyl is more expensive than PVC but longer lasting. It is also less easily punctured, but both PVC and butyl can be repaired if necessary. To calculate the width the liner needs to be, measure the pond's maximum width and add twice its maximum depth plus 15cm (6in) for overlap. For the length, measure the maximum length of the pond plus twice the maximum depth plus 15cm (6in).

Raised ponds

Raised ponds can be constructed of stone, brick or concrete. The construction must be sufficiently strong to support the pressure of the water inside it. A double-skinned cavity wall is preferable – the two skins are linked with wall ties and the inside is lined with butyl or laminated PVC before filling. The walls should be high enough to allow a minimum depth of water of 45-60cm (18-24in). It is important that the top of the walls are dead level, since the water will show up the slightest slope and this will be a constant source of irritation. For a neat finish to the inside of the pond, put the liner in position before laying the top two courses of bricks on the interior wall. A layer of builders' sand on the base of the liner will protect it from sharp stones, which could cause punctures or uneven wear. Lay the liner fairly loosely over the pool, weighting the edges with bricks. Run water in slowly through a hose, lifting the bricks as necessary to allow the liner bit by bit into the pond; it will stretch to form a tight, almost wrinkle-free fit. When the pool is almost full, lay the remaining two courses of bricks on the interior wall, over the liner, to hold it in place. Then fold up the edge of the liner over the final two courses toward the interior of the pond and top it off with coping stones, trimming the liner so that it does not show. Be careful not to drop mortar into the water, and allow the mortar to dry thoroughly before filling the pond to the top.

Sunken ponds

You need to excavate a sunken pond reasonably accurately. If you are using a pre-formed fibreglass mould, turn the mould upside down on the site and run a stick around the edge to mark its shape in the soil before starting to dig. Excavate the hole slightly wider and deeper than the size of the mould, allowing for any marginal shelves. Line the base of the hole with sand to bring it up to the correct depth and check the level of both the base and top of the excavation with a spirit level. Lower the mould into place, check the level again and begin slowly to fill it with water using a hose. As the mould fills up, backfill the excavation with soil or sand, firming it thoroughly, and continue to check the level of the pond at intervals. When the pool is full, lay paving stones around the edge, so that they slightly overlap the top of

MAKING A MINI-POND

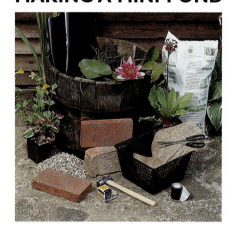

1 *Assemble the equipment you need to prepare your mini-pond: wooden half-barrel, black polythene liner, hammer, nails, your chosen plants, planting baskets, soil and some coarse gravel.*

2 *Cut a circular piece of polythene considerably large than the size of the barrel. Position it centrally over the top of the barrel and push it in so that it fits loosely. Fold the edge under, then nail it to the barrel with galvanised nails.*

3 *Half-fill the barrel with water. Line the planting baskets with hessian, which will help to prevent the soil being washed out. Fill the baskets two-thirds full with soil, then cut away the excess hessian level with the top of the baskets.*

the mould to disguise it. If you are using a flexible liner for a sunken pond, excavate the pond accurately, smooth the sides (which should slope outwards slightly) and put a layer of sand in the base, then lay the liner loosely over the hole and fill it in the same way as for a raised pond.

Mini-ponds

The most popular container for a mini-pond is a wooden half-barrel. These are usually waterproof (they were originally used for holding liquid, after all), but once they have been allowed to dry out, the wood shrinks slightly, opening up gaps between the staves. If the barrel can be submerged in water, or filled and refilled several times, the wood should swell sufficiently to stop leaks. The inside can be lined with heavy-duty polythene (preferably black), or painted with bitumen paint to ensure that it remains watertight. Before beginning to plant the barrel after painting, empty and refill it several times to wash away any residue from the paint.

Other containers can also be used for mini-ponds, but they should be at least 38cm (15in) deep; algae will be difficult to control in anything shallower. A container with the volume of a half-barrel can support a basket of oxygenators, a couple of submerged aquatic plants, a marginal plant and a goldfish or two. Compact types of plant should be chosen – a miniature water lily and the dwarf reed mace, *Typha minima*, for instance – and only one or two common goldfish, or the confines of a barrel become too restrictive.

The question of balance

A pool that is well cared for will contain sparklingly clear water in which fish and water plants can easily be seen and enjoyed. Often, however, particularly in new pools, the water is a thick murky green, or sometimes reddish brown. This is caused by a sudden explosion in the growth of algae. In a newly filled pond, the algae feed on the abundance of mineral salts present in tap water, and make use of the sunlight that at this stage can enter the water unimpeded by plant growth.

Although this "pea soup" stage does not look attractive, resist the temptatation to interfere. As plants become established, they (and the algae themselves) will use up the excess minerals. The leaves of floating plants will also cut down the amount of sunlight entering the water, and the algae will die out. This often happens literally overnight, but it may take a few days or weeks. Emptying the pool and refilling it will simply introduce a new supply of mineral-rich water and delay the clearing process; although commercial algicides may kill existing growth, until a good balance is achieved naturally, the problem will only recur.

To keep the water clear you need some oxygenating plants. Plants with floating leaves that cover part of the water surface will also help to control algal growth – waterlilies are the favourites. Both of these types should be planted at the bottom of the pond. Floating plants, such as fairy moss, *Azolla caroliniana* (*A. filiculoides*), can also help to reduce algae by shading the water.

4 *Set the plants in the soil and add a layer of gravel to stop the soil washing away. You will need oxygenators, a miniature waterlily and perhaps a marginal plant such as miniature reed mace, a water iris, or marsh marigolds.*

5 *Lower the baskets gently into the barrel. Set the basket containing the marginal plant on submerged bricks to raise it to the right height. In a short while the water will clear, and your mini-pond will begin to flourish.*

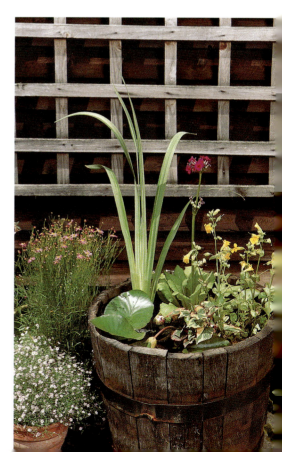

Design and planning

Water features

The sound and movement of water can be enjoyed without having a pool; a recirculating pump will enable you to have an attractive water feature in a very small space. However, a header pool of some sort is needed to supply sufficient water for the pump to circulate; this can either be a part of the feature or can be hidden behind or below it.

Water pumps

There are two main types of pump – surface or submersible. Surface pumps run off mains voltage and are useful for moving large volumes of water. They must be housed in a waterproof, ventilated pump chamber near the water feature and should be installed by a professional electrician. For small water features, submersible pumps are much easier. They require a transformer to reduce the mains voltage (transformers are usually included as part of a kit) and are simply lowered into the water they are required to pump. They must remain submerged while they are working.

Decorative water features generally make use of falling water, as in waterfalls and cascades. Here the pump is sited in a small pool or container, and the water is pumped upwards through a hidden hose to the top of the feature, where it is allowed to spill out. Slightly different is a fountain, where both the upwards movement and fall of the water provide the decorative effect.

Fountains

A fountain is often part of a formal rather than an informal feature, although it can be used in both. It is easy to install, since the fountain jet generally fits directly on to the pump, so no pipework is required. For most effects, the top of the jet should be just above the water surface; the pump can be raised on bricks to reach the correct level. Many different types of jet are available, to give a variety of water patterns, some complex, others quite simple; most can also be adjusted to raise or lower the height of the water. Merely lowering the pump so that the fountain jet lies just below the water surface also gives a different effect – like that of a spring bubbling up. Fountain ornaments can be situated in the centre or at the side of a pool or they can be free-standing, with the falling water being collected in a chamber beneath the ornament to be recirculated. A word of warning: in very windy locations, water will be blown away from the pool, making the surroundings wet, and the pump will burn out if the pool empties.

A wall fountain, with the water falling into a basin or into a miniature pond makes a charming focal point in a small area.

Cascades

Like a fountain, a cascade may be part of a pool or it may form a feature on its own. It consists of a step or series of steps over which water falls to provide a splash. The abrupt fall of water from one level to another is critical, so it is important that the water does not simply run down a sloping course, since this provides little sound or noticeable movement.

Plastic or fibreglass waterfall sections are available in many garden centres but, being poor imitations of stone, they are not entirely successful. It is better to use a flexible liner to cover steps which have been cut into well-firmed earth, topping the liner with an overhanging stone on each step to form a lip from which the water will fall cleanly. A submersible pump sited in the bottom pool pumps the water back up to the top through a hose buried in the soil behind the steps. With a little imagination, a variety of attractive individual features can be constructed using the principles of the fountain or cascade.

Other features

A large, waterproof, decorative pot filled with water can bubble at its surface by means of a jet, or water can spill out continuously from a tilted urn or through an old-fashioned hand pump. A foaming water spout emerging through a circle of cobbles or the centre of a millstone has become a popular feature, and there are many different types of mask or gargoyle which will spout water from a wall or poolside. Some ingenuity will often be needed to ensure that the working parts (the electricity cable and hoses) are concealed, but this need not be a major problem.

Water features

A simple fountain bubbling up over pebbles in a small container, set within a larger stone circle, makes an imaginative water feature and provides perfect conditions for marginal plants.

Maintaining water features

Where oxygenating plants cannot be used to keep the water clear, algae are likely to be a nuisance, and algal growth is often a particular problem with millstones or pebble fountains, since a film of algae will soon form on stone that is constantly wet. Regularly switching off the pump to let the stones dry out completely will help to delay its formation, but an algicide is also likely to be needed – plus occasional scrubbing, or even replacement, of the affected stones.

Several chemical algicides will do the trick, but the treatment needs to be repeated at intervals. Chemical algicides are not normally recommended for use in ponds, but with a very small or shallow area of water, you may sometimes need to use them. Remember that treating heavy algal growth can pollute the water because the algae die and decompose, and you may need to replace the water.

Design and planning

Food from small areas

Many gardeners feel that home-grown vegetables and fruit are too much to expect from a tiny garden area, but it is surprising just what can be achieved. Selecting the right crops is of paramount importance. There is no point in trying to grow varieties that need a deep root run, wide spacings and a long growing season, or those that produce a small crop in relation to the amount of space they take up. Nor is there much point in growing fruit and vegetables that can be bought cheaply and easily in the shops.

The types to go for are those unusual varieties that are difficult or very expensive to buy: crops that give a heavy harvest from a small area; varieties that are especially noted for their superior flavour; and those in which absolute freshness is of vital importance to the quality. They should be compact, quick-maturing and easy-going. Most importantly, they should be crops that you enjoy eating – there's no point in producing a bumper harvest if your family doesn't like them.

Growing in containers

It is quite possible to grow a reasonable selection of vegetables in a hanging basket or window box, so no one need feel that their "no-garden" is too small. As with most plants, the more space you can provide, the better the plants will grow and the wider the choice of suitable subjects you will have.

Growing bags are sold largely for growing tomatoes, but these, or any low, wide container, are suitable for other crops,

Cherry trees are best grown trained into fan-shapes on a warm wall or fence. This has the added advantage of making them easier to protect from raiding birds.

such as lettuce, beans, aubergines (eggplants) and sweet peppers (capsicums). They can be placed quite comfortably on balconies, patios and the tops of low walls. Ordinary plant pots can also be used: 38–45-cm (15–18-in) pots will support most fruit trees and bushes and a reasonable number of vegetables, depending on the variety. Nearly all fruits and vegetables prefer an open, sunny position, and growing in containers enables you to select the best spot for them.

Growing in the ground

Growing plants in beds in the open ground will increase the number of types and varieties you are able to try. In many "no-gardens" these beds will be raised beds, which can be excellent for edible crops as long as you remember that they are free draining, so frequent watering will be necessary. The depth of soil or compost is limited also, so plants will require regular feeding.

All plants in tiny garden areas have to work hard to earn their place, and fruit and vegetables are no exception – they should be attractive to look at as well as to eat. Select varieties with striking, bright colours, frilly leaves or fruits with interesting shapes. Grow them in a pattern – not necessarily in straight rows – and edge the beds or pots with plants such as curly-leafed parsley, or flowers such as pinks. Beds of edible plants grown in this way become potagers, and can be just as ornamental as any beds of flowering plants.

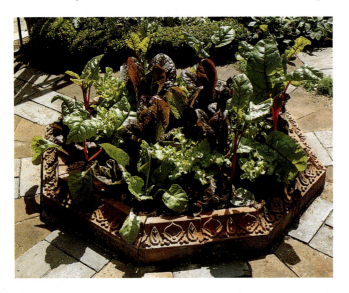

A miniature potager with Swiss chard (silver beet), beetroot and lettuce forms the centrepiece in this small paved plot.

Herbs for containers

The fragrant foliage, attractive appearance and fascinating history of herbs make them popular plants with most gardeners. Most varieties form compact plants which are perfect for small areas. Many grow well in containers and some, such as mint, are actually more manageable when their natural exuberance is restrained by containing their roots.

The most useful herbs are those we rely on in the kitchen to add flavour to meals, and these are the ones that are best grown close at hand – perhaps in pots near the back door, or in a window box outside the kitchen window. Herbs also lend themselves to being planted in raised beds, in cracks in paving, in crevices in walls, as well as in small, formal beds in courtyard gardens and patios. Chamomile and thyme can even be grown as aromatic lawns or fragrant "seats", and some herbs, such as lavender and rosemary, perform well as low hedges.

Most herbs need light, free-draining soil – they cannot stand being waterlogged – and a sunny, open, but protected position. Containers must have sufficient drainage holes and be well crocked, with a good layer of gravel or stones on top of the compost. For the best flavour and aroma, do not feed the plants too frequently.

Recommended culinary herbs

BASIL An excellent culinary herb, with a strong, warm, clove scent. It forms a small bush with pointed, tender, rich green leaves. There are many different varieties with subtly different scents, leaf sizes and shapes. 'Dark Opal' is an attractive purple type. Basil likes warmth and will grow well in small pots.

A pot of fresh herbs for cooking, such as this one containing sage, chives and parsley, can easily be grown on a sunny kitchen windowsill.

SAGE A bushy, wide-spreading perennial with grey-green leaves and blue or pink flowers; there are also gold- and red-leafed varieties. Given plenty of sun, sage will grow well in pots, window boxes or hanging baskets.

PARSLEY Perhaps the best-known herb. The deep green, tightly curled leaves make a good ruffled edging for decorative beds. The flat-leafed form is less attractive but has a more pungent flavour. Excellent for pots.

MINT A vigorous, spreading plant with underground runners which should be contained in a pot or tub. There are many different types, including spearmint, eau-de-cologne mint and golden variegated ginger mint. Likes moist soil and will grow well in light shade.

THYME A short upright bush or low-growing, spreading plant, depending on variety. These include types with gold and silver variegated leaves. Small leaves on wiry stems have a warm, spicy scent, and the pretty pink, purple or white flowers are very attractive to bees. Will grow in tubs, window boxes or borders; makes a good edging plant.

MARJORAM Sweet marjoram is a low, spreading herb which does well in gaps in paving. The golden-leafed form is especially attractive. Trim the plants back after flowering to keep them neat.

CHIVES Round, pink, papery flowerheads make this a decorative plant. Its clumps of slender, grassy leaves have a mild onion flavour and are useful in cooked dishes and salads. Chives prefer slightly moister soil than most other herbs.

ROSEMARY The spiky, silvery leaves are strongly aromatic, and plentiful hooded blue flowers enliven the plant's appearance in summer. Grows best in a large container or raised bed. Can be clipped to form a low hedge.

BAY Unusual in that it forms a tree when allowed to do so, but amenable to being grown in pots and clipped into standards, pyramids, globes and other decorative shapes. It is slow growing, so trained plants are usually expensive. The dark green, lance-shaped leaves have a characteristic aroma. Bay is rather tender, and needs a protected position in cool areas.

Design and planning

Vegetables for containers

Most vegetables are annuals that are fairly easy and cheap to raise each year. If the crop is a failure, it's disappointing, but it has not usually cost you too much; you can try again, or try something different, next year.

You can buy popular varieties of vegetable seeds at any garden centre or store, but a far more comprehensive range can be provided by mail-order specialists. Some catalogues give much more detailed information than that found on the backs of seed packets, and many catalogues have a section devoted to varieties suitable for container growing. You can also buy many types of young vegetable seedlings, which are simpler to grow if you don't have the patience or facilities for raising seed at home.

Many modern varieties are F1 hybrids, which are often the best option where space is limited. The seed is much more expensive than open-pollinated types, but the resulting plants are more consistent in size, growth habit, season and cropping. The varieties specified here are particularly suitable for gardening in a small space, but every year the catalogues are filled with new varieties and improvements. Don't be afraid to experiment; it's part of the fun.

As well as being delicious when home grown and picked as they ripen in the sun, tomatoes are extremely decorative, and some varieties, such as 'Sweet 100' and 'Gardener's Delight', can be trained on a support to form a tower of small red fruits.

Recommended vegetables for container growing

POTATO Try the "gourmet" varieties. Sprout the tubers in a light, cool room. Set them on a 10-cm (4-in) layer of compost in a deep tub or barrel and cover them with another 10cm (4in) of compost. Continue adding compost to keep the shoots just covered as they grow through until the tub is full.

BEETROOT Use globe varieties for baby beets. Sow the seed clusters in spring and thin the seedlings to one plant per station. Harvest at golf-ball size. 'Detroit 2 – Tardel' is a good, uniform shape, while 'Burpees Golden' or 'Golden' is a dual-purpose variety with attractive, deep yellow roots and leaves that can be cooked like spinach.

KOHLRABI Produces turnip-like swollen stems which should be harvested at golf-ball to tennis-ball size: the smaller they are, the sweeter and less woody they are. 'Rolano' is a compact, fast-maturing variety; 'Purple Vienna' is an attractive deep violet colour. Sow seed in spring.

CARROT Sow very thinly in spring and pull as soon as they are large enough to eat. Choose short-rooted types for limited soil depth. 'Suko' is a fast-maturing variety suitable for a window box; 'Parmex' is almost round, like a radish.

TOMATO Always popular and not difficult to grow in a sunny spot. Start seeds indoors and plant out after frosts, or buy plants. Does well in growing bags, tubs, pots, and even window boxes and hanging baskets when the right varieties are chosen. 'Tumbler' is specially bred for hanging baskets, while 'Totem' is recommended for containers, and 'Tiny Tim' can be grown in windowsill pots or window boxes. Liquid-feed every 10 days once the first flowers are setting.

AUBERGINE (EGGPLANT) Grown like a tomato, the aubergine needs a warm, sunny position. Raise seed on a windowsill or buy plants, setting two plants in a 38-cm (15-in) pot or three in a growing bag once frosts are over. Tie them to stakes as they grow if support is necessary. Pinch out the growing tips at 30cm (12in) tall to encourage bushy growth. Keep the compost moist and liquid-feed every 14 days.

PEPPER (CAPSICUM) Sweet peppers, grown like tomatoes, carry lantern-shaped, mild-flavoured fruits which can be eaten green or allowed to ripen to yellow or red. 'Jingle Bells' and 'Baby Belle' are ideal for small spaces, carrying loads of miniature red peppers. Chilli peppers are much more fiery in flavour; 'Super Cayenne' bears long red fruits in great profusion on a compact plant. They are good for pots.

Vegetables for containers

Nothing tastes better than freshly picked vegetables – plump small beetroot, crisp lettuce, succulent tomatoes, green or red peppers, and courgettes (and their flowers, which are perfect for stuffing to make an unusual savoury dish).

COURGETTE (ZUCCHINI) Does well in a growing bag or container. Set plants out after the risk of frost is over. Keep the compost moist and liquid-feed every 10–14 days. Cut the fruits young and regularly for continued cropping.

BEANS Dwarf french (snap) beans carry heavy crops on compact plants. Yellow and purple varieties add interest to plain green types. Climbing or runner (pole) beans can be trained up a tripod of canes and are very productive. Sow beans outside in late spring in tubs and growing bags, as well as in raised beds. Keep all beans well watered while flowering and pick them regularly.

LETTUCE Particularly good when eaten super-fresh – within a few minutes of picking. Sow in spring, summer and into autumn for a succession of crops. 'Blush' is a baby 'Iceberg', tinged with red and ready at tennis-ball size.

CHARD (SILVER BEET) A decorative spinach-like vegetable with crinkly leaves and broad leaf-stems – white in silver chard and red in ruby chard – excellent for dotting among flowers. Grows better in beds than in pots; sow in early spring, and thin to 20cm (8in) between plants.

SALAD ONIONS Sow from early spring onwards and pull when pencil-sized. Keep moist for a mild flavour. Good for growing bags and window boxes. 'White Lisbon' is an old standby; the stems of 'Santa Claus' ('Red Bunching') are rosy pink towards the base.

RADISH One of the fastest and easiest crops to raise. Sow in spring, in pots, beds, window boxes or growing bags; keep moist and harvest while they are small and crisp. Many varieties are available, in different shapes and sizes. 'French Breakfast' is red and cylindrical with white tips, 'Cherry Belle' is a rosy red globe. Mixtures, with red, pink, white, purple and bicolours, are also popular.

SALAD MIXTURES (MESCLUN) Several varieties of "cut-and-come-again" salad leaves to be harvested while they are young and tender. Sow throughout spring and summer. Mixtures may contain various types of lettuce, herbs, purslane, rocket, cress, chervil, chicory and so on. Colourful and useful for small spaces.

Design and planning

Fruit for containers

There is space for at least a few types of fruit even in very small areas. Crops are grown on trees, bushes, climbing stems and canes, and ground-hugging plants. Use as large a pot as possible, filled with soil-based compost, and pay careful attention to watering and feeding.

Tree fruits obviously present most problems in a limited space, but their size can be controlled by using the right rootstock and training the trees correctly. Most tree fruits consist of a rootstock, which determines the size and rate of growth of the tree, on to which is grafted the variety chosen for its fruit quality. For a fruit tree grown in a small area, a dwarfing rootstock is required. Several types of tree fruit can also be grown as restricted forms against a support; cordons, espaliers and fans are the most common (*see* pp.130–131 for further information). You can use existing walls and fences against which to grow the trees, or erect simple post-and-wire supports. Step-overs are low, single-tier espaliers and are used to edge beds and borders – they are novel and attractive, but don't expect a lot of fruit. The trees are kept to shape by regular summer and winter pruning.

Apples and plums are among the tree fruits suitable for growing in containers as Minarettes, and it is possible to have several heavily fruiting trees in a severely restricted space.

Recommended fruit for container growing

APPLE Compact, columnar forms of apple known as Ballerina and Minarette trees have been developed especially for small areas and pot culture; they are like upright cordons. Best rootstocks are the very dwarfing M27, which produces trees up to about 2m (6ft) tall, and M9, which allows them to grow slightly taller. Trees need to be staked firmly throughout their life, and must be fed and watered regularly. They will begin cropping at two to four years old. There are dozens of varieties available. Since nearly all require pollinating by a different variety in order to set fruit, grow two or three different trees, making sure that they are compatible – flower at the same time; the supplier will advise you. A "family tree" has three or four different, compatible varieties grafted on to the same rootstock – a neat way to ensure pollination and achieve a selection of fruits.

CRAB APPLE Several varieties of crab apple are available on dwarfing rootstocks. As well as being decorative and useful in their own right, they also act as pollinators for eating apples. 'John Downie' has white spring blossom and yellow and red fruits which make excellent jelly; 'Golden Hornet' bears a heavy crop of cherry-sized yellow fruits.

PEAR Pears are rather more difficult to grow than apples, particularly in containers. Quince C is the most dwarfing rootstock, but trees will still grow to around 2.5m (8ft) or more. Pear trees can also be grown as fans, cordons and espaliers. As with apples, pollinating varieties are required. 'Beth' and 'Concorde' are two comparatively new varieties that can be relied on to crop well, as can 'Winter Nellis'.

Fruit for containers

What could be more satisfying than a bowl of currants, strawberries and blueberries grown in your own "no-garden"? The plants take up little room and the freshly picked fruit is likely to be far better than the bought variety in terms of flavour and colour. It is also easy to protect the fruit from birds, and standing the pots on trays of gravel will keep them safe from slugs and snails.

PEACH Fan-trained trees against warm, sunny walls usually give the best results. The flowers open in early spring and may require hand-pollination in cooler areas. Peaches fruit on one-year-old wood, so pruning to remove fruited wood and encourage its replacement is necessary. Peach leaf curl disease can be a problem. You may be able to find trees grafted on to the dwarfing Pixy rootstock, but the taller St Julien A is more common. 'Rochester' or 'Red Haven' are popular, while 'Peregrine' has a good flavour. 'Early Rivers' is a nectarine – a smooth-skinned form.

PLUM Plums grow well as fans on warm walls; they can be grown as cordons but tend not to crop heavily. Like peaches, they flower early in spring. Do not prune trees in winter, since this may encourage infection by silver leaf disease. Pixy is the rootstock for small spaces; choose a self-fertile variety if you have room for only one tree. 'Victoria' is an old favourite, with red and yellow fruit; 'Early Transparent Gage', or 'Greengage', has an especially good flavour.

CHERRY Dwarfing rootstocks Inmil and Damil are now available to keep cherries to around 2m (6ft) or so; trees on Colt grow up to twice that size. The acid cooking cherry 'Morello' is self-fertile and will do well as a fan against a wall or fence, even a fairly shady one. Several self-fertile sweet varieties are also being introduced. 'Stella' was the first, and it has been joined by others, such as 'Cherokee' and 'Sunburst'.

GRAPE Grape vines can be grown over pergolas, against walls and fences, or on post and wire supports. They need training and pruning and a warm, sheltered position to crop well and are not suitable for cold areas unless grown purely for decoration.

BLUEBERRY An attractive bush which grows well in a container but needs lime-free (ericaceous) soil. Creamy, urn-shaped spring flowers are followed by round, sweet fruits, which are deep purple with a blue "bloom". The foliage has excellent autumn colour. Pollinating varieties are not essential, but growing two or more different varieties may improve the yield. The fruits will need protection from birds as they start to ripen. 'Bluecrop' and 'Earliblue' are among the most popular and reliable varieties.

CURRANTS Black, red and white currants are available and do well in cool winter climates; black currants are the most popular, but red and white are more suitable for growing in pots. Black currants produce the best fruit on one-year-old branches; an easy way to prune them is to cut out the whole branch bearing fruit at picking time, encouraging strong growths to be produced. 'Ben Sarek' is a good compact variety. Red and white currants produce fruits on spurs on older branches, allowing them to be trained as cordons. 'Stanza' and 'Red Lake' are good red varieties; 'White Versailles' is the most commonly found white one.

STRAWBERRY This is the fruit that everyone can find room for. Strawberries can be grown in pots, growing bags, as edgings to borders, even in window boxes and hanging baskets. Plant in summer or, in mild areas, in autumn for cropping the following year. Some varieties can be raised from seed sown indoors in early spring and planted out to crop the same summer; the tiny-fruited alpines can be grown like this, but seed of large-fruited varieties is now also available. Most strawberries fruit for a short season in summer, but the season can be extended with perpetual or autumn-fruiting varieties, which bear a smaller flush in late summer or early autumn.

77

Design and planning

Raised beds

Brick is one of the most long-lasting and attractive materials for raised beds and paving. Its warm tones are a perfect foil for plants, and by setting low-growing types in pockets in the brick, the hard outline of the bed can be softened.

A raised bed is really just an extra-large, permanent container for your plants. Where you have no soil, but concrete or a similar hard surface, a raised bed allows you to achieve a better approximation of natural growing conditions than pots and tubs do. Even if you have a soil base, it can be useful to make a raised bed which is isolated from the existing soil so that a different range of plants can be grown.

Why build a raised bed?

There are many advantages in building a raised bed. It can be filled with a specific type of soil enabling you to grow specialist plants. It will also bring the plants up closer to you. This is of special benefit with low-growing fragrant plants, whose scent may otherwise go unnoticed, and with small, delicate plants, such as alpines, which often repay closer inspection. If a suitable coping is used on the top of the walls, they double up as seating areas, making efficient use of space. Changes of level provided by the beds improve the garden's appearance, and can make a small area look larger.

Disabled gardeners often find raised beds particularly handy. When constructed at a suitable height, they can be worked on from a wheelchair, or simply from a garden seat for those who find it difficult to bend or stand for a long time. As long as they are no wider than an arm's length – or two, if there is access from both sides – planting, weeding and general maintenance is easier and less tiring. Gardeners with poor eyesight will appreciate the increased visibility of plants, and everybody will be encouraged to touch textured and tactile plants when they are within easy reach.

Use imagination when designing your raised beds. They do not have to be built singly – ascending tiers can be very successful. Neither do they have to be in formal shapes, flowing curves can look most attractive. In a small space, simplicity is usually far more effective than an intricate design, but that does not mean you have to limit yourself to a rectangular box.

Raised beds

In the greater depth of soil in a raised bed, small trees and shrubs will thrive, giving a patio or balcony the appearance and feel of a much larger garden.

Topsoil can be delivered by the lorryload, but access is often a problem in many "no-garden" situations. The quality of topsoil is also variable and it is likely to contain a lot of weed seeds. Bagged compost is expensive, and buying sufficient to fill a large bed may be uneconomic, so estimate the amount required before staring on the building work.

Compost is generally packed in litres, so you will need to find out the volume of the bed by multiplying together its height, breadth and length in centimetres. Divide the answer by 1000; this will give the number of litres of compost required. For example, a bed 60cm high, 150cm long and 100cm wide would require 60x150x100 = 900,000÷1000 = 900 litres of compost. You can then find out the cost of the compost you require, and adjust the dimensions of the bed accordingly.

Plants for a raised bed

There are few limits on the types of plant that can be grown in a raised bed, but some are more suitable than others. Avoid very deep-rooted and invasive types. Trees, shrubs and perennials can be left in the bed permanently, so plants that spread rapidly by underground runners or suckers are soon going to become a nuisance. Among the lime-hating plants are many choice subjects which you will be able to enjoy if you fill the raised bed with ericaceous (lime-free) compost: azalea, rhododendron and pieris among them. Free-draining soil with plenty of grit mixed in provides ideal conditions for alpine plants. A lightly shaded bed filled with moisture-retentive compost will provide a home for plants that like cool, moist, woodland conditions. Lining the bed with polythene – with holes

Because a raised bed is a type of container, it shares some of the same problems of cultivation. The depth to which the roots can penetrate is limited (unless there is soil beneath the bed), which will in turn limit the size of the plants to some extent. Drainage tends to be free, so plants can suffer from drought unless watered regularly. Roots are not as well insulated as they would be in the ground, and in colder areas tender plants may be damaged or killed by a cold snap.

The main advantage of a raised bed over other types of container is its greater size, but this can also be a drawback when it comes to finding suitable soil with which to fill it.

Design and planning

Raised beds

punctured in it for drainage – will even enable you to turn the bed into a bog garden, in which you can grow plants such as primulas, marsh marigold, astilbes, hostas and irises.

Bricks

Raised beds can be constructed from a variety of materials, so choose one which blends happily with your house and surroundings. Brick is fairly easy to build with – use frost-proof bricks. Dry (unmortared) brick beds are often seen, but for all except very low walls it is more satisfactory to bond the bricks properly and mortar them together. Most beds will use single bricks laid lengthways, known as a half-brick wall; for this a simple running bond can be used in which the joints are staggered on each course. More decorative effects can be provided by full-brick walls, which are two bricks thick. Leave unmortared gaps between the bricks on the lowest course to act as weep holes, which will allow excess water to drain away.

Concrete and stone

Concrete blocks in a range of finishes can be used in a similar way to bricks. Stone-effect blocks, with textured finishes in various colours, are popular. Sometimes these come in "units" constructed to give the appearance of several stones already mortared together, which makes laying the blocks quick and easy. Natural stone is more expensive but the variation in its shades, textures and shapes gives it a more pleasing appearance. Dry-stone walls form an ideal bed for rock plants, but are not easy to build; the stones can be mortared into place for extra security.

Logs and peat

Whole or half logs make a pleasant, informal-looking raised bed; the height of the logs can be varied to give it a flowing outline. Preservative-treated logs can be used; sometimes sections of log bound together with wire, which simply need rolling out, are available. Logs may need to be partly buried in soil for stability. Acid-loving plants were at one time grown in beds in which the retaining walls were made from blocks of peat. These blocks were soaked and allowed to drain before being used to build walls one or two courses high. The beds were filled with compost made from peat mixed with acid topsoil and a small amount of grit, but the peat blocks tended to dry out and shrink. Some peat substitutes come in blocks, but beds are probably better formed from logs and filled with compost based on a peat substitute, such as coir.

How to build beds from brick and stone

The weight of damp soil within a raised bed will exert considerable outward pressure on the walls – the amount of pressure depends on the height of the walls. Most raised beds are at least 30cm (1ft) high, and to raise them to an easy

MAKING A RAISED PEAT-TYPE BED FROM TIMBER

1 Timber is particularly appropriate for peat-type beds for lime-hating plants. Lengths of 10 x 12.5cm (4 x 5in) timber, bought from a timber yard and treated with preservative, are the easiest to use.

2 Choose a place that provides a firm base on which to build, and one that will suit the plants – the petals of camellias will turn brown if they receive morning sun when wet or frosted. Bond the timber in staggered rows, like bricks.

3 For extra security, drill holes through the timber and insert steel rods to pin them together. Use a hammer with a heavy metal head and, if possible, drive the rods through the timber and into the ground for several centimetres.

Raised beds

A raised bed made from logs with an integral seat provides a resting place from which to contemplate your handiwork. Logs are particularly suitable for informal beds and woodland subjects.

working height means making them 60–100cm (2–3ft) high. For walls over 30cm (1ft) high, a proper foundation is recommended, except where you are building on a level concrete surface in good condition. Where foundations are to be used, mark out strips at least twice the width of the wall with pegs and string, and dig a trench 20–30cm (8–12in) deep. Consolidate the soil base well and drive in pegs to show where the top of the concrete should be. Make sure the tops of the pegs are level. Half-fill the trench with concrete, tamping it down and levelling the surface. Allow it to harden for a few days before starting to build the wall.

The first course or so of bricks, stones or concrete blocks will be below ground level where this type of foundation has been used. When building the wall, check both vertical and horizontal levels frequently, using a spirit level. Use posts and taut string stretched between them as a horizontal guide for each course of bricks or stones. Leave some unmortared joints between the building blocks on the course at ground level, to act as weep holes. Topping the walls with coping stones gives a finished appearance and the overlap affords the wall some protection from the weather.

It helps to conserve moisture if you line the base of the interior with heavy-duty polythene, but you need to make holes in it with a garden fork to enable water to drain out. On a concrete surface, a layer of hardcore will ensure sufficient drainage. If you want to grow lime-hating plants in a bed with a mortared wall, paint the inside of the wall with bitumen paint to prevent lime leaching into the soil from the mortar.

If you are not sufficiently skilled to build your own beds, you can pay professionals to do the work – but make sure they know your requirements and use appropriate materials.

4 *To suit plants such as rhododendrons, heathers and azaleas, the compost must be acidic, so fill the bed with moist peat-based compost, or one based on a peat substitute. Water the bed well before starting to plant.*

5 *Remember that even if you choose smaller varieties, the rhododendron, camellia and azalea will grow into quite large plants, so do not overcrowd them.*

6 *Finish the planting by adding some heathers and primulas that are already in flower, to complement the shrubs and to provide extra instant colour.*

Design and planning

Choosing containers

Visit any garden centre in order to pick a container for your plants and you are likely to be spoiled for choice. While appearance is important – the container is often just as much on show as the plant inside it – the style of the container must also be practical and suitable for the purpose you have in mind. What plants need from a container is an adequate volume and depth of soil and an efficient method of drainage to prevent waterlogging. Choose the size and shape of the container to suit the plant; a shallow pan is fine for alpines but hopeless for a vigorous, deep-rooted shrub. Check that the drainage holes are sufficient; sometimes, particularly with plastic pots, you can add extra holes yourself, but this is not always possible. Having catered for the plants' requirements, you then need to concentrate on picking a container of a material, shape and design that you find pleasing to look at and that will blend comfortably with its surroundings.

1 Blue earthernware pot with a shiny blue-glazed exterior and a cream interior. Best planted with an architectural plant, such as yucca, or a shrub or tree. 2 Terracotta pot with lipped holes for growing strawberries, herbs or alpines. 3 Traditional terracotta, or clay, pots, one plain and one embossed with a design of swags of leaves and flowers. Terracotta is an excellent material for plant pots, since it is porous and breathes and also looks good, especially when it has weathered; it is, however, brittle, prone to frost damage and plants need frequent watering in hot weather. 4 Novelty basket made from cement, then painted. Cement containers should be allowed to weather before being planted up. 5 Terracotta pot with a

Choosing containers

decorative wrought-iron stand, which would be attractive standing on a patio or in a sunroom. **6** Wide, shallow container, ideal for growing alpines. It is made from reconstituted stone, a mixture of crushed stone and concrete, which is much cheaper than real stone, although the appearance of good-quality pots is similar. **7** Stoneware pot – when weathered, stone is probably the most attractive of all materials for containers, but it is also the most expensive. **8** Terracotta feet, useful for raising pots off the ground to ensure good drainage. **9** Partially glazed earthernware pot, with a chequered pattern. A good sturdy pot for a larger specimen plant. **10** Traditional square terracotta planter; planted up with bay trees or clipped box; a pair of these planters would add a formal note to an entrance porch. **11** Shallow terracotta bowl, ideal for alpines and low-growing plants, such as pansies or miniature daffodils. **12** Terracotta stand with a shallow bowl – useful for adding height to an arrangement of containers. **13** A deep urn made from reconstituted stone, which would make an eye-catching feature in a small area, especially if raised on a pedestal. **14** Low glazed pot, which is large and deep enough to accommodate some summer salad crops or decorative winter cabbages.

Design and planning

Choosing containers

The typical round, sloping-sided plant pot has proved itself a practical and efficient shape for growing and working with plants, but other shapes can often be particularly useful for small spaces. Rectangular troughs fit on or under window ledges, or close up against a wall; half-round pots can be hung on walls or fitted on narrow ledges.

Hanging baskets, which are perhaps the ultimate in space-saving plant growing, come in a range of styles, some of which are much easier to keep watered than others. When considering less traditional types of plant container, avoid those with narrow necks or waists, such as Ali-baba jars. They may look attractive, but when it is time for the plant to be potted on, it is virtually impossible to remove it with its roots intact without breaking the container. If a container has sufficient style, it can be used as a garden ornament in its own right and does not need to be planted up.

Hanging baskets

SOLID-WALL BASKET
This type of container, made from plastic or terracotta, is really a flowerpot suspended on chains, rather than a basket. The bare wall can look unattractive, and you need to set trailing plants all around the edge of the pot so that the outside is quickly covered up. The great advantage of such solid-wall baskets is that they often have a drip tray built in, or one that can be clipped on. This is particularly useful in places where people either sit or walk underneath the hanging basket.

Tubs and troughs

1 *Deep blue-glazed trough, excellent for use on a patio or on the top of a wall.* **2** *Small terracotta window box, with a moulded pattern of acanthus leaves. This type of container is suited to more formal planting, perhaps with evergreens and other foliage plants.* **3** *This plastic window box with two built-in reservoirs for water would be a good choice for anyone with little time for watering.* **4** *A wooden half-barrel makes a good container for large plants needing special treatment, such as lime-hating camellias or rhododendrons, which must have ericaceous compost to thrive.* **5** *A large and substantial tub, such as this treated wooden one, is essential if you plan to grow trees in your "no-garden".*

Wall pots

Pots that can be mounted on the wall usually have flat backs with a hole or two in them so that they can be screwed to the wall or a batten, or hung on hooks. Shapes vary from round to half-round, to the novelty "swallow's nest" pot with a high back, which holds so little compost that it is suitable only for succulents and cacti.

Choosing containers

SELF-WATERING BASKET

Several versions of this type of solid-wall hanging basket are in use. However, the general principle is the same: a reservoir for water is built in at the base, and capillary matting is laid above this and below the compost. The matting is kept damp by water from the reservoir, which means that the basket needs to be watered only once every week or so.

TRADITIONAL BASKET

The hanging basket made from plastic-coated wire is the most popular type. Originally such baskets were lined with sphagnum moss, and moss may still be used today, usually in combination with plastic sheeting to prevent it drying out so rapidly. Other types of liner include those made from coconut fibre, wool, plastic foam and pre-formed compressed fibre. The great advantage of the wire basket is that plants can be inserted through the holes in the sides.

Hayrack

Also known as a manger, the hayrack is another, generally larger, type of wall-mounted container. It is made from flat strips of metal, possibly coated with black or white plastic to prevent it from rusting. The container must be lined with plastic sheeting and sphagnum moss before being filled with compost and plants.

Window boxes

Window boxes are the nearest some city dwellers come to having somewhere to grow plants. They need to be about 20cm (8in) wide and deep so that they will hold sufficient compost to sustain plants during the season, although if plants are set in the window box in their own individual pots, they can be replaced as they fade. In addition to the usual unlined plastic window box, it is possible to find wooden containers that contain plastic liners (left above), which can be planted up and put into the box when they are at their best. Watering can be a problem, but plastic window boxes are now available with a built-in water reservoir (left below).

Design and planning

Plant partners

Finding a pleasing combination using different types of plants is one of the joys of garden planning. Often you will accidentally discover a particularly happy association, but careful consideration before planting will usually pay dividends. Take into account the contrasts and similarities of shapes, colours, textures and sizes of the various plants, remembering the effect of the different seasons, and you will be able to create a garden where the whole really does seem to be greater than the sum of its parts.

Size and scale: The intense blue of grape hyacinths is offset perfectly by the cool lemon yellow of dwarf narcissi. Relative sizes of the flowers are important; in this situation large-flowered narcissi would tend to overpower the grape hyacinths so that a major part of the effect would be lost.

Winter planting: *Winter is often a difficult time of year in a small garden, but this terracotta container will be a season-long delight. The creamy white of the frilly-edged ornamental kale plants dominates the arrangement, but bright spots of colour are provided by the red skimmia berries, while trails of ivy soften the overall outline. The branching central brachyglottis provides height and structure.*

Plant partners

Colour and contrast: Acid yellow euphorbias and bright primroses make an effective colour contrast with deep blue forget-me-nots, but what gives this plant grouping its real impact is the brilliant scarlet of the lily-flowered tulips, which rise above the low-growing plants.

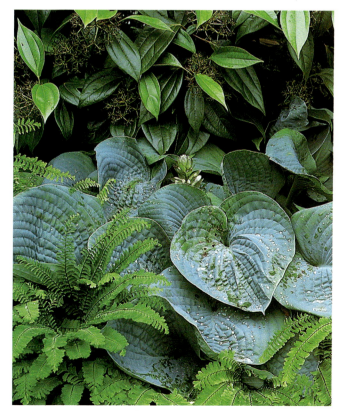

Cool shade: Perfect partners for a cool, shady spot, the lush, bold leaves of hostas form an effective contrast with lacy fern foliage. A variety of shades of green can be just as effective as brighter colour combinations.

Texture and foliage: The texture of flowers and foliage is an aspect that is often overlooked when planning plant combinations. The blue and white heads of nigella rise from a feathery mist of foliage and bracts, complemented by the acid-green, foamy flowers of alchemilla in the background. A ribbon of rosy red wallflowers brings solidity to the association.

Design and planning

Containers for all situations

Few plant lovers are lucky enough to have perfect growing conditions, but usually plants can be found to suit even the most difficult situations. A cold, exposed, windy spot demands particularly tough plants that are adapted to water loss as well as cold conditions.

In many ways, a sunny position is one of the easiest to plan for as far as plants are concerned. There are many that revel in full sun, although frequent watering will be needed to keep the compost moist. Plants with delicate flowers and foliage are also more likely to be scorched in a sunny situation, particularly if water droplets remain on the plant tissue to act as a magnifying lens for the sun's rays.

In the hottest, brightest areas, unrelieved sun can be difficult for most plants to cope with, particularly in an enclosed courtyard or patio garden, where the heat is reflected off stone or tile floors and walls. In these situations, opt for succulents or desert plants that are well adapted to bright, hot, dry conditions.

Many "no-garden" areas may have the opposite problem – little or no direct sun and generally low light levels. But there are also plenty of plants, whose natural habitat is under the shady canopy of trees, that are perfectly adapted to these conditions. They may not be as brilliantly coloured as sun lovers, but their subtle shades are still very attractive.

The plans shown here offer suggestions for planting, but it is easy to design containers to suit your own situation.

Plants for a cold, exposed position

Plants with leathery, waxy or needlelike leaves are well adapted to cold, drying winds. By choosing varieties with variegated and coloured leaves, you can make sure that such robust and sturdy plants will not look dull.

The roots of plants in containers are more susceptible to damage in extremely cold conditions, but by insulating the containers you can help to protect your plants.

THE PLANTS
1 *Aucuba japonica* 'Gold Dust'
2 *Euonymus fortunei* 'Emerald 'n' Gold'
3 *Hedera helix* 'Goldheart'
4 *Juniperus communis* 'Compressa'

Containers for all situations

Sun-lover's trough

This is a trough for a really hot spot, which uses just three succulent plants well able to cope with the conditions. The contrast of form and size makes this a very effective combination.

THE PLANTS
1. *Agave americana* 'Striata'
2. *Sedum spathulifolium*
3. *Sempervivum tectorum*

A tub for shade

Hostas are among the best plants for shade, with their heart-shaped leaves in a wide variety of sizes, textures and colours. In contrast to the fleshy-leafed hosta, Alchemilla mollis *has delicate lobed leaves and frothy heads of lime green flowers, while trailing* Vinca minor *is a vigorous grower with bright blue flowers.*

THE PLANTS
1. *Alchemilla mollis*
2. *Hosta* 'Shade Fanfare' or other variety
3. *Vinca minor*

89

Design and planning

Plants to catch the eye

Planting for visual impact involves not only the considered use of colour, but also of plant form and texture. Frequently a container is required to make a dramatic statement, particularly in a confined area where there is no room for a lot of other plants. Here, a simple arrangement is often most effective, relying on the individual plants themselves to provide the punch, and so-called "architectural" plants, with their bold shapes and plant forms, come into their own. A simple but striking container will reinforce the effect.

A traditional "riot of colour" from a window box or hanging basket is the aim of many a gardener, but colour theming of containers usually gives a far more pleasing effect than the random mixing of shades, though it need not be unduly restrictive. Boldest, brightest shades are the "hot" colours of the colour wheel – reds, oranges, yellows. "Cool" colours are blue, green and purple, which have a more restful effect.

Pastel tones can come from any part of the spectrum and are simply much paler tints of a particular colour; like cool colours, they are quiet and restful. Pastel colours are often particularly successful in slightly shaded situations, where their delicate colours will not be bleached out by brilliant sunshine.

Dramatic urn

Cordylines can be relied upon to provide a strong, dramatic shape – like an exploding firework. Both variegated and plain-leafed forms are successful, and in mild areas will continue to provide winter interest. The silvery cascades of **Lotus berthelotii***, parrot's beak, with its red and yellow flowers do not detract from the bold shape of the cordyline, but they do help to disguise the bare stem that this plant tends to develop.*

THE PLANTS
1 *Cordyline australis* 'Torbay Red'
2 *Lotus berthelotii*

Plants to catch the eye

Hanging basket in pastel colours

Subdued pastel tones have a quiet, relaxing effect. Here, pale blues, pink and white are complemented by silvery foliage plants for a cool summer basket. Don't position containers of pastel-coloured plants too close to plantings in bright colours or the paler tones may be overwhelmed.

THE PLANTS
1 *Bacopa* 'Snowflake'
2 *Felicia amelloides*
3 *Helichrysum petiolare*
4 *Impatiens*
   (pale pink variety)
5 *Lobelia* 'Fountain'
   (mixed blue and white shades)
6 *Pelargonium* (white variety)
7 *Petunia* Surfinia Series 'Blue Vein'

Trough in "hot" shades

This is a well-packed trough with plenty of contrast in flower shapes and plant forms to add to the liveliness of the brilliant colours. The trough uses colours from the "hot" range of the spectrum – intense reds, yellows and oranges. Take care to use the compact forms of rudbeckia and bidens, some varieties are too vigorous for container use.

THE PLANTS
1 *Begonia* (scarlet tuberous variety)
2 *Bidens ferulifolia*
3 *Fuchsia* 'Thalia'
4 *Lysimachia nummularia* 'Aurea'
5 *Pelargonium* 'Balcon Red'
6 *Petunia* (creamy yellow variety)
7 *Rudbeckia* 'Toto'

91

Design and planning

The value of foliage

Flowers are often the most colourful and eye-catching parts of a plant, but the value of foliage should not be underestimated. Apart from providing a useful foil to the flowers, the leaves can be a striking feature in their own right. They may be large and showy, with bold, dramatic shapes, or tiny and numerous, forming an overall cloudy haze of green. Their arrangement on the stalk can provide distinctive and attractive plant outlines; they can be coloured, variegated, spiky, leathery, hairy or fragrant.

Sometimes a foliage plant on its own makes a perfect container specimen, its simplicity being the key to its effectiveness. A container of mixed foliage plants enables textures, colours and forms to be complemented or contrasted, making an arrangement of long-season interest.

Single variety planting

Depending upon the type of plant, a single specimen or a small group of one variety – even a simple grass or bamboo – can make a striking display. This variegated hakonechloa makes a spectacular fountain of colourful foliage.

THE PLANT
Hakonechloa macra 'Alboaurea'

Colour from foliage

Leaves sometimes have surprisingly intense and unusual colours. In this planting, plummy purple and red shades of euphorbia and grey-mottled heuchera are highlighted by the silver filigree foliage of artemisia and the almost black, strap-like leaves of ophiopogon.

THE PLANTS
1 *Artemisia* 'Powis Castle'
2 *Euphorbia amygdaloides* 'Rubra'
3 *Heuchera* 'Pewter Moon' or 'Palace Purple'
4 *Ophiopogon planiscapus* 'Nigrescens'

Scented and aromatic plants

The smaller your growing space, the more important it is that plants should earn their keep. As well as looking good, they can please some of the other senses too.

Selecting strongly scented flowering plants gives you an opportunity to gain immense pleasure from a container that is situated near a sitting area, where the plants' fragrance can be enjoyed in moments of relaxation. But it is not only flowers that are aromatic – foliage can be scented, too. A trough of herbs is attractive, fragrant and practical, since many of the herbs can be used in the kitchen or home.

Herb trough

Herbs are perfect for container growing, and, if picked reasonably sparingly, will provide sprigs for use in the kitchen over an extended season. There are plenty of contrasting forms and foliage colours to give visual interest to the trough.

THE PLANTS
1 *Origanum vulgare* (oregano, marjoram)
2 *Petroselinum crispum* 'Curlina' or similar compact, curled variety (parsley)
3 *Salvia officinalis* 'Tricolor' (variegated sage)
4 *Satureja hortensis* (summer savory)
5 *Thymus x citriodorus* 'Aureus' (golden lemon thyme)

Tub with scented plants

Many flowers are most strongly scented in the evening, but this tub contains sufficient variety of plants to be fragrant throughout the day. The colour scheme has been kept simple, with purple, pink and the pure white of the lily.

THE PLANTS
1 *Glechoma hederacea* 'Variegata'
2 *Heliotropium* (heliotrope)
3 *Lilium regale*
4 *Nicotiana* 'Havana Apple Blossom'
5 *Petunia* (purple-pink variety)

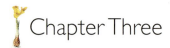# Chapter Three

Basic gardening

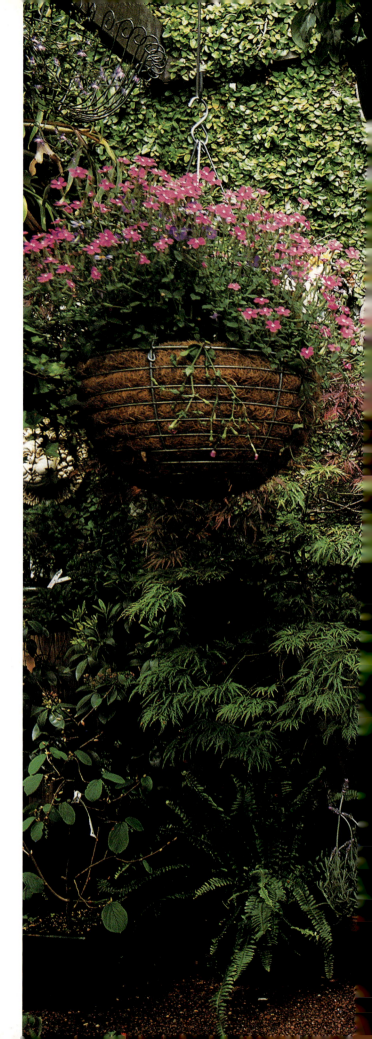

Green plants have a major advantage over many other types of organism – they can manufacture food from sunlight by converting the sun's energy directly into energy for their own maintenance and growth. To do this, they need certain chemicals, water, moderately warm temperatures and physical support.

In the natural world, soil provides a reservoir of rainwater and suitable chemicals for the plants' needs. It also forms a support system for the roots, enabling them to anchor plants firmly in place while they grow outwards and upwards above the soil surface. In the growing conditions of a "no-garden" space, a good depth and expanse of soil is exactly what is missing. So the plant-grower must provide the necessary pieces of the jigsaw to enable the plants to thrive in unnatural conditions.

This tiny, lavishly planted space is deceptively casual: it features dozens of different ways of growing plants. To achieve such a rich effect in a small corner, you need a sensitive and creative understanding of the way plants work.

Basic gardening

How plants grow

Plants that grow in a garden usually benefit from receiving much more light than houseplants do, but light can still prove a problem in our "no-garden" growing areas. Small plots may be bounded by high walls or fences, or overhung by neighbouring trees; basement areas become increasingly dull the deeper they are; walls may never receive direct sunlight.

Light

All green plants need light in order to grow, but plants need a particular quality of light in order to photosynthesize, or manufacture carbohydrates. The different parts of the spectrum are split into wavelengths, and the varying wavelengths of the visible spectrum consist of light of different colours. The portion of the light spectrum that is useful to the plant is absorbed by it, while the light that is of no value is reflected. The fact that plants are green shows that green light is of little use to them and is being reflected – the most valuable light for photosynthesis is an orange-red shade.

As far as gardeners are concerned, the practical application of this is to ensure that plants receive an adequate amount of ordinary daylight, a large proportion of which is useful to them. Artificial lighting, while it is valuable for adding to the visual appeal of a plot, is unlikely to be of any benefit for plant growth unless special growth-promoting light bulbs are used, and these are only really practical for use with indoor plants.

For the most part, plants try to maximise the amount of light they can absorb. This is why leaves are usually flat and thin, and are arranged on the branches in such a way as to present the maximum surface area to the sun. The basic outline of many plants is a conical shape, which ensures that the lower leaves are not overshadowed by the upper branches. Plants may also be able to turn the surface of their leaves to follow the sun during its daily journey across the sky. They can also adjust them to the variations in light intensity resulting from cloud cover.

Plant species vary in the intensity of light they require. Some thrive only in full sun, while others are well adapted to low light conditions – those plants that form the understorey of forest or woodland, for example, where little light penetrates the dense tree canopy. Such shade-loving plants are adapted to absorb what little light there is, and would soon be scorched and damaged by a position in strong, bright sunlight. Plants which in nature grow in open positions in full sun have a variety of mechanisms to protect their leaves from excess exposure, including dense silvery hairs and shiny reflective surfaces. These impede light absorption, so the plant is unable to cope with shaded conditions. Choosing the right varieties of plant for the quality of light in any given situation is, therefore, the first important step to growing them successfully.

The effect of varying light intensity is most easily observed on variegated plants. In bright conditions, there is ample light for the leaves to absorb, and the active, green portions of the leaves can afford to be relatively small, with large, well-defined coloured areas (usually yellow or white), which do not photosynthesize. Where light levels are lower, however, the amount of variegation decreases as the green areas increase, in an attempt by the plant to improve the overall absorption of light. Frequently, a plant in shady conditions will lose its variegation altogether and revert to an all-green form.

Air

Air is vitally important to plants because the carbon dioxide it contains forms part of the equation for photosynthesis (in a simplified form, $CO_2 + H_2O \rightarrow CH_2O + O_2$, or carbon dioxide plus water gives carbohydrate plus oxygen).

Air is also necessary for respiration, another process carried out by plants. This is almost the reverse of photosynthesis: as carbohydrates are broken down for use by the plant, oxygen is taken in and carbon dioxide is given out.

There is no need to worry about enough air being available for plants to undertake these functions, but sufficient fresh air can be vital in preventing fungal diseases. These tend to thrive in humid conditions with little air movement, such as those found in overcrowded plantings. When gardening in small spaces there is a great temptation to cram in as many plants as possible, but being a little more generous with plant spacing can often prevent a display being ruined through damping off, grey mould or other similar diseases.

How plants grow

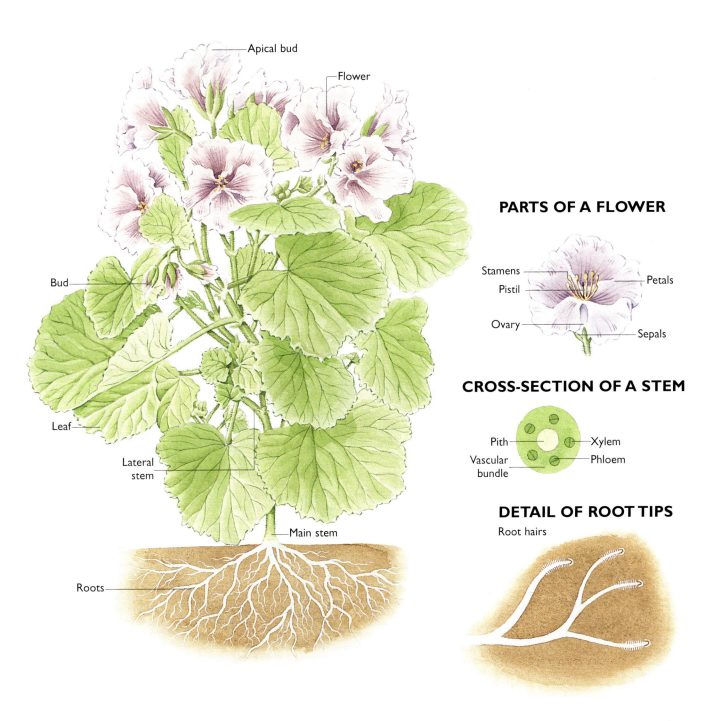

PARTS OF A FLOWER

CROSS-SECTION OF A STEM

DETAIL OF ROOT TIPS

Plants vary greatly in form, but the main parts are evident on almost every type of plant. The plant's food is made in the leaves, while the flowers carry the reproductive organs. The female reproductive organs, known collectively as the pistil, are the ovary (usually hidden by the petals), the style, or stalk, and the stigma, which receives pollen grains from another flower. The male reproductive organs are the stamens, made up of filaments, topped by pollen-bearing anthers.

The stems, shoots and roots contain vascular bundles which act like veins and arteries, carrying food to all parts of the plant. Xylem carries water from the roots, phloem transports nutrients and the pith provides support. Apical buds are the growth buds at the tips of shoots.

Fine hairs on the roots absorb water and nutrients from the soil. The root system, which may be extensive and fibrous or a tap root, also anchors and supports the plant.

Basic gardening

How plants grow

Water

Another essential element of photosynthesis is water, but it also performs other important functions. The various chemicals needed and used by the plant are dissolved in water, enabling them to be transported in solution to different parts of the plant so that the correct chemical reactions can take place. The pressure of water within each cell also keeps the whole plant turgid, or swollen, and erect. If a plant has insufficient water, the leaves and stems lose their turgor and begin to go limp – in other words, the plant wilts.

The natural water supply for plants is rain, which is held in the soil in spaces between the soil particles. The plant's tiny rootlets and root hairs penetrate these spaces and absorb water as part of a process known as transpiration. The wide, flat leaf surfaces that are such a good shape for absorbing sunlight are also a good shape for the evaporation of water to take place, so a plant is constantly losing large amounts of water from its foliage. Water is carried through the plant in a continuous pipework of cells called xylem; as water evaporates from the cells of the leaf, more water is automatically sucked up through the pipework from the soil. This system works well until the reservoir of soil water is empty; moisture continues to evaporate from the leaves but cannot be replaced, leading to the wilting and eventual collapse of the plant.

Even in natural conditions, and in areas with relatively high rainfall, the death or stunting of plants due to drought is common; in "no-garden" situations, the problem is particularly acute. Soil depth is shallow; the soil in containers drains freely and is exposed to all-round evaporation. Dense plantings lead to heavy competition for water as the soil becomes filled with roots; profuse leaf cover prevents rain from reaching the soil, and, anyway, little rain may penetrate to the sheltered positions in which we try to grow our plants. As a result, frequent watering is likely to be necessary throughout the growing season. Hot sun obviously increases the rate of evaporation from plants, but windy conditions can be just as damaging, whipping away moisture from the leaf surface. Increased watering is likely to be necessary in both sets of conditions.

EVAPOTRANSPIRATION

Water taken up by the roots of the plant travels up the xylem system to all parts of the plant and evaporates through the foliage. The water removed from the soil is replaced by rain or by frequent watering.

Nutrients

Plants cannot survive solely on the energy they derive from sunlight, and a variety of chemicals is also needed to carry out a wide range of functions within the plant. These chemicals are usually referred to as plant nutrients. They are normally present naturally in the soil, but where artificial composts and only small amounts of soil are used, many of the chemicals will have to be provided or supplemented by the gardener.

Three major plant nutrients are required in relatively large quantities – nitrogen, phosphorus and potassium – and they are commonly in short supply in heavily cropped soils. The role of these chemicals is quite complex and they play a part in many aspects of the plant's growth. In broad terms:

NITROGEN is responsible for the leafy growth of plants.
PHOSPHORUS is needed for good seed germination and healthy root development.
POTASSIUM is required for flower and fruit formation and general hardiness. Calcium, magnesium, sulphur and iron are also required, but in lower doses.
CALCIUM is an important constituent of the cell and has a particular role to play in the development of shoot tips (for example, the death of the tips of developing tomato fruits, known as blossom end rot, is due in part to calcium shortage). But for most gardeners, the main importance of calcium is the way in which it interacts with other essential nutrients, making some of them unavailable to the plant. Some plants are particularly sensitive to this and will not grow satisfactorily in soil in which calcium (in the form of lime) is present – they are called calcifuges, or lime-haters, and include rhododendron, pieris and camellia.
MAGNESIUM is essential for photosynthesis to take place and a shortage leads to yellowing of the leaves (especially the older ones) between the veins.
SULPHUR plays a part in cell division and protein structure, but it is rare for it to be in short supply in the soil.
IRON is also rarely in short supply, but plants often show signs of iron shortage because they cannot use what is available, generally because of the presence of calcium. The characteristic yellowing between bright green veins that results is known as lime-induced chlorosis. Like magnesium, iron is necessary to enable photosynthesis to take place.
TRACE ELEMENTS (micronutrients) are also required in tiny amounts. They are, nevertheless, essential to the plant and will cause symptoms of distress if not available. They include elements such as molybdenum, boron, manganese, copper and zinc, but any one trace element deficiency is normally dealt with by using a fertiliser containing the complete range. Because deficiencies are frequently caused by calcium rendering minerals in the soil unavailable to the plant, these fertilisers are often formulated as foliar sprays, to be taken up directly by the leaves.

Warmth

The climate around the world produces widely varying temperatures, but most of the plants we grow do best within the range of 5°–25°C (41°–77°F). Above and below these temperatures, growth will be much slower. For most plants, 10°–20°C (50°–68°F) provides the optimum temperature range for growth.

In what we think of as the "warmer" areas of the world, it is not the temperature peaks that promote lusher, faster growth, but the fact that the temperature range stays within the plant's optimum growth range for a larger proportion of the year. In temperate climates, growth is virtually halted for several months when the temperature drops in winter; similarly in hot, desert regions plants grow much more slowly as temperatures rise.

Ferns such as Nephrolepis *can tolerate widely fluctuating temperatures.*

Because high temperatures cause greater evaporation of water, plants tend to suffer from water stress as well. In "no-garden" situations, plants growing in enclosed areas, on balconies in full sun and against sunny walls can become much hotter than in larger, more open gardens. As long as plants have sufficient soil moisture and humidity, high temperatures on their own are not likely to cause too much damage, although sun scorch may be a problem.

In temperate regions, the onset of cold weather must be contended with. Some particularly tender plants will die when the temperature drops to a certain level above freezing, but usually it is frost that sounds the death knell. As the plant's tissues freeze, the cell membranes rupture and the soft growth collapses and turns black. Firmer growth, such as older stems, can withstand the effects of freezing to a certain extent, but hard frosts may eventually kill this too.

Shrubs and trees, which have woody stems and branches, are more resistant to the effects of frost, and although leafy growth may be killed, the framework of branches may sprout again from dormant buds the following spring. Roots are also protected from cold by the soil, and some plants survive freezing weather as dormant rootstocks, even when the top growth has been killed. Different species of plant have different degrees of cold tolerance, or hardiness.

Basic gardening

How plants grow

Tender plants, with little cold tolerance, can often be grown in cooler climates in summer, being discarded at the end of the season. Half-hardy plants will not withstand long periods of cold but are more tolerant than tender plants, while hardy plants should survive spells of freezing temperatures.

The role of the roots

A plant's roots have two functions. They take up moisture and nutrients, and they also anchor the plant. In nature, plants usually grow in soil, but they can grow on other plants, like some orchids in tropical jungles; in water, like aquatic plants; and in gravel, shingle or fissures in rocks, like alpines. But if they are going to photosynthesize, they usually need to be able to stay in one place and to spread their topgrowth to maximize its exposure to sunlight. If its roots are not firmly anchored, the plant runs the risk of falling over.

The qualities of soil

Soil varies widely from place to place, but it has usually developed from weathered rock, which has gradually been eroded down to fine grains. Most soil also contains organic matter in the form of dead animal and plant remains, which are broken down by bacteria and soil organisms to form humus.

The type of rock from which soils have developed, and the amount of humus they contain, give them different qualities. The size of the soil grains, and therefore the spaces between the grains, are all-important; large grains, as in sandy soil, have large spaces between them, so water and dissolved nutrients drain away rapidly.

Small grains, as in clay and silt soils, have only small spaces between them which trap water and nutrients. Plants in sandy soil often suffer from drought and nutrient deficiencies; plants in clay soil may suffer from waterlogging of the roots. Humus – decayed organic matter – improves both types of soil, acting as a sponge to soak up moisture and make it available to the plants.

Since "no-garden" gardens contain no (or very little) natural soil, the growing medium has to be imported in the form of pre-packed compost of different types.

A colourful summer display of pansies and lobelia in a hanging basket will do best in lightweight compost with Perlite or other water-retaining granules added.

TYPES OF COMPOST

Most composts are generally of a reliable standard if a reputable brand is bought. Soil-based composts are very like garden soil; soilless composts are based on peat or a peat substitute. For larger areas, such as raised beds, topsoil can be bought, but the quality is often variable and it is difficult to check it before buying. Special composts are also available.

Because varying amounts of fertilisers are added to pre-packed composts, check the packs to see when you need to start feeding plants with extra fertiliser. Soil-based compost generally has the longest-lasting nutrient reserve.

Different ingredients give different amounts of support to a plant's roots, with the heavier, soil-based compost offering the most stability. You can also provide root support with pebbles, stone chippings, sand, tree bark, rock, clay granules and so on. But few of these offer nutrients as well, so you will have to adapt your fertiliser programme accordingly.

Soil-based compost

This is similar to garden soil. It contains a higher level of nutrients than other composts and retains water well. Use it for trees and shrubs, such as buddleja.

Peat-based compost

Lighter and cleaner to handle, peat-based compost runs out of nutrients quickly and dries out easily. Use it for annuals, bulbs, and tubers.

Peat-substitute compost

Made from substances such as tree bark or coir, with added nutrients, this can be used instead of peat for plants such as florist's chrysanthemums.

Ericaceous compost

This is compost without free lime, which calcifuge plants (lime-haters), such as azaleas, pieris, heaths and heathers, need in order to grow well.

Perlite and compost

Lightweight compost with water-retaining granules, such as Perlite, mixed in, is ideal for hanging baskets and window boxes, where weight is critical.

Basic gardening

Types of plant

Plants are divided into a number of general categories according to their physical characteristics and the way in which they grow. Knowing which category a plant belongs to will help you to care for it correctly and enable you to plan for future years. The different categories are not always straightforward – there is often some overlap between them.

Annuals
These are plants which germinate, flower, set seed and die within one year. Some hardy annual plants, such as candytuft and cornflower, can be sown in autumn and will overwinter to flower and die the following season; although they seem to span two growing seasons they still complete their life cycle within 12 months. Plants sown in autumn will flower earlier and give a longer display than those sown outdoors in spring.

Hardy annuals will tolerate frost; half-hardy annuals will not. In cold areas, half-hardy annuals are often sown indoors and transplanted to their flowering positions once the likelihood of frost has passed. They may be raised at home in a greenhouse or conservatory, or sometimes on a sunny window-sill, or they can be produced commercially and bought as young plants from garden centres in spring. Some half-hardy annuals can be sown outdoors where they are to flower once the danger of frost is over.

Many of the plants that appear in seed catalogues as annuals are, in fact, perennials – if left to do so, they would survive for a number of years. However, because the display they give is much less attractive after the first year, they are treated as annuals and replaced at the end of the season.

Biennials
Plants that produce only leafy growth in their first season, then overwinter to flower the following spring or summer, are known as biennials; they need two seasons to complete their life cycle. They are sown in autumn or spring to

Two commonly grown biennials are the stately summer-flowering hollyhock (above left), and the cheerful honey-scented spring-flowering wallflower.

Lupins, with their close-packed heads of pea-like flowers and handsome foliage, are among the most rewarding perennials.

early summer, depending on climate and germination temperature, and transplanted later. Where space does not allow them to be raised at home, like half-hardy annuals, they can be bought from garden centres. Popular examples include wallflower, daisy and forget-me-not. As with annuals, some plants treated as biennials are actually perennials which are discarded after their first flowering season.

Bedding plants
This is a loose term for young plants which are set out in beds and borders in spring and discarded at the end of the flowering season. Many of them are annuals and biennials, but plants from other groups may also be included. They are always temporary residents.

Perennials
Unlike annuals and biennials, these plants do not die once they have flowered, but live for a number of years, given appropriate conditions. Many perennials are herbaceous – they die down in winter in cool climates, reappearing from the rootstock again in spring. However, some perennials, such as bergenia and some species of hellebore, are evergreen.

An increasingly popular bedding plant is the vivid annual zinnia (right), which is also an excellent flower for cutting.

Basic gardening

Types of plant

Shrubs

These plants maintain a woody framework of branches above ground all year round, although some species may be killed by frost in colder climates. The distinction between shrubs and trees is not clear cut, and there is some overlap; there are also some small, low-growing shrubs, such as garden thyme and lavender, which are generally known as subshrubs, or sometimes as shrubby perennials.

Shrubs may be deciduous or evergreen, and have a wide variety of attractive features, being grown for their foliage, flowers, berries or attractive stems, as well as their general shape and form. Foliage can be variegated or plain, or have spectacular autumn tints; flowers can be carried at every season of the year.

Even in small spaces, shrubs are valuable to create a basic framework for the overall garden design. And where there is no space for a tree, a large or medium-sized shrub can act as an eye-catching feature. The secret is to find the right shrub for the purpose you have in mind.

Consider the shape and the eventual height and spread of the plant. Do you want an evergreen that will contribute to the form of the garden all year round? Do you want spring flowers or autumn colour, or both? In a small "no-garden" area it will pay you to take time in selecting the perfect shrub for what may be the only spot in which you can plant one.

There is an enormous range of shrubs available, so try to choose one that offers more than one attractive feature – flowers, fruits, autumn coloration, beautiful bark – so that it will earn its place in your garden all through the year.

The mop-head hydrangea, with its great heavy heads in pink, blue or white, is an accommodating shrub, which will grow happily in a container and in almost any type of soil.

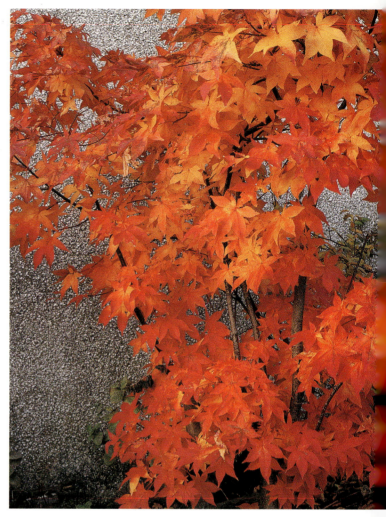

The Japanese maple Acer palmatum *'Osakazuki', with its dazzling display of autumn colour, welcomes the shelter of a wall.*

Trees

The main distinction between a tree and a shrub is the tree's larger size and its single stem, which forms a trunk, but this does not always hold true. Some vigorous shrubs grow far larger than some small species of tree, and a tree may grow several stems while a shrub sometimes develops (or is trained as) a single stem. Plants which would form large trees in their native habitat remain small and shrubby when grown in different climates, and some trees are regularly pruned back to keep them bushy – eucalyptus, for example, when it is grown for its juvenile foliage.

Large, spreading trees are obviously not suitable for "no-garden" areas, but that does not mean that all trees are out of bounds. Some smaller species adapt quite easily to growing in containers and provide useful height and vertical emphasis. Maples (*Acer* spp.), some birches, bay (*Laurus nobilis*) and conifers, such as yew (*Taxus baccata*) or white cedar (*Thuja occidentalis*), make ideal trees for small spaces.

Types of plant

Bulbs, corms, tubers and rhizomes

All of these plants have underground storage organs which enable the dormant plant to survive. There are subtle differences between them, although they are often lumped together as "bulbous plants". Bulbs consist of fleshy leaves wrapped around an embryo flower bud, all usually covered by a dry, papery, protective skin – daffodils and tulips are well-known examples.

Corms are swollen stem bases which are renewed each year, and include plants such as crocus and gladiolus. Tubers are either swollen stems, as in begonias and cyclamen, or tuberous roots, such as dahlias.

Rhizomes look like roots, but are, in fact, swollen underground stems, which generally grow horizontally, so they tend to move forwards through the soil. Irises are probably the best-known rhizomatous plants.

Tuber

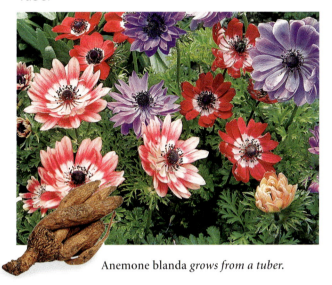

Anemone blanda grows from a tuber.

Bulb

Bulbous tulips enliven late spring days.

Corm

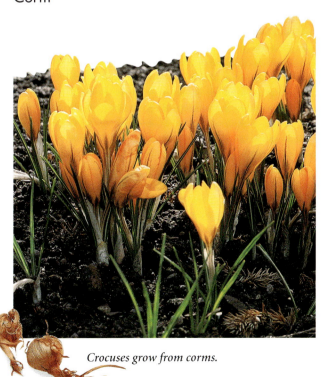

Crocuses grow from corms.

Rhizome

The beardless Iris versicolor *has a rhizome.*

Basic gardening

Choosing plants

There are many different ways to obtain plants, and your choice will depend, among other things, on how much money you want to spend, what facilities you have, and how much work you want to do. Your first choice is between raising your own stock from seed or cuttings, and buying in ready-to-plant specimens.

Raising your own plants is satisfying, usually cheaper, and often gives you a greater selection of varieties and flower colours. However, you do need to be able to provide the right facilities for germination or rooting and growing on. Some seeds will germinate quite easily in a dark, warm place, for others you will need a heated propagator. If you are to be successful, you also need to have sufficient space and time to allow the plants to develop, and be reasonably skilled in the propagation and care of young plants (*see* pp.142–149 for details of propagation techniques).

Sowing seeds

If you want only one or two packets of seed, a reduced selection of varieties from seed companies is available at garden centres and stores. From them you can also obtain seed which has been treated in various ways to make it easier to sow and germinate.

PELLETED SEED is covered in a clay mixture that separates the seeds and makes them a more suitable size for easy handling and space sowing. It is useful for plants which have very small seeds, such as petunias.

SEED STICKS contain single seeds glued to the ends of paper "matchsticks", which can be torn apart and inserted separately into the soil.

SEED TAPES have the seed evenly spaced along a length of paper tape, which is laid where you want the plants to grow and then buried.

SAVING SEED The cheapest way to obtain seed is to save it from flowers grown by yourself or by friends, but not all varieties will give good results. Hybrid varieties do not breed true from seed, so if you save seed from them you will end up with something quite different from what you were expecting.

Seed gathered straight from flowers often needs to be sown immediately to give a good germination rate – commercially collected seed is specially treated and kept in carefully controlled conditions to preserve its viability.

BUYING SEED BY MAIL ORDER

Mail-order seed catalogues provide a wealth of ideas and information about plants, as well as offering a good selection of varieties, some old favourites, some new introductions. Flowers are generally available in single colour selections, making it easier to plan themed plantings – plants on offer at garden centres are often available only as mixed colours, so you have to take pot luck. There is usually an excellent selection of annuals, biennials and vegetables, enabling you to choose varieties according to size, habit of growth, foliage colour and so on. Most catalogues also offer seeds of perennials, although not in the same abundance as annuals, and some seeds of shrubs and trees.

Choosing plants

compost, increase the heat and amount of water they are given to start them into growth, and take cuttings from the new shoots as they develop. Pelargoniums, begonias, fuchsias, and many other plants can be propagated in this way. As well as using your own plants, you can also ask for cuttings from the plants of friends and neighbours.

Buying in plants

Plants can be bought at various sizes and stages of growth, either by mail order or from nurseries and garden centres. Generally, the smaller the plants supplied, the cheaper they will be, but the more difficult to grow on to flowering size. Plants for growing on are usually sold as seedlings or "plug plants".

SEEDLINGS have been germinated under the correct light and temperature conditions, and they are supplied to you at a time of year when it is easy to provide the necessary warmth and light for their continuing development. They are normally available in small trays of compost which contain different numbers of plants according to variety. Within a short time of their arrival the seedlings will need pricking out (replanting into seed trays so as to give them more room to grow), and you will need to have sufficient well-lit space to grow them on unless they are large enough to plant in their flowering positions. You will also need compost and small pots or trays into which to prick out the plants.

"PLUG PLANTS" do not need pricking out – they have been raised in individual cells containing a small "plug" of compost. They will need potting up into larger containers, but there is not the same urgency as with other seedlings, and the individual plants are much easier to handle. Plug plants are usually available in a range of different sizes.

READY-TO-USE PLANTS are large enough to plant out into beds or containers – ideal if you don't have the facilities for growing on. Some mail-order suppliers offer larger-than-normal plug plants for setting out immediately, and will deliver them at a time when you can do this without worrying about frost. There are many ready-to-use plants at nurseries and garden centres, including herbs, advanced seedlings, climbers and rock plants. A large range of perennials, shrubs and trees are sold in individual pots. The larger the plant, and its pot size, the more expensive it tends to be. Such plants, which have been raised in containers, can be planted out at virtually any time of year.

Quite large specimens of popular plants such as fuchsias and pelargoniums (above left) are usually potted up individually. Small seedlings for growing on (above right) are usually sold in trays. Plug plants (right) can be bought in different sizes in lightweight plastic or polystyrene trays. Seedlings of annuals ready for planting out (below) are also sold in trays or strips.

Taking cuttings

Many plants are easy to root from cuttings and will give you a good stock of young plants for little outlay. Plants that have performed particularly well can be propagated in summer, and the young plants overwintered in frost-free conditions for setting out the following spring. If space for overwintering is a problem, retain just one or two of the best original specimens, keeping them frost-free and just moist during the winter. In early spring, repot them in fresh

Basic gardening

Choosing plants

BARE-ROOT PLANTS This used to be the only form in which most plants were available, and they are still obtainable from various nurseries and may sometimes be supplied by mail order. Bare-root plants can be planted only in the dormant season. They are often "lined out" in nursery rows, and when the dormant season arrives they are lifted and transplanted as required. It is a cheaper way of buying relatively large quantities of plants. When a plant has been lifted, efforts should be made to prevent the roots from drying out (in the dormant season, wind is the major drying factor). Wrap the roots in plastic or in a paper sack for the journey home, then set the plant in its permanent position as soon as you arrive there. If it is not possible to plant it immediately, cover the roots with moist soil or compost and keep the plant in a sheltered, frost-free place until you can.

ROOT-BALLED PLANTS Root-balled shrubs and trees are similar to bare-root specimens, but the plants have been undercut while growing in the nursery bed to encourage them to form a compact ball of fibrous roots. They are then lifted with as much soil as possible around the intact root ball, which is generally wrapped in sacking or netting to hold it together. This method of growing plants helps to avoid the root damage that can occur when the plants are lifted, and so prevents any subsequent check to establishment and plant growth.

Where to buy plants

The main options for buying plants are mail order, garden centres or specialist nurseries.

MAIL ORDER is convenient; you can choose plants from a catalogue at home and they are delivered to your door, saving you the trouble of making a special journey and possible problems in transporting the plants. For rare or specialist plants, mail order may be the only option, since unusual plants may not be available at any outlet within travelling distance. The drawbacks of mail order are that you have to rely on catalogue descriptions and you cannot see the size or quality of the plants you are ordering. You usually have no control over the date they will arrive (although some specialist firms allow you to specify despatch dates). Plants may be damaged in transit, and though you can normally obtain replacements or refunds, this involves extra trouble and loses valuable growing time. You also have to pay for the carriage of the plants, which can be fairly expensive.

GARDEN CENTRES are popular, since most have a good range of competitively priced plants and also stock many of the sundries you are likely to need, making "one-stop shopping" possible. However, they are unlikely to stock unusual species or varieties, and they can quickly sell out of seasonal items. The quality of the plants is also sometimes indifferent at poorly run outlets, but you can at least select them yourself.

SMALLER NURSERIES where plants are raised on the premises are dwindling in number, but here you can usually buy from a knowledgeable seller who gives advice freely. This type of nursery usually specialises in specific groups or species of plants (clematis, or hostas, for example) and you are likely to find a much better selection of those particular plants than you would at garden centre chains.

The range of types of seedlings in a garden centre is often rather limited, but you can check them over and choose strong, healthy plants.

Choosing plants

WHAT TO LOOK FOR

GOOD SIGNS

BAD SIGNS

- Plenty of flowers and buds
- Healthy foliage
- Concise labelling
- Roots just emerging from the bottom of the pot

- Drooping blooms
- Damaged shoots
- Signs of pest damage
- Poor-coloured and wilting foliage
- Weed growth
- Dry compost and broken container
- Long roots pushing through the pot

Look for a plant that appears healthy, with good-sized, evenly green leaves (poor-coloured leaves indicate that the plant has been starved). Select a well-balanced, sturdy specimen with stocky stems, avoiding those that are one-sided or have soft, elongated stems. Bigger is not necessarily better; smaller, sturdier plants grow more quickly and can often overtake initially larger specimens after a short time in their permanent positions.

With container-grown plants, check the base of the pot; root tips should be just emerging from the drainage holes. If long, matted roots are protruding, the pot is too small, and the plant's growth will have been checked. If there is no sign of roots, try gently tipping the rootball from the pot – after one or two taps the whole rootball should slide out cleanly. If it does not, it could indicate that the plant has only recently been potted up and should be left a little longer to establish itself. The surface of the compost should be free from weeds, which will have been competing with the plant and which could be a nuisance if they get established among your plants at home. The compost should also be evenly moist; do not buy plants where the compost is dry and has shrunk away from the sides of the pot.

Check the undersides of the leaves for signs of pests and diseases, and reject any plants that are damaged or infested.

Basic gardening

Tools and equipment

Only a few tools are essential for "no-gardens", which is just as well, since tool storage can be a problem where space is limited. Tools can be expensive, but it's worth buying the best quality you can afford – buying cheap brands often proves to be a false economy.

Caring for the tools properly will extend their life and improve their performance. Small hand tools can usually be found a place in the home, or you can keep them outside in waterproof wooden or plastic storage bins and boxes. A useful way to keep long-handled tools tidy is to hang them on a wall rack with hooks. Some manufacturers supply sets of tools with one handle and a number of interchangeable heads (hoes, brushes, forks and so on), and these are particularly good where storage space is limited.

Always clean your tools properly after use. Remove all soil and mud, wipe the tools over with a damp cloth, then dry them and rub the bright parts over with a little oil to prevent rust. Stainless steel blades are expensive but long lasting, and there are various other metal finishes that are claimed to improve performance and prolong the life of the tools.

What you will need

What tools you will need depends on the space you have and the type of gardening you are going to do; if your plant-growing is limited to containers, you will need fewer tools than if you have larger areas of raised beds to cultivate.

TROWEL AND HAND FORK A trowel is not essential for planting in containers, but it does make life easier and is useful for planting in beds or in the ground. It is probably the tool that is going to get the most use in a "no-garden" situation. As well as digging holes for planting, it can be used for digging out weeds, mixing compost and incorporating fertiliser. A hand fork is useful for "titivating" soil in containers. Make sure you buy sturdy tools that will not bend when pressure is applied.

SECATEURS These are necessary to keep plants within bounds in limited spaces, for general pruning work, and to help with clearing up at the end of the season. There are two basic types of secateur: by-pass (parrot-billed), where the two parts of the blade pass each other like scissors, and anvil, where the blade meets a flat surface when cutting. It is usually easier to obtain a clean cut with the parrot-billed type. Test out the feel of secateurs when buying them, since it is important that they fit your hand comfortably and are easy to use. Check that the handles are not likely to pinch the fleshy part of your hand. Brands with a rolling handle may be worth considering if you find constant squeezing tiring, although they are really intended for people who are likely to be pruning for hours at a time. If you have a weak grip, ratchet-action secateurs make tough cuts with the minimum of effort.

Along with your secateurs you may like to use a knife occasionally, but in small spaces it is not the essential gardening tool it is often made out to be. For most functions, secateurs, a pair of scissors or a single-sided razor blade are just as satisfactory. If you are planning to use a knife to take cuttings or carry out pruning, it must be really sharp.

BORDER FORK AND SPADE In most small-space gardens these are not needed, but if you have a raised bed you may find a fork useful for turning over the soil, and the spade for shovelling compost into containers, cleaning up debris and so on. Choose "border", or "lady's" models, rather than "digging" tools, since they have smaller blades and are easier to manage.

WATERING CAN Choose a can that is well balanced and easy to carry when full, with a long spout to enable you to reach awkward spots. Brass cans are expensive; galvanized cans last longer than plastic but they are heavier and noisier.

SPRAYER A hand mister can be used for applying foliar feeds, pesticide sprays and water. Have several misters and keep those used for pesticides and weedkillers separate. For small areas, pesticides and weedkillers are best bought as ready-to-use sprays, since it is often difficult to mix up small amounts of concentrate for a hand sprayer.

RAKE This is sometimes useful for levelling and crumbling soil in larger beds, as well as refreshing and aerating the surface soil and removing plant debris such as fallen leaves. For crumbling the soil, a type of small hand rake is available, which can also be used for stirring up the surface of the compost in larger containers.

SUPPORTS You will need various types of trellis for climbing plants, and link supports and stakes to hold up the stems of heavy-headed plants. Soft twine or raffia will do the job of tying most plants to their supports, but soft garden wire is better for more robust plants and for thick-stemmed climbers.

This hand weeder is one of many tools that can be slotted into the same handle, saving storage space.

Tools and equipment

Basic gardening

Growing in the ground

Soil containing a lot of clay will form a ball if you roll a small amount of it in your hand.

To be able to grow plants in the ground in the "no-garden" garden is something of a luxury. By our definition, the ground space available will be small, and there could be problems with the planting itself and with getting the plants established. The quality of the soil present could also leave something to be desired. Builders' rubble or infertile subsoil are common, any good-quality topsoil having been taken away and sold when building work started.

If you have some ground space in which you may be able to grow plants, your first step should be to take a closer look at the soil. If possible, excavate a deep hole to expose the soil strata; usually several distinct layers can be identified. You may be able to see the depth of topsoil; how stony it is; whether there is a chalk layer, making the soil alkaline; or a bed of clay, making drainage slow and poor. The topsoil is the most important layer, for it is here where the plant roots develop and obtain their nutrients and moisture. You can carry out several simple tests to learn a little more about the nature of your soil.

Testing the soil

Take a sample of soil from just below the surface, using a trowel. As we have already noted, there are several different types of soil. It may be predominantly clay, sand, silt or a mixed loam, and contain varying amounts of humus, or organic matter. Rub a small quantity of wet soil between your thumb and forefinger; does it feel gritty to the touch, or sticky or slippery? Sandy, free-draining soils feel gritty, while heavier clays and silts feel sticky or slippery.

Take a small handful of moist soil and squeeze it tightly in your palm. When you open your hand, does the soil crumble and fall apart, or does it hold together? If it crumbles, it is sandy soil; if it holds together it contains a quantity of clay. Try to roll the handful into a ball, then rub the ball with your thumb to see if it will take a polish. Roll the ball into a long snake, then try to join the ends together. The more of these steps you can achieve, the higher the quantity of clay the soil contains.

CHECKING THE pH CONTENT OF YOUR SOIL

1 *The most common type of soil-testing kit consists of a container in which to place the soil sample, a dropper, capsules of chemicals and a chart against which to compare the results of your test.*

2 *Take a soil sample 5–7.5cm (2–3in) below the surface. Put the contents of a capsule into the test chamber, and add two capsules of dry soil. Fill the chamber with distilled water.*

3 *Make sure the water comes up to the level of the dotted line. Then fit the cap securely on the tester and shake it until the powder and soil are thoroughly mixed in the water.*

Growing in the ground

Soils are hardly ever pure sand or pure clay, but a mixture. Put another trowelful of soil into a glass jar with a screw lid, and half-fill the jar with water. Shake it up well, then leave the jar on a level surface for several hours or overnight so that the contents settle. The soil will separate into layers, with the largest particles (stones, grit and sand) on the bottom, and fine particles of silt and clay at the top. This is a particularly useful test because it shows you at a glance the different proportions of the various soil constituents. The organic matter the soil contains will float on the surface of the water.

These tests will tell you about the physical make-up of the soil. Sandy soils are light, easy to work, warm up early in spring and drain freely. Clay soils are heavy, slow to warm up, and prone to waterlogging. Extremes of both types of soil can be improved by the addition of well-rotted organic matter (such as garden compost), which will open up clay soil and improve its drainage, and, with its absorbent, spongy texture, will help sandy soil to retain more moisture.

Checking the soil's chemical content
The chemical constituents of the soil are also important, for it is these that provide plants with their nutrients and determine how fertile the soil is. The quantities of these chemicals are not so easy to establish, but already you will have an idea of the fertility from the physical structure tests; free-draining, sandy soils tend to contain fewer nutrients than clays because the soluble chemicals are washed away. Kits for testing the soil are widely available, and these give an idea of the proportions of the major plant nutrients, nitrogen, phosphorus and potassium (*see also* pp.98–99), but the results of the tests should be viewed only as a rough guide. Truly accurate results depend on more sophisticated and rigorous sampling and testing procedures than are possible at home.

One chemical test that it is worth your while to perform is that for soil acidity, or pH. This measures the amount of calcium in the soil and will tell you whether your soil is acid or alkaline, indicating the type of plants you may be able to grow. Neutral or alkaline soils rule out the possibility of growing lime-hating plants such as rhododendrons and camellias. Although electronic meters for measuring the pH are available, a more accurate result can generally be obtained by using a solution that will change colour according to the degree of acidity or alkalinity of the soil.

Sandy soil will separate out and remain crumbly if you squeeze a small amount of it tightly in your hand.

4 *Let the tester stand for a few minutes to allow the colour to develop fully in your sample.*

5 *Against a white background and using natural daylight, but not direct sunlight, compare the coloured solution in the test chamber with the colours on the chart. This will tell you whether your soil is alkaline or acid.*

pH CHART

pH 7.5 Alkaline
pH 7.0 Neutral
pH 6.5 Slightly Acid
pH 6.0 Acid
pH 5.5 Acid
pH 5.0 Very Acid
pH 4.5 Very Acid

Basic gardening

Planting techniques

You may be lucky and have a narrow strip of soil in your "no-garden", but generally you will be faced with a hard surface. If the surface is paving slabs or bricks, it is usually possible to prise up one or two of them and to plant in the gap that is created. If the slab has been cemented into place you may need to break it up with a sledge hammer so that you can extract it piece by piece. If the surface is solid concrete, use a cold chisel and hammer to chase out the area you want to expose, then break up the inside of the area with hard blows on the chisel and remove the bits of broken concrete. Wear protective goggles and gloves when carrying out either of these processes.

Cracks between slabs can often be widened sufficiently to take a small plant by chiselling away one edge, but lifting an entire slab allows you to make a much better job of improving the soil and planting than simply chipping off one corner and squeezing the plant in there. In the same way, when breaking up concrete, be sure to make a hole larger than is needed to allow for the existing plant roots.

Once you have cleared a large enough area for planting, dig out as big a hole as is practical and fill it with fertile soil or compost. Add some slow-release fertiliser and water-retaining granules, whether you are using existing soil or replacing it.

Set the plant in the hole and firm it in, then water it. You can topdress around the plant with pebbles or gravel to avoid moisture loss and improve its appearance, or you may wish to replace a lifted slab, having reduced its size to allow for the plant's stem.

All plants growing in holes in paved areas are likely to be in shallow, fairly infertile soil (apart from the improved soil in the immediate planting area), so they will benefit from liquid-feeding during the growing season.

Planting against walls

Several climbing plants are suitable for setting in relatively small holes in paved areas; clematis, in particular, thrives with its roots in cool shade and its head in the sun. When planting a climber, insert a cane to lead the growth up to the wall you want it to grow on. In such positions, plants need regular watering, since sufficient rain is unlikely to reach them.

By sinking a length of plastic piping or a small plant pot in the soil near the plant and running the water into it, you will ensure that water gets to the plant roots, especially in the early days. Later, the roots will penetrate the soil farther away and extract some additional nutrients and moisture from that.

PLANTING AMONG BRICKS

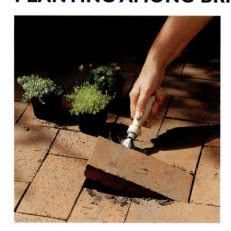

1 When you have decided where you want to place your plants in the paved area, work a brick loose, prise it up and remove it.

2 The soil immediately beneath the brick is likely to be poor quality, sandy, stony, or even builders' rubble, so dig the hole out to a depth of at least 10–15cm (4–6in).

3 Make sure that the drainage at the base of the hole is adequate. Mix some slow-release fertilizer and water-retaining granules into fertile soil or good-quality compost and fill the hole with it.

Planting techniques

Precautions

Take care when planting larger plants in slabs, concrete or tarmac, since the plants could become a hazard if they are badly positioned, and their root growth could also cause problems, lifting slabs unevenly and raising or breaking through tarmac and concrete. Don't plant anything which makes very strong, vigorous growth, and check slabs regularly to ensure that they are level, re-laying them if necessary.

Always be particularly careful what subjects you plant against a house wall, especially in clay soil. Roots can undermine foundations, and vigorous growth can cause structural damage by altering the moisture content of the soil, leading to subsidence.

Take care also when planting against walls that form garden boundaries – roots penetrating the earth in neighbouring properties can cause problems. Never plant moisture-greedy trees, such as poplars or willows, in the ground near buildings, but confine them to large containers where their growth can be kept in check.

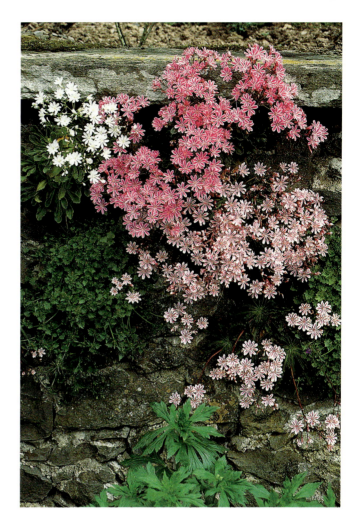

A free-draining dry-stone wall is an ideal place to grow lewisias. Gouge out some of the soil between the stones, pack the space with compost, tuck the plants into it, and they will thrive.

4 *Water the compost thoroughly, then set the plant in the soil, firming it in gently with your fingers. A good depth of fertile, moisture-retentive soil around the roots will enable the plant to make strong initial growth.*

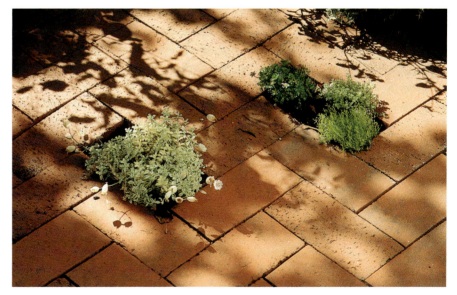

5 *Spreading rock plants, which flourish in well-drained conditions, are ideal for planting among bricks, and low-growing plants with aromatic foliage, such as thyme and chamomile, are pleasant set where they may occasionally be trodden on by passers-by, releasing their scent into the air.*

Basic gardening

Growing in containers

Growing any plant in a container is very different from growing it in the open ground, and it will have an effect on both the way the plant develops and the way we need to care for it. A container has a limited amount of space in which the plant's roots can develop, and it contains relatively small amounts of compost or soil. If the roots are restricted, this will limit the overall size of the plant; as an extreme example, the small containers and careful root-pruning used in bonsai culture are able to reduce a potentially towering forest tree to a perfect miniature replica of itself.

The small volume of compost in containers also reduces the amount of moisture and nutrients available to the plant, which in turn has an effect upon the plant's size and development. By watering and feeding plants in containers we can, to an extent, overcome some of these effects, but this can produce further problems; it promotes the size of the topgrowth of the plant while the spread of roots is still limited by the boundaries of the container. This leads to an unbalanced plant, which could be blown over easily by wind, for example, since it does not have the firm below-ground support system to balance its above-ground growth. It will also lead to problems with water supply, since the increased leaf surface is likely to lose water by evaporation more rapidly than the roots can take it up, or sometimes more rapidly than the gardener can supply it.

The trick of growing plants in containers successfully is to maintain a balancing act. It is necessary to promote healthy root growth, especially of the young feeding roots, and well-shaped, balanced topgrowth; to supply sufficient water at all times without overwatering; to start feeding once the original supply of nutrients in the soil is beginning to run low; and to provide the right nutrients both for the plant's health and for the best display of the plant's outstanding features. Container-grown plants often need extra support because of their limited root system, and they may need pruning to keep them balanced and shapely.

Drainage

This is a priority for all containers, since water must be able to drain away freely for healthy root growth. Wherever possible, the container should have drainage holes in the base, but on their own these may not be sufficient. You can add a layer of drainage material, such as broken clay pots, coarse gravel or stones, in the bottom of the pot. Containers on the ground will drain more freely if they are raised slightly on bricks, or decorative plastic or clay "feet" can be bought.

Some plastic tubs or wooden containers are intended for use as decorative pot covers and do not have drainage holes. But if you want to use these as plant pots, it is usually fairly simple to drill a number of holes at least 1cm (½in) across in the base.

TIPS FOR CONTAINER PLANTING

1 Choose a suitable container and make sure there are sufficient drainage holes in it. It is fairly simple to drill extra holes in wood, plastic or fibreglass.
2 Stand the container on bricks or feet to raise it off the ground so that it will drain freely and the compost will not become waterlogged. This also helps to prevent wooden containers from rotting.
3 Cover the drainage holes with crocks or large pebbles so that they do not become blocked by the compost.
4 Fill the container to the bottom of the pot rim with damp compost, then press it down with your hands. Make a hole in the compost to take the plant, firm it in with your fingers, water it well and, if desired, add a top layer of gravel.
5 Choose good-quality, sturdy plants with well-developed root systems. This is especially important if your container is to hold a single specimen plant.

Growing in containers

A striking container is a decorative feature in itself, so keep the planting simple and let it echo the colours of the pot.

Growing in containers

An extra-deep, very sharp-draining layer of crocks at the base of a container may enable you to grow plants satisfactorily, but watering must be carried out carefully. A better system is to grow the plant in a smaller pot inside the container without drainage holes, setting the inner pot on the deep layer of crocks. Then, if the plant is overwatered and the water level comes above the crock layer, the inner pot can be removed and allowed to drain.

Compost

Garden soil is not the best choice for containers. It is usually full of weed seeds and often disease organisms that can cause havoc among the plants. In addition, its texture and structure may be completely unsuitable for container growing. Various growing composts are available from garden centres and plant shops; these are sterile, so they are free of weeds, insects and diseases, and they contain known quantities of nutrients.

The main choice is between soil-based, or loam-based composts, and soilless (also called loamless or peat-based) composts. The soil-based composts have the appearance of garden soil. They are heavy, making them awkward to handle in the sack, and the weight of filled containers makes them difficult to move around. Some gardeners prefer these composts because they behave in a similar way to garden soil; they absorb water well and contain a relatively long-lasting supply of nutrients.

Soilless composts used to be based on peat, and although peat types are still available there are now several composts based on peat substitutes, such as coir or coconut fibre, in order to preserve dwindling peat supplies and wildlife habitats. These are similar to peat in that they are lightweight, clean and easy to handle. Soilless composts contain relatively low levels of nutrients and hold limited supplies of water; they can be difficult to re-wet if they are allowed to dry out. Supplementary feeding must be started soon after potting up, and watering must be carried out frequently.

There are also one or two specialist composts: hanging-basket compost, for example. Some brands are soil-based, but this compost is often soilless, to ensure that the filled baskets are not too awkward to handle and that they will not prove too heavy for their supports. The compost is likely to contain a slow-release fertiliser and may also contain water-retaining granules to help avoid the common problem of drying out. Ericaceous compost is formulated without lime, enabling it to be used for lime-hating plants such as heathers, pieris and rhododendrons.

Fertiliser

In order to keep producing a good display despite a limited volume of compost in which to grow, container plants need supplementary feeding. The full range of nutrients and fertilisers is discussed on page 137, but perhaps particularly useful for containers are slow-release fertilisers and liquid feeds. There are some natural slow-release fertilisers, such as blood, fish and bone meal, which gradually breaks down to make nutrients available to the plants, or there are specially formulated granules which are manufactured in such a way that particular combinations of ambient temperature and moisture levels allow the nutrients to be released slowly throughout the growing season.

Liquid feeds are at the opposite end of the spectrum; they provide a quick pick-me-up for plants, since they are rapidly absorbed. They are easily applied, being measured into the watering can every 10 days or so, or a more dilute application can be made with every watering.

Evergreen plants in large containers are best potted in soil-based compost, which is heavier, providing stability for the roots, as well as holding water well and containing more nutrients.

Growing in containers

A symmetrical grouping of identically painted pots, filled with neatly clipped box, contrasts pleasingly with the otherwise informal planting in this corner of a patio garden and creates an attractive formal focal point.

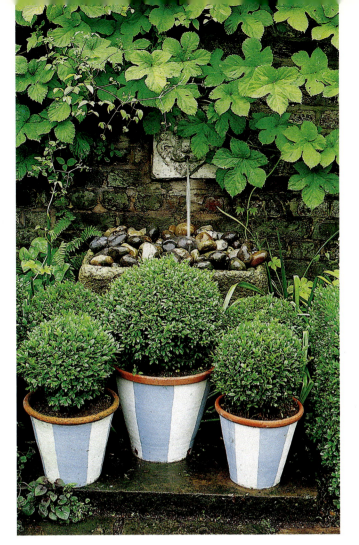

large, it is worth putting it in its final position before you begin – it could be too heavy to move afterwards.

If you know you are going to need to move a large container from time to time, you can buy a plant trolley with castors on which to transport it. You will probably have to put it on the trolley before planting and leave it there throughout the season, since lifting a ready-planted pot on to the trolley could be difficult.

Cover the base of the pot with crocks and a layer of coarse gravel for drainage, then fill the container two-thirds full with your selected compost. If you want to use fertiliser and water-retaining granules, you can either mix them in before you begin to ensure that they are evenly distributed, or you can add them to the compost in the container at this point and mix them in with your hands.

Gather the plants you intend to use and work out their positions in the container before removing them from their pots. Group them together, standing the pots on the compost surface, and check the effect from all sides, adjusting their positions as necessary. Once you have arranged them satisfactorily, knock them out of their pots and plant them with a trowel or your hands, firming them in lightly but thoroughly, and adding compost as necessary. Begin planting from the centre to avoid damage to plants already planted.

When the planting is complete, the level of the compost should be just below the rim of the container, to make watering easier. Water the completed pot gently, and if possible shade it from bright sun for a day or two to give the plants a chance to get established.

Watering

Containers need regular watering during the growing season, and you should apply sufficient water each time to moisten the compost thoroughly, right down to the base of the pot. In many instances, watering may need to be done twice a day or more in high summer. For perennial plants, watering may still be necessary during the dormant season in order to prevent the container drying out completely, but care must be taken not to overwet the compost or the roots will rot. Check the state of the compost 5–7.5cm (2–3in) below the surface before watering in winter.

Planting up containers

Several hours before planting your containers, thoroughly water the plants you intend to put in them. This will ensure that they are easy to turn out of their pots and will get them off to a good start.

Before planting, always check that there are enough, reasonably large drainage holes in the container and make more or make them bigger if necessary. If the container is

This trough of alpines, in which each plant can be seen at its best, demonstrates the value of working out a plan before planting.

Basic gardening

Growing in containers

Pots, tubs and troughs

These are some of the most popular of all plant containers. They are very versatile, coming in a wide range of shapes and sizes and in a variety of colours and decorative finishes. They are free standing, and smaller containers can be moved from place to place without too much difficulty. They can support many different types of plant.

The traditionally shaped plant pot is cylindrical with gently sloping sides. Its height is normally equivalent to the width across the top of the pot, tapering to about two-thirds that width at the base. There are, of course, many variations on this, including square pots and tall or wide pots. The point at which a pot becomes a tub is something of a grey area; a tub is larger than a pot, but there is no specific size at which one becomes the other. A tub is a container that is often rather more squat than a pot, with less steeply sloping sides, and probably contains something over 15 litres of compost. (Plant containers are generally measured according to their volume in litres or their width in centimetres across the widest part of the top.) A wooden half-barrel is perhaps most people's idea of a typical tub.

Decoratively shaped urns and jars such as "Ali-baba" jars also fall into the category of pots and tubs, while a trough is oblong and tends to be shallow – the typical window box shape, but used as a free-standing container on the ground.

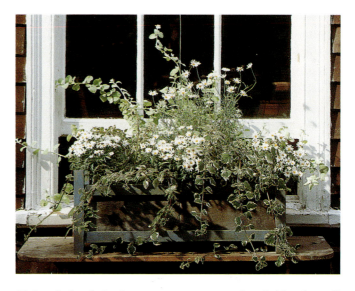

If the window ledge is narrow, you can attach a shelf to the wall below the level of the ledge and safely stand a window box on it; since the box is lower down, the plants will block out less light.

A trough for alpines is an even shallower rectangle, and is wider than a window box – an old stone sink is a typical example.

Pots, tubs and the like have usually been designed according to tradition and for convenience rather than to suit plant growth; the tapering shape of the traditional plant pot facilitates repotting and enables the empty pots to be stacked, for instance, rather than being of special value to the plant.

AN ALPINE TROUGH

1 *A wooden trough makes an attractive container, but it needs lining, otherwise the compost will fall between the slats. You will need a quantity of crocks, broken terracotta flowerpots and the like, to put at the bottom to ensure drainage.*

2 *Line the trough with sphagnum moss, which is in keeping with the rustic look of the wood. Staple plastic sheeting to the top of the trough, cut holes in it so that excess water can escape, add the crocks, and half-fill the trough with compost.*

3 *Water the pots of plants well an hour or so before planting. When you have decided on your planting plan, put your fingers around the base of each plant and carefully tip up the pot. Try to keep a good ball of soil around the plant roots.*

Growing in containers

Some containers are designed simply to be decorative; tall jars, with their narrow necks and bulbous middles, have a graceful and elegant appearance but are not particularly practical for growing plants, especially when it comes to repotting.

Keeping the display going

As individual plants start to die off, they can often be removed and replaced with another plant that is just coming into flower. This is made easier if the seasonal plants are kept in their individual pots, sunk into the surrounding compost and disguised with a thin layer of compost over the top. Once they are ready to be replaced, the pot can just be uncovered and lifted out, leaving a planting space for the next occupant. A little advance planning is necessary to have replacement plants in the correct size pots at the right time.

Semi-permanent or permanent plants will generally need moving on to their final size container in stages, as they grow. A plant with a small rootball set in a large pot will not grow well – it should be moved into a container only slightly larger than the current one each time. If a plant is already in its final size pot, it can be repotted into the same pot, but with a little fresh compost to give it a boost to growth.

Topdressing is a useful way to perk up large plants which cannot easily be removed from their containers. Without removing the plant from its pot, remove as much of the compost from the surface as possible, then top up with a layer of fresh compost, with added slow-release fertiliser granules. These techniques are explained on pages 138–139.

Window boxes

A window box is one plant container that nearly every home can use. Different types of box are available (*see* pp.84–85). They can be made from a variety of materials, but wood or plastic are the most common, since they are reasonably light in weight and not too difficult to fix securely to the wall or window ledge. Wooden boxes can be painted with a plant-safe wood preservative to extend their life, but it is better to choose a type that has two or three plastic inserts which will actually contain the compost and plants.

WINDOW BOX SAFETY It is important that a window box is fixed in place securely. You risk ruining your display and wasting your time and money if the box topples off a ground-floor window ledge; there are more serious implications with an upper-storey window ledge because of the damage a falling box can do to people or property below.

There are various ways of securing a window box, depending on the style of the box itself and the surface on which it is to be fitted. If there is an outside window ledge, it is sometimes wide enough to take a window box, but it will need to be fixed in position with brackets screwed to the wall for safety. Since window ledges slope downwards to allow water to drain away, some wooden wedges should be inserted under the front of the box to keep it level.

4 When all the plants have been set in place, fill up the trough with compost, water it well and add more compost if it settles too far. A layer of coarse gravel on the top will keep the compost moist and improve the appearance of the trough.

5 Stand the trough in a bright, sunny spot, and within a week or two the plants will begin to flourish and grow over the edges of the trough.

Basic gardening

Growing in containers

Standing the box on the the window ledge is fine as long as the windows open inwards or slide, but many open outwards, making this position impractical. And as the plants grow, much of the view and light from the window will be obscured.

A position below the window is more suitable if there is no window ledge or only a narrow one. A casement window can still be opened outwards, but this may become difficult as the plants get taller. Even if you don't usually open the window in question, you will need to do so to water and feed the plants in the window box.

Use metal brackets to support the box from below, and either screw the back of the box to the wall (or, preferably, to a wooden batten fixed to the wall) or attach chains and hooks between the window box and wall to keep it in position. (*See* pp.16–19 for tips on securing baskets and window boxes to walls.) A permanent wrought-iron container can be fixed securely to the wall and a wooden or plastic window box placed inside it.

Do bear in mind that you need to have easy access to a window box for deadheading, watering, feeding and so on; don't put it in a position where it will be difficult or dangerous to reach.

PREPARING A WINDOW BOX As with other containers, plants in a window box need to be grown in free-draining compost. If there is no obstruction below, holes can be drilled directly into the base of the box for drainage. If water draining from the box is likely to cause a nuisance, use a drip tray below the box which can be emptied as necessary, or fill the undrilled base of the window box with drainage material and stand drilled plastic liners on this to hold the plants. Self-watering window boxes are useful; they have a reservoir for water at the base with capillary material to take the moisture up to the plants.

Window boxes should be planted up in the same way as pots, tubs and troughs.

Hanging baskets

These can be spectacular when well grown, and nearly every home can manage to find a suitable spot for a hanging basket. They can, however, be a big disappointment if they are not properly cared for.

Plenty of different types are available, but the main distinction is between wire-mesh baskets and "hanging plant-pot" types with solid sides (*see* pp.84–85).

WIRE-MESH BASKETS The traditional basket is open plastic-coated wire mesh, hanging from three chains. This has the advantage that plants can be pushed through the wire in the sides of the basket so that the basket itself can be completely disguised with plant growth. Its disadvantages are that it is trickier to plant up, needs a liner, dries out quickly, and watering can be a messy process. Traditional lining for a wire basket is sphagnum moss, but this is not always easy to

A TRADITIONAL HANGING BASKET

1 Set the plastic-coated wire basket on top of a fairly large flower pot or bucket to keep it steady. Start to line the basket with sphagnum moss. If you prefer, you can use plastic sheeting with holes pierced in it, or a fibre or plastic foam liner.

2 Put a plant saucer in the bottom of the basket. This will act as a water reservoir and will help to keep the compost moist, so the basket will not need watering so often. It will also help to stop it dripping when it is watered.

3 Half-fill the basket with compost. Take the plants you plan to set in the sides of the basket out of their pots. Gently wash off some of the soil, and push the plants, roots first, through the wire and lining; lay the roots flat on the compost.

Growing in containers

get hold of or to use. Various alternatives have been developed commercially, including coconut fibre, plastic foam and recycled fabric liners. Some of these can look ugly and it is difficult to plant the sides of the basket so as to hide them. When planting, either use special hanging basket compost or mix some slow-release fertiliser and water-retaining granules with soilless compost. This is almost essential with hanging baskets unless you are prepared to water two or three times daily at the height of the summer.

HANGING POTS These are squat pots or bowls, often with an integral clip-on saucer, hanging from three plastic or wire chains. If you want to disguise the basket you need to plant it carefully with plants that will hang over the edge, since you cannot plant through the sides of the basket. On the other hand, the solid walls prevent the compost from drying out so quickly, and the saucer provides a reservoir of water. Self-watering baskets have a deeper reservoir and may have a covering of capillary matting to wick up water into the compost. They also have a filler tube through which to fill the reservoir.

A hay rack, or manger, makes a handsome plant container, so be sure not to obscure the metalwork when filling it with plants.

PLANTING THE BASKET Work out a rough planting plan, bearing in mind that the basket will be viewed from below as well as the sides and possibly above. Set low-growing and cascading plants towards the edge at the top of the basket, a more upright specimen in the centre, and small trailing plants, which will help to conceal the basket, around the edge or between the wires of a traditional basket.

When planting the sides of a wire-mesh basket, wrap the plants' roots in a small piece of newspaper to neaten them so that they can be tucked in easily. If the basket is big enough, make two layers of trailers through the wires, and when planting the top of any basket, remember to allow for the position of the chains when it is hanging.

Water tends to run off the surface of a hanging basket, so before you add the plants at the top of a traditional basket, sink a small plant pot or piece of tube near to the edge and level with the surface of the compost. By watering through this, you can be certain that the water will penetrate to the roots of the plants.

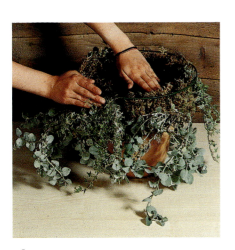

4 *Cover the roots with compost and fill the basket with compost. Before planting the top of the basket, insert a small plant pot or piece of tube level with the top of the compost. This will make it easier to water the basket.*

5 *Plant up the top of the basket, being careful not to obstruct the plant pot. Water the completed basket gently and keep it in a sheltered place for a week or two for the plants to become established. Hang it where you can enjoy it all season.*

Basic gardening

Growing in containers

Growing bags

A growing bag is simply a plastic sack of compost, but instead of transferring the compost to a pot, the plants are set directly in the sack. Where growing bags are not available, you can make your own, using a potting mix. Growing bags are widely used for raising tomatoes on patios and in greenhouses, but they are far more versatile than this.

The bags are laid flat where the plants are to be grown. Opinion is divided over whether it is advisable to cut drainage slits in the base of the bag. They were first used for commercial tomato growing when the border soil in greenhouses had become diseased, and it was important to keep the bags intact in order to isolate plant roots from the contaminated soil below. If this is not an issue, no harm is done by cutting slits in the base, especially if you are prone to overwatering containers. It is possible to conceal the bag itself by setting it in a specially designed shallow trough. Instead of the gaudily coloured bags which are common, it is sometimes possible to obtain plain green ones. Trailing plants set at the edges will soon help to disguise the bag.

Cut planting holes in the upper surface of the bag with a sharp knife. If you intend to grow a lot of plants close together – a bedding plant display, for instance – it is easiest to cut one large rectangle from the top of the bag. Because the depth of compost a growing bag contains is shallow, it dries out quickly, so leaving as much of the compost surface covered by the plastic as possible will help to prevent this. Mix a small amount of water-retaining granules with the compost in the bag to cut down the frequency of watering.

Plant up the bag in the normal way. Tall plants that need staking can be a problem, since the depth of compost is often not sufficient to support a cane, but there are specially designed frames, which are anchored underneath the bag, and these should be put in place at an early stage. Because the bag is well-filled with compost it tends to have a rounded upper surface, which can make watering difficult since the water runs off; again, various watering devices to overcome this can be found in most garden centres. Growing bags contain similar amounts of fertiliser as general-purpose sowing and potting composts. Once the plants have become established, regular liquid feeding will help to prolong their productive period and keep them looking healthy.

Converted containers

Plants can be grown in almost anything that will hold enough compost, and inventive growers have given many different items new leases of life as plant containers. Antique lead cisterns, washtubs, chimney pots, stone sinks, boats,

PLANTING UP A GROWING BAG

1 *You will need a growing bag, a trough to contain it in if you intend to use one, the plants – here tomatoes, french beans, basil and parsley – canes to support them, as well as string to tie them in to the canes.*

2 *Put the growing bag into the trough. If you want to grow two or three specimen plants, rather than a show of annuals, cut equally spaced crosses in the bag and tuck the flaps under to form diamond-shaped planting holes.*

3 *Water the compost in the growing bag with a rose on the can until it is thoroughly moist but not waterlogged. With a trowel, dig out a sufficient quantity of the compost to make holes big enough to take your plants.*

wheelbarrows – even worn-out walking boots and old car tyres have been converted to horticultural use. If you want the container to last for several years, you may need to treat it in some way. Wood can be coated with bitumen paint on the inside to prevent it rotting, and varnished on the outside to protect it from the weather. Metal or painted surfaces may benefit from a coat of acrylic varnish to prevent flaking. Remember that many objects may be stained, scratched or otherwise spoiled by a single season as a container, so don't use a valuable item unless you are sure it can stand up to the conditions without sustaining too much damage.

The biggest problem with many "novelty" containers is their failure to provide adequate drainage. Ensure that suitable drainage holes can be made, and use drainage material at the base. Make sure, also, that it will hold sufficient compost for good growth, and that you will be able to water the plants easily. The rules for cultivation are then the same as for any other container – water regularly and liquid feed as necessary throughout the growing season.

Plastic or terracotta tower pots (left) extend the growing area upward; a long hanging plastic tube (above left) can double hanging basket space, and drainpipe pots (right) full of cascading plants will turn even that mundane object into an asset.

Miscellaneous containers

Each year new systems of container growing are introduced. Often these promise more spectacular displays, but they may also offer easier cultivation; because container-grown plants need watering so frequently, self-watering systems are often incorporated.

Tower pots clip together to make a free-standing, vertical column in which plants can be grown to cover the pots completely. Another system uses a perforated plastic tube which is suspended to form a hanging "tower". Always follow the instructions on these kits, since the way in which they are assembled can be critical to achieving proper watering. Most have a reservoir at the base and are self-watering to an extent, but check regularly that moisture penetrates evenly all the way down the tower.

Containers that disguise unsightly items are also popular. Manhole covers or sewer vents are a feature of some yards, and while they are easy enough to conceal with a planted trough, make sure it is not so heavy and awkward to move that it prevents access or air flow. Drainpipes can be graced with pots clipped to them by plastic rings, and the drains into which they flow can be fitted with a planted cover as well. These are valuable for making full use of all the available space in a small area, but you must take care to ensure that they don't interfere with the function of the object they are disguising.

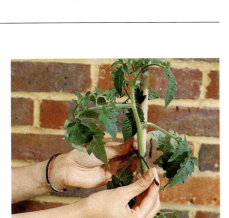

4 *Set the plants in the holes and push in canes to support the tomatoes. As the plants grow, gently tie in the stems. The underplanting of herbs will quickly form bushy growth which will help to hide the plastic growing bag.*

Basic gardening

Plant supports

When plants are grown in a small space, you usually need to pay more attention to their support and training than you do in a larger garden. Supports are necessary for a several reasons. They keep plants tidy and prevent them from obstructing pathways so that they are less likely to be damaged by people pushing through or past them. Supports can also help plants to grow into pleasing shapes – perhaps more attractive or practical than their natural ones.

Many plants need support to combat damage by wind and rain, which may otherwise flatten or break their branches. Flowers such as delphiniums and lupins are soon spoiled if a heavy shower beats the stems down. The tips of the flowerheads continue to grow in a strongly vertical direction within hours, so even if you are able to gather up the stems and restore them to their normal position later, the flowerheads will have a permanent kink in them which will ruin the display.

In exposed, windy positions, it is not just the above-ground parts of the plant that may suffer. Constant rocking of the main stem as it is blown to and fro will also cause movement of the rootball, preventing the roots from establishing themselves in the soil – a condition known as wind-rock. A stake is even more necessary where larger plants are growing in shallow soil, as is the case in containers or shallow raised beds. Here, the roots cannot penetrate deeply enough to give them the anchorage they would achieve in deeper soil. While trees or shrubs in the open garden are often staked for only their first two or three years, until they become established, some plants in shallow soil are likely always to need a stake.

Plants often require staking in order to show off their best features, such as flowers which may otherwise be hidden behind foliage. Occasionally, plants are bred which carry flowers that are too large and full for their stems to support; many varieties of double daffodil, for instance, have stems that fold under the weight of the blooms, particularly after rain. Careful staking at an early stage can prevent such problems.

Standard roses and small trees in raised beds or containers will need permanent staking. Insert the stake into the soil or compost before planting, and attach the plant to the stake with a couple of small tree ties. Check the ties regularly as the plant grows to make sure that they are not too tight.

Not every plant needs support; many types have spreading growth, or short or stout stems that will hold up quite well on their own. Climbers and ramblers and other plants with tall, lax growth or weak stems should nearly always be provided with some form of support, but otherwise experience will tell you which plants would do better with staking in your own particular conditions.

How to support plants

The "no-garden" often has particular problems when it comes to supporting plants, since it can be difficult to find a firm base in which to secure the support because there is little or no natural soil, only a hard surface. For example, it is usually recommended that a tree stake should extend a good 50cm (20in) below the soil surface – well below the base of the rootball. In a "no-garden" situation, this is usually impossible – the base of the rootball is as low as you are likely to be able to get. Obviously this does not provide the stability that a deeper stake does.

Lightweight composts, such as those based on peat or peat substitutes, do not make things any easier. Because they are light and fluffy in texture, they do not hold a stake as firmly as a soil-based compost does. One way to overcome these problems of stability in a large container or raised bed is to set a cane or stake in a plastic plant pot filled with a stiff cement mix. Once this has set, the weighted stake can be buried in the container or raised bed, or even positioned behind a container, to provide a relatively stable support.

Stake set in concrete

The main rule is that the supports should be unobtrusive. Use natural-looking materials, preferably in dull green or brown shades, and arrange them so that plant growth will cover them as much as possible. They may be fairly obvious initially, but once the plants they are supporting have grown they should be almost invisible. The plant's habit of growth should always appear natural, even if it isn't – few things look worse than a bunch of stems which have been gathered tightly together and firmly trussed to a single, overlarge stake. Don't be mean with materials; three or four stakes or canes, placed among the stems of a shrub or tall perennial, give a much more natural effect than if you try to make do with one.

Plant supports

CREATING A SUPPORTING FRAMEWORK

1 Spreading plants, such as Impatiens, busy lizzie, can be supported by inserting several small, green, wooden split canes into the compost at strategic positions among the stems.

2 Once you have made a framework of canes, tie one end of a length of green garden twine to one of them, then carefully loop the twine around the rest of the canes.

3 The twine will contain and support any sprawling, wayward stems, and as the plant grows and becomes more bushy, both twine and canes will disappear among the leaves and flowers.

TYING IN PLANTS

1 Soft-stemmed perennials, such as geraniums, can be tied in to a cane. Loop green garden twine or raffia around the cane, cross the ends behind it, then bring them around the stem just above a leaf stem, and knot them against the cane.

2 Make further ties at 10–15cm (4–6in) intervals up the stem, with the last one about 5cm (2in) from the top of the cane. Try to make your ties as unobtrusive as possible by choosing places that are hidden by leaves and by cutting off any ends of twine or raffia to neaten them.

SUPPORTING PERENNIALS

1 Bushy herbaceous plants that tend to flop over or produce very heavy flowerheads are best supported by one of several types of metal frame. The most common consist of a crisscross framework, supported on legs (left), or of a series of linked metal stakes that can be bent around and joined to form a support (below).

2 The legs of the frames must be pushed into the ground in the spring, when the plant starts into growth. As the plant increases in size, the stems will grow through the framework and eventually obscure it.

Plant supports

Always support plants from an early stage; if you leave it until they need support it is often too late to achieve a pleasing effect. The plants should grow up into the support to give a natural outline, with branches well clothed with foliage. If you try to gather in branches later on, you will often be given away by a lack of foliage at their base or on one side.

Once you have provided a plant with its support, it is not the end of the story. Its growth needs to be tied in regularly and gently encouraged to grow in the right direction. Further supports may need to be added, or existing ones moved, as the spread of the branches increases. At all times aim for a natural-looking result.

Types of plant support

Use different methods of support according to the types of plant that are being grown, and where they are growing.

In containers

CANES Bamboo canes have the advantages of being relatively cheap and having a pleasant, natural appearance. They do not last for ever, though, since they eventually split, and rot where they have been below ground. Their life can, however, be extended by dipping the base (the thicker end of the cane) in a plant-safe wood preservative. Unobtrusive green plastic "canes" are also available, which do not rot. Because bamboo canes are hollow, they can form a good hiding place for plant pests, such as woodlice and earwigs;

Support sweetpeas and tall runner beans on a wigwam of canes, tied together at the top. Otherwise, you can buy a plastic ring with holes in it through which you pass the canes to hold them together at the top.

stopping up the ends with Plasticine or putty helps to keep out undesirable creatures.

A single, central cane may be sufficient, or, for climbers, a wigwam of three or more canes evenly spaced around the edge of the pot and tied together at their tips. Sometimes a ring of canes at the edge of the pot with twine twisted around them is appropriate.

SPLIT CANES Made from wood, rather than bamboo, these are thinner and shorter than bamboo canes and are square in section and usually stained green. They are useful for smaller plants and can be inserted among the branches of the plant wherever they are needed.

Many serious injuries are caused by people bending down among plants and being poked in the eye by the top of a cane. Using small plastic pots, cotton reels, corks or one of the proprietary cane tops available will help avoid this.

FIXING WIRE TO WALLS

1 *Plastic-covered wire stretched horizontally on a wall provides good support for climbers. Using a drill with a masonry bit, drill holes in the wall and insert vine eyes – screws with a loop at one end – large enough to hold the wire slightly away from the wall surface, or screw them into battens. Thread the wire through the first eye and twist the end tightly with pliers to secure it.*

2 *Screw the rest of the vine eyes into position, with one every 2m (6ft) or so, spacing the horizontal wires about 45cm (18in) apart. Thread the wire through each intermediate vine eye, looping it back on itself so that it can be tensioned; when the final vine eye is reached and the wire twisted off, the tension can be adjusted by turning the vine eye itself with pliers.*

TWIGGY STICKS Perfect for annuals and perennials, twiggy sticks provide plenty of support while being unobtrusive. Finding suitable sticks in the city can be a problem, but sometimes they are sold as pea-sticks or tomato sticks at garden centres. Normally they last for only one season.

FREE-STANDING TRELLIS Usually made into a fan or other decorative shape, a wooden or plastic trellis for containers has long prongs at the base which are inserted into the compost in the pot. Trellises are used for supporting climbing plants.

MESH CYLINDER Climbers such as sweet peas, grown in a pot, can be trained around a central cylinder made from rigid plastic mesh or chicken wire. Cut a piece of mesh to the appropriate size, roll it into a cylinder and fasten it with wire or string. Place it in the centre of an empty pot, allowing room for the plants to be set around the outside. Fill the pot with compost and plant it up; the climbers will soon cover the cylinder and form an attractive flowering column.

In beds and in the ground

STAKES Where the depth of soil allows, a heavier wooden stake can be used to support a tree or tall shrub. Dig the planting hole, then drive the stake into position before planting; this avoids the root damage that occurs when a stake is inserted after planting. It used to be recommended that the stake should be tall enough to come just below the head of the plant. This is still the case for thin-stemmed subjects such as standard roses, but otherwise short stakes about 60cm (24in) above ground are considered better because they allow some movement of the trunk, which helps to strengthen and thicken it. In an exposed position, two or three short stakes can be used around the plant.

When planting a container-grown tree with a dense rootball, or if staking is necessary after planting, use an angled stake, driven in so that the tip of the stake avoids the plant roots. Cut off the top of the stake just beyond the top of the trunk once the tree has been fixed to it.

Fix a tree to a stake with an adjustable tree tie, which will prevent chafing of the trunk and can be loosened as the tree grows and its girth increases.

CANES AND TWIGGY STICKS Bamboo and plastic canes can be used in open ground in the same ways as they are in containers. Twiggy sticks or tomato sticks are also useful for low perennials, annuals and bulbs in beds and borders.

COMMERCIAL SUPPORTS Various supports, such as a circle of wire mesh on legs, or angled wire stakes which link to each other with hooks and eyes to form a range of shapes and sizes, can be useful for a wide variety of plants. Many save time and labour, being easier to use than traditional methods of staking, though they may not have such a natural appearance. As with all supports, for the best effect it is important to have them in place before they are needed. Some commercial products would be very expensive if used in quantities in a large garden, but are more suitable for small areas where few are needed.

On walls and fences

Self-clinging climbers, such as ivy and parthenocissus, do not need supports in order to climb rough surfaces such as walls, but you will have more control over the plants and will find it easier to train them if you do provide some form of support. Where it is necessary to maintain the surface over which you wish to grow the plants – painting a wall, for instance, or treating a wooden fencing panel with preservative – you will find maintenance easier to carry out if climbing plants are grown on a trellis which can be let down from the wall. This is especially important if the wall or fence forms a boundary with an adjacent property and is the responsibility of your neighbours, since they may wish to carry out maintenance at a time of year that is not the most suitable from the point of view of the plants.

WOODEN TRELLIS This is available in a range of different shapes and styles, some of them purely functional, some more decorative. However, some wooden trelliswork is very lightweight; make sure you choose a sturdily constructed type if you need to support heavy, vigorous plant growth. Plastic trellises are also available. Chicken wire can be used to provide a base for lightweight climbers to scramble over, but it will sag under the weight of heavy stems.

FIXING A TRELLIS TO A WALL

Rather than fixing the trellis directly to the wall, screw wooden battens or spacing blocks about 8cm (3in) thick to the wall and secure the trellis to these. This will maintain a flow of air behind the plant, leading to healthier growth; it will also help to prevent self-clinging plants attaching themselves to the wall. If you need access to the wall behind the plants, you can unscrew the trellis from the battens and lay it carefully on the ground, so make sure the sections of trellis are a suitable size to make this practicable. Otherwise you can use hooks and screw eyes to fix the trellis to the battens, which will make lowering it even simpler.

Basic gardening

Training plants

Plants are usually trained in order to make them look attractive, but various training methods can also help to display a plant's best features more prominently, to promote flowering and fruiting by restricting leafy growth, and to expose fruit or branches to maximum sunshine in order to ripen them. "Training" means making a plant grow in a way that it would not do naturally. It usually means that regular attention is required from the gardener throughout the plant's life to maintain its form.

Growing plants up the types of support previously discussed is training at its simplest. Climbing plants may need to be encouraged to climb by twisting their shoots around the support, or threading them through trelliswork. Plants will usually need to be attached to the support at intervals; this can be done with plastic-covered wire ties, which are twisted into place, or soft garden twine, loosely tied. It is usually best to tie the stems just below a leaf node, and they should always be tied to the support with a figure-of-eight loop to prevent them being crushed. Spread the branches out equally over the supports, and train shoots into place to fill in any gaps. When it is necessary to cut back plants, make the cut just above a bud that is pointing in the direction you want the the new growth to take.

Training fruit trees

Vigorous plants often produce a lot of leafy growth at the expense of flowers and fruit. This can be remedied by slowing down the passage of plant foods in the stems by keeping the stems horizontal or sloping downwards. Side-shoots, or laterals, are trained horizontally, or they can even be trained downwards; this method is used by commercial fruit growers, who attach weights to the tips of branches of apple trees to pull them down and so increase the fruit crop. Shoots off the laterals are known as sub-laterals.

Fruit trees are often candidates for specific training techniques aimed at improving the crop and forming attractive plants. Many of these trees are ideal for small spaces, allowing a range of fruit to be grown where it would otherwise be impossible. They are often known as restricted forms, and need dwarfing or very dwarfing rootstocks.

These restricted forms all need support. Training in the early stages can be complex, and it is best to buy trees which have been specifically produced to be grown in these forms. The initial training should then have been done for you.

TRAINED FRUIT FORMS

CORDONS

These are single-stemmed trees, usually grown at an angle of 45 degrees. Compact columnar trees, such as Minarette and Ballerina trees, are a type of vertical cordon. When planting cordons, make sure that the grafting point remains well above soil level, otherwise the grafted variety will root and overcome the effects of the dwarfing rootstock.

ESPALIERS

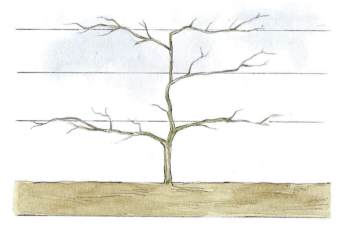

For an espaliered tree, suitable branches are trained horizontally to form a tree with a central stem and regular tiers of branches about 45cm (18in) apart. Crops of fruit are potentially more abundant than with a cordon, but espaliered trees require considerably more space.

Training plants

Grow trained trees in containers or in the open ground on wires against a wall or fence, or on posts and wires.

Pruning trained trees

This is all-important for restricted forms. Most pruning is done in summer, since this slows down growth; avoid winter pruning, which tends to lead to vigorous growth the following spring.

On cordons, prune the tip of the main stem lightly in late spring once it has reached the top wire of its support. Once the shoots have reached about the thickness of a pencil, start to prune them, carrying out the whole operation over a period of several weeks in midsummer. Prune laterals, or shoots off the main stem, fairly lightly, cutting them back to the third leaf above the cluster of leaves at the base of the stem. Prune sub-lateral shoots (shoots arising from main-stem side-shoots) more severely.

Fan-trained cherries should be pruned more lightly, with the laterals cut back to four or six leaves. Badly placed buds should be removed in early spring. Retain those that will grow on in the same plane as the wall, and rub out any that point in towards the wall or straight outwards.

PRUNING CORDONS

Every year, in late spring, cut off the tip of the main stem of cordons, leaving about 1cm (½in) of new wood. Tie the stem to its support.

In midsummer, when laterals (side-shoots on the main stem) are about 23cm (9in) long, cut them back to the third leaf above the basal cluster. On sub-laterals, cut above the first leaf beyond the basal cluster.

STEPOVERS

The ultimate in small trees, the stepover is an espalier with just one tier of branches. It can be grown as an edging to a bed and will bear a small crop of fruit.

FANS

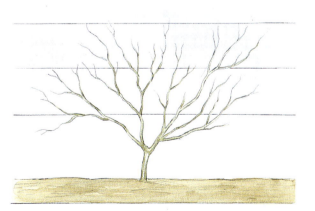

Cherry trees are perhaps the most commonly found fan-trained trees. They are normally grown against a wall or fence, with the branches spread out in a regular fan shape and the tree kept flat against the wall.

Basic gardening

Training plants

Standards

A standard – a plant with a clear stem topped by a head – makes a good focal point in a group of plants, adding height and a touch of formality. Many foliage and flowering plants can be trained as standards; bay, fuchsia, rose, willow and marguerite are popular choices. Half-standards have shorter clear stems than standards; the accepted height varies from species to species.

It requires a lot of skill to produce some standard plants. With roses, for example, one variety provides a strong-growing stem while the flowering variety, which will form the head, is budded on to the stem later, when it has reached an appropriate height. Slow-growing bay trees need several years of painstaking training before they produce a reasonably sized specimen. Usually such plants must be bought ready-trained – producing them is beyond the scope of most gardeners, let alone "no-garden" gardeners.

Training a standard plant

Other plants, however, are much easier to train, and anyone with a little patience can produce a standard within a season or two, depending on the type of plant. Fuchsias make a good starting point.

Select either a young rooted cutting or a slightly older plant that has been produced specifically for training as a standard. Make sure the growing point is undamaged. Provide the plant with a cane and allow it to continue growing upwards, tying it to the support regularly in order to keep the stem as straight as possible. As side-shoots start to grow, pinch them back to one pair of leaves. Do not rub the shoots out completely; they help to build up the main stem. Pot the plant on in the normal way as necessary, taking extra care not to damage the growing point or stem. Continue in this manner until the stem has reached the required height. Allow the leading shoot to produce another four pairs of leaves, then pinch out the tip to stimulate the buds beneath into growth to form the head. Pinch out the tips of the shoots that develop when they have reached 15cm (6in) or so in length to encourage a bushy head to form. Thereafter, pinch out the tips of shoots to keep the head well shaped and even, and rub out any shoots that develop on the main stem.

The stem lengths generally recognised for standards are 25–45cm (10–18in) for a quarter-standard; 45–75cm (18–30in) for a half-standard; and 75–107cm (30–42in) for a full standard.

TRAINING A STANDARD FUCHSIA

1 Choose a strong cutting 15–23cm (6–9in) high with an intact growing tip. Pinch out any side-shoots that grow in the leaf axils (where the leaves join the main stem).

2 Provide the plant with a cane and tie it to the cane to produce a straight stem. Continue to pinch out the side shoots as they appear, leaving one pair of leaves.

Topiary

Small-leafed evergreens can be clipped into ornamental shapes, known as topiary. Some specimens are extremely complex, taking the form of intricately spiralled corkscrews or painstakingly produced birds and animals, but for the "no-garden" situation, simpler spheres, cones and pyramids are more effective. Topiary specimens are particularly suitable for growing in containers, but take care that the shape and style of container chosen will complement the eventual form of the plant. Good plants for clipping are yew, box-leafed honeysuckle *Lonicera nitida* and, perhaps most popular, box.

Corkscrew frame

Select a strong, healthy container-grown plant with an even shape. If you have a good eye, simple shapes can be clipped freehand, but a better result is likely to be achieved by placing a wire frame – obtainable from many garden centres – over the young plant, and simply clipping back shoots with secateurs as they grow through the frame. Clip regularly during the growing season to maintain dense, bushy growth. It is also possible to "cheat" by growing vigorous, small-leafed ivies over a moss-covered wire frame, training the shoots carefully over the wires to cover it completely, and tucking in or clipping back untidy growth as it forms. In this way, complex shapes can be clothed in greenery in a short time to give an effect very similar to that of traditional topiary. Water the plants frequently and mist the leaves to keep the moss damp.

Spherical frame

Training plants

3 When the fuchsia is as tall as you want it, allow it to produce three more sets of leaves, then pinch out the growing tip of the plant.

4 As side-shoots form at the top of the stem, pinch out their growing tips. This will make them branch, and gradually a bushy head will form at the top of the stem.

MAKING A TOPIARY CONE

1 *Small-leafed box*, Buxus sempervirens, *is especially suitable for small topiary because it has densely packed, small shiny leaves on woody stems. Choose a sturdy plant and clip it roughly into the shape with sharp secateurs.*

2 When the plant has grown sufficiently, either buy a wire frame or make a cutting guide from canes held in a cone shape with wire. Place the frame over the plant and cut the stems to the shape.

3 Once the cone shape is established, you will need to clip it at least twice a year to maintain it. In between, cut off new growth or pinch off the leaves with your fingers to prevent cutting marks on the leaves.

TRAINING IVY ON A FRAME

Make a frame from a double layer of chicken wire with a layer of sphagnum moss about 2cm (¾in) thick in between. Shape the frame and put it in position, leaving room at the edge of the pot for the ivies. As they grow, train the tendrils over the frame.

Basic gardening

Plant maintenance

One of the main objects of pruning plants is to keep their growth within bounds and to prevent them outgrowing their allotted space, and nowhere is this more necessary than where space is in short supply. But you need to prune carefully, not just cut back branches wherever they encroach.

This is not, however, the only consideration. It is important to prune plants to keep them flowering, fruiting and looking attractive. Pruning plants correctly helps to stimulate vigorous growth, encourage more profuse flowering, improve the shape of the plant and keep it healthy. But be wary; prune incorrectly, and it can have exactly the opposite effects to those you intend.

What is meant by "pruning"?

The term is usually associated with woody-stemmed subjects, where cutting-back has an effect on the main framework of the plant. Shrubs and climbers are the chief candidates for regular pruning, although in small spaces, some trees may require attention, too.

If a plant needs frequent, drastic pruning to keep it small enough for its space, it is probably better to replace it with a more compact, less vigorous variety. Before replacing it, however, check your pruning technique. Severe pruning in winter or early spring encourages strong, vigorous growth, so you may be making the problem worse by cutting the plant back hard. The removal of selected whole branches is often more successful than clipping back branch tips, as long as you take care not to spoil the plant's shape.

The timing and type of pruning required varies according to the particular plant, but when pruning flowering shrubs, note when the flowers are produced and on what type of wood – prune early bloomers right after the blooms fade and summer bloomers in late winter to early spring.

PRUNING RULES

1. Know why you are pruning.
2. Use well-sharpened tools to avoid damage to stems.
3. Cut out dead, damaged and diseased branches.
4. Cut back healthy stems to a strong bud.
5. Prune at an appropriate time of year.

HARD PRUNING

Where plants are grown for characteristics other than flowers, they may need especially hard pruning. Dogwood, Cornus alba, *for example, has attractive winter stems, and eucalyptus,* Eucalyptus gunnii, *round, blue, juvenile leaves. The stems of both these plants can be cut down to within a few centimetres of the ground in spring to promote the production of strong young shoots, rather than leaving them to form large plants. Butterfly bush,* Buddleja davidii *also benefits from hard pruning, which improves the quality of flowers and appearance of the plant.*

DEADHEADING

The removal of faded blooms, known as deadheading, improves virtually all plants that do not produce attractive or useful fruits or berries. It enhances the plant's appearance, saves it wasting energy on setting seed, and often prolongs flowering. Pinch off dead flowerheads with your finger and thumb, or snip them off with a pair of secateurs.

Plant maintenance

Follow these steps when pruning

1 Take out dead, dying and diseased branches completely and cut right back to healthy wood. For many shrubs, this will be all that is necessary, but if the plant is too large, or failing to give a good display of flowers, coloured foliage or stems, further pruning may be needed.

2 Check when the plant flowers. Deciduous flowering shrubs fall into two main groups: those that flower in spring on last year's shoots, and those that flower in summer on the current season's growth.

Prune plants in the first group immediately after flowering, in late spring or early summer, cutting back the branches that have just flowered. This promotes the growth of strong young shoots which will overwinter and carry next season's flowers. Prune plants in the second group in late winter or early spring, as they are about to start into growth.

Evergreen trees and shrubs are usually best pruned in spring or early summer.

3 On most plants, cut back branches to within a few buds of where they join the main stem, using sharp secateurs. Cut just above a bud with a straight cut or one sloping away from the bud. Before cutting, envisage the direction in which the bud will grow away – it is usual to choose an outwards-facing bud so as to keep the centre of the plant open.

4 If a plant is encroaching on an open area, neighbouring plant or pathway, cut back the overhanging branches to an appropriate bud. You may need to cut back the opposite side of the plant in a similar way to retain a balanced shape. Remember to allow for regrowth when deciding how hard you need to prune.

Clipping

Some plants are grown as hedges or formal shapes, which require frequent pruning of the growing tips during the growing season. This clipping can be done with secateurs, shears or a powered hedge trimmer, depending on the size of the plants. The constant cutting back of the tips of the branches encourages new shoots to grow, forming a dense, leafy bush.

Pinching out

Many plants, particularly herbaceous and annual types such as marigolds, asters, antirrhinums and chrysanthemums, naturally produce a single stem with a flower on top. A more attractive and free-flowering plant will be produced if the growing point is pinched out while the plant is still young, since this stimulates buds lower down the stem to start into growth, resulting in a bushy specimen with many more flowers. This technique is also known as stopping.

BASIC PRUNING

Terminal bud
SUB-LATERAL BRANCH
Lateral bud
Last year's growth (2nd-year wood)
New wood
LATERAL BRANCH
Growth made the year before last (3rd-year wood)
Fruit bud
Make a clean sloping cut 6mm (¼in) above an outwards-facing bud
Secateurs
MAIN STEM
Cut off the branch close to the main stem
Small folding pruning saw
Cut the branch a quarter of the way through underneath before cutting from above

Basic gardening

Plant maintenance

In one way or another, your plants will need care all through the year. In cold climates there may be little to do in the worst of the winter (*see* pp.140–141 for details of winter care), but the growing season, from early spring to late autumn, can be as busy as you like to make it. Gardening in a small space means that jobs rarely have a chance to become tedious.

Watering

One thing almost all "no-garden" situations have in common is that there is a limited amount of soil around the plants' roots. Even when plants are not in containers but planted out they will tend to be at the base of walls, or in raised beds or cracks in paving, where the soil is shallow and often of poor quality. The most important consequence of this is that water available to the plants' roots is almost certain to be in short supply, so regular watering will be an essential task. Estimating the correct amount of water to give a plant can be difficult for inexperienced gardeners, but giving too much will eventually kill the plant just as surely as not giving enough. The aim should be to keep the growing medium moist, not wet. The spaces between the soil particles must contain air as well as water. Unimpeded drainage is necessary to let excess water run away. Containers must have sufficient drainage holes in the base, and be raised off the ground if necessary. Crocks, in the form of broken clay pots or stones, covering the drainage holes will enable the water to percolate through easily; similar crocks and rubble should form the base of a raised bed. The soil or compost used for the plants must also be of the right consistency, usually containing a proportion of sand or grit to ensure efficient drainage. These drainage precautions may seem ironic when the supply and conservation of water is usually a gardener's biggest worry, but they are essential for healthy growth nonetheless.

Soilless composts tend to be most popular for "no-garden" situations because they are light and relatively clean to handle. They do, however, dry out more quickly than soil-based types. Once peat or peat substitutes are allowed to dry out completely, they are often difficult to rewet – the water simply runs off the top of the compost or drains away down the sides of the container where the dry compost has shrunk, leaving a gap. Many brands contain a wetting agent to help overcome this, but sometimes the entire container needs to be immersed in water for several hours before it will start to take up water normally again. To prevent the problem arising, make sure the compost never dries out completely.

Water plants sufficiently to keep the soil or compost just moist; if necessary, dig a little hole with a trowel so that you can check the state of the soil a few centimetres below the

Fertilisers are available for every type of plant. Those shown here are, clockwise from the left, potassium-rich fertiliser for tomatoes and roses; liquid concentrate for ericaceous plants; organic seaweed extract and high-potash fertiliser to promote vigorous root growth, flowering and berrying; sulphate of aluminium for blueing hydrangeas; sequestered iron for acid-loving plants such as azaleas; general-purpose concentrated manure and bonemeal.

Plant maintenance

surface. The best time to water is in the evening, when the sun is off the plants, since less water is wasted through evaporation. But if plants show signs of lack of water, they should be watered immediately.

Feeding

In the same way that finding sufficient water can be a problem for plant roots in confined spaces, plant nutrients are usually in short supply, too. Plants in "no-garden" situations are usually grown at high densities, as gardeners try to cram quarts into their pint pots. This increases the competition for food and water, making the plants ever-more reliant on the grower providing frequent top-ups.

We have already noted which nutrients plants require (*see* p. 99), and although good soil or compost contains sufficient nutrients to start the plants off, after a while they will require supplementary feeding. A balanced fertiliser, with more or less equal quantities of the major nutrients, is a good basic plant food, while high-potassium feeds encourage prolific flowering and berrying and high-nitrogen feeds are suitable for foliage plants to ensure healthy, lush, leafy growth.

All fertiliser packs should display the nutrients they contain as an NPK (nitrogen, phosphorus, potassium) ratio – 7:7:7, for instance, indicates a balanced fertiliser, while 14:4:22 is a high-potash (potassium) feed. Most fertilisers also state on the pack the types of plant and applications for which they are particularly useful, but you will find some are interchangeable if you study their NPK ratio. Rose and tomato fertilisers, for instance, are often identical, both being high-potash feeds.

PLANTS NEED FEEDING MORE OFTEN IF THEY ARE:

- vigorous growers
- planted in soilless compost
- growing in small containers
- planted very closely
- given short-acting fertilisers

PLANTS NEED FEEDING LESS OFTEN IF THEY ARE:

- slow growing and compact
- growing in good-quality loam-based compost
- spaced well apart
- have a good depth of soil for their roots
- fed with slow-release, long-acting fertilisers

Pay special attention to watering and feeding plants growing between paving slabs and in other confined spaces. The soil will be sparse and probably poor, and little rain will reach the roots.

Fertilisers are formulated in a variety of ways. Powders are usually dissolved in water before application, although some can be applied dry to the soil; granules are applied to the soil surface and watered in, or mixed with the compost when the plant is potted up; sticks and tablets are pushed just below the soil surface. Liquid fertilisers are diluted with water and applied to the soil around the plants and sometimes to the foliage as well. Specially formulated foliar feeds usually contain trace elements, which are taken up rapidly by the leaves. It is important to follow the directions for the application of all fertilisers carefully – they can harm the plants if wrongly applied. Powder and granule fertilisers should always be kept off leaves, since they may scorch them.

How often you need to feed plants depends on their type and the density at which they are being grown, the type and volume of compost or soil, and the brand of fertiliser.

Basic gardening

Plant maintenance

Plants growing in containers in a small volume of soil will soon fill that soil with roots and exhaust the supplies of plant nutrients. Feeding will replace the nutrients, but in order to make healthy new root growth, fresh soil or compost must be supplied from time to time. This can be done by potting the plant on into a larger container, cutting the roots of the plant back and simply replacing the compost or topdressing with fresh compost.

Potting on

A plant should always be supplied with a container in proportion to its size. Tempting though it may be to place a small plant in a large tub because that is where you want it to end up, it is not a good idea. It will be difficult to regulate the amount of moisture held by the large volume of compost that the plant's roots do not penetrate. This leads to the unused compost becoming sour and not suitable for plant growth.

Young plants should be moved progressively to slightly larger containers as they grow, enabling their roots to extend quickly into the new compost provided. How soon they need potting on varies according to the vigour of individual plants, but generally a good sign that it's time to move them is when roots start to emerge from the drainage holes in their current containers.

To pot on, prepare the new container by placing crocks or other drainage material in the base, then add a layer of a similar type of compost to the one in which the plant is already growing. You may want to change over to a compost containing a higher level of nutrients but it is not generally a good idea to swap between soilless and soil-based composts when repotting plants.

Remove the plant from its existing pot by turning the pot upside down and striking the rim against a firm edge, or if the pot is too large for this, turn it on its side and run a large knife or thin piece of wood between the sides of the pot and the rootball and ease the plant and its rootball out carefully. (The plant will come out of its pot more easily if it has been well watered several hours in advance.)

Stand the rootball on the layer of compost in the new container and check that the top of the rootball is at the correct level. Fill in around the sides with fresh compost, firming it down with your fingers or a piece of wood to ensure there are no air pockets. Cover the top of the rootball with a fairly thin layer of compost and water the plant.

POTTING ON A PLANT

1 To remove a plant from its pot, water it well some time beforehand. Turn it upside down, place your hand around the top of the plant to prevent it falling, and give the rim of the pot a firm tap against the edge of a table or a window ledge.

2 Put a layer of crocks in the bottom of a pot one size larger than the old one, and cover it with fresh compost. Gently tease out the roots of the plant if they are very constricted, then set the plant in the pot.

3 Fill the gap between the side of the pot and the plant with fresh compost, dribbling it in carefully by hand so as not to damage the plant. Press the compost down firmly. Then water the plant thoroughly with a rose on the can, or stand the pot in a bucket of water to soak the compost. Finally, drain the pot.

Plant maintenance

Repotting and topdressing

If the plant is already in the largest practical size of pot, it can be repotted into a new container of the same size. Some plants, such as clivia, need to be slightly pot-bound in order to flower well. They, too, should be repotted into a pot of the same size, but only when roots appear on the surface of the compost.

If you cannot turn the plant out of its pot, simply topdress it by scraping away and replacing the top layer of compost.

Staking plants

Tall or weak-stemmed plants may need staking as they grow. The earlier the supports are provided, the better the effect. It is much more difficult to achieve a natural-looking shape if stakes are put in position only when it becomes essential. Check plants frequently as they grow so that supports can be moved or ties adjusted. Never let a tie bite into the stem of a shrub or tree, and tie soft stems with garden string or use a plastic-covered twist-tie. Details of supports and training are given on pages 126–133.

Most weedkillers can be sprayed, or watered, on to plants and paths.

Weeding and pest control

Weeds are an ever-present problem in even the tiniest pocket of soil. As well as looking untidy, they compete with your plants for nutrients, moisture and space, and should be removed, preferably while they are still in the seedling stage. In "no-garden" areas, a hoe is unlikely to be practical, and weeds should simply be pulled out by hand. This is easiest to do when the soil is moist.

Weeds with a deep taproot which cannot be pulled up easily; those such as bindweed, which are difficult to disentangle from plants without damage; and others, like creeping grasses, which are difficult to remove from the soil entirely, can be spot treated with a weedkiller such as glyphosate, but care must be taken to keep the weedkiller off cultivated plants. Weedkillers are produced as sprays, sticks and gels for easy use.

Regular monitoring means that any pests can be detected early, so treatment is more likely to be successful. Further details on possible pests and their control, as well as some common diseases, are given on pages 150–155.

REPOTTING INTO THE SAME SIZE POT

1 *Remove the plant from its old pot and crumble away some of the old compost from the roots and top of the rootball. Use a pointed piece of wood if necessary, or cut off part of the rootball with a sharp knife to encourage the growth of strong new roots.*

2 *Put a layer of drainage material in the bottom of the pot, then a layer of compost, and set the plant on it so that the top of the rootball comes just below the bottom of the pot rim. Fill in around the rootball with fresh compost and press it down firmly. Add fresh compost to the top of the rootball, too, but don't bury the stem any deeper. Water thoroughly.*

TOPDRESSING

If a plant is too well established and large to turn out of its pot, you can simply topdress it. With a kitchen fork, or a small garden fork, gently scrape away the top 5-7.5cm (2–3in) of compost, being careful not to damage the roots. Fill the pot up to the old level with fresh compost to which slow-release fertiliser has been added, press it down and water the plant.

Basic gardening

Winter care

Preparations must be made for the winter season in climates where frosts and prolonged cold spells are likely. Plants vary in their degree of hardiness, or ability to cope with cold. Even those that are generally acknowledged to be fully hardy will often be killed by frost if they have not been accustomed to cool weather – plants that have been grown in a greenhouse, for example. The growth they produce is soft and sappy, and much more prone to frost damage than if they had been growing in the open, when the stems would have become firmer and more resilient.

Caring for plants

Having assessed your particular situation, as discussed on pages 38–39, you should have a good idea of the likelihood of damage to your plants. If you are growing annuals or bedding plants that are easy to replace, the plants can be discarded when they are past their best, or as soon as frost spoils the display. Containers can then be cleaned and put away for the next summer season or, where climate permits, filled with plants for winter interest such as winter-flowering pansies and heathers, or with spring bulbs. If you are replanting for the winter, don't wait for the frost before getting rid of your summer plants; it helps to have winter-flowering subjects well established before the coldest weather begins. Make sure that the new plants are fully hardened off before putting them out.

Some of the container plants you have grown may be tender but not easily replaced. Perhaps they are unusual varieties, or particularly expensive, or perennials that must be grown for several years before they assume an attractive shape or reach a reasonable size, or are able to flower or fruit.

These plants can sometimes be successfully brought into the home to overwinter – they usually require a cool, frost-free environment with plenty of light. The aim is to prevent them from being killed by frost rather than to keep them growing all the year round, and many species will not thrive in centrally heated rooms. A frost-free greenhouse or conservatory is ideal, and you may know someone who would be willing to board out your plants until the spring. Large specimens are not easy to move and are not so adaptable to changes in conditions, so keep your most tender plants in practical-sized containers and prune them back well if necessary so that they are manageable.

Those plants which are "dubiously hardy" are in some ways less easy to deal with. They may survive outside for several years quite happily, only to be killed off by an especially sharp

Snow will do less damage to sturdy stone containers and to hardy plants such as box than frost and biting winds.

WINTER PROTECTION

A large tender shrub can be protected by covering it in horticultural fleece and tying rope firmly around the bush.

Place stakes in a square around a young tree, then wrap hessian or plastic sheeting around the stakes.

Winter care

spell one winter, just as you have become confident of their hardiness. As an insurance policy, always take a few cuttings of treasured varieties during the summer and keep them under cover for the winter so that you have replacements if the worst happens. Give a little extra protection to borderline plants by heaping peat, dry leaves or straw over dormant rootstocks, or by constructing shelters around them.

Be careful about applying fertiliser. High-nitrogen fertilisers promote soft, vulnerable growth; high-potash feeds help to ripen and toughen up stems for the winter. Towards the end of the summer, switch from nitrogen to potassium-based fertilisers for all the plants that you want to overwinter; withold fertiliser while plants are dormant.

Wrap vulnerable pots in bubble plastic or sacking stuffed with straw for winter protection.

Caring for containers

Plant containers can be expensive, and they all need regular maintenance and occasional cleaning. While plants are growing in them, the outside can be hosed down, scrubbed with a stiff brush or wiped with a cloth. In winter, when they are empty, scrub the pots inside and out with a mild disinfectant solution to help prevent the carry-over of pest and disease problems. A stiff toothbrush is useful for cleaning raised decorations. Any other treatment that pots may require depends on the material that they are made of.

PLASTIC Wash and scrub the pots. Discard any pots that have become brittle or cracked after exposure to sunlight.

FIBREGLASS Fibreglass can also be brittle and needs careful handling. Like plastic, it can be scrubbed and washed. On white or light-coloured containers, ornate decorations often become grimy; scrubbing empty containers with a weak solution of household bleach usually solves this.

CLAY AND EARTHENWARE Clay, or terracotta, pots are fragile, so handle them carefully. They can also be prone to frost damage, and in cold areas you should buy those that are guaranteed frost-proof. Because the clay absorbs moisture, algae often grow on the outside and salts are deposited on the surface, giving a patina of age which many people find attractive but others prefer to scrub off. There is no problem of algal growth with glazed earthenware pots; they are easy to wipe clean, but, like terracotta, are prone to frost damage.

If you are worried about a pot's frost resistance, it will help to line the inside of the container with polythene sheeting before filling it with compost, but remember to cut drainage holes in the base of the polythene. A piece of plastic-coated wire encircling a pot and twisted tight before winter sets in will help to hold the pot together if it does crack.

WOOD Wooden containers will rot if they are constantly damp, so treat them with a plant-safe wood preserver and raise them off the ground so that water can drain away from the base. In winter, repaint the outside with wood preserver or gloss or emulsion paint.

METAL Treat metal containers inside and out with a suitable preservative against rust before planting. Any signs of rust that appear later can be spot-treated with an oxidising paint.

Caring for ponds and water features

If the surface of a pond freezes over for more than a day or two in winter, you will need to melt a hole in the ice to allow oxygen in and other gases out. Don't break the ice with a heavy implement, since this causes shock waves that will harm any fish. Electrically operated pond heaters can be used to keep a small area free of ice, or you can stand a metal pan of boiling water on the surface to melt a hole.

Floating a plastic ball on the surface of the water absorbs the pressure from ice and helps to prevent the sides of a concrete pond from cracking.

In cold regions, mini-ponds are at risk of more than just the surface of the water freezing. It is safest to transfer the fish to an indoor tank for the winter. In marginal climates, partially sinking the mini-pond into the ground can help to keep a sufficient depth of water free from ice.

Where there is a high risk of freezing weather, the pumps for fountains and the like should be switched off and any exposed pipes emptied so that they do not freeze and burst.

Straw packed around a wigwam of canes makes good protection for half-hardy plants such as yucca.

Basic gardening

Propagation

Raising your own plants is always satisfying; it can also save money and enable you to perpetuate those that have done particularly well for you. Although propagation on a grand scale is not possible in a "no-garden" situation, some methods require a minimum of space and special equipment.

Seed

A vast number of seeds of vegetables, flowering, and foliage plants is available, many of which are very simple to raise. Annuals or plants grown as annuals are particularly popular and you can produce large numbers for a small outlay.

Seeds can be sown in ordinary pots, but seed trays are more useful. Sterile seed and cuttings compost, with a low level of nutrients, or a general-purpose compost, is essential to prevent the seedlings being attacked by fungal diseases. Seed kits, which contain all you need to grow the plants on a window-sill indoors, are often available. Trays should be watered with a can fitted with a fine rose, or with a hand mister, to avoid disturbing the surface and dislodging the seeds. For pricking out young seedlings, a plastic dibber is handy, but a pencil will do the job just as well. For those seeds that are sown directly into the soil out of doors, a rake is useful to break up the soil into fine crumbs, and garden string stretched between a couple of canes will help you to obtain straight rows in beds.

If you intend to raise a lot of plants from seed, and want to try some of the more difficult species that require high temperatures to germinate, you can buy electrically heated propagators for indoor use. You will, however, need sufficient space indoors to grow on the seedlings before they are ready to be planted out, so it is probably worth investing in a heated

HANDLING VERY FINE SEEDS

The best way to sow very fine seeds is to mix them with a tablespoon or two of fine silver sand in a clean jar and spread the mixture evenly over a tray of damp compost. Then simply cover the tray with glass and newspaper.

PROPAGATING BY SOWING SEED

1 *Most seeds do not need special treatment. Simply fill a seed tray with moist compost, level the surface, and press it lightly with the base of another seed tray to firm it. Spread the seeds thinly and evenly over the surface, either tapping them from the packet or scattering pinches of seed by hand.*

2 *Cover the seeds carefully with a layer of fine compost, preferably through a sieve, or a layer of sharp sand. This will hold them in place and keep them moist, though some seeds (very fine ones, or those that need light in order to germinate) should not be covered – the seed packet will tell you if this is the case.*

3 *Water the sown tray carefully with a fine rose on the watering can or a coarse mist from a hand sprayer until the compost is thoroughly moist, but not waterlogged.*

Propagation

propagator only if you have a conservatory or sunroom. In order to germinate, seeds require warmth and moisture. The amount of warmth varies according to the plant and its country of origin. Some seeds need a heated propagator, others the warmth of an indoor room, while yet others can be raised in trays outdoors.

The seeds of hardy annuals can be sown where they are to flower. Break down the soil until it is fine and crumbly, then make a series of shallow, parallel drills using a cane or tool handle. Sprinkle the seed evenly along the drills, rake soil over to cover, and water with a fine rose. When the flower seed germinates, the plants will be easy to distinguish from any weed seedlings because they will be growing in straight rows. As the seedlings develop, gradually thin out the rows, eventually leaving the strongest plants at the correct spacing.

Once seeds have germinated, the young plants need light, nutrients and water, just as adult plants do, but like all babies young plants need special care in their early stages.

To speed the germination of hard-coated seeds, such as those of some sweetpea varieties, nick the side opposite the eye with the point of a sharp knife (left), or soak them in a bowl of water for 12 hours (right).

Sow large seeds by hand, spacing them about 2.5cm (1in) apart to avoid having to prick them out too soon. Push the seeds into the compost – the larger the seed the deeper it should be sown – then gently water the tray.

4 *Cover the seed tray to create a warm, humid atmosphere, which will induce the seeds to germinate. The traditional method is to use a sheet of glass topped with newspaper, but an upturned seed tray will also do. Best of all is a plastic propagator top with sufficient headroom for the seedlings to develop; cover it with newspaper until germination begins.*

5 *Remove the cover as soon as the first seedlings show through. Once they are up, they need bright, diffused light, but must not be exposed to direct sunlight. Tissue paper taped to the window glass makes a good shade for plants on a window-sill. As the seedlings grow and become stronger, remove the shading. Give them enough water to keep the compost just moist.*

6 *Thin out the seedlings as soon as they are large enough, handling them by their seed leaves (the first pair of leaves), never by their stems. Water the tray, then gently lever the plants up with a dibber, tease the roots free, and carefully pull the seedlings apart. Set them in fresh compost in another tray so that the space between them is about the same as their height.*

Basic gardening

Propagation

Cuttings

Not all plants can be raised from seed. Some plants are sterile and do not produce seeds; others produce seed but do not breed true – plants raised from the seed they produce will not have the same characteristics as the parent. Sometimes growing plants from seed can be too slow, difficult or laborious to be practical. In this instance, cuttings can often be used to produce plants instead. A young plant raised from a cutting is larger and more robust than a seedling and has the advantage of being genetically identical to its parent.

Many different types of cutting can be taken at various times of year, using roots and leaves as well as stems, but for the "no-garden" gardener the most useful are softwood and semi-ripe cuttings.

SOFTWOOD CUTTINGS These are taken mainly in spring and early summer, using vigorous young shoots. Almost any plant can be increased by this method, but perennials and bedding plants are probably the most common candidates.

First, prepare pots or trays of seed and cuttings compost or general-purpose compost in the same way as for sowing seed, and sprinkle a thin layer of sharp sand on the surface.

Select a strong, healthy young shoot, preferably without any flower buds, and cut or break it from the plant – cuttings of some plants, such as chrysanthemum, root better if they are snapped rather than cut. The length of the stem varies, but most softwood cuttings carry one or two pairs of fully expanded leaves when trimmed. Using a sharp knife or blade, trim the cutting just below a node (the point where the leaves join the stem) and remove the lower leaves flush with the stem.

Rooting powder or gel is optional with softwood cuttings; most root just as well without it, and some root better. If you are trying to propagate a particularly difficult species you may like to try it. Choose a brand that contains a fungicide as well as rooting hormones, since this will help to prevent the base of the cutting from rotting. Tip out some powder into the lid of the tin, dip the base of the cutting in it, then tap the stem lightly to shake off all but a fine dusting of powder.

Insert the prepared cutting into the compost and firm it gently but thoroughly with your fingers to ensure that the base of the cutting is in close contact with the compost – don't leave an air space beneath it. Once the pot or tray is filled, water well with a fine rose on the can and cover it with a propagator top if you have one, or a tent made from a clear plastic bag supported on split canes. Because cuttings still

SOFTWOOD CUTTINGS

1 Soft-stemmed pelargoniums are excellent subjects for softwood cuttings. Cut a stem about 7.5cm (3in) long with three or four leaf nodes between the tip and the base. Remove the lower leaves with a sharp knife (inset) and trim the stem to just below a node. Fill a pot with compost and sprinkle a thin layer of sand on top. Make a hole with a dibber or pencil and insert the cutting, gently firming the compost around it with your fingers.

2 If you put several cuttings into the same pot, make sure that their leaves do not touch. Water the pot well. Then cover it with either a propagator top or with a clear plastic bag held away from the cuttings with canes, and seal the opening with sticky tape to provide the humid atmosphere the plants need to form roots. Remove the bag when the cuttings begin to show signs of growth.

SEMI-RIPE CUTTINGS

1 Shrubs are suitable plants from which to take semi-ripe cuttings. In summer, select a 7.5–15-cm (3–6-in) long sideshoot of the current season's growth that is firm but still pliable, and tear it away from the main stem with a heel of the old wood.

Propagation

have their leaves, they continue to lose moisture through them, so it is essential to provide a humid atmosphere. Shade the tray from direct sunlight. It is common for the leaves to droop immediately after the cuttings have been inserted, but they should pick up after a few hours.

A reasonably warm position will speed rooting, and some plants may produce new roots in only a few days. Two to three weeks is normal, but some species may be much slower. Once the cuttings have recovered from their initial shock, the ventilators on a propagator top should be opened to help avoid fungal disease; covers can often be removed altogether after a short while, as long as the compost is kept moist. Do not overwater – this will cause the base of the cuttings to rot.

It is usually easy to see when the cuttings have begun to root as they start to look fresh and "growy" at their tips. Be patient; never pull up a cutting to check its root development. You can check for signs of roots through the pots' drainage holes, but in general it will be obvious from the cuttings' appearance when they have rooted and need potting on.

SEMI-RIPE CUTTINGS Woody plants, such as trees and shrubs, usually produce better results from semi-ripe cuttings, which are taken in summer from the current season's growth, when the stems have begun to firm up and ripen.

Prepare pots or trays in advance as for softwood cuttings. Select a side-shoot of the current season's growth; it should be firm at the base, but still pliable. Side-shoots of a suitable length can be torn away from the stem to leave a small "heel" of bark attached, otherwise they are trimmed with a sharp knife just below a node. Semi-ripe cuttings are generally rather larger than softwood cuttings, but again usually consist of two pairs of fully expanded leaves. If the plant has very large leaves, it is best to reduce them to a single pair to avoid excessive water loss.

Dip the base of the cutting in hormone rooting powder or gel and tap off the excess. Insert in compost, firm in and water as before. Cover with a propagator top to start with, but this can be removed once the cuttings have recovered from the initial shock; the atmosphere does not need to be as humid as for softwood cuttings.

Semi-ripe cuttings do not root as quickly as softwood cuttings, but are more resilient. Keep them in a sheltered position out of direct sun for the rest of the summer, moving them to a cool position under cover before the first frosts if necessary. Keep the compost just moist during the winter and remove any fallen leaves. The cuttings will not generally be rooted and ready for potting on until the following spring.

2 Trim the base of the cutting cleanly with a sharp knife and neaten the heel if necessary. Remove the lower leaves and stalks and, if the plant has particularly large leaves, take off all but one pair and the terminal bud. Dip the base of the cutting in hormone rooting powder or gel, leaving only a fine dusting on the stem.

3 Insert the cutting into a prepared tray of compost covered with sand, using a dibber or pencil to make a hole, and firm it in with your finger. It is a good idea to take more than one cutting at a time, since they may not all root.

4 Water the cuttings with a fine spray and cover the tray with a propagator top. Keep the tray in a shady spot and, after a few days, open the vents in the top. Water the cuttings as soon as the compost begins to dry out. Overwinter the cuttings in the tray indoors or in a cold frame and pot them on the following spring.

Basic gardening

Propagation

Layering

Layering is a simple way to produce new plants. It is similar to taking cuttings in that a portion of a plant is encouraged to produce its own roots, but the layer is not separated from the parent plant while rooting takes place. This means that its food and water supply are unchanged, so there is little stress on the new plant.

Plants that are generally increased by layering are those that have branches which can be bent down to soil level easily, or that produce plantlets on long runners. Shrubs such as rhododendrons and dogwoods, and climbers like clematis or wisteria are common candidates.

There are various methods of layering, according to the type of plant being increased:

SIMPLE LAYERING This is used for spreading shrubs, such as dogwoods and rhododendrons. In spring, select a healthy, vigorous branch of the previous year's growth which can easily be pulled down to ground level, allowing a portion of the stem to be buried while leaving 15cm (6in) or so of the tip above ground. If the shrub is growing in a raised bed, it can be layered into the surrounding soil; if it is in a container, you will have to bury the layer in compost in a pot.

Use soil-based compost, since this is less likely to dry out and will hold the layer in place more firmly. If necessary, raise the pot to a suitable level by standing it on another upturned pot or a pile of bricks. Stems layered in this manner can take

SIMPLE LAYERING

1 In early spring, select a healthy shoot of the previous year's growth which is firm, yet still pliable. At a point about 30cm (12in) from the tip bend the stem down to the soil and mark the spot where it touches. Dig a hole about 10cm (4in) deep and 20–25cm (8–10in) long and work in some peat and sharp sand.

2 Starting some 15cm (6in) from the tip trim the leaves and leaf stems off the branch for about 60cm (24in). Then make an angled cut in the bare stem so that the tip can be bent at a right angle. This will encourage roots to grow from the stem just above the cut.

3 With a bent piece of wire, pin the stem firmly into the hole so that the tip with leaves on it is above the ground. This will help to prevent the stem from springing up out of the soil.

4 Fill in the hole with soil to which you have added some peat and sharp sand. Roots will form only in the dark, so cover the stem thoroughly. Lightly firm the soil down to help hold the stem in place, and water it well.

5 Insert a cane close to the tip of the layer that is showing above ground and tie the shoot to it. This will keep the layer upright so that it will form a straight-stemmed plant. Water frequently during the summer. When the layer has rooted, cut it away from the parent, but do not lift it or pot it up for six weeks or so.

Propagation

up to 18 months to root. Some may have rooted by the first autumn after layering; others need to be left undisturbed until the following autumn.

Whether or not layers have rooted can often be assessed by looking at the amount of growth the tip has made compared to the other unlayered shoots on the shrub; where a branch is layered into a pot, root growth may be seen through the base of the pot. When a strong root system has developed, cut the stem between the layer and the parent plant with secateurs, lift the layer carefully and pot it up individually.

SERPENTINE LAYERING Climbers with long, sinuous stems, such as clematis, can be layered by this method, which has the advantage of producing a number of plants from one shoot. Each leaf node has the potential to form roots if buried, but two or three nodes must be left intact between buried portions – these will provide the shoots for the new plants. The completed layer, with its series of loops, looks like a snake making its way across the soil – hence the name. If you do not have a suitable patch of soil, the stem can be layered into a large pot, curling it round to take up less space.

RUNNERS Strawberries; bugle, *Ajuga reptans*; sweet violets, *Viola odorata*; and saxifrage, *Saxifraga stonolifera (sarmentosa)*, are among the plants that produce new plantlets on stolons, or runners. If left to their own devices, they produce a thick mat of plants, since they root readily into the surrounding soil, but by selecting the best plantlets and pinning them down into pots of soil-based compost in spring and summer, you can produce strong young plants ideal for transplanting.

SERPENTINE LAYERING

Choose a long, healthy stem of a plant such as clematis and strip off the leaves around the nodes you have selected for layering, leaving two or three nodes on the stem between each of them. With a sharp knife make a small nick in the underside of the stem to encourage rooting. Lay the stem on the soil and bury each of the prepared sections of stem, leaving the intact nodes above the ground.

LAYERING RUNNERS

1 *Disentangle the runners around the parent plant. Choose those that bear strong plantlets and cut off the other runners. Select the plantlets nearest to the parent and cut off the rest of each runner.*

2 *Sink small plant pots filled with soil-based compost into the ground around the parent plant and pin each plantlet down with a bent piece of wire. Keep the pots moist, and the new plants should be ready for lifting by autumn.*

Propagation

Division

Many groups of plants can be increased by division, including those that form clumps, such as herbaceous perennials, bulbs and succulents that form offsets, and tubers and rhizomes, which can be cut into sections. It is a simple and usually very successful method of propagation.

SIMPLE DIVISION Many herbaceous plants become woody in the centre of the clump after a few years, and they can be divided as they are dying down in autumn, or as they are starting into growth in spring. Discard the woody centres, and keep only the strong growths around the edge for replanting.

RHIZOMES Swollen underground stems of plants such as border irises, known as rhizomes, grow horizontally along the ground, producing leaves from their upper surface and roots from the lower. They can be cut into sections to form new plants when older parts become woody and unproductive. Lift irises once they have finished flowering. Using a sharp knife, cut 15-cm (6-in) sections of plump rhizome, each with a fan of leaves and some healthy roots; discard any shrivelled, woody pieces. Then cut down the fan of leaves to about 10cm (4in) to balance the reduced stem and roots. Replant the sections, leaving the top of the rhizome just clear of the soil.

OFFSETS Many bulbs increase by forming smaller bulbs, known as offsets, around the parent. With bulbs such as narcissi, the offsets remain attached to the parent at the basal plate – the ring of tissue where the roots form. If the bulbs are not lifted, flowering is likely to deteriorate after a few years since the offsets cause overcrowding of the clump. Offsets are also produced on short runners or around the base of the parent by several rosette-forming, succulent plants, such as echeveria. The offsets are normally left to form clumps, but one or two can be removed to provide new stock.

TUBERS Plants such as begonias and cyclamen grow from disc-shaped tubers with a dished upper side where the shoots arise. When it is time to start the tuber into growth, press the lower side into a pot of moist compost. Mist the upper side with water once or twice, but do not overwet it – its dished shape collects water, which can lead to rotting. When clusters of growth buds appear on the surface, lift the tuber from the compost and divide it into sections.

SUCKERS Several shrubs produce suckers – shoots that arise from the roots – which can be removed and grown on individually to produce new plants. Plants that sucker freely include *Kerria japonica* and dogwood.

Carefully dig away the soil to expose the root from which the sucker is growing. Ensure that the sucker has plenty of fibrous root growth, then cut it off close to the parent with secateurs. Dig under the sucker so it can be lifted with the roots intact, cut off surplus lengths of the main root and pot up the sucker in fresh compost.

DIVIDING HERBACEOUS PLANTS

1 If the plant is growing in an open bed, lift it carefully, using a fork, retaining as much soil around the roots as possible. If it is in a container, loosen the soil around the edge of the container with a stick or knife, and turn the plant out.

2 With your hands, split the plant into several sections, each with at least one healthy shoot and some good fibrous roots. Patiently tease the sections apart without damaging them.

3 If the crown is too tough to tear apart with your hands, use a pair of hand forks. Split the crown carefully, then pull the sections apart.

DIVIDING BULBS

Some species of lily produce bulbils, tiny black bulbs, on the stem. Remove them after the flowers have faded and plant them, well spaced, in seed and cuttings compost with their tips just beneath the surface. Keep them in partial shade, and they should flower in three or four years.

DIVIDING TUBERS

Divide tubers with a sharp knife. Most tubers can be cut into two or three pieces, each of which must have a group of plump buds. Dust the cut sides of the sections with fungicide powder and then replant them in individual pots of compost.

When the foliage begins to die down, lift bulbs of plants such as narcissus. Shake off loose soil to expose the offsets – there are usually two or three per bulb – and separate them from the main bulb by pushing them off gently with your thumb. Store them with the original bulbs for replanting in autumn.

TAKING OFFSETS

Offsets are produced by some rosette-forming succulent plants, such as echeveria and sempervivum. Plants with small plantlets directly around the base should be lifted carefully and the offsets gently teased away. The offsets should be potted up in sandy compost.

4 The crowns of some plants are so tough and the roots so entangled that they must be cut into segments with a sharp knife.

5 Discard the old sections of the crown. Straightaway, before the roots dry out, replant the newer sections into fresh compost to which slow-release fertiliser has been added. Water them in well.

DIVIDING CHRYSANTHEMUMS

In autumn, lift half-hardy florist's chrysanthemums, trim the rootstocks, or stools, then pack them in compost for the winter. In spring, new roots and leaves will grow on the edges of the stool; detach them and pot them up to form new plants.

Basic gardening

Keeping plants healthy

Plants seldom make it through a whole growing season without showing some disfiguring signs of infestation by disease or attack by pests. Pest and disease organisms are everywhere, even in the most sterile urban environment, just waiting for a suitable victim to arrive.

Growing plants in a "no-garden" situation has some drawbacks as far as plant health is concerned. Damage that would be insignificant in a larger area is all too obvious, and one or two unhealthy plants can ruin an entire display. The temptation to pack as many plants as possible into a limited space leads to overcrowding, which provides fungal diseases with ideal conditions in which to develop. Remedies are sometimes difficult to apply to only a few plants, and chemicals can drift on to neighbouring properties.

But there are benefits to small-scale gardening, too. When you are caring for a small number of plants, it is relatively easy to spot the early signs of trouble and deal with them promptly. In a large garden, problems can go unnoticed until they are well established and far more difficult to deal with. Using sterile compost helps you to avoid a range of potentially harmful soil-living organisms. In addition, plants grown in containers are less likely to be attacked by some pests and diseases than those growing in the open ground. But no matter how many plants you grow, and whatever the size of your "no-garden", the key to healthy plants is keen observation, and prompt, appropriate action when it is needed.

Look after your plants

It is generally thought that weak, undernourished, badly grown plants are more likely to be attacked by pests and diseases than flourishing, well-cared-for specimens. This is not usually the case – in fact, the opposite may well be true. However, the thriving plant is in a much better state to throw off the damaging effects of infestation than one which is already undermined by poor growing conditions, so the visible effects of the problem are usually less obvious.

Keep plants healthy by providing them, as far as possible, with ideal growing conditions. Choose subjects that are suitable for the situation in which they will have to grow – exotic plants that love high temperatures are never going to do well in a cold, exposed site, and shade-loving, woodland natives will find it hard to cope with a sun-baked balcony. A relatively minor pest or disease problem could be the final straw for plants that are already struggling to survive. Keep them adequately watered at all times, apply fertilisers and repot when necessary.

Most problems occur in the growing season, particularly spring and early summer. Pay close attention to your plants; those that are failing to make strong, healthy growth, could be showing the first signs of a pest or disease attack. Favourite places for pests are the undersides of the leaves and the soft young growing tips, so check these carefully if you suspect a problem. And don't forget the roots; if a plant wilts, soil-living pests such as vine weevil and diseases like verticillium wilt could be responsible.

Control without chemicals

It is not always necessary to rely on chemical products to keep plants healthy. You cannot avoid pests and diseases entirely, but you can take simple steps to make it more difficult for them to attack your plants, and to minimise the effects if they do. Taking early action helps to prevent a problem getting out of hand, and several non-chemical means of control give excellent results, particularly where a small number of plants is involved.

KEEP PLANTS TIDY Remove dying leaves and flowers, which can be a focus for fungal diseases. Leaf litter provides a perfect hiding place for slugs, snails, woodlice and other pests, and clearing up regularly can significantly cut down their numbers, and the damage they do.

HAND-PICK PESTS If a pest is identified, hand-picking is often a surprisingly successful way to eliminate it, provided you act promptly. Leaf-eating caterpillars can be picked off individually (if you are not too squeamish), and one or two greenfly-encrusted shoots can usually be cut away without spoiling the plant. Occasionally an entire plant may have to be sacrificed in order to prevent the spread of a problem. A strong jet of water from a hand sprayer can sometimes be enough to dislodge pests. For example, this is often a good way of dealing with aphids on young growing points.

"NATURAL" PESTICIDES Pests can often be controlled organically, with pesticides such as soft soap and pyrethrum.

BIOLOGICAL CONTROL The deliberate introduction of natural predators and parasites to control plant pests is most suitable for the enclosed, controlled environment of greenhouse growing. However, recognising and encouraging common beneficial insects like ladybirds, lacewings and ground beetles will certainly help to protect your plants against severe pest attacks.

Chemical control

There is no doubt that modern pesticides are both effective and safe – as long as they are used correctly. But garden centres carry a bewildering range of products, and it is often difficult to know where to begin when looking for the best remedy.

The first step is to identify the problem. There's no need to be too precise – although there are several different species of moth whose larvae can cause damage, it is enough to know that caterpillars are the culprits. It is also helpful to know the plants that are affected, since not all chemicals are suitable for all groups of plants.

Having identified the problem, you can find out how to treat it. New chemicals are being developed all the time, and manufacturers' literature is generally freely available in garden centres to keep you up to date. The same chemicals are available in several different combinations and formulations under a wide variety of brand names, but the active ingredients should be stated on the packaging to enable you to compare the various brands. The packaging should also tell you the range of pests or diseases the product will control.

Products are formulated in a variety of ways, some of which are much more convenient for use in small areas than others. Chemicals may have systemic or contact action. Systemic chemicals are taken up by roots and foliage and transported within the vascular system to all parts of the plant. Chemicals with contact action will affect only those pests or parts of the plant to which they are directly applied.

SAFE USE OF CHEMICALS

Garden chemicals are tested to ensure their safety, but they can still be harmful to plants, animals and people if they are misused. Follow common-sense safety precautions.
- **Choose the right product for the job.** Spraying caterpillars with a product designed to kill greenfly is a waste of time and money.
- **Mix different chemicals** only if the labels tell you it is safe to do so.
- **Choose the right pack size.** Large economy packs may seem cheaper but, remember, they have a limited shelf life.
- **Read the instructions.** Note any precautions, including recommended protective clothing; storage; and how long you should keep children or pets away from treated plants.
- **When treating edible crops**, observe the stated harvest interval or withholding period between spraying and eating.
- **Don't spray plants in windy conditions.** Spray might drift on to neighbouring plants or properties.
- **Store chemicals in a cool, dry place** away from children, pets and foodstuffs, preferably in a locked cupboard.

CONCENTRATES Chemicals are easier to store in concentrated form and have a longer shelf life. However, care must be taken when storing and handling the concentrate, and it must be diluted correctly before application. Check the minimum amount that can be made up; it is often not practical to prepare the small quantities needed for very small areas. Surplus solution made up from concentrates cannot be stored and it is a problem to dispose of it safely.

Liquid concentrates are the most common; look for packs with easy-to-use measuring devices. Dry concentrates can take the form of wettable powders or granules, or effervescent tablets to make dilution particularly quick and simple. Don't be tempted to add a little extra concentrate to the solution to make it more effective – it won't, and it may damage your plants. Don't make up weaker solutions than recommended, either. They won't do the job properly and could encourage resistance to develop in pests or diseases.

READY-TO-USE CHEMICALS These are particularly useful in "no-garden" situations. Although they tend to be expensive, their convenience, and the fact that there is no wastage, makes them an attractive option. They are often in the form of a liquid in a trigger spray, or as aerosols. Insecticides applied to the soil may come as granules, and some insecticides and several fungicides are available as powders in puffer packs. Some systemic insecticides may be obtainable as tablets or cardboard pins which are pushed into the compost to allow the active ingredients to be taken up by the plant's roots.

- **Keep products in their original containers.** Never decant garden chemicals into a different container because the packaging is damaged. If the label and instructions have become unreadable, dispose of the product properly.
- **Don't store diluted concentrates.**
- **Mix only enough concentrate** to do the job – surplus solution is very difficult to dispose of. Do not pour it down drains, sinks or lavatories. If possible, spray it on bare soil, gravel, or unsurfaced paths and drives.
- **Contact your local authority** to find out how to dispose of concentrates safely if you cannot get rid of them in the ways suggested above.
- **Wash your hands** after you have handled chemicals.
- **Wash out any equipment you have used**, preferably under an outside tap or using a bucket of clean water.
- **Don't mix chemicals** or rinse out equipment in the kitchen sink.
- **Dispose of sprayer rinsings** in the same way as surplus solution.

Basic gardening

Plant pests

Aphids

Commonly known as greenfly or blackfly, aphids may also be pink, yellow, brown or white. Females can reproduce without fertilisation by males, leading to rapid population increases. Aphids feed on plant sap and can usually be found clustered on growing tips or the undersides of young leaves. Plant growth may be distorted and stunted, and the sticky honeydew excreted by aphids is often colonised by sooty mould, which forms a black deposit on the foliage and stems. Aphids also help to spread viral diseases.
CONTROL In the early stages of infestation, a strong jet of water may be enough to wash away aphids. There are many chemical controls; pirimicarb is specific to aphids, but derris, insecticidal soaps and pyrethrins can also be used.

Caterpillars

Caterpillars are often clearly visible on plants and can cause considerable damage by eating irregular holes in foliage. Some species produce grey webbing at their feeding sites, often near the shoot tips. They may be present in large numbers when clusters of eggs are laid, or they may occur singly. Most caterpillars are the larvae of moths, although one species of butterfly – the cabbage white – is a serious pest of brassicas.
CONTROL Hand-picking of the caterpillars is often sufficient. Prolific infestations can be sprayed with a biological control agent, *Bacillus thuringiensis*. The chemical pesticides fenitrothion, pirimiphos-methyl and carbaryl are also very effective.

Flea beetles

These pests may attack seedlings of the brassica family, as well as wallflowers and stocks; radishes, too, are often badly affected. Leaves are peppered with very small holes, and large numbers of the tiny adult beetles can often be seen leaping from the plants when the foliage is disturbed.
CONTROL Keep the growing area free from weeds and plant debris, such as dead leaves, in which the beetles can overwinter. Bad infestations can be treated with insecticides such as derris dust, pyrethrins and pirimiphos-methyl.

Leaf miners

Characteristic meandering white or brown lines may appear on the foliage of a number of plants, indicating the presence of a small larva eating its way through the plant tissue between the upper and lower leaf surfaces. Chrysanthemums, tomatoes and hollies are among plants affected.
CONTROL Pick off and destroy affected leaves as soon as the miners are seen.

Red spider mites

Usually a problem in greenhouses and indoors, sap-sucking red spider mites (two-spotted mites) can also be troublesome outside, particularly in hot, dry conditions. Affected foliage loses its lustre and becomes dull; tiny yellow or white speckling covers the surface. Very fine webbing may be present at shoot tips or on the undersides of leaves. The tiny mites are only just visible to the naked

Keeping plants healthy

eye, but can sometimes be seen on the underside of the leaf or in the webbing.
CONTROL Increase the humidity by spraying plants and damping down paving with water. Pirimiphos-methyl and other chemicals can be used, but repeated applications are usually needed. Insecticidal soaps are not usually very efficient.

Sawflies

Damage is caused by the caterpillar-like larvae, which can be particularly troublesome on fruit. The foliage of gooseberries and currants is often reduced to a skeleton of veins. Other species of sawfly bore into the young fruits of apples and plums. On infested roses, the leaves become tightly rolled into narrow tubes.
CONTROL Pick off and destroy rolled rose leaves. Spray fruit at the first signs of attack with pirimiphos-methyl or permethrin or carbaryl.

Scale insects

Limpet-like brown scales attached to stems and the undersides of leaves are the most visible stage in the life cycle of this pest. Scale insects weaken the plant through sucking sap, and the sticky honeydew they excrete attracts sooty mould fungus. Bay *(Laurus nobilis)* and succulents are very commonly attacked.
CONTROL Scrape off the scales with a fingernail. Insecticides are effective only against the mobile nymph stage, so spraying is best carried out when they are active, in late spring and early summer, using pirimiphos-methyl or malathion.

Slugs and snails

Virtually all soft-leafed plants can be attacked by these pests, often with devastating results. Seedlings may disappear entirely; older plants can have foliage reduced to tatters. They feed at night, slimy trails on and around plant remains giving away their presence the following day. They are generally less troublesome on plants growing in containers than in open ground. Young, tender plants are most at risk: lettuce and hostas are particular favourites.
CONTROL Keep the growing area free of weeds and plant debris. Use a torch, and hand-pick the pests after dark, or lure them into traps baited with beer for disposal. Several organic controls and deterrents are available, or methiocarb or metaldehyde slug pellets can be used with care (these are poisonous to pets and wildlife).

Vine weevils

The greyish black adults eat holes from the edges of leaves of a variety of plants, particularly rhododendrons, while their larvae damage roots. A collapse of the plant may be the first sign of a problem.
CONTROL Keep the area free of weeds and plant debris. Mix insecticide dust, such as gamma-HCH, into the compost. Pirimiphos-methyl or permethrin may control adult weevils. Biological control in the form of nematodes is available.

Woodlice (pill bug, slaters)

These pests may attack seedlings, but they are mainly a secondary problem, enlarging damage caused by another pest or disease. Fruit such as strawberries can be ruined when large numbers of them begin feeding on decaying tissue.
CONTROL Keep the area free of weeds and plant debris and remove damaged foliage and fruit promptly. Treat bad infestations with an insecticide dust such as methiocarb or pirimiphos-methyl.

Blossom-end rot

This disorder affects tomatoes and sweet peppers (capsicums) and is the result of a shortage of calcium, generally caused by irregular watering. A brown or black, hard, shrunken patch of tissue develops at the base of the fruits, often making them inedible. Only fruits at a certain stage of development during a period of water shortage will be affected, and provided adequate water is given afterwards, subsequent fruits will not be affected.
CONTROL Never let plants dry out; those in growing bags and containers are particularly at risk. Nothing can be done for fruits already affected.

Damping off

This fungus disease affects young seedlings. Damping off usually occurs where seedlings are overcrowded and causes plants to collapse at soil level.
CONTROL Sow thinly and maintain a buoyant atmosphere (not stagnant air) around seedlings. Spray the seedlings with a general-purpose fungicide at the first sign of trouble.

Downy mildew

There are two types of plant mildew, downy and powdery (*see* facing page); downy mildew is the less common. It occurs on lettuce and grapevines, and sometimes on a range of bedding plants. Leaves are marked with yellow or pale green patches on their upper surface, with downy grey or purplish mould on the lower surface. The disease is most damaging when plants are young.
CONTROL Pick off and destroy diseased leaves as soon as you see them; destroy badly affected plants completely. Spray with mancozeb, making sure that the undersides of the leaves are treated.

Grey mould (botrytis)

Usually this fungus attacks dead or damaged parts of a plant first, but it soon spreads to the rest of the plant. Affected parts become covered in grey fluffy mould. Grey mould thrives in cool, damp conditions and is a serious disease of annuals in wet seasons.
CONTROL Remove damaged and dying plant material promptly. Ensure that there is good air circulation among your plants, and do not splash water on to foliage and stems, especially in cool weather. Outbreaks can best be treated with a general-purpose fungicide such as carbendazim or thiophanate methyl.

Leaf spots

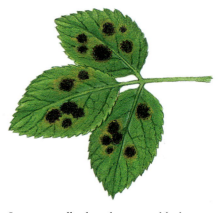

Leaves usually show brown or black spots or patches, with yellowing tissue between them; leaves fall early and the plant loses vigour. The best-known disease in this group is blackspot in roses, but similar fungal or bacterial leaf spots may affect a large number of plants.
   Leaf spot – brownish round or oval spots – affects pansies, phlox, and polyanthus.
   Leaf blotch – rings of dark spores – is common on columbine.
CONTROL Pick off and destroy diseased leaves, and clear up and destroy fallen leaves in autumn. Subject susceptible plants to a programme of preventive spraying with fungicides, or treat plants at the first sign of attack.

Keeping plants healthy

Powdery mildew

This common disease affects trees, shrubs, perennials and bedding plants, fruit and vegetables. It is frequently seen on Michaelmas daisies (asters) and forget-me-nots (myosotis), particularly in hot, dry seasons; roses and apples may also be badly affected. A white powder covers the upper surface of leaves, especially new shoots; growth is stunted and the plant's appearance is spoiled.
CONTROL Make sure plants are not overcrowded. Clear up and destroy all plant debris in autumn to prevent the infection surviving during the winter. Many chemical fungicides can be used to treat mildew, including the broad-spectrum systemic carbendazim.

Spraying with sulphur is a long-established treatment, but it is not suitable for use on some plants and should be used only in temperatures below 27°C (80°F).

Rust

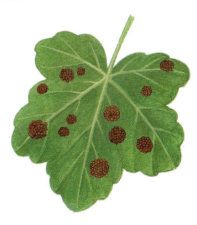

Rusts affect a large number of plants and are usually quite distinctive. Typically, pale yellow spots appear on the top surface of the leaf, and rings, or pustules, of orange or dark-brown powdery spores are present on the underside. The leaves fall early and the growth of the plant is weakened. Rusts are caused by a variety of fungi and can be difficult to control. Roses, chrysanthemums and pelargoniums are among the plants most commonly affected.
CONTROL Ensure that plants are not overcrowded. Remove and destroy affected leaves, and spray affected and nearby healthy plants with propiconazole, mancozeb or copper compounds.

Scab

Scab is common on apples and pears. The fruit is disfigured by dark brown or black, corky scabs, and leaves develop round brown spots and often fall early. Scab also affects potatoes and some other root vegetables; although it is not related to apple scab, the symptoms are similar, with widespread corky brown spots on the potato tubers. It is a particular problem in dry summers, especially with free-draining soils.
CONTROL For apples and pears, a programme of preventive spraying with fungicides is necessary, starting when the blossoms open and continuing every two weeks until petal fall. Many fungicides are suitable, carbendazim, mancozeb and bupririmate plus triforine among them.

Clear up and destroy fallen leaves in autumn, since the fungus overwinters on them and will reinfect trees the following year. Spray trees with lime-sulphur in late winter.

Planting resistant varieties will reduce the incidence of potato scab. Add plenty of organic matter to light soils and water often in dry spells; potatoes grown in containers also need regular watering. Don't apply lime to the soil – this creates ideal conditions for scab to develop.

Viruses

There are many plant viruses, causing a wide range of symptoms on a large number of plants. Typical symptoms include the yellowing, mottling and streaking of leaves, which may also be malformed, often with curled and crinkled margins. Flowers can be affected, with colour-breaking causing streaks and flames, which are sometimes decorative – many bi-coloured tulips owe their origins to virus infection. Viruses can also affect fruits; mosaic virus is common on courgettes (zucchini) and marrows, and can cause distorted crops.
CONTROL There is no chemical control for viral diseases, and affected plants should be destroyed. Many viruses are spread by aphids, so controlling these pests will help to prevent infection. Weeds may also be hosts, so keep the growing area weed free. Wash your hands after touching virus-infected plants, since the infection may be spread by handling.

Chapter Four

Plant directory

So many plants are perfect for small-space gardens that the list here can offer no more than selected suggestions, which should whet your appetite and encourage you to find out more.

In most instances, the species and cultivars particularly suitable for growing in confined spaces are mentioned, but the availability of particular cultivars will change. Don't be afraid to experiment, but remember that plants within a genus can vary in their speed of growth and ultimate size. "Dwarf", "slow-growing" and "compact" are among the plant descriptions you should look for.

Where plant size is given in the directory, it is only a very rough guide. The size of the container or available root run, the type and quality of soil, the amount and type of watering and feeding, climate and many other aspects of cultivation will also play a large part in governing a plant's ultimate size.

The cactus-flowered dahlia 'Explosion' produces a riot of small, brilliantly coloured blooms from midsummer through to autumn.

Plant directory

Plants for special places

Trees for containers

Most trees have a limited life in containers, but many species can make a very attractive show for several years, adding height and an important air of maturity to the overall plant display. A reasonably large tub is required to enable the plant to assume tree-like proportions.

Acer
Maple

Citrus
Citrus

Eucalyptus
Gum tree

Ilex
Holly

Prunus
Flowering cherry, cherry laurel

Salix
Willow

Several types of citrus tree, particularly Citrus sinensis, *the orange, (right) and* C. limon, *the lemon, will flourish and bear prolifically in a container.*

The rounded juvenile leaves of Eucalyptus gunnii, *cider gum, are more attractive than the older foliage, so the tree should be cut back hard annually, which also prevents it becoming too large for a "no-garden" situation.*

Conifers for containers

Choose slow-growing, well-shaped conifer species and varieties for the best results. Some dwarf forms are compact enough for very small containers, including window boxes and troughs.

Abies
Silver fir

Chamaecyparis
False cypress

Juniperus
Juniper

Picea
Spruce

Pinus
Pine

Taxus
Yew

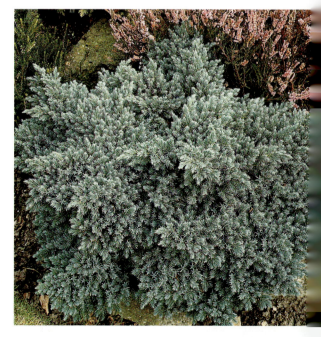

Juniperus squamata *'Blue Star', with its fine blue-grey needles, is extremely slow growing and will take decades to form a dense mound some 60cm (2ft) across and 1m (3ft) high.*

Plant directory

Groundcover plants

These plants are ideal for awkward planting situations such as sloping banks; they also cut down work by suppressing weed growth. Remember that many varieties may be invasive in the wrong situation.

Ajuga Bugle	*Cornus canadensis* Creeping dogwood	*Hedera* Ivy
Aubretia Aubretia	*Cotoneaster congestus* Cotoneaster	*Hypericum* St John's wort
Bergenia Elephant's ears	*Erica* Heath, heather	*Lamium* Dead nettle
Campanula Bellflower	*Euonymus fortunei* Euonymus	*Thymus* Thyme
Ceanothus repens Californian lilac	*Geranium* Cranesbill	*Vinca* Periwinkle

An excellent, but not rampant, groundcover plant, **Hedera helix 'Buttercup'** *has bright yellow-green leaves when it is grown in the sun and pale green leaves in a shady situation.*

Early-flowering plants

After a dull, cold winter, the sight of some of the earliest flowering plants is always a delight. Several of the following species bring the promise of spring to even the chilliest winter weather.

Anemone Anemones	*Erica* Heath, heather	*Narcissus* Daffodils and narcissi
Camellia Camellia	*Erythronium* Dog's-tooth violet	*Primula* Primrose, polyanthus
Chionodoxa Glory-of-the-Snow	*Galanthus* Snowdrop	*Prunus* Prunus
Crocus Crocus	*Helleborus* Hellebore	*Tulipa* Tulip
Eranthis Winter aconite	*Leucojum* Snowflake	*Viola* Violet, pansy

In late winter, the large yellow-green, cup-shaped flowers of **Helleborus lividus** *appear in clusters above pale green leaves that are tinged with purple on the underside.*

Plants for special places

Scented plants

Plants with fragrant flowers are especially suitable for sitting-out areas near the house, where their perfume can be fully appreciated. Many are scented most strongly in the evening.

Brugmansia
Datura, Angel's trumpet

Buddleja
Butterfly bush

Choisya
Mexican orange blossom

Cytisus
Broom

Daphne
Daphne, mezereon

Dianthus
Pink, carnation

Hamamelis
Witch hazel

Hyacinthus
Hyacinth

Jasminum
Jasmine

Lavandula
Lavender

Lilium
Lily

Lonicera
Honeysuckle

Mahonia
Oregon grape

Nicotiana
Ornamental tobacco

Philadelphus
Mock orange

Rosa
Rose

Viburnum
Viburnum

The short, magenta-coloured blooms of Buddleja davidii *'Dartmoor', full of nectar, scent the air and act as a magnet for butterflies.*

Dianthus *'Emile Pare' is a relatively modern pink, which resembles the Old-fashioned pinks in its tendency to sprawl and in its fully double flowers with a sweetly spicy perfume.*

Choisya *'Aztec Pearl' has almond-scented white flowers, which are pink in the bud, and darker, more finely divided leaves than those of* C. ternata, *whose flowers are pure white and citrus scented.*

161

Plant directory

Plants tolerant of air pollution

Air quality in crowded and industrial areas is often poor, leading to difficult growing conditions. The following plants have been found to grow well in polluted areas.

In spring, the arching, spiny stems of **Berberis x** stenophylla *'Corallina Compacta' are covered with strongly fragrant, bright yellow flowers. It is a useful plant which rarely grows taller than 30cm (12in).*

Acer Maple	*Cornus* Dogwood	*Euonymus* Spindle bush		
Berberis Barberry	*Cotoneaster* Cotoneaster	*Fatsia japonica* Japanese aralia	*Lonicera* Honeysuckle	*Pyracantha* Firethorn
Buddleja Butterfly bush	*Cytisus* Broom	*Hibiscus* Hibiscus	*Magnolia* Magnolia	*Pyrus* Ornamental pear
Buxus Box	*Elaeagnus* Elaeagnus	*Hypericum* St John's wort	*Malus* Crab apple	*Robinia* False acacia
Camellia Camellia	*Escallonia* Escallonia	*Ilex* Holly	*Philadelphus* Mock orange	*Salix* Willow
Chaenomeles Flowering quince	*Eucalyptus* Gum tree	*Laburnum* Golden chain	*Prunus* Prunus	*Viburnum* Viburnum

Shade-tolerant plants

Few plants thrive in permanent, dense shade, but those that grow naturally in woodland conditions are well adapted to low light levels, and will do especially well in dappled shade.

Adiantum Maidenhair fern	*Camellia* Camellia	*Fritillaria* Fritillary
Ajuga Bugle	*Dryopteris* Male fern	*Hedera* Ivy
Alchemilla mollis Lady's mantle	*Elaeagnus* Elaeagnus	*Hosta* Hosta
Aucuba japonica Spotted laurel	*Euonymus fortunei* Spindle bush	*Lamium* Deadnettle
Bergenia Elephant's ears	*Fatsia japonica* Japanese aralia	*Vinca* Periwinkle

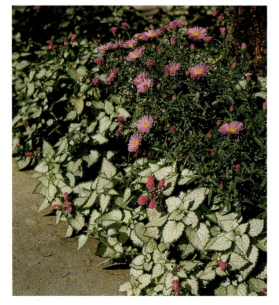

Hardy, herbaceous **Lamium** *'Beacon Silver' is a low-growing plant with silvery leaves, ideal for planting at the front of a shady bed. Here it is teamed with purple-pink asters.*

Plants for special places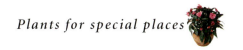

Sun-loving plants

The following plants will thrive in bright light and direct sun; full sunlight is often necessary to ensure the flower buds open.

Anemone coronaria
Anemone

Cistus
Rock rose

Cytisus
Broom

Dimorphotheca
African daisy, Star-of-the-veldt

Dorotheanthus
Mesembryanthemum, ice plant, Livingstone daisy

Eschscholzia
Californian poppy

Genista
Broom

Hakonechloa
Hakonechloa

Hebe
Veronica

Helichrysum
Everlasting, paper daisy, strawflower

Ipomoea
Morning glory

Kniphofia
Red hot poker, torch lily

Lavandula
Lavender

Rosmarinus
Rosemary

Salvia
Salvia, sage

Yucca
Yucca

Shrubby Salvia officinalis purpurascens, *is the purple-leafed culinary sage. It is also reputed to have medicinal value, and an infusion of two sage leaves in a cup of boiling water will act as an aid to digestion either before or after a heavy meal.*

Plants for dry places

Plants which are naturally adapted to dry growing conditions usually have silver-grey, succulent or waxy foliage to enable them to cope with water shortages.

Achillea
Yarrow

Agave
Agave

Aloe
Aloe

Armeria
Thrift

Buddleja
Butterfly bush

Buxus
Box

Cistus
Rock rose

Lavandula
Lavender

Sedum
Stonecrop, ice plant

Sempervivum
Houseleek

Senecio
Senecio

Yucca
Yucca

Waxy-leafed aloes are excellent for growing in dry conditions, but they should be planted in pots and brought indoors where winters are cold and frosty.

Plant directory

Plants for autumn colour

Just before many deciduous plants lose their leaves for winter, the foliage may turn remarkable shades of red, yellow, orange and gold, making a short-lived but spectacular display. Autumn is also the time when some of the most showy flowering plants are at their best and many plants are full of fruits or berries, or, in the case of some roses, brilliantly coloured hips.

Acer
Maple

Berberis
Barberry

Cercidiphyllum
Katsura tree

Cotinus coggygria
Smoke bush

Cotoneaster
Cotoneaster

Dahlia
Dahlia

Dendranthema
Chrysanthemum

Euonymus europaeus
Spindle bush

Hamamelis
Witch hazel

Malus
Crab apple

Parrotia
Iron tree, Persian ironwood

Parthenocissus
Virginia creeper

Prunus
Flowering cherry, cherry laurel

Pyracantha
Firethorn

Rosa rugosa
Species rose

Sorbus
Rowan, mountain ash

Vitis
Vine

In midsummer, Cotinus coggyria *'Flame' produces clouds of pinkish flowers, which turn grey later in the season, hence its name of smoke bush. In autumn, the dark green rounded leaves change to many shades of orange and red.*

Cotoneaster horizontalis, *the fishbone cotoneaster, has bright green leaves, which turn red in autumn, when a mass of red berries also appears.*

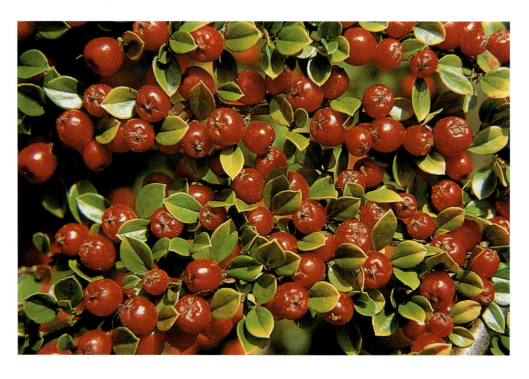

164

Plants for special places

Plants for winter interest

It is not only evergreens that maintain interest in the garden during the winter; berries, flowers, stems and bark also play their part, coming into their own in the dormant season.

Acer griseum (bark)
Paperbark maple

Calluna (foliage)
Ling, heather

Chimonanthus praecox (flowers)
Wintersweet

Cornus (stems)
Dogwood

Corylus avellana '**Contorta**' (stems)
Corkscrew hazel

Erica (flowers)
Heath, heather

Eucalyptus (bark)
Gum tree

Hamamelis (flowers)
Witch hazel

Iris unguicularis (flowers)
Winter iris

Lonicera x *purpusii*, *L. standishii*, *L. fragrantissima* (flowers)
Shrubby honeysuckles

Mahonia (flowers)
Oregon grape

Prunus serrula (bark)
Prunus

Salix alba 'Britzensis', *S. matsudana* 'Tortuosa' (stems)
Willow; twisted willow

Viburnum (flowers)
Viburnum

Viburnum tinus 'Gwenllian' *is a bushy evergreen shrub with shiny leaves. The buds appear from mid-autumn and the pinkish flowers, which open from midwinter onwards, are followed by blue-black berries.*

Plants for year-round interest

Some plants maintain their good looks throughout the year, even in the dormant season. A selection of the following will help to give continuity of interest from month to month.

Euphorbia characias *is evergreen and hardy except where winters are very wet and cold. It forms a large shrubby plant with yellow-green flowerheads up to 20cm (8in) long in mid- to late spring.*

Arundinaria (foliage)
Bamboo

Berberis (evergreen varieties – foliage, flowers, berries)
Barberry

Calluna (foliage, flowers)
Ling, heather

Choisya (foliage, flowers)
Mexican orange blossom

Cordyline (foliage)
Cabbage palm, cabbage tree

Erica (foliage, flowers)
Heath, heather

Euphorbia (evergreen varieties – foliage, flowerheads, architectural shape)
Spurge

Festuca glauca (foliage, flowerheads)
Blue fescue

Hedera (foliage)
Ivy

Ilex (foliage, berries)
Holly

Mahonia (foliage, flowers, architectural shape)
Oregon grape

Pyracantha (foliage, flowers, berries)
Firethorn

Plant directory

Climbers and wall plants

Climbing plants are an ideal way to make maximum use of growing space in small areas, and many other plants will also benefit from the protection offered by a sunny wall. There are some plants which will thrive when planted in deep shade, although most prefer at least a little sunshine. You need to choose the plant to suit the aspect. In the Northern Hemisphere, north- and east-facing walls are usually cool and shady, while south- and west-facing walls are suitable for plants that love warmth and sun; in the Southern Hemisphere south- and east-facing walls are cool, while north- and west-facing walls are warm.

Climbers and plants for warm, sunny walls

Rosa *'Mme Grégoire de Stachelin'* is a vigorous climber, which produces quantities of strongly scented double flowers. It is a particularly useful rose, since it will also do well on a cool, shady wall.

Grown in a warm, protected position, such as that offered by a warm sunny wall, the edible fig, Ficus carica, *will produce a rewarding crop.*

Actinidia kolomikta
Kolomikta vine

Bougainvillea
Bougainvillea

Campsis
Trumpet vine

Ceanothus
Californian lilac

Chaenomeles
Japonica, flowering quince

Eccremocarpus scaber
Chilean glory flower

Fatsia
Japanese aralia

Ficus carica
Fig

Hebe
Hebe

Hibiscus
Hibiscus

Humulus lupulus 'Aureus'
Golden hop

Ipomoea
Morning glory

Plants for special places

Jasminum officinale
Summer-flowering jasmine

Lathyrus
Sweet pea

Magnolia liliiflora
Magnolia

Passiflora caerulea
Passion flower

Rosa
Rose

Climbers and wall plants for cold walls with little sun

Garrya elliptica *produces festoons of silky, silver-grey catkins from midwinter to early spring. Those on male plants are more showy, but after flowering the branches of female plants are hung with long tassels of purple-brown fruits.*

Aucuba japonica
Spotted laurel

Bergenia
Elephant's ears

Cotoneaster horizontalis
Fishbone cotoneaster

Euonymus fortunei
Euonymus

Garrya elliptica
Silk tassel bush

Hedera
Ivy

Hydrangea petiolaris
Climbing hydrangea

Jasminum nudiflorum
Winter-flowering jasmine

Mahonia
Oregon grape

Parthenocissus
Virginia creeper

167

Plant directory

About the plants

Lack of space means that this list of plants suitable for "no-garden" gardens contains no more than suggestions to whet your appetite and encourage you to find out more.

The plants are listed alphabetically by botanical name; the family name and the most frequently used common name are also given. In most instances, the species and cultivars that are particularly suitable for growing in confined spaces are discussed. Don't be afraid to experiment, but do remember that plants within a genus can vary greatly in their speed of growth and ultimate size. Dwarf, miniature, slow-growing and compact are among the catalogue descriptions to look out for. Sizes are usually those likely to be attained by established plants growing in open ground; plants growing in containers or confined spaces will generally be much smaller.

Brief notes about the type of soil, situation and general care the plants require, with details of how they may be propagated, are given under the heading "Cultivation". If plants are liable to suffer from any particular pest or disease this is also mentioned (see also pp.150–155).

A plant's suitability for the "no-garden" situations identified in this book is indicated alongside the common name. Where a genus is noted as suitable for situation 1, this usually means that only selected species will be appropriate.

① **No ground space** (window boxes; hanging baskets; wallpots)
② **Small amount of ground space** (standing room for a small tub; planting space for climbers)
③ **Slightly larger ground space** (roof garden; patio)

Abies Pinaceae
Silver fir ③

* Evergreen conifer
* Various dwarf and slow-growing forms
* Hardy

Abies generally makes a large forest tree, but several dwarf types are suitable for growing in small spaces. Dense, needle-like foliage is often silvery; the tree outline is rounded or flattened according to variety.

Abies balsamea f. *hudsonia* makes a rounded shrub growing slowly to around 60–90cm (2–3ft). The spreading, low-growing *A. cephalonica* 'Meyer's Dwarf' reaches some 60cm (2ft) high and will spread to 1.5m (5ft).

A. lasiocarpa arizonica 'Compacta' has a more conical outline; it eventually reaches some 4m (12ft) but is very slow growing. 'Roger Watson', another conical variety, grows to only 75cm (30in) and has whorls of silver-blue needles.

Cultivation
Free-draining but moisture-retentive soil is required; strongly alkaline soils are not suitable. Give young plants some shelter from cold winds until they become established.

Prune lightly, if necessary, to keep a compact shape in early to mid-spring. New plants can be raised from seed sown outdoors or in a cold frame in spring.

Like other conifers, silver firs may be attacked by adelgids, sap-sucking pests that leave waxy white tufts on the branches. A systemic insecticide may be necessary to control severe infestations.

Acanthus Acanthaceae
Bear's breeches ③

* Herbaceous perennial
* Bold, striking foliage and imposing spikes of summer flowers
* Hardy

Bear's breeches, with a mound of large, deeply cut, dark green leaves tipped with spines, makes a good specimen plant for a border or large container. The hooded, funnel-shaped flowers are purple and white, and are carried in tall, stately spires. *Acanthus spinosus* grows 1–1.2m (3–4ft) tall, and has a spread of around 60cm (2ft).

Cultivation
Grow in a sunny or lightly shaded position in fertile but free-draining soil. In cold areas, protect the roots with a mulch of organic matter or chipped bark over winter, particularly until young plants get established. Plants in containers need moderate watering in summer.

Clear away topgrowth and cut the stems back to within a few centimetres of ground level in autumn. Plants can be increased by division in the dormant season.

Acer palmatum dissectum

Acer Aceraceae
Maple ② ③

* Deciduous tree
* Ornamental foliage, often with brilliant autumn leaf colour
* Attractive bark
* Hardy

There are hundreds of species and varieties of maple, many of which are excellent compact specimens that grow as medium to large shrubs. Commonly grown types are deciduous, with palmate leaves which usually colour well in autumn.

The Japanese maple, *Acer palmatum*, has given rise to many cultivars. 'Osakazuki', known for its fine autumn colour, is one of the most popular. 'Atropurpureum' has purple-red leaves, which turn bright scarlet red in autumn, while '**Dissectum Atropurpureum**' has finely divided, lacy leaves and eventually forms a mound up to 1.2m (4ft) high and the same across. '**Butterfly**' is variegated with creamy white, and spreading '**Garnet**' has finely cut red foliage. All can be kept to under 2m (6ft). '**Senkaki**' ('**Sango-kaku**') is valuable for its pinkish red winter stems and pink-tinged spring foliage.

Cultivation
Acers colour best in full sun but will grow in light shade. Shelter from strong winds will extend their autumn display. They need fertile, free-draining, preferably acidic soil. Plants in containers need regular watering.

Prune in early spring if necessary and pinch back wayward growths in summer. Propagation is not practical for small-scale gardeners.

About the plants

Achillea Compositae
Yarrow ③

* *Herbaceous perennial*
* *Flat head of long-lasting, colourful flowers*
* *Deeply cut, ferny, aromatic foliage*
* *Hardy*

The tall border plant *Achillea filipendulina*, with wide flat heads of many tiny yellow flowers, is perhaps the best-known yarrow, but many new and more compact varieties have been bred in recent years, extending the colour range and suitability of these plants for small spaces. Some plants are semi-evergreen and their feathery foliage can be attractive throughout the winter.

A. 'Moonshine', growing to about 60cm (24in), has silver foliage and heads of light yellow flowers in summer; 'The Beacon', growing to a similar size, has crimson blooms. For smaller spaces, *A.* x *lewisii* 'King Edward' forms a rounded, spreading plant only 10cm (4in) high, with tightly packed heads of light yellow flowers from early summer. *A. ptarmica* 'The Pearl' has abundant, round, white pompons of blooms in large sprays; it grows to 75cm (30in) but can be invasive.

Cultivation
Achilleas are generally best in borders and raised beds rather than containers, although the compact 'King Edward' can be grown in pots as well as in walls and rock gardens. Full sun and well-drained soil are required. Cut back the flower stems in autumn; tidy up foliage as necessary. Plants can be divided in spring.

Achillea filipendulina 'Gold Plate'

Actinidia kolomikta

Actinidia Actinidiaceae
Chinese gooseberry,
Kolomikta vine ② ③

* *Climbing plant*
* *Bold or colourful foliage*
* *Edible fruits sometimes produced*
* *Hardy or slightly tender*

Actinidia is a vigorous twining plant with bold, heart-shaped leaves. It grows well on walls or over pergolas.

In suitable conditions, *Actinidia deliciosa* (*A. chinensis*), the Chinese gooseberry or kiwi fruit, produces edible, egg-shaped fruits that are densely covered in brown hairs. A male and female plant must be grown close together if fruits are required; in cool temperate areas fruiting is unreliable in the open, but these plants do well in sheltered, enclosed garden spaces. The coarse, strong stems and mid-green foliage are covered in bristly hairs. More decorative is the less vigorous *A. kolomikta*, with heart-shaped leaves that are pink at the tips, merging to creamy white, then green.

Cultivation
Actinidias will grow well in sun or light shade, but *A. kolomikta* needs full sun for the best leaf coloration. Moderately fertile, well-drained soil is required.

Train the young shoots on wires or trelliswork on walls. If pruning is necessary, thin out the branches in early spring and tip back the leading shoots.

Adiantum Adiantacae
Maidenhair fern ① ② ③

* *Deciduous or evergreen fern*
* *Delicate, attractive foliage*
* *Shade loving*
* *Hardy or tender, according to species*

The maidenhair fern is well known as a houseplant in cool temperate regions, but there are also fully hardy members of the family. They are good for damp, shady, or sun-filtred spots, and in sheltered positions and mild climates, even the tender species may survive outside.

Adiantum capillus-veneris, maidenhair fern, is frost tender, but can be grown outdoors in warm, sheltered areas. The individual triangular, pale green leaves, are carried in dainty fronds on very slender black stems. It reaches a height of about 30cm (12in).

A. pedatum is taller, at up to 45cm (18in), with pale green, arching fronds. It is hardy, but dies down after the first frosts. The broadly triangular, delicate fronds of the hardy *A. venustum* turn rusty brown after frost, and persist until the new foliage emerges in spring. The plant grows to around 23cm (9in), with a greater spread.

Cultivation
Maidenhair fern grows well in containers. Plant in light shade in moisture-retentive, fertile, preferably lime-free soil, containing plenty of well-rotted organic matter. Keep the soil moist – but not waterlogged.

Remove dead leaves unless they are kept for winter interest. In cold areas, move container-grown tender varieties indoors in the winter. Plants can be divided in spring.

Agapanthus Liliaceae
African lily ② ③

* *Herbaceous perennial*
* *Striking summer flowers*
* *Good specimen plant*
* *Hardy or half-hardy*

Agapanthus is an eye-catching plant, with rounded heads of blue, funnel-shaped flowers carried on tall, stout stems, which rise above long, strap-shaped, glossy leaves.

'Headbourne Hybrids', with variable blue flowers, is among the hardier strains, with plants reaching some 90cm (36in). Particularly suitable for small spaces is 'Lilliput', which grows to around 30cm (12in) and has deep blue flowers. There are also white-flowered varieties, including 'Bressingham White', 'Snowdrop' and 'Alice Gloucester'.

Cultivation
It needs a fairly sheltered position in full sun in a mild region to thrive outdoors; in cold areas, winter protection will be required. Use free-draining but moisture-retentive, fertile soil; feed and water plants regularly during the growing season.

Cut down the flower stems when the flowers have faded, and protect the crowns with a mulch in winter in all but very mild areas. Divide every few years as required.

169

Plant directory

Agave — Agavaceae
Agave

* *Succulent, rosette-forming plant*
* *Specimen plant with exotic appearance*
* *Sword-shaped, spine-tipped leaves*
* *Half-hardy*

These bold, succulent plants lend an exotic touch to a warm, sheltered spot. All are rosette-forming perennials with spiny leaves; take care if planting them where there are children or other vulnerable groups. Agaves are not frost hardy and need winter protection in cold areas.

Agave americana, the century plant, is one of the most popular species, growing to some 1–1.5m (3–5ft). Its narrow leaves are armed at the tips with tough, needle-like spines. *A. americana* 'Striata' (often sold as 'Marginata' or 'Variegata') has broad creamy bands along the leaf edges. In warm, frost-free zones only, it may flower in summer, producing creamy yellow, bell-shaped flowers on towering 5m (15ft) stems; but as a container plant it will remain reasonably compact for some years.

The smaller *Agave filifera* has mid-green leaves edged with white, which peels away to hang in attractive fibrous threads.

Cultivation
Agaves require very freely drained soil; container-grown plants need regular watering in summer, but take care not to overwater or the roots will rot. A sheltered position in full sun is essential.

Mulch around the base of the plant with chipped bark or similar material in autumn, and protect the roots from excess rain during the winter. Where temperatures fall to freezing and below, overwinter the plants in a frost-free place. The plants can be propagated by offsets in spring.

Ajuga — Labiatae
Bugle

* *Herbaceous perennial*
* *Spreading groundcover*
* *Semi-evergreen with colourful foliage*
* *Hardy*

This mat-forming, groundcover plant has rounded, toothed leaves and short spikes of purple-blue, hooded flowers in late spring. *Ajuga pyramidalis* grows to about 15cm (6in) high, with deep green leaves, but more popular are *A. reptans* and its many cultivars. 'Atropurpurea' has bronzy purple, metallic foliage; 'Multicolor' ('Rainbow') has leaves marked and splashed with cream, pink and purple. 'Catlin's Giant' has particularly large, lush, shiny bronze leaves.

Ajuga reptans 'Multicolor'

Cultivation
Bugle prefers light shade and a fertile, moisture-retentive soil, but will grow adequately in most conditions.

The spikes of flowers can be picked off as soon as they appear if a low carpet is required, otherwise they can be removed when the flowers have faded. Tidy up the foliage in late autumn; in all except very cold areas, the foliage persists throughout the winter. Plants are easily propagated by division of the roots in spring.

Alchemilla — Rosaceae
Lady's mantle

* *Herbaceous perennial*
* *Attractive, scalloped leaves and summer flowers*
* *Hardy*

The light green, palmate, lobed leaves of alchemilla have a furry texture and scalloped edges; they are particularly attractive after light rain or heavy dew, when glistening drops of water are held by the hairs around the edges and on the surface of the leaf. In summer, loose sprays of tiny, lime-green flowers (bracts) are carried in frothy profusion.

Alchemilla mollis, growing in loose, rounded clumps to about 30cm (12in) high, is the most popular species. Smaller and more dainty is *A. alpina*, reaching some 15cm (6in) high. The leaves are finely pleated as they open, and more densely covered with silky, silvery hairs. The flowers are similar to those of *A. mollis*, though on a smaller scale.

Cultivation
Plant alchemilla in free-draining soil, in full sun or partial shade. It grows well in containers.

Cut down the faded flowers and foliage in late autumn to tidy the plant for winter. Divide plants in spring or autumn to increase your stock.

Allium — Liliaceae
Ornamental onion

* *Perennial bulb*
* *Spring and summer flowers in a wide range of forms and colours*
* *Foliage smells of onion when crushed*
* *Hardy*

There are many species of allium, providing a wide range of attractive plants. Flowers are generally carried on tall stems, and may be in tightly rounded umbels or loose sprays. Colours range from purple and blue through pink and rose to white and yellow. Dried umbels of taller species are good for flower arrangements.

Among the many species appropriate for small spaces are *Allium oreophilum* (*A. ostrowskianum*), with rounded, loose umbels of rosy red flowers in late spring and summer, and *A. moly*, with sprays of bright yellow, star-shaped flowers in early summer. Both are suitable for containers, raised beds and rock gardens, growing to no more than 25cm (10in) high.

Slightly larger is *A. narcissiflorum*, with nodding, bell-shaped, pink flowers. *A. cristophii* (*A. albopilosum*) reaches some 45cm (18in) and has rounded heads of narrow-petalled, star-shaped purple-pink blooms. Among the most dramatic specimens is *A. schubertii*, growing to around 60cm (24in). The large umbels carry dozens of purple-pink, starry flowers on slender stems of varying lengths, which create the impression of an exploding firework.

Cultivation
Alliums like an open position in full sun, in free-draining soil. Plant the bulbs to a depth of three times their size; keep the soil moist in dry weather but do not overwater. Remove faded flower stems; some make good dried flowers for the home. Divide crowded clumps in autumn.

About the plants

Aloe Liliaceae
Aloe ① ② ③

* Succulent, rosette-forming perennial
* Exotic summer-flowering plant for warm areas
* Half-hardy or tender

Aloes have succulent, sword-shaped leaves and bear some resemblance to agaves. Like agaves, they are useful to give an exotic appearance to warm, sheltered garden areas. They are not frost hardy, and in cool areas need to be overwintered under cover.

Aloe aristata is one of the hardiest species, suitable for a summer trough in a sunny spot. It grows 10cm (4in) high, and has grey-green, pointed leaves spotted with white and spiny leaf margins.

A. arborescens has long, bluish leaves with spiny margins; there is also a variegated form with creamy striped leaves.

Cultivation
Plant aloes in full sun in a sheltered position in free-draining soil. Water regularly during the summer, but make sure that the soil is never waterlogged. Overwinter at a minimum temperature of 5°C (40°F) and water very sparingly during the winter.

Plants can be propagated during the summer from offsets, which are freely produced.

Mealy bugs may attack aloes, forming white tufts like cottonwool on the leaves. It is usually necessary to treat severe infestations with a systemic insecticide.

Anemone Ranunculaceae
Windflower ① ② ③

* Herbaceous perennials with tuberous or rhizomatous roots
* Cup-shaped or daisy-like spring and summer flowers
* Some species good for shaded areas
* Hardy

Many different species of windflower exist, nearly all are easy to grow and trouble free.

Anemone blanda produces bright, daisy-like flowers from late winter through to mid-spring in shades of blue, white, mauve and pink. Growing to around 15cm (6in), with grey-green, attractively lobed leaves, it makes good groundcover under deciduous trees or shrubs, as well as being an excellent container plant.

A. coronaria, growing to 10–30cm (4–12in), has more deeply divided, ferny foliage and cup-shaped spring flowers. The **De Caen** and **St Bridgid** strains have particularly large blooms in clear shades of red, white and blue.

For late summer and autumn flowers, *A.* x *hybrida* (*A. japonica*) is a border plant up to 1.5m (5ft) tall, with cup-shaped single or double blooms in white or pink on delicate, branching stems.

A woodland plant, *A. nemorosa* produces a profusion of delicate, white, starry flowers above deeply cut foliage, to form a 15-cm (6-in) high carpet in early spring.

Cultivation
A. coronaria does best in full sun, but most other varieties prefer light shade. Plant in well-drained, humus-rich soil which should be kept moist during the growing season. Leave *A.* x *hybrida* undisturbed as far as possible, but *A. coronaria* is best discarded and replaced after a year or two.

Viral diseases can cause mottling of the foliage and stunting and distortion of plants. Destroy affected specimens and control aphids, which spread the diseases.

Aquilegia Ranunculaceae
Columbine, granny's bonnet ③

* Herbaceous perennial
* Delicate, nodding, spurred flowers
* Suitable for rock gardens, raised beds and borders
* Hardy

These old-fashioned, cottage garden favourites have been much improved by selective plant breeding. The lobed, grey-green, ferny foliage forms a soft mound, topped with graceful, pendent, usually long-spurred flowers.

There are several alpine species especially suitable for small spaces, including the dainty *Aquilegia flabellata* 'Alba' ('Nana Alba'), with white-spurred spring flowers, which is about 15cm (6in) tall. The early summer-flowering border varieties grow to around 1m (3ft), and are usually represented by hybrids such as the **Mrs Scott Elliott** and **McKana Hybrids**, which have more upwards-facing flowers in a good range of colours and bicolours.

Cultivation
Alpine species like partial shade and moisture-retentive, humus-rich soil; border varieties prefer open, sunny positions and free-draining soil. Plants cross-pollinate and self-seed freely and can become a nuisance. They tend to be short-lived.

Plants are easy to raise from seed, or clumps can be divided in autumn or spring.

Aphids often attack the flower stems and young growth, but can be controlled with a non-persistent, contact insecticide.

Anemone blanda

Aquilegia McKana Hybrids

Plant directory

Argyranthemum — Compositae
Marguerite ② ③

* Evergreen perennial
* Daisy-like spring and summer flowers and ferny foliage
* Excellent for training as a standard
* Half-hardy

Also sometimes called chrysanthemum, *Argyranthemum frutescens* is a frost-tender evergreen with aromatic, ferny, deep green foliage and large, daisy-like flowers. It produces a woody stem and, supported by a cane, can be trained as a standard, which makes an imposing container specimen.

The species has white flowers, but named varieties with coloured flowers are available, including the pale yellow '**Jamaica Primrose**' and pink '**Mary Wootton**'.

Cultivation
Plant in spring in a fertile, free-draining soil; in cool regions, keep plants under protection until warm weather arrives, then set out in a sunny, sheltered position. Water freely in summer.

Pinch leading shoots regularly to form a rounded bush, or train one shoot upwards for a standard. Move plants back under cover before the first frosts, and take stem cuttings in spring to provide the following season's plants.

Aphids may attack the young growth and can be controlled with a non-persistent contact insecticide.

Armeria maritima 'Snowball'

Armeria — Plumbaginaceae
Thrift ① ② ③

* Evergreen perennial
* Cushion-like mounds of foliage and summer flowers
* Hardy

A native of coastal areas, thrift is an easily grown, undemanding plant which has a long flowering season. *Armeria maritima* forms a neat, compact (15–23-cm/6–9-in) hummock of slender, mid-green leaves.

Artemisia ludoviciana latiloba

From this arise many stiff stems topped with round heads of papery pink flowers during the summer. Named varieties include '**Bloodstone**', '**Vindictive**' and the white-flowered '**Snowball**'.

A. juniperifolia (*A. caespitosa*) grows to only 5–8cm (2–3in), with greyish leaves and an abundance of round pink flowerheads in early summer. Varieties include the deep pink '**Bevan's Variety**' and white '**Alba**'.

Cultivation
Well-drained soil and full sun suit these plants. Water container-grown specimens fairly sparingly during the growing season.

Remove the faded flowerheads in late autumn to enjoy the neat mounds of evergreen foliage throughout the winter. Increase plants by taking semi-ripe cuttings in mid- to late summer.

Artemisia — Compositae
Wormwood, southernwood ② ③

* Shrubby perennials
* Finely cut, aromatic, silver foliage
* Hardy or half-hardy

There are several species of artemisia, mostly grown for their attractively ferny, silver foliage. They withstand drought well and most are reasonably hardy. Plants often become leggy and ungainly after a few years and many are best replaced by new cuttings annually.

Artemisia ludoviciana, which grows to 1m (3ft) or more, usually has entire, lance-shaped leaves covered in woolly white hairs, which give it a striking silver-white appearance. The topgrowth dies down in winter.

A. schmidtiana '**Nana**' is a low-growing, semi-evergreen perennial, with very finely cut, thread-like silver foliage that forms a spreading, 8-cm (3-in) high dome. It is suitable for a rock garden or the top of a wall, as well as for pots.

The well-known '**Powis Castle**' is a vigorous, woody, evergreen shrub with deeply cut, aromatic, silver leaves. It reaches about 1m (3ft) and becomes leggy after a year or two.

Cultivation
Full sun, light, free-draining soil, and a sheltered position are required for the smaller species. Take care not to overwater container-grown plants.

Prune evergreen species back hard in early spring to promote neat growth. In summer, take semi-ripe cuttings, and overwinter them in a frost-free place to guard against winter losses, which can occur in severe weather.

About the plants

Arundinaria Poaceae
Bamboo ③

* Evergreen
* Good container plants for an oriental look
* Can be invasive
* Hardy

The bamboos have undergone a variety of confusing name changes, and some species of *Arundinaria* are also known as *Pleioblastus*. Many species of bamboo are very invasive and unsuitable for small areas, but dwarf species of arundinaria make excellent container plants.

Arundinaria fortunei (*A. variegatus, Pleioblastus variegatus*) is a slow-spreading, tufted variety growing to around 1.2m (4ft). The narrow, mid-green leaves are striped white along their length. Although this species is not as invasive as some, it should nevertheless be confined to a container in small gardens.

Cultivation
Fertile, moisture-retentive soil is necessary for bamboos; keep the soil moist at all times. Plants can be grown in full sun or light shade, but need protection from winds, which can discolour the foliage.

Divide crowded plants in spring to keep growth healthy and vigorous.

Arundinaria fortunei

Aster x frikartii

Aster Compositae
Michaelmas daisy ③

* Herbaceous perennial
* Late season, daisy-like flowers
* Good for cutting
* Hardy

Michaelmas daisies are the best known of the asters, but there are also some excellent dwarf alpine species. Asters are valuable for their colourful flowers, which are produced well into the autumn; the cultivars of *Aster x frikartii* are particularly free flowering.

A. alpinus is a spreading rock plant growing to 15cm (6in). It has dark green foliage and in summer bears purple flowers with yellow centres; there are also lilac-pink and white varieties.

A. amellus reaches about 45cm (18in) and is usually represented by purple-flowered 'King George', although there are several other purple and pink varieties.

The true Michaelmas daisies are *A. novae-angliae* and *A. novi-belgii*. There are many varieties; red 'Jenny', 'Little Pink Beauty', 'Royal Ruby', white 'Snowsprite', 'Lady in Blue' and 'Audrey' are good dwarf specimens. *A. thomsonii* 'Nanus', with pale lilac flowers, reaches about 40cm (16in).

Cultivation
Asters like a rich, free-draining, but moisture-retentive soil. In containers, they need frequent watering while flowering.

Grow in an open, sunny position, and support the stems with twiggy sticks where necessary. Cut down and remove the topgrowth in autumn, and divide plants after two or three years to maintain vigour. Asters are very prone to powdery mildew, and preventive spraying with a suitable fungicide is often necessary.

Aubrieta Cruciferae
Aubrieta ② ③

* Evergreen perennial
* Trailing stems with colourful spring flowers
* Useful for the tops of walls and banks
* Hardy

This popular rock plant makes a carpet of colour in spring and early summer, and is trouble-free to grow. The grey-green leaves are elongated; the small, four-petalled flowers, in shades of red and purple, are carried in great profusion and last well.

There are several varieties in different shades, including 'Dr Mules', 'Gurgedyke' and 'Cobalt Violet', all forming spreading mats under 10cm (4in) high. Even more compact is *Aubrietia deltoidea* 'Argenteo-variegata', which has leaves edged with creamy white and pale purple flowers.

Cultivation
Grow aubrieta in full sun in free-draining soil. Water sparingly if required.

Keep plants tidy by cutting them back hard once the flowers have faded.

Soft tip cuttings can be taken in early summer, or plants can divided in autumn.

173

Plant directory

Aucuba   Cornaceae
Spotted laurel   ② ③

* Evergreen shrub
* Shade tolerant
* Female plants produce colourful berries
* Some varieties have coloured leaves
* Hardy

Although *Aucuba japonica* will form a shrub up to 3m (10ft) high when allowed to, it makes an excellent container plant, and with regular pruning will remain small and compact for many years. The leathery, glossy green foliage tolerates dense shade but will also cope with considerable sun. You need both male and female varieties for berries to form on the female plants.

'Nana Rotundifolia' is a very compact, small-leaved female variety. 'Rozannie' is also small and usually berries well; it is unusual in that it is self-pollinating, although berrying is usually better with a male plant for pollination.

There are several coloured-leafed varieties, of which the male 'Crotonifolia', with large, gold-spotted foliage, is one of the most reliable. 'Gold Dust', with oval leaves speckled with gold, is a berry-bearing female.

Cultivation
Moist, but not waterlogged, fertile soil is required. Variegated varieties are best in sun, but aucubas grow well in shade and are useful for gloomy areas.

Prune the branches back hard in early spring to maintain a neat, compact shape. Semi-ripe cuttings can be taken in summer.

Begonia   Begoniaceae
Begonia   ① ② ③

* Perennial, sometimes tuberous
* Summer flowers in a wide colour range
* Tender

There are many species and varieties of begonia, but the two groups most suitable for growing outside are *Begonia* x *tuberhybrida* and *B. semperflorens*. Stems are soft and succulent, and the colourful flowers may be single or double.

B. semperflorens is a low, bushy, branching plant with rounded, often bronze-red foliage. Small, simple flowers are carried in loose panicles in shades of red, pink and white.

The flowers of *B.* x *tuberhybrida* are much larger; the central, male flower in each group of blooms is the most showy, and the females each side are often pinched off. Many named varieties exist.

Cultivation
Plant tubers dished side up, with the top above soil level; water sparingly until growth starts, then more frequently. Start the tubers into growth under cover in early spring. Plant out *B. semperflorens* after all risk of frost has passed. Both types like fertile, free-draining soil, and are excellent for containers.

Lift *B.* x *tuberhybrida* before the first frosts; let the leaves die down and store the tubers in dry peat for replanting the following spring.

Begonias are often affected by powdery mildew, which can be treated with fungicide.

Begonia x tuberhybrida

Bellis perennis 'Pomponette'

Bellis   Compositae
Double daisy   ① ② ③

* Perennial, usually grown as a biennial
* Very double, daisy flowers in spring
* Hardy

Bedding daisies, *Bellis perennis*, are grown for their cheerful, button-like flowers carried on short stems in spring and summer. The leaves are mid-green, oval, with toothed edges; flower stems about 20cm (8in) high carry fully double blooms in shades of red, pink and white, with a yellow eye. These little plants are good for bedding out, for containers and as edging plants.

Varieties include 'Goliath', with extra-large flowers, and 'Pomponette', a compact, miniature-flowered type.

Cultivation
Double daisies grow best in the sun but will tolerate light shade. They prefer fertile, freely drained soil. Deadhead the plants to keep them neat and encourage flowering. Divide established clumps in spring.

Berberis   Berberidaceae
Barberry   ③

* Evergreen, semi-evergreen or deciduous shrub
* Prickly foliage, spring or summer flowers
* Autumn colour (deciduous types)
* Hardy

This versatile group of plants may be grown for a variety of purposes. They make good hedges, their spines deterring intruders; and

About the plants

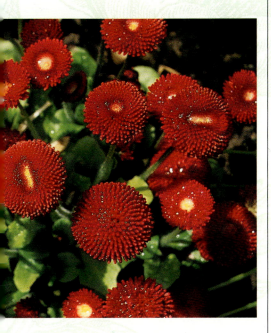

many varieties have a spectacular flowering season, with bright yellow or orange flowers carried in great abundance, followed by blue-black or red berries.

Among the varieties particularly suitable for small spaces are *Berberis* x *stenophylla* 'Corallina Compacta', a dwarf evergreen growing only to some 25cm (10in), with plenty of orange-yellow flowers in spring; *B. thunbergii* 'Atropurpurea Nana', a purple-foliaged, deciduous plant up to 60cm (24in) tall; and the similar but smaller 30-cm (12-in) high 'Bagatelle'.

Cultivation
Berberis will grow in most soils, even poor soil, but cannot stand waterlogging. Plant in sun or light shade; deciduous varieties give better autumn colour in full sun.

To maintain a neat shape, prune plants in early spring or after flowering (depending on type). Propagate from semi-ripe cuttings in summer.

Bergenia Saxifragaceae
Elephant's ears ③

* Evergreen perennials
* Large, leathery leaves
* Good groundcover
* Shade tolerant
* Hardy

The rounded or heart-shaped, leathery leaves of *Bergenia* form a mound up to 60cm (24in) high; some varieties turn attractive red and russet shades in autumn and winter. Panicles of pink or white drooping flowers are carried in spring.

Most popular varieties are hybrids, and include 'Abendglut', with luminous rosy flowers and deep crimson foliage, and 'Silberlicht', with mid-green leaves and white flowers. 'Baby Doll' is a particularly compact variety, with low-growing foliage and clusters of pale pink flowers.

Cultivation
Elephant's ears are not fussy about soil or position, and will tolerate sun or shade. Foliage colours are most pronounced in full sun and on well-drained, not-too-rich soils. Plants in containers need regular watering during the growing season.

Remove any damaged or yellowed leaves in autumn and winter, and cut down faded flower stems. Crowded clumps can be divided in spring or autumn, but plants should otherwise be left undisturbed if possible.

Bougainvillea Nyctaginaceae
Bougainvillea ② ③

* Evergreen or semi-evergreen climber
* Colourful flower-like bracts in summer
* Tender

This climber has woody, scrambling stems, which are sometimes thorny, and oval, mid-green leaves. Plants bear showy clusters of bracts in several shades including purple, crimson, scarlet, salmon-orange, cream and white. In some varieties the bracts are bicoloured, and some have double bracts.

Bougainvillea x *buttiana* has given rise to several double-flowered cultivars 'Mahara Double Red' ('Klong Fire'), 'Mahara Off-White' ('Limberlost Beauty'), 'Mahara Orange' ('Thai Gold'), 'Mahara Pink' ('Pagoda Pink'), and the well-known crimson-magenta 'Mrs Butt'.

B. glabra has rosy purple bracts with a conspicuous, long-tubed, cream flower in the centre; *B. g.* 'Harrissii' ('Variegata') has a narrow cream margin to the leaves.

Cultivation
Bougainvilleas need free-draining soil and a bright, sunny position. Train the stems up a trellis or similar support, or around a hoop. Keep the plants well watered during the active growing season, but water sparingly when dormant.

Bougainvilleas are grown outdoors in warm climates, but they are frost tender and in cold climates container-grown plants must be moved under cover before autumn.

Prune the previous year's lateral shoots to within 2.5cm (1in) of the main stem in spring or after flowering. When grown outdoors, it is better to keep them regularly and lightly pruned, trimming long shoots in summer if necessary. Propagate plants by taking semi-ripe cuttings in summer.

Whiteflies can be a problem. Spray with a suitable insecticide; several applications will be necessary to control an infestation.

Brassica Cruciferae
Ornamental cabbage and kale ① ② ③

* Biennial grown as an annual
* Attractive, colourful foliage throughout the winter
* Hardy

Ornamental forms of *Brassica oleracea* (cabbage or kale) make neat, compact plants for winter containers and bedding. Plants form curly-leafed rosettes, with pink or green central leaves, which become green towards the edge, or have deeply cut, feathery foliage in shades of rose, pink and white. They are easy to raise from seed but are usually bought as potted plants in autumn or spring.

Varieties include 'Tokyo', 'Northern Lights', 'Red Peacock', 'White Peacock', 'Red Feather' and 'White Feather'. Particularly suitable for containers is 'Kamome', a dwarf type with tightly packed, frilly foliage in red or white.

Cultivation
Plant in full sun in fertile, moisture-retentive soil. Cold conditions (nights below 5°C/40°F) produce the most intense coloration of the foliage. Discard plants when they are past their best or begin to show signs of flowering. Plants can be raised from seed sown outdoors in spring or late summer and autumn in mild areas.

Ornamental kale is not usually troubled by insect pests, but, like all brassicas, it is subject to clubroot disease.

Brassica oleracea

175

Plant directory

Briza maxima

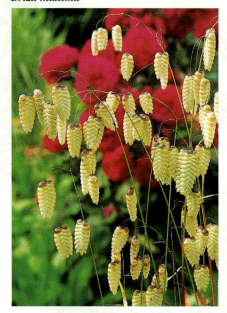

Briza Gramineae
Quaking grass ② ③

* *Annual or perennial grass*
* *Delicate, pendent panicles of spikelets*
* *Good for cutting and for drying*
* *Hardy*

These tuft-forming grasses grow up to 60cm (24in) tall, and have very slender stems carrying gracefully drooping heads which give a delicate, shimmering effect when planted in a mass.

Briza maxima (pearl grass) is an annual species with a dozen or so purplish green heads to each stem, while *B. media* is a hardy perennial, bearing more numerous but smaller purple-brown spikelets. Both flower in summer.

Cultivation
Grow *Briza* in well-drained soil and in a sunny position. *B. maxima* can be raised from seed sown in situ in spring; *B. media* can be increased by division in mid-spring. Once established, it will often seed itself.

Brugmansia Solanaceae
Angels' trumpet ② ③

* *Semi-evergreen shrub*
* *Fragrant flowers in midsummer*
* *Good for containers*
* *All parts poisonous*
* *Frost tender: minimum 7°C (45°F)*

Often still known by its old name of *Datura*, *Brugmansia* produces large, trumpet-shaped, exotic flowers with a heady scent. The mid-green, oval leaves are rather coarse in appearance; the plant makes a rounded or conical shrub up to 2.5m (8ft) tall. The white, cream, orange, yellow or peach pendulous flowers, often with attractively waved rims, may be up to 25cm (10in) long.

Among popular species are *Brugmansia arborea*, with white flowers, and *B.* x *candida* 'Grand Marnier', with orange-red blooms.

Cultivation
Angel's trumpet needs a warm, well-lit spot and frost-free conditions. Light, free-draining but fertile soil is required. Water plants moderately while in growth, sparingly at other times; in cold areas, grow plants in containers that can be taken under cover to protect them in winter.

Prune stems back hard in early spring. Propagation is possible from semi-ripe cuttings in summer.

Red spider mites and whiteflies often attack the plants: spray with plain water to increase humidity and use a suitable pesticide when necessary.

Buddleja Loganiaceae
Butterfly bush ③

* *Deciduous or semi-evergreen shrub*
* *Strongly scented summer flowers*
* *Attractive to butterflies*
* *Hardy or half-hardy*

These spreading, easily grown shrubs produce panicles of small, strongly fragrant flowers in white, purple, lilac, purple-red or orange. Buddlejas are also valuable because they attract large numbers of butterflies, which feed on their nectar.

The most popular species is *Buddleja davidii*, a vigorous, arching shrub with long panicles of flowers. Many cultivars have been raised, including the deep purple 'Black Knight' and compact 'Border Beauty'. 'Harlequin', with variegated leaves, is also reasonably low growing. *B. globosa*, the orange ball tree, grows to 3m (10ft) and has attractive, spherical heads of fragrant orange flowers in early summer.

Cultivation
Grow in full sun in a moderately fertile, free-draining soil in a reasonably protected position.

Prune *B. davidii* hard each spring, cutting all the branches back to within a few centimetres of the older wood; this keeps plants compact and improves flowering. *B. globosa* should be pruned after flowering, by cutting back flowered branches by about one-third. Semi-ripe cuttings can be taken in summer.

Buxus Buxaceae
Box ② ③

* *Evergreen shrub*
* *Good for hedging and topiary*
* *Hardy*

Box has small, neat, deep green leaves and forms a compact bush which responds well to clipping. It is widely used for dwarf hedges and edging borders; container-grown specimens can be clipped to ornamental shapes.

Buxus microphylla is the small-leafed box, which forms a dense shrub about 1m (3ft) high. 'Compacta' is a tiny, rounded, dwarf form suitable for rock gardens and containers; 'Green Pillow' is slightly larger but still forms a low, dense mound of bright green foliage. *B. sempervirens*, the common box, has given rise to many named varieties, of which 'Suffruticosa' is widely used as an edging plant or low hedge. It will grow to just under 1m (3m) tall, but is generally clipped to keep it lower.

Cultivation
Box grows well on most soils, except very heavy ones, in sun or light shade.

Prune to shape in late spring and clip hedges and trained forms as necessary throughout the summer. Take semi-ripe cuttings in summer.

Buxus sempervirens

Calluna vulgaris 'Golden Feather'

About the plants

Calluna   Ericaceae
Ling, heather   ① ② ③

* *Evergreen sub-shrub*
* *Valuable for both foliage and flowers*
* *Good winter colour*
* *Requires lime-free conditions*
* *Hardy*

This versatile plant forms a bushy, low evergreen shrub up to about 60cm (24in) tall, but there are many lower-growing cultivars. Slender branches are densely packed with needle-like leaves in red, orange and yellow, as well as green and grey-green; some varieties have foliage which changes colour during the year. Spikes of small, bell-shaped flowers are carried at the tips of the branches from late summer into autumn. The dead flower spikes may persist and remain attractive throughout the winter.

There are hundreds of cultivars of *Calluna vulgaris,* varying in their size and habit, as well as in their leaf colour and flower form and colour. Reliable varieties include '**Anthony Davis**' (grey leaves, white flowers); '**Beoley Gold**' (golden leaves, white flowers); '**Blazeaway**' (gold leaves turning red in winter, purple flowers); '**County Wicklow**' (compact, double, pale pink flowers); '**Darkness**' (compact, purple-pink flowers); '**Elsie Purnell**' (grey-green leaves, double, silvery pink flowers); '**Foxii Nana**' (compact, mid-green leaves, sparse pink flowers); '**Golden Feather**' (gold to orange foliage, purple flowers); '**Gold Haze**' (bright gold leaves, white flowers); '**H. E. Beale**' (mid-green leaves, double, rose pink flowers in long spikes); '**Spring Cream**' (bright green leaves tipped cream in spring, white flowers); and '**Wickwar Flame**' (yellow and orange leaves intensifying in colour in winter, mauve flowers).

Cultivation
Heather requires free-draining, lime-free (ericaceous) soil. Add a little sharp sand to heavier soils to improve them. Grow the plants in full sun. Regular clipping over keeps plants compact. This is usually done in spring, but trim varieties grown for colourful spring foliage in early autumn to give a good flush of new growth for spring.

Camellia   Theaceae
Camellia   ② ③

* *Evergreen shrub*
* *Very early spring flowers*
* *Hardy or slightly tender*

The large, showy flowers of camellias are well known, but because they are carried so early in the season plants often need a protected position to prevent the blooms being damaged. The foliage is leathery, dark green and oval or lance-shaped; flowers are cup shaped and may be double, semi-double or single in shades of pink, red and white. Plants grown in the open ground may reach 9m (30ft), but they grow well in large pots or tubs where they can usually be kept below 2m (6ft).

There are many cultivars of *Camellia japonica,* including the old favourite '**Adolphe Audusson**' with semi-double, deep red flowers; '**Donckelaeri**', slow-growing with red, semi-double flowers marbled white; and '**Mary Charlotte**', with pale pink, anemone-type flowers.

Camellia japonica 'Akashigata'

The hybrid *C. x williamsii* has produced a large number of very successful varieties such as '**Brigadoon**', with rosy-pink, semi-double flowers; '**Donation**' with large, semi-double pink flowers and '**J. C. Williams**', a pure pink single variety.

Cultivation
Grow in fertile, lime-free (ericaceous) soil with some added organic matter. In cold areas, plant in a sheltered position where the flowers will not receive early morning sun, which will damage them in frosty weather or where there is heavy dew. Most camellias grow well in semi-shade.

Remove dead flowerheads and prune back long shoots in mid-spring after flowering if necessary to maintain the shape. Propagation by semi-ripe cuttings is often tricky, but plants can also be layered.

Campanula   Campanulaceae
Bellflower   ① ② ③

* *Annuals, biennials and herbaceous perennials*
* *Bell-like flowers in spring and summer*
* *Hardy or half-hardy*

There are many different types of campanula, from prostrate or trailing alpine varieties to tall, stately border plants. They mainly have lance-shaped, mid-green leaves and blue or white, bell-like flowers.

Among species suitable for rock gardens, troughs and baskets are *Campanula isophylla,* which is tender but invaluable, and *C. portenschlagiana*, which forms mats of mid-green, heart-shaped leaves and violet-blue, open bell-shaped flowers, and can be invasive. *C.* '**G. F. Wilson**' is a mound-forming plant with rounded, light green foliage and large blue bells; low-growing *C. cochleariifolia* has small, round leaves and dainty bells on slender stems.

The Canterbury bell, *C. medium,* is a biennial border plant growing to 1m (3ft) or more, but dwarf selections such as '**Bells of Holland**' remain under 60cm (2ft). Perennial *C. glomerata*, with violet or purple flowers, is another good border plant.

Cultivation
Campanulas prefer free-draining, fairly fertile soil and full sun. Remove the flower spikes of tall varieties once the flowers have faded. Divide plants in autumn or spring, or take basal cuttings in spring.

Border varieties are often attacked by froghoppers (cuckoo spit, spittlebugs), but they rarely cause damage and can be washed off with water. If slugs and snails damage young growth, they can be controlled with slug bait or an organic alternative.

Plant directory

Campsis radicans

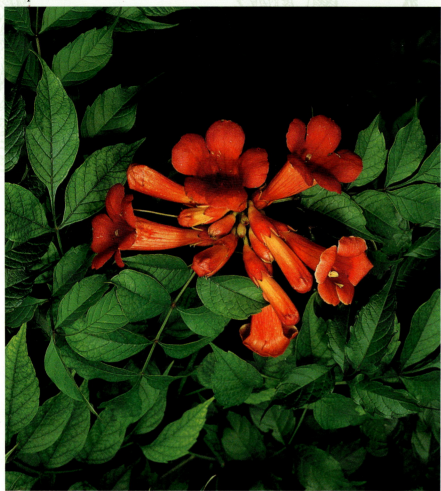

Campsis Bignoniaceae
Trumpet vine ② ③

* *Deciduous climber*
* *Showy, trumpet-shaped flowers*
* *Hardy or slightly tender*

An attractive climbing plant with light green, pinnate, toothed leaves and clings by aerial roots. In summer, large, red, yellow or orange flowers are produced. *Campsis radicans* is the most popular species; *C. grandiflora* is less hardy and flowers well only in warm locations. The hybrid *C.* x *tagliabuana* '**Mme Galen**' has attractive salmon pink blooms, but can be invasive.

Cultivation
Grow in fertile, moisture-retentive but free-draining soil in a sunny, sheltered position; against a warm wall is ideal. Water generously in dry spells during the growing season.
   Prune back shoots to within a few centimetres of older growth in late winter. New plants can be raised from semi-ripe cuttings, by layering or from seed.

Canna Cannaceae
Indian shot ② ③

* *Herbaceous perennial*
* *Showy foliage and flowers*
* *Striking specimen plants*
* *Tender*

The exotic appearance makes canna a good plant to grow as a specimen in a container. The roots are rhizomatous, sending up a strong stem clasped by broad leaves which may be mid-green, variegated or purplish brown. Tall flower spikes, up to 1.2m (4ft), carry large, orchid-like flowers in shades of red, orange, pink and yellow.
   Hybrids are most commonly available under the name *Canna hybrida*, or more recently *C.* x *generalis*. '**President**' has scarlet flowers; the red flowers of bronze-leafed '**Lucifer**' are edged with yellow, while '**Orange Perfection**' has orange flowers and mid-green leaves.

Cultivation
A moisture-retentive soil with added organic matter suits these plants best. Plants in containers need regular watering during the growing season. Start the rhizomes into growth in pots under cover in early spring, setting them out in a sheltered, warm position once all risk of frost has passed.
   Lift the plants before the first frost, remove the topgrowth, and store the rhizomes in just-moist peat in a frost-free place over winter. Do not lift in mild areas.
   Plants can be increased by dividing the rhizomes in spring, once they have started into growth.
   Slugs and snails find the succulent leaves attractive; to deal with these pests, use slug bait or an organic alternative.

Ceanothus Rhamnaceae
Californian lilac ③

* *Evergreen or deciduous shrub*
* *Dense heads of blue flowers in summer*
* *Hardy or half-hardy*

Ceanothus is grown for its clouds of tiny, powder-blue flowers, which appear in early summer. In cool areas, the plant appreciates the protection of a sheltered wall.
   Some species, such as '**Trewithen Blue**' tend to make large, spreading bushes, but there are reasonably compact varieties. '**Blue Mound**' is evergreen, making a dense, bushy mound up to 1.5m (5ft) high, which is covered in deep blue flowers in early summer. '**Burkwoodii**', growing up to 1.5m (5ft), with deep blue flowers in midsummer and autumn, is hardier than some. Growing to a similar height, '**Gloire de Versailles**' is deciduous, with powder-blue flowers throughout summer and autumn.
   C. thyrsiflorus var. *repens* is a dense, spreading evergreen less than 1m (3ft) high, which bears abundant light blue flowers in spring and early summer.

***Ceanothus* 'Trewithen Blue'**

About the plants

Cultivation

Light, free-draining soil, preferably lime free, is required. In cold areas, plant evergreen varieties in the shelter of a wall.

Deciduous varieties should be pruned back almost to the old wood in spring; evergreens can be pruned lightly after flowering to keep them within bounds.

Increase plants from semi-ripe cuttings taken in summer.

Cercidiphyllum Cercidiphyllaceae
Katsura tree ③

* *Deciduous tree*
* *Spectacular autumn colour*
* *Hardy*

Only one species of this small to medium-sized tree is grown – *Cercidiphyllum japonicum.* The leaves are deep green in summer, turning to attractive yellow, purple and pink shades in autumn, when they give off a strong and distinctive smell of burnt sugar. Suitable for growing in slightly larger garden spaces.

Cultivation
Plant in moisture-retentive, fertile soil, preferably lime free. Cercidyphyllum will grow in sun or light shade. Light pruning can be carried out in late winter or early spring when the tree is dormant.

Propagation is by seed sown in autumn, but it takes several years to produce a good-sized plant.

Chaenomeles Rosaceae
Japonica, flowering quince ③

* *Deciduous shrub*
* *Early spring flowers*
* *Hardy*

These spiny, spreading shrubs grow particularly well against walls or fences. Long before the rounded, toothed, glossy green leaves appear, cup-shaped, bright red or orange-red flowers can be seen in clusters on the bare stems. They are often followed by small, aromatic, quince-like fruits.

Chaenomeles japonica grows to about 1m (3ft), with a spread of twice that. Orange-red flowers appear in early spring. *C. x superba* grows to about 1.5m (5ft) and is particularly free flowering: '**Crimson and Gold**', '**Knap Hill Scarlet**' and '**Rowallane**' are among award-winning varieties.

The taller *C. speciosa* flowers earlier, in late winter, with slightly larger, deep red flowers: '**Geisha Girl**' and '**Moerloosei**' are popular cultivars.

Chaenomeles japonica

Cultivation
Well-drained, moderately fertile soil and an open, sunny position, preferably against a wall or fence, suits flowering quince.

Keep plants tidy by cutting back the previous season's branches to two or three buds in late spring after flowering. Take semi-ripe cuttings in summer.

Fireblight disease, which causes branches to look as though they have been scorched, does attack flowering quince. Cut out affected branches as soon as they are seen.

Chamaecyparis Cupressaceae
False cypress ② ③

* *Evergreen conifer*
* *Exhibits a range of different shapes, foliage colours and textures*
* *Hardy*

False cypress can grow to 15m (50ft) or more, but there are many excellent dwarf and slow-growing forms. The aromatic leaves, whose colour varies widely, are carried in flattened sprays.

Chamaecyparis lawsoniana '**Ellwoodii**', with grey-green foliage, is slow growing; it eventually makes a 3-m (10-ft) column, but can be grown successfully in a container or rock garden for many years. '**Gnome**' is a true dwarf, making a blue-green sphere some 50cm (20in) tall. '**Minima**', growing to 1m (3ft) tall, is another rounded variety, with fresh green foliage.

C. obtusa provides several good dwarf varieties. '**Kosteri**' is a spreading bush growing very slowly to some 1.2m (4ft)

Chamaecyparis lawsoniana 'Gnome'

high, while the tiny '**Minima**' makes a flat cushion of dense, mossy-green foliage. '**Nana**' forms a small, flat-topped, rounded bush growing slowly to 1m (3ft); '**Nana Aurea**' has golden foliage. *C. pisifera* is probably most commonly represented by '**Boulevard**', a medium-sized bush with soft, silver-blue foliage.

Cultivation
This conifer is happy in most soils as long as they are not waterlogged. An open, sunny position is preferred, although light shade can be tolerated.

Plants may need occasional pruning in late spring to keep them in shape. Conical varieties sometimes produce forked leaders, which should be reduced to the strongest to give the best effect. Semi-ripe cuttings with a heel of older wood may be taken in summer.

Chimonanthus Calycanthaceae
Wintersweet ③

* *Deciduous shrub*
* *Sweet-scented winter flowers*
* *Hardy*

Chimonanthus praecox, which grows up to 2.5m (8ft) tall and forms a rounded, bushy shape, is grown primarily for its winter flowers, carried on bare stems. They are cup shaped, yellow with a central purple blotch and strongly fragrant. The leaves that follow are oval and dark green.

Cultivation
Plant in fairly fertile, well-drained soil in full sun. Although the plants are hardy, a sheltered position against a warm wall will protect the flowers in cold regions.

Shoots which have carried flowers can be cut back hard once the flowers have faded to keep plants neat. Low-growing shoots can be layered to provide new plants.

Plant directory

Chionodoxa forbesii

Chionodoxa Liliaceae
Glory-of-the-snow

* *Bulb, producing early spring flowers*
* *Suitable for rock gardens, containers and raised beds*
* *Hardy*

These bulbs generally produce two long, narrow, erect leaves and clusters of open-faced blue or pink flowers with a central cluster of stamens. *Chionodoxa luciliae* (*C. gigantea*) has relatively large, blue flowers with white eyes, and is less than 10cm (4in) tall. *C. forbesii* (*C siehei*), formerly known as *C. luciliae,* is slightly taller, with pale blue flowers, but the most popular form is the large-flowered 'Pink Giant'. *C. sardensis* has pendent, rich blue flowers with no contrasting eyes. All flower in late winter or early spring.

Cultivation
Well-drained soil with added organic matter is preferred. Chionodoxa thrives in full sun. Seed germinates freely in autumn, or plants can be divided in late summer or autumn.

Choisya Rutaceae
Mexican orange blossom

* *Evergreen shrub*
* *Fragrant flowers in spring*
* *Aromatic foliage*
* *Hardy or slightly tender*

This plant makes a rounded shrub some 2m (6ft) high, with glossy, fresh green leaves, consisting of three leaflets. They have a pleasant aroma when crushed. Small, starry, very fragrant white flowers are carried in spring and early summer, often with a further flush in autumn that sometimes persists throughout a mild winter. *Choisya ternata* 'Sundance' has bright yellow leaves, while 'Aztec Pearl' has finely divided foliage which gives it a delicate appearance, but plants can become straggly after a few years.

Cultivation
Grow in free-draining soil in a sunny but sheltered position, especially in colder areas. Prune straggly shoots where necessary in late spring, removing frost-damaged shoots. Propagate by semi-ripe cuttings in summer.

Cistus Cistaceae
Rock rose

* *Evergreen shrubs*
* *Excellent for seaside areas*
* *Late spring and summer flowers*
* *Slightly tender*

These plants can form a spreading, lax shrub up to 2m (6ft) high where conditions suit them, but most remain smaller than this. The long, crinkled, grey-green leaves of cistus are sometimes sticky to the touch. In summer, open, cup-shaped flowers, with delicate, paper-thin petals, cover the branches. Flowers may be white or pink, often with contrasting blotches at the base of the petals, and with a showy golden boss of stamens. Each flower lasts only a day, but further buds open in quick succession to give a long season of interest.

Cistus x *corbariensis* grows to about 1m (3ft) but spreads more widely; it carries white flowers with a central yellow blotch. Slightly taller is *C. ladanifer,* with slightly tacky leaves and white flowers with maroon blotches at the base of each petal.

C. x *purpureus* has rose-pink flowers with deeper red markings at the centre.

The popular hybrid 'Silver Pink' has grey-green foliage and large, clear pink flowers with golden stamens, which are produced in abundance in early summer.

Cultivation
Provide cistus with light, very free-draining soil and a position in full sun. Some shelter is necessary in colder areas, and plants should be protected from prolonged frosts.

Prune back dead wood in spring. Plants can be increased by softwood cuttings taken in summer.

Citrus Rutaceae
Citrus

* *Evergreen shrubs*
* *Fragrant spring flowers and colourful fruit*
* *Excellent in containers*
* *Tender*

Members of the citrus family have deep green, glossy, ovate leaves, which are aromatic when crushed, and starry, fragrant white flowers in spring and later. These are usually followed by attractive, often edible fruits. Plants are not frost hardy, and should be overwintered under cover in cold areas.

The calamondin, x *Citrofortunella microcarpa* (*Citrus mitis*), is one of the most successful plants, with small, orange-yellow fruits freely carried. It grows to 60–100cm (2–3ft) in a container. *C. limon* (lemon) and *C. sinensis* (orange) can also be grown; they will reach 1.2m (4ft) in suitable conditions.

Cultivation
Citrus plants need a minimum temperature of 5°C (40°F) to do well, although established plants will sometimes withstand short periods of lower temperatures. In cold regions, they are best grown in a sunroom or conservatory or a light position indoors during the winter; place them in a sunny, sheltered spot outdoors when all risk of frost has passed.

Use free-draining, soil-based compost and water plants freely during the growing season, sparingly in cooler weather.

Cut back or cut out straggly shoots in spring where necessary.

Plants can be increased from semi-ripe cuttings in summer, but a heated propagator is generally needed to produce good results.

Citrus sinensis

About the plants

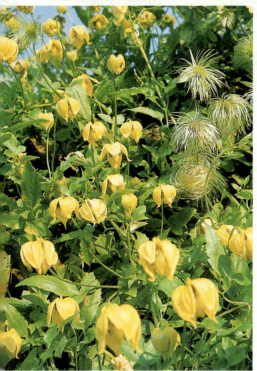

Clematis 'Bill Mackenzie'

Clematis — Ranunculaceae
Clematis ② ③

* Evergreen or deciduous climber
* Showy flowers from early spring to autumn, depending on species
* Hardy

There are three main groups of clematis: early-flowering species, which are largely evergreen and have small, nodding flowers in early spring; early-flowering hybrids, with larger, flat-faced flowers with colourful sepals in early to midsummer; and late-flowering hybrids, which flower in late summer or early autumn.

The early-flowering species such as *Clematis alpina*, with pendent, purple-blue flowers, and *C. armandii* with small, white, strongly scented blooms, are particularly suitable for containers and small gardens.

C. montana is a vigorous scrambler with an abundance of small to medium, white spring flowers; **'Tetrarose'** is a less rampant form, with deep pink blooms and reddish-tinged leaves. *C. florida* **'Sieboldii'** needs a sheltered position and is not a strong grower, but its unusual blooms – ivory-white sepals with a prominent central cluster of purple stamens – are eye-catching.

Among the larger-flowered types, the compact **'H. F. Young'** has medium-sized, pale violet-blue blooms in early summer.

The yellow *C.* **'Bill Mackenzie'** blooms from midsummer to early autumn and often bears flowers and seedheads together.

Cultivation
Clematis like their heads in the sun and their feet in the shade, so give them a cool, moist root run. Keep containers moist at all times; never let the compost dry out. Give high-potash liquid feeds regularly.

When necessary to keep them within bounds, spring-flowering species can be pruned after flowering by removing all the flowered wood.

Early flowering hybrids should have young shoots shortened by up to one-third in spring; and the previous season's shoots on late-flowering hybrids should be pruned back to a pair of healthy buds near the base in spring.

Plants can be increased by semi-ripe cuttings in summer, or by layering low-growing shoots in spring.

Clematis wilt causes the sudden, dramatic wilting of the topgrowth; affected plants should be mulched. Heaping the mulch around the base of the plant encourages adventitious roots from the base of the stem and new shoots are often produced. Do not plant replacement clematis in affected soil or compost.

Colchicum — Liliaceae
Autumn crocus, naked ladies ② ③

* Corm
* Crocus-like autumn flowers appearing before the leaves
* Hardy

Although similar in appearance, colchicum and crocus are not related. Colchicum produces relatively large, goblet-shaped flowers in early autumn. The flowers rise on slender, fragile-looking stems directly from the ground; the untidy mounds of broad leaves are produced in spring. There is one spring-flowering species, but it is not widely grown.

Colchicum agrippinum grows to some 10cm (4in) high and has deep, rosy-pink, chequered flowers with pointed petals. The 15-cm (6-in) high *C. autumnale* has pink, white or purple flowers on delicate stems. Free-flowering *C. byzantinum* has funnel-shaped, pale lilac flowers and grows to some 15–20cm (6–8in). *C. speciosum*, at about the same height, is a vigorous grower with purple-pink flowers; **'Atrorubens'** has purple-red flowers; **'Album'** is a pure white form. The hybrid **'Waterlily'** produces fully double flowers which are often too heavy for their slender stems, while **'The Giant'** has large, mauve-pink flowers, fading to white at the base.

Cultivation
Plant the corms 10cm (4in) deep in groups in late summer. Colchicums like an open, sunny position, and may be grown in free-draining soil in borders, containers and raised beds or naturalised in grass. Remember, however, that the spring foliage may look untidy and can smother grass.

Lift the corms in early summer and break away the offsets to increase your stock before replanting.

Colchicum speciosum 'Atrorubens'

Plant directory

Cordyline australis 'Albertii'

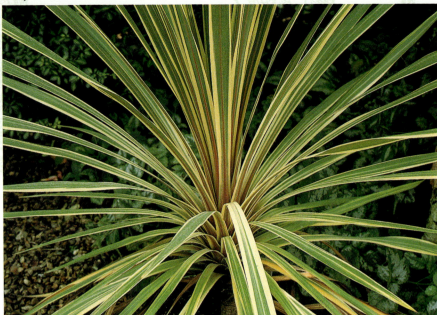

Cordyline   Agavaceae
Cabbage palm, cabbage tree ② ③

* *Evergreen shrub*
* *Foliage plant with a tropical appearance*
* *Excellent for containers*
* *Hardy or slightly tender*

The long, strap-shaped leaves of cordyline are carried in rosettes at the ends of the stem, giving the plant a palm-like appearance. The most commonly grown species is **Cordyline australis,** which can grow slowly to become a branching tree more than 8m (25ft) tall, but usually remains restricted to below 2m (6ft) in a container. Many forms with coloured and variegated leaves are available, including '**Atropurpurea**' with bronzy green leaves, and the **Torbay Series** in a wide range of colours.

C. indivisa produces a single stem up to 3m (10ft) high, with long, greyish green leaves in loose rosettes.

Cultivation
Well-drained soil and a warm position are necessary; in cold regions young plants need winter protection.

Cordylines prefer full sun, but will tolerate light shade. Water moderately in the growing season, but sparingly otherwise. Prune only to remove frost-damaged growth. Plants can be propagated by potting up suckers in spring.

Red spider mite may attack plants in summer although they are more common on specimens grown as houseplants. Spraying the foliage with plain water helps to avoid infestation.

Cornus   Cornaceae
Dogwood ② ③

* *Deciduous shrub*
* *Colourful winter stems*
* *Hardy*

There are several useful members of the dogwood family, but perhaps the most popular is **Cornus alba,** grown for its bright red winter stems. Plants reach about 2m (6ft), forming a cup-shaped bush. '**Sibirica**' (also known as '**Westonbirt**') has shining red bark, while '**Kesselringii**' has deep red bark and colourful autumn foliage. '**Elegantissima**' has white-variegated foliage and '**Spaethii**' golden-variegated leaves, giving these two varieties summer interest in addition to their red winter stems.

Cornus alba 'Spaethii'

Cultivation
Dogwoods like fertile, moisture-retentive soil in sun or light shade. Plants grown for their winter stems should be pruned back hard in spring, cutting them to within a few centimetres of the ground; this ensures the formation of vigorous young shoots, which have the best colour.

Propagate plants by semi-ripe cuttings in summer, or by layering low-growing branches in autumn.

Corylus   Corylaceae
Hazel ③

* *Deciduous shrub*
* *Attractive catkins in late winter and spring*
* *Bears edible nuts*
* *Hardy*

Corylus avellana is a vigorous plant, forming a large bush which bears hazel nuts in autumn. The most attractive form for gardens is '**Contorta**', the corkscrew hazel, which forms a bushy shrub 2m (6ft) or more in height. Sometimes known as Harry Lauder's walking stick, its shoots are curiously twisted and corkscrewed, making it very attractive in winter, particularly when it is hung with catkins. Oval, toothed leaves cover the branches in summer.

Cultivation
Plant in free-draining soil in a sunny or lightly shaded spot. Position the plant against a suitable winter background that will display the stems well.

Cut out at the base any straight shoots and suckers that develop.

Plants can be increased by layering low-growing branches.

Cotinus   Anacardiaceae
Smoke tree ③

* *Deciduous shrub*
* *Attractive foliage and flowers*
* *Good autumn colour*
* *Hardy*

Cotinus makes a bushy shrub, eventually growing to about 3m (10ft), with soft, oval, mid-green leaves which often colour well in autumn.

Cotinus coggygria bears fluffy, feathery plumes of flowerheads in midsummer, which persist until autumn and give the plant its common name of smoke tree. The variety '**Royal Purple**' has deep purple foliage, which goes light red in autumn, and clusters of pink flowers.

About the plants

Cultivation
Light shade is tolerated, but purple-leafed forms have better colour in full sun. Grow in free-draining, light soil; over-rich soil leads to disappointing autumn colour.

Prune lightly to shape, if required, in early spring. Plants can be increased by semi-ripe cuttings or layering in early autumn.

Cotoneaster   Rosaceae
Cotoneaster   ② ③

* Evergreen or deciduous shrub
* Attractive foliage, flowers and fruits
* Hardy

This is a large and varied family, containing many valuable plants. Cotoneasters can be grown as groundcover, specimen shrubs, hedges or wall plants, depending on variety. On deciduous species, the small, round, deep green leaves generally turn bright red in autumn, and the small, pink-tinged white flowers are followed by little, round, red fruits.

Among the groundcover types are *Cotoneaster congestus,* a dense-growing, spreading evergreen forming low 10-cm (8-in) hummocks with sparse red berries. *C. salicifolius* 'Gnom' has more pointed, glossy green leaves; and 'Autumn Fire' is a slightly taller, spreading plant with arching stems, evergreen or semi-evergreen, and freely-borne bright red berries. *C.* x *suecicus* 'Coral Beauty' is a compact, arching, evergreen shrub up to 1m (3ft), with orange-red berries in autumn, which can be grown as a specimen shrub or as groundcover.

C. horizontalis, the fishbone cotoneaster, is a wall plant which produces flattened branches in a herringbone arrangement. The deciduous, dark green leaves turn flame-red in autumn. A profusion of pale pink flowers is carried in early summer, and these are followed by bright red berries clustered tightly on the stems.

'Hybridus Pendulus' (*C. salicifolius* 'Pendulus'), a prostrate evergreen, can be grown as a weeping standard to form an attractive specimen in a container. Pink flowers are followed by plentiful red berries.

Cultivation
A sunny position and light, free-draining soil will give good results. Evergreen species are tolerant of light shade.

Prune back overlong shoots in early spring when necessary. Plants can be propagated by semi-ripe cuttings in summer.

Fireblight disease often attacks cotoneasters, causing leaves, flowers and berries to shrivel and blacken suddenly, with a scorched appearance. Cut out and destroy affected branches immediately.

Crocus   Iridaceae
Crocus   ① ② ③

* Corm
* Spring, or occasionally, autumn flowers
* Ideal for containers
* Hardy

Crocus is one of the best-known flowering corms, with low-growing, goblet-shaped flowers in a wide range of colours in early spring. However, one or two species do flower in autumn. The leaves are narrow, stiff, deep green and pointed, and usually accompany the flowers.

There are dozens of species and hundreds of varieties. Among the early spring-flowering species are *Crocus ancyrensis* (golden bunch crocus) with deep yellow flowers; *C. angustifolius* (cloth-of-gold crocus), with yellow flowers that are marked bronzy brown on the outside; and *C. tommasinianus,* with flowers in a range of purple-blue shades. *C. vernus* has given rise to a large number of popular spring-flowering cultivars, among which are the reliable 'Blue Pearl' (pale lavender-blue petals, white inside with a deep gold blotch in the centre); 'Cream Beauty' (cream with a yellow throat and brown markings on the outside); 'E. A. Bowles' (deep yellow with bronzy brown shading outside); 'Jeanne d'Arc' (large, white flowers); and 'Pickwick' (striped purple and white).

Autumn-flowering types include *C. kotschyanus,* with purple-pink, yellow-centred flowers; *C. laevigatus* which has pale lilac with gold and white centres; and *C. speciosus,* with purple flowers and a prominent orange stigma.

Cultivation
Plant corms in autumn, in well-drained soil in full sun or light shade, about 8cm (3in) deep. They can be grown in containers and beds, or naturalised in grass.

Once the foliage has died down, the corms can be lifted, cleaned and dried for storage before replanting, or they can be left in situ. Increase plants by dividing clumps of corms. Birds may damage the flowers by shredding the petals; use bird scarers if they are a problem.

Cyclamen   Primulaceae
Cyclamen, sowbread   ① ② ③

* Tuberous perennial
* Autumn, winter and spring interest from flowers or foliage
* Hardy

The dainty flowers of cyclamen have a very distinctive form, having strongly reflexing, swept-back petals and nodding heads. As well as their attractive flowers, many species have strongly marked, decorative foliage, with heart-shaped, marbled leaves. Plants grow from tubers, which can become very large; some species self-seed freely. Height is around 10–15cm (4–6in).

There are many valuable hardy species, but the best known is *Cyclamen hederifolium* (*C. neapolitanum*). Pale to deep pink flowers are produced in autumn, usually before the slightly pointed, silver-marbled leaves appear. 'Album' is a white variety. The foliage remains attractive until early summer. *C. coum* has more rounded, sometimes marbled foliage; the winter flowers are a stronger, deeper pink shade, and not quite so dainty as those of *C. hederifolium.*

C. repandum, with purple-pink or white flowers and heart-shaped, silvery leaves, flowers in spring.

Cultivation
Plant the tubers shallowly in early autumn. Cyclamen like light shade, and a free-draining but fertile, humus-rich soil. Allow the tubers to dry off in summer. For best results, do not disturb the tubers.

Propagate by seed collected in summer.

Crocus vernus

Plant directory

Cytisus Leguminosae
Broom

* *Deciduous, evergreen or semi-evergreen shrub*
* *Pea-like flowers carried in profusion*
* *Hardy*

For the most part, cytisus are spreading shrubs with wiry, green, arching branches and three-lobed or linear leaves. The flowers, typical of the pea family, appear in large numbers in spring or summer, in shades of cream, yellow or red.

Cytisus battandieri, Moroccan broom, will grow into a small tree up to some 4m (12ft) high. The three-lobed leaves are covered in silvery hairs, and racemes of golden yellow flowers are carried in early summer. The blooms have a strong, rich pineapple scent.

The Warminster broom, *C. x praecox*, forms a mound of slender, arching branches eventually reaching some 1.2m (4ft); in spring the branches are densely packed with pale, creamy, scented flowers. The variety '**Allgold**' has deeper yellow flowers.

C. x kewensis, with pale yellow flowers in late spring, is smaller, growing to 60cm (24in) high and spreading to 1.2m (4ft).

C. scoparius is the common broom, of vigorous, upright habit. Several named varieties exist, with flowers in varying shades of yellow, cream, red and brown. Most suitable for small spaces is *C. s. maritimus*, a mound-forming shrub some 20cm (8in) high, with small, greyish leaves and quantities of golden yellow flowers in late spring and early summer.

Cultivation
Grow in full sun in very free-draining, light soil; cytisus do not mind lime. Try to leave plants undisturbed; some species tend to be short lived.

If necessary, thin out the branches after flowering to produce shapely plants. Increase plants by semi-ripe cuttings taken in summer.

Dahlia Compositae
Dahlia

* *Tuberous-rooted, herbaceous perennial*
* *Colourful late-summer and autumn flowers*
* *Good for cutting*
* *Half-hardy*

Towards the end of summer, dahlias produce long-lasting, colourful flowers that persist until the first frosts. There are many different forms of border dahlia, classified according to the type of flower: pompon, collerette, anemone-centred, cactus and so on. Colours include red, orange, yellow, pink, white and purple. More compact types suitable for small spaces, which usually grow to less than 1m (3ft), include: '**Bishop of Llandaff**' (single, deep red flowers, bronzy foliage); '**David Howard**' (deep orange flowers and dark foliage); '**Fascination**' (with pale violet-pink flowers); '**Giraffe**' (with strikingly marked, orange-yellow flowers); and '**Small World**' (a white pompon type).

Bedding dahlias are raised from seed and are usually treated as annuals. They are more compact and shorter growing than border varieties; the flowers may be single, double, or semi-double, and colours are usually mixed. '**Redskin**', growing to 30cm (12in), has bronze-tinted foliage and double flowers in many colours; **Coltness Hybrids** have single flowers and reach 45cm (18in). '**Explosion**' is a small cactus-flowered type.

Cultivation
Dahlias like a rich, moisture-retentive soil and full sun. Border dahlias are planted out as dormant tubers in mid-spring or as young plants or rooted cuttings in late spring, after the risk of frosts has passed. Bedding dahlias are planted out after the frosts. Keep the plants well watered during dry spells and feed with a high-potash fertiliser every 14 days.

Stake the flowering stems of taller varieties. When flowering is over and frosts have blackened the topgrowth, lift the tubers and store them in dry peat or similar material in a frost-free place over winter, ready for planting out the following spring. Bedding dahlias also form tubers which can be stored, but the plants are often discarded and replaced with fresh stock.

Aphids can be a problem on young growth and flower buds; wash them away with water or spray with a non-persistent contact insecticide. Earwigs may eat holes in petals and cause malformed flowers. They feed at night and hide among the plants during the day; check flowerpots and shake out the earwigs and destroy them.

Daphne Thymelaeaceae
Daphne

* *Deciduous or evergreen shrub*
* *Very sweet-scented winter or early summer flowers*
* *Poisonous*
* *Hardy or slightly tender*

Daphnes range from small, creeping alpines to medium-sized shrubs, all with tubular, pink or white, fragrant flowers. *Daphne alpina*, a small, upright, deciduous plant, with slightly furry, greyish green leaves and white flowers in late spring, grows to 45cm (18in). *D. x burkwoodii* '**Variegata**' grows to 1.5m (5ft); it is semi-evergreen, with abundant clusters of pink flowers in early summer. Evergreen *D. cneorum* is usually represented by '**Eximia**'; the small, deep green leaves and deep pink and white spring flowers are carried on a plant some 15cm (6in) high, spreading to 60cm (2ft).

D. mezereum (mezereon) makes a rounded bush about 1.2m (4ft) tall; in winter and spring its bare stems bear thick clusters of deep pink flowers. The purple-pink flowers of evergreen *D. odora*, appearing from midwinter to early spring, are among the most fragrant of all. This species can be rather tender and needs a protected position; the variety '**Aureomarginata**', with a fine gold rim to the leaves, is a hardier selection.

Cultivation
Plant in full sun in fertile, well-drained but moisture-retentive soil containing plenty of organic matter. The smaller species of daphne are very suitable for rock gardens and containers. Prune plants lightly to shape, if required, in early spring.

Daphnes can be propagated by semi-ripe cuttings taken in summer, but they are not particularly easy to root.

Dendranthema Compositae
Chrysanthemum

* *Herbaceous perennial*
* *Colourful late summer and autumn flowers*
* *Half-hardy*

These plants are more familiarly known as florists' chrysanthemums, and along with dahlias provide a bright show of colour in late summer and autumn. There are many different flower forms and hundreds of

Daphne odora

184

About the plants

Dendranthema 'Cherry Emily'

cultivars. Mid-green foliage is lobed and aromatic; the stems can be tough and woody.

Suitable for smaller spaces are the pompon types, which grow to 30–45cm (12–18in). They include varieties such as **'Fairie'**, pink, and its bronze, purple and salmon sports; and the pink **'Maria'** and its bronze, salmon and cream sports. Korean chrysanthemums are low growing and particularly free-flowering; **'Agnes Ann'** is double, with deep red flowers; **'Fred Raynor'** is double, cream tinged pink; **'Raquel'** is single, lilac, and **'Starlet'** single, bronze, with spoon-shaped petals.

Cultivation
Grow in free-draining but moisture-retentive, fertile soil, in full sun. Water plants regularly and feed with a high potash fertiliser every 14 days.

In late autumn, when flowering is over, cut down the stems and lift the roots to store in dry peat or similar material over winter. Plant out again in spring, or start the roots into growth under cover and take cuttings of the young shoots that arise.

In cool, damp weather, botrytis can be a problem on incurving varieties, causing the petals to rot. Shelter blooms from excessive rain to try to prevent it.

Dianthus   Caryophyllaceae
Pink, carnation   ① ② ③

* Evergreen perennials
* Scented, summer flowers
* Hardy or half-hardy

Mainly cushion-forming plants, with narrow, blue-grey leaves, dianthus have flat-faced or double, sweetly scented flowers in red, white or pink shades. Tallest members of the group are the carnations, including border and perpetual-flowering carnations. These grow up to 1m (3ft) high, with semi-double or double flowers, some of which require greenhouse cultivation. Suitable for smaller spaces outdoors are varieties such as **'Bookham Fancy'**, which is yellow and red; **'Golden Cross'**, yellow; and **'Merlin Clove'**, white and red.

Pinks provide a large number of plants suitable for small gardens and containers. The alpine pink, *Dianthus alpinus*, forms a compact bun of rosy pink flowers in summer; the deep green, narrow leaves make an attractive evergreen mat. The maiden pink, *D. deltoides*, has 15-cm (6-in) high summer flowers over tufts of evergreen foliage; **'Flashing Light'** is a brilliant cerise shade.

Old-fashioned pinks form spreading mats of grey foliage and produce huge numbers of flowers in summer; they are often heavily laced or have fringed petals, and all are strongly fragrant. **'Dad's Favourite'** is white with purple-brown lacing; **'Mrs Sinkins'** is a double white with fringed petals and **'Sops-in-wine'** has single, purple flowers with white markings.

Modern pinks have been bred to combine the best attributes of old-fashioned pinks with robust growth and repeat flowering. Good examples are **'Doris'**, pale pink semi-double, marked with deeper pink; **'Houndspool Ruby'**, cerise-pink semi-double; and **'Becky Robinson'**, pale pink laced with deeper pink.

Cultivation
Pinks and border carnations like light, free-draining soil, preferably containing some lime. An open, sunny position is necessary.

Cut down dead flower stems to encourage repeat flowering. Propagate plants by "pipings" – soft-stem cuttings – in summer.

Dicentra   Papaveraceae
Bleeding heart   ③

* Herbaceous perennial
* Attractive foliage and early summer flowers
* Hardy

Dicentras are among the earliest border plants to push up their shoots in spring. The leaves are fresh green and attractively fern-like; the flowers are heart-shaped in shades of pink and white.

The best-known species is *Dicentra spectablis*, which has arching flower stems some 60cm (2ft) or more tall, bearing racemes of dainty rose pink and white flowers in spring and early summer. By midsummer the topgrowth has usually died away completely. **'Alba'** has creamy white flowers. *D. eximia* is a more compact plant, up to 45cm (18in), with finely divided greyish green foliage and narrow pink

Dicentra spectabilis

flowers all summer; *D. formosa*, about the same height, has bright green ferny leaves and deep pink blooms in early summer.

The several hybrid varieties include **'Adrian Bloom'**, with compact mounds of foliage and sprays of rose-pink crimson blooms; **'Bacchanal'**, with relatively short-stemmed flowers of deep crimson; and **'Spring Morning'**, with almost tubular pink flowers on a compact plant 30cm (12in) tall.

Cultivation
Dicentras thrive in well-drained soil containing plenty of organic matter, in sun or light shade. Early spring foliage can be damaged by late frosts, so choose a reasonably sheltered position.

Divide plants in the dormant season, but otherwise avoid disturbing the roots.

Dimorphotheca   Compositae
African daisy,
Star-of-the-veldt   ① ② ③

* Annual
* Daisy-like summer flowers
* Hardy or half-hardy

Many of the plants previously known as dimorphotheca have now been reclassified as osteospermum. *Dimorphotheca pluvialis* (*D. annua*) is a bushy annual up to 30cm (12in), with deep green, downy leaves. The daisy-like flowers have white petals with purple undersides and purple-brown centres. *D. sinuata* (*D. aurantiaca*), Star-of-the-veldt, has similar daisy flowers in a range of orange and red shades.

Cultivation
Dimorphothecas cope well with poor, dry soils; they must have free-draining conditions and full sun (the flowers will not open in shade). They grow best in a warm, sheltered spot.

Deadhead the plants to prolong the flowering season. Raise new plants from seed sown in spring. Plants may rot in cool, wet weather, particularly in heavier soils.

Plant directory

Dorotheanthus Aizoaceae
Mesembryanthemum, ice plant, Livingstone daisy ① ② ③

* *Annual*
* *Succulent plant suitable for very dry conditions*
* *Brightly coloured summer flowers in profusion*
* *Hardy or half-hardy*

Dorotheanthus bellidiformis is probably still better known under its previous name of *Mesembryanthemum criniflorum*. It is a 15-cm (6-in) high spreading plant, with fleshy, succulent leaves. These have a crystalline appearance, which gives the plant its common name of ice plant. Many-petalled, daisy-like flowers in white, red, yellow and pink shades, often with centres of a contrasting colour, are carried throughout the summer.

Dorotheanthus is usually available in mixed colours, including selections such as **'Magic Carpet'**, **'Sparkles'** and **'Harlequin Mixture'**.

Cultivation
These plants must have very free-draining soil and full sun; they are excellent subjects for poor, light soils. The flowers will not open in dull weather or in shade.

Deadheading the plants will prolong the flowering season. Raise from seed sown in mid-spring.

Over-moist soil conditions will lead to rapid rotting of the roots and collapse of the plants. Slugs and snails are serious pests, and plants should always be protected with slug bait or an organic alternative.

Dryopteris Aspidiaceae
Buckler fern, male fern ② ③

* *Deciduous or semi-evergreen perennial fern*
* *Frond-like, divided foliage*
* *Hardy*

These generally easy-to-grow ferns have mid-green, pinnate, arching fronds arising from a woolly brown crown. In a sheltered position the foliage may last well into the winter. *Dryopteris filix-mas,* the male fern, grows to around 1m (3ft); there are several cultivars, including **'Crispa Cristata'**, with frilled leaf margins. *D. erythrosora*, the Japanese shield fern, with coppery red young foliage is a little more tender.

Cultivation
Dryopteris likes shade or semi-shade and rich, moist soil. Keep the plants well watered (but not waterlogged) in dry spells.

Dead foliage is useful as protection for the crowns of *D. erythrosora* during the winter, and the brown, crisp fronds can also be attractive. Divide plants in mid-spring.

Eccremocarpus Bignoniaceae
Chilean glory flower ② ③

* *Evergreen perennial climber*
* *Showy, tubular flowers*
* *Half-hardy*

The only species commonly grown is *Eccremocarpus scaber*. Although this is a perennial in warm areas, it is often grown as an annual. The dark green leaves are bipinnate, with twining tendrils at the tips that coil around any convenient support to enable the plant to scramble upwards. It is a fast grower, soon covering a pergola or growing over a wall or fence. In summer, and into early autumn, clusters of scarlet, orange or yellow tubular flowers are freely produced. Selected colour forms can sometimes be obtained, including *E. s. aureus, E. s. carmineus* and *E. s. roseus*.

Cultivation
Plant against a suitable support in a sunny, sheltered, warm position, in free-draining soil. Trellis or netting should be provided. Water plants regularly in dry conditions.

Deadhead the plant to encourage prolonged flowering. Plants may be killed by frost and are usually raised afresh from seed each year.

Elaeagnus Elaeagnaceae
Elaeagnus ② ③

* *Deciduous or evergreen shrub*
* *Attractive foliage*
* *Insignificant but strongly scented flowers*
* *Good for coastal or exposed areas*
* *Hardy*

These tough, medium-sized shrubs are often grown for their attractively variegated leaves. They are not fussy about soil, and several species are useful for shady spots or exposed positions.

Elaeagnus x *ebbingei* is a hybrid with leathery, evergreen, greyish leaves; the cultivar **'Limelight'** has leaves with golden central markings, while **'Gilt Edge'** has golden margins to the foliage. Both are more compact than the species, growing to about 3m (10ft). Scented white flowers are carried in autumn.

E. pungens is slightly more vigorous in growth. The tough, evergreen leaves are glossy above, with grey, scaly undersides; those of **'Maculata'** have a broad, golden centre. White, bell-shaped, fragrant flowers appear in autumn.

Cultivation
Free-draining, light soil and a sunny position are preferred, although elaeagnus will grow well in light shade. Variegated varieties need bright light to maintain their coloured foliage.

Shrubs can be shaped if necessary and overlong shoots reduced by pruning in mid-spring. Variegated varieties tend to produce all-green shoots, which should be cut out at the base as soon as they are noticed.

Plants can be increased by semi-ripe cuttings in summer.

Dorotheanthus bellidiformis

About the plants

Eranthis Ranunculaceae
Winter aconite ① ② ③

* *Tuberous perennial*
* *Winter or early spring flowers*
* *Hardy*

The bright golden, buttercup-like flowers of winter aconite have glossy, lacquered petals, backed by bracts which form an attractive green ruff. The blooms appear in winter or very early spring, growing to some 10cm (4in) high, and the plant dies away in summer. *Eranthis hyemalis* is the true winter aconite; *E. x tubergenii* is a robust hybrid with larger, slightly later, golden yellow flowers. *E. x t.* 'Guinea Gold' has bronze-tinted bracts and foliage.

Cultivation
The oddly shaped tubers should be planted in moisture-retentive soil containing plenty of organic matter, preferably in partial shade. Keep them well watered during dry spells in spring.

Plants can be increased by lifting and dividing clumps in the green (after flowering, but while the plants are still in leaf), when they are easier to establish than dormant tubers.

Erica Ericaceae
Heath, heather ① ② ③

* *Evergreen sub-shrub*
* *Winter or summer flowers and attractive foliage*
* *Good ground cover*
* *Prefers lime-free soil*
* *Hardy*

These are some of the most useful plants for year-round colour in small-space gardens. Some varieties flower in summer, others during the winter months; some are grown mainly for their attractive foliage.

Probably the most popular species is the winter-flowering *Erica carnea*, which contains dozens of different cultivars. Plants can reach 30cm (12in), but are usually about half that height. The foliage consists of whorls of tiny, deep green needles; flowers are bell shaped in shades of white, red and pink. Unlike most heaths, this species will tolerate some lime in the soil.

Among the many excellent cultivars are 'Ann Sparkes', purple flowers and bronze-gold foliage; 'Foxhollow', yellow foliage with orange-red winter tints and pale pink flowers; 'Myretoun Ruby', deep purple-red flowers and deep green foliage; 'Springwood White', long stems packed with white, brown-tipped flowers; and 'December Red', deep rose-pink flowers in winter.

E. ciliaris, the Dorset heath, which flowers from midsummer through to autumn, carries its rounded, bell-shaped flowers at the tips of the branches. 'Corfe Castle' has salmon-pink flowers and bronze-tinged winter foliage; 'David McClintock', white flowers with pink tips and grey foliage; and 'Mrs C. H. Gill', prolific red flowers and deep green foliage.

The bell heather, *E. cinerea*, blooms from midsummer to mid-autumn. 'Atrorubens' has long stems of ruby-red flowers; 'Eden Valley' bears white flowers, tipped with lavender, and 'Rock Pool' has coppery foliage, turning orange and red in winter.

Bushy, winter-flowering *E. x darleyensis* grows up to 45cm (18in) or so; the tips of the young shoots are often creamy white or pink in late spring. Like *E. carnea*, this hybrid tolerates lime. 'Arthur Johnson' has rosy pink flowers and creamy pink spring foliage; 'Darley Dale', clear pale pink, long-lasting flowers; 'Ghost Hills', pink flowers and cream-tipped spring foliage; and 'Silberschmelze' (Molten Silver) has long-lasting, fragrant, white flowers and creamy spring foliage.

E. tetralix (cross-leaved heath) produces dense heads of usually deep pink flowers from summer to mid-autumn. 'Con Underwood' has crimson flowers over grey-green foliage; 'Hookstone Pink' has greyish foliage and pale pink flowers.

Cultivation
Heathers grow best in a sunny position in free-draining but moisture-retentive, acid soils containing plenty of organic matter. Varieties of *E. carnea* and *E. x darleyensis* will tolerate lime, but usually perform better in lime-free conditions. Water the plants regularly in dry spells.

Prune lightly after flowering or in early spring to keep the plants compact. Heathers can be propagated by semi-ripe cuttings in summer, or by layering.

Erica carnea 'Foxhollow'

Erysimum 'Bowles Mauve'

Erysimum Cruciferae
Wallflower ① ② ③

* *Annuals, biennials and evergreen perennials*
* *Spring flowers*
* *Hardy or half-hardy*

These plants are related to, and sometimes listed as, cheiranthus. Best known are varieties of *Erysimum cheiri* (*Cheiranthus cheiri*); many selections are available, including the dwarf **Tom Thumb Series**, orange-scarlet 'Fire King', yellow 'Golden Monarch' and the compact, dwarf **Prince Series**. *E. hieraciifolium* (*C. x allionii*) is the slightly taller Siberian wallflower, of which 'Orange Bedder' and 'Golden Bedder' are popular varieties. These wallflowers are grown as biennials for spring bedding.

Several attractive perennial varieties exist, including 'Bowles Mauve', with dark green leaves and mauve flowers, growing to some 60cm (2ft) tall; 'Harpur Crewe', with scented, double, yellow flowers, to 30cm (12in); 'Moonlight', a low-growing, spreading plant about 10cm (4in) high with pale yellow flowers; and 'Jacob's Jacket', with flowers which change through pale pink, yellow, red and bronze tones. All these varieties tend to be short lived.

Cultivation
Grow in full sun in light, free-draining soils containing some lime. Varieties grown as perennials need a sheltered position. Deadhead after flowering.

Sow seed of varieties grown as biennials in early summer or sow as annuals in warm areas, planting later. Perennial types are increased by softwood cuttings in early or mid-summer. Take cuttings each year as a precaution against unexpected losses.

Plant directory

Erythronium 'Pagoda'

Erythronium Liliaceae
Dog's-tooth violet ① ② ③

* *Tuberous perennial*
* *Spring flowers and attractive foliage*
* *Hardy*

Dog's-tooth violets have attractive, nodding, spring flowers in shades of white, pink or yellow. The leaves of some varieties are attractively mottled and marbled.

Erythronium dens-canis (dog's-tooth violet) grows to 15cm (6in) and has lilac or purple-pink, pendent flowers with lightly reflexed petals. The leaves are often mottled grey and deep purple.

E. californicum is usually represented by 'White Beauty'; spikes of several slightly pendent flowers are white, marked with reddish brown in the centre, and leaves are lightly mottled.

'Pagoda' is an attractive hybrid with lightly mottled leaves and a flower stem up to 45cm (18in) tall, bearing 8–10 pendent, yellow flowers with reflexed petals and prominent stamens.

E. revolutum can reach 30cm (12in) tall, with brown and green mottled leaves and spikes of pink flowers. *E. tuolumnense* has plain green, shiny leaves and bright yellow flowers in clusters of half a dozen or more.

Cultivation
Erythroniums prefer cool, moist soil containing plenty of organic matter, and a position in light shade. Do not let the tubers dry out during the growing season.

Plants can sometimes be increased by offsets in late summer; replant the offsets immediately after detaching them.

Escallonia Escalloniaceae
Escallonia ③

* *Evergreen or deciduous shrub*
* *Early summer flowers and glossy foliage*
* *Good for coastal regions*
* *Hardy or slightly tender*

This medium-sized shrub generally requires a sheltered spot in a mild climate; in colder areas it can be grown against a wall. Leaves are oval, glossy and mid to deep green; white or pink flowers are carried from early to midsummer.

Most of the commonly grown types are evergreen hybrids. Good choices include 'Apple Blossom', a bushy shrub up to 2m (6ft), with pink and white flowers; 'Langleyensis' with arching branches to 2m (6ft), loaded with deep pink flowers in early summer; 'Donard Beauty', 1.5m (5ft) tall, with deep pink flowers and glossy, dark leaves, and 'Donard Gem', a compact grower with large, pink, scented flowers.

Cultivation
Free-draining soil is required, and an open, sunny position in mild gardens, or the shelter of a wall in more exposed areas. Plants can be clipped lightly to keep them shapely after flowering.

Increase escallonia by taking semi-ripe cuttings in summer.

Eschscholzia Papaveraceae
Californian poppy ③

* *Annual*
* *Brightly coloured, poppy-like flowers*
* *Tolerates poor soils*
* *Hardy*

Eschscholzia californica, Californian poppy, has finely cut, fern-like, blue-green leaves and open, cup-shaped flowers in summer. The poppy-like flowers have silky petals and are carried on slender 20–30-cm (8–12-in) stems; they may be white, cream, yellow, red or orange. Mixed shades are common; 'Monarch Art Shades' is a popular variety but single colour selections are also available, including 'Apricot Bush', 'Rose Bush', 'Apricot Chiffon', 'Rose Chiffon' and the scarlet and gold, semi-double 'Dali'.

E. caespitosa has smaller, rather less showy yellow flowers in late summer and grows to some 15cm (6in).

Cultivation
Free-draining soil is essential; eschscholzia copes well with poor, thin, sandy soils. The plants need a position in full sun.

Deadheading will help to ensure a long-lasting display of flowers.

Grow from seed sown in early to mid-spring; earlier flowering plants can be obtained from an autumn sowing in all but very cold, exposed areas.

Eucalyptus Myrtaceae
Gum tree ② ③

* *Evergreen tree*
* *Attractive foliage and bark*
* *Hardy or slightly tender*

Fast-growing, vigorous trees from Australia, eucalyptus can top 30m (100ft) in their natural habitat. However, if they are cut back hard annually, they make attractive shrubs suitable for smaller spaces. The grey-green leaves have a characteristic aroma when crushed.

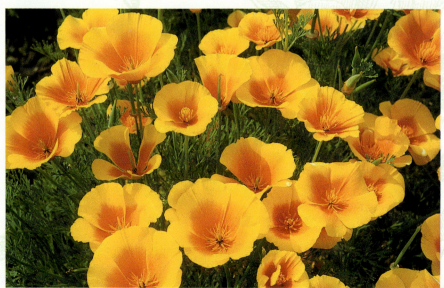

Eschscholzia californica

About the plants

One of the most popular eucalypts is the cider gum, *Eucalyptus gunnii*. It is one of the hardiest eucalypts in cool climates and grows rapidly to make a large tree. The juvenile foliage is round and a bright silver-blue; adult foliage is sickle shaped and blue-green. The plant can be cut back to within a few centimetres of the base each year to maintain the juvenile foliage and keep it a manageable size. The bark is attractively patched cream and tan on larger plants.

E. pauciflora subsp. *niphophila,* the snow gum, grows relatively slowly. The bark is a striking silver-white on young plants; on older trees it peels to form green, grey and cream patches. Young shoots are bright red.

Cultivation
Eucalyptus likes well-drained, reasonably fertile soil and a sunny, sheltered position, especially when young; the vigorous growth is prone to wind damage. Make sure the soil does not dry out during the summer.

In small spaces, plants will need frequent pruning. Cut them back to the base in early spring and pinch out the strongest-growing branches regularly to form a rounded shrub. Plants may need cutting back twice a year if they start to outgrow their space.

Plants can also be grown as small trees by allowing them to reach just over the required height before removing the growing tip. Rub out most of the new shoots that appear on the stem as soon as they develop, leaving those at the top of the stem to form a head. These shoots can then be cut back close to the main stem every spring, to form a pollarded tree.

Severe frosts or cold winds can damage or even kill plants, so give winter protection if necessary until they become established. Plants can be raised from seed sown in spring.

Euonymus Celastraceae
Spindle bush

* *Deciduous or evergreen trees and shrubs*
* *Attractive foliage*
* *Suitable for groundcover*
* *Hardy*

These are versatile plants with a wide range of uses. *Euonymus alatus*, the winged spindle bush, is a slow-growing, deciduous shrub; it has unusual branches with attractive corky wings. The leaves colour well in autumn. Inconspicuous white flowers are followed by showy, fleshy, purplish red fruits with exposed, bright orange seeds. The form **'Compactus'** is particularly suitable for small spaces, growing to about 1m (3ft) tall, although it will spread to two or three times that.

Euonymus fortunei 'Emerald 'n' Gold'

E. fortunei is a popular evergreen, with prostrate, creeping stems which will climb if they are provided with a suitable support. Leaves are oval, glossy and dark green. When the stems reach the top of their climb, a different, adult form of growth develops, with larger foliage and green-white flowers followed by pink and orange fruits. **'Emerald 'n' Gold'** forms a dense, bushy shrub to 60cm (2ft) or so tall, with bright, gold-margined leaves. **'Kewensis'** is a dainty miniature form with slender stems and very small leaves; it is ideal for a rock garden, raised bed or container.

Cultivation
Moisture-retentive, reasonably fertile soil and sun or light shade are required. Variegated types need full sun to maintain good leaf colour. Cut plain green shoots to their base as soon as they are seen.

Plants can be propagated from semi-ripe cuttings in summer.

Euphorbia Euphorbiaceae
Spurge

* *Evergreen, semi-evergreen or deciduous perennials and shrubs*
* *Striking flowerheads and foliage*
* *Good for cutting for flower arrangements*
* *Hardy*

The large family of spurges contains many different types of plant, including succulents and popular houseplants, but they excel as striking border perennials. *Euphorbia amygdaloides* **'Purpurea'** (Rubra) is semi-evergreen, with stems up to 30cm (12in) long clothed with narrow, oblong, deep reddish purple leaves. The colour is particularly pronounced in spring.

The stems of *E. characias wulfenii* are upright or rather lax, growing up to 1.5m (5ft), with evergreen, blue-grey foliage. In spring, it bears large, elongated heads of long-lasting lime-green flowers with brown centres in spring. The plant is a good architectural subject.

E. griffithii has mid-green leaves, and in late spring and early summer, the small flowers are surrounded by showy, orange-red bracts. **'Fireglow'**, reaching about 1m (3ft), is a particularly good form.

Cultivation
Plants need well-drained soil but should not be allowed to dry out, particularly in spring and early summer. Full sun or light shade are suitable.

Cut down the flower stems once the flowers have faded to maintain a compact, bushy shape. Plants can be propagated from seed, or by softwood cuttings of basal shoots in late spring.

Fatsia Araliaceae
Japanese aralia

* *Evergreen shrub*
* *Bold, palmate leaves and late-summer flowers*
* *Architectural value*
* *Hardy or slightly tender*

Fatsia japonica makes a rounded shrub up to 3m (10ft) tall. It is valuable for its large, glossy, dark green, deeply lobed leaves. In late summer it bears distinctive round umbels of tiny white flowers, followed by blue-black fruits. **'Variegata'** has narrow, creamy white margins to the leaves.

Cultivation
A sheltered position is required for this plant, with protection from cold winds. Any reasonably fertile soil is suitable, and plants grow well in shade or full sun.

Propagate by semi-ripe cuttings in summer. Severe frosts can damage plants, killing shoot tips and causing distorted growth. Prune back damaged branches.

Fatsia japonica in flower

Plant directory

Festuca Gramineae
Blue fescue ① ② ③

* *Evergreen perennial grass*
* *Colourful foliage gives year-round interest*
* *Hardy*

This grass makes neat tufts of narrow, steely blue foliage around 15cm (6in) high. By far the most popular species grown is *Festuca glauca*, with fine, silver-blue foliage and dainty panicles of pale fawn spikelets in summer. 'Golden Toupee' has pale green and gold foliage, with dense golden panicles. *F. amethystina* grows to 30cm (12in) high, with spreading tufts of blue-green leaves.

Cultivation
Light, free-draining soil and an open, sunny position are preferred.
 Flower spikelets are sometimes thought to detract from the foliage and they can be cut off if they are not required.
 Plants should be divided and replanted in autumn or spring every few years, to keep growth neat and vigorous.

Ficus Moraceae
Fig ② ③

* *Deciduous shrub or small tree*
* *Attractive, bold foliage*
* *Edible fruits in favourable conditions*
* *Slightly tender*

The common edible fig, *Ficus carica*, has large, lobed leaves on spreading branches. Fruits are regularly produced in warm climates, but in cool temperate zones fruiting is not reliable.
 The fruits are carried towards the ends of the branches; in cold areas only, small, undeveloped fruits should be allowed to remain on the bush over winter to ripen the following summer. Large, unripe fruits still on the tree in late autumn should be removed, since they will not mature.
 'Brown Turkey' is the most popular fruiting variety; 'White Marseilles' ('White Genoa') is good for warmer areas.

Cultivation
Grow figs in the shelter of a warm, sunny wall or a similar position. Restricting the roots ensures better fruiting, so these plants are ideal for container culture. Use moisture-retentive, fertile soil and water regularly during the growing season, giving liquid fertiliser every 14–21 days.
 Remove frost-damaged branches in early spring.
 Plants can best be propagated by layering the lower branches.

Fritillaria imperialis 'Rubra Maxima'

Fritillaria Liliaceae
Fritillary ① ② ③

* *Perennial bulbs*
* *Showy spring flowers*
* *Hardy*

The showiest of the fritillarias is the crown imperial, *Fritillaria imperialis*. The large, lily-like bulb, with overlapping scales, has a hollow centre; both the bulb and the shoots it sends up have a distinctive foxy smell. The tall 1-m (3-ft) high stems, with linear, mid-green leaves, bear clusters of large, pendent, bell-shaped flowers in late spring; these are topped with a leafy cluster. The flowers may be orange, yellow or orange-red; 'Lutea' has yellow flowers, while 'Rubra Maxima' is deep orange-red.
 The snake's head fritillary, *F. meleagris*, is quite different. Growing to some 30cm (12in), it has linear leaves, with dainty, pendent flowers on slender stalks; the petals may be white, purple or pink, and usually show an attractive white chequered pattern.
 F. persica 'Adiyaman' grows to around 1m (3ft) or more and has grey-green leaves and a dozen or more deep plum-purple, bell-shaped flowers at the top of the stems.

Cultivation
Fritillaries like free-draining but moisture-retentive soil, in full sun or light shade. *F. meleagris* grows well naturalised in grass, in rockeries or in the front of a border; *F. imperialis* and *F. persica* are good border plants or focal points. All these plants are suitable for containers.
 Plant the large bulbs on their sides to avoid water collecting in the hollow centres, which can lead to rotting. Do not disturb the bulbs unless essential. Plants can be raised from seed or from offsets, which take several years to reach flowering size.
 Slugs and snails can damage both the bulbs and the young shoots as they emerge; use slug bait or an organic alternative.

Fuchsia Onagraceae
Fuchsia ① ② ③

* *Deciduous shrub*
* *Summer flowers*
* *Hardy or tender*

There are hundreds of different varieties of fuchsia, some tender, some hardy in temperate regions. Flowers, which are carried throughout the summer, are usually pendulous and tubular, with overlapping petals and colourful sepals forming a bell shape. Petals may be single or double, waved and ruffled; the sepals are often of a contrasting shade. Leaves are oval and mid- to dark green, sometimes tinged red. Plants usually grow to around 60–90cm (2–3ft), but hardy varieties often exceed that in mild, sheltered locations.
 Some types are bushy and upright, others trailing; they are excellent in containers and can be trained as standards. The choice of varieties is vast and increasing. Good forms include 'Alice Hoffman', semi-double, red sepals, white petals; 'Dollar Princess', double, red sepals, purple petals; 'Mrs Popple', red sepals, violet petals; and 'Tom Thumb', dwarf 45cm (18in), red sepals, purple petals. *Fuchsia magellanica* 'Tricolor' has cream, green and pink variegated foliage and small flowers with red sepals and purple petals.
 Among good varieties for use in containers and as summer bedding are 'Lye's Unique', white sepals, pale salmon-pink petals; 'Marinka', trailing, red sepals and petals; 'Swingtime', lax, semi-trailing, full double flowers with white petals and red sepals; and 'Thalia', very long tubes with orange-red sepals and petals.
 Relatively recently introduced are giant-flowered hybrids with blooms 7.5cm (3in) or more across, such as 'Holly's Beauty', white sepals and pale lilac petals; and 'Snow Burner', magenta sepals and white petals. There are also several compact, bushy varieties with unusual, starry, upwards facing flowers, such as the pink and white 'Twinkletoes'.

Cultivation
Plant hardy varieties in a fairly sheltered position in sun or light shade, in free-draining but fertile soil. Tender varieties should not be planted out until all risk of frost is past. Keep plants well watered during the flowering season and feed every 14 days with a high-potash liquid fertiliser.
 Move tender varieties under cover before the first frosts; softwood cuttings can be taken from new growth in spring. Leave the old stems on hardy plants over winter for protection, cutting them down to near the base in early spring. Buds may grow from the old stems or spring directly from the

About the plants

roots. In cold areas, extra protection can be given by mulching the root area with peat, chipped bark, straw or similar material.
Take softwood cuttings in early summer.
Aphids may infest young shoots and can be sprayed with a non-persistent contact insecticide where necessary.

Galanthus   Amaryllidaceae
Snowdrop

* *Bulb*
* *Very early, pendulous flowers*
* *Hardy*

For many people, snowdrops are the first sign of approaching spring. The bulbs send up pairs of spear-shaped, mid-green leaves and pendent white flowers on slender stems. The flowers have three large, all-white outer petals and three short inner ones which are white tipped with green. They grow to about 10–15cm (4–6in).

The common snowdrop is *Galanthus nivalis*. There are many cultivars, including '**Viridapicis**', with pronounced green markings, '**Sandersii**' ('**Lutescens**'), with yellow markings instead of green, and the double, frilled '**Flore Pleno**'.

G. elwesii, with broader, strap-shaped leaves and larger, more rounded flowers, can reach 25cm (10in). The hybrids '**Atkinsii**' and '**S. Arnott**' are robust and vigorous. An oddity is *G. reginae-olgae*, which flowers in autumn, usually before the leaves appear.

Cultivation
Plant bulbs in late summer in moisture-retentive soil in light shade; they can be difficult to establish if they have dried out.

The most reliable time to plant snowdrops is in-the-green, just after flowering, when established clumps can also be split up.

Garrya   Garryaceae
Silk tassel bush

* *Evergreen shrub*
* *Long, showy catkins in winter and spring*
* *Grows best against a wall*
* *Hardy*

Garrya elliptica forms a bushy shrub up to 3m (10ft) or so if given the shelter of a wall in cool climates. The deep green, leathery leaves are oval, with waved edges; in winter and spring the branches are profusely draped with long, pale green catkins.

Male and female plants exist; the males produce longer, more handsome catkins, although the females' short, grey catkins are followed by long, knobbly clusters of purple-black berries, which can be an attractive feature. The sexes must be grown in close proximity for the berries to be produced.

'**James Roof**' is a vigorous male variety with particularly long, striking catkins with yellow anthers.

Cultivation
Plant in spring in well-drained soil in a sheltered position, preferably protected from freezing winds. Container-grown plants will establish more quickly and garrya does not like being transplanted.
Plants will grow in sun or shade.
Cut back overlong or damaged shoots once the catkins have shrivelled.
Take semi-ripe cuttings in summer.

Genista pilosa

Genista   Leguminosae
Broom

* *Deciduous shrub*
* *Profusion of flowers, often fragrant, in early summer*
* *Grows well in poor soils*
* *Hardy or slightly tender*

Brooms generally make spreading shrubs with slender green branches; the leaves are thin and linear, and the stems often appear leafless. In late spring and early summer, typical pea-like, usually yellow, flowers are carried in great numbers.

Some species of broom make small trees, but there are several low-growing, compact forms particularly suitable for small spaces. The Spanish gorse, *Genista hispanica*, must be positioned carefully, since it is extremely spiny. It grows some 60cm (2ft) high and forms a mound of dense clusters of golden flowers in early summer.

G. lydia is a dwarf shrub less than 1m (3ft) high; its pendulous shoots are covered with yellow flowers in late spring and early summer. *G. pilosa* makes a neat hummock around 30cm (12in) high and the same across, with yellow flowers in early to midsummer. It is particularly good on dry banks or in rock gardens.

Cultivation
Plant in full sun in well-drained, light soil. Brooms resent being transplanted and fairly small, container-grown plants will establish most quickly.
Plants do not normally require watering or feeding, but watering will probably be necessary if they are in containers.
Shoots can be clipped over with secateurs after flowering to keep the bushes in shape.
Softwood or semi-ripe cuttings can be taken in summer, but are not particularly easy to root.

***Galanthus nivalis* 'Flore Pleno'**

Plant directory

Gentiana Gentianaceae
Gentian ① ② ③

* *Semi-evergreen or evergreen perennial*
* *Intensely blue flowers in early summer or autumn*
* *Excellent for rock gardens*
* *Hardy*

Well known for their brilliant blue flowers, gentians also have a reputation for being difficult to grow. They are fussy about soil and position and are sometimes reluctant to bloom; among the easiest and most reliable is *Gentiana acaulis*.

The plants produce dense mats of slender or oval leaves; the flowers are relatively large, trumpet shaped, and often of a deep, intense blue. The most commonly grown species are the evergreen *G. septemfida* and *G. sino-ornata*, which flower in late summer or autumn. *G. septemfida* has oval leaves and grows to about 30cm (12in); the mid-blue flowers have white centres. *G. sino-ornata* has narrow leaves and deeper blue flowers with less conspicuous white throats than those of *G. septemfida*, and the outsides of the petals are strongly marked with purple-black and greenish white stripes.

Cultivation
Plant gentians in lime-free, moist, humus-rich soil in full sun or semi-shade. Water as necessary to keep the soil moist but not waterlogged during the growing season.

Divide plants every few years in spring.

Gentiana acaulis

Geranium 'Johnson's Blue'

Geranium Geraniaceae
Cranesbill ① ② ③

* *Herbaceous perennial*
* *Flowers carried freely in summer*
* *Hardy*

The cranesbills are colourful, easy-to-grow plants, ideal for rock gardens and paved areas, as well as containers. They form low mounds 15–60cm (6–24in) high, with downy, deeply cut or lobed leaves. In summer, they carry open, cup-shaped flowers, often with prominent stamens, in shades of pink, purple and blue.

Among the best known are *Geranium cinereum* 'Ballerina', with pink, strongly veined petals; *G. clarkei* 'Kashmir Purple' and 'Kashmir White', with finely cut foliage and nodding flowers. *G. x oxonianum* 'Wargrave Pink' is often evergreen, with a long season of bright pink flowers. 'Ann Folkard' has golden yellow foliage and deep magenta, black-eyed and veined flowers. 'Johnson's Blue' has attractively divided foliage and lavender-blue flowers. The scented foliage of *G. macrorrhizum* makes it ideal for small gardens. *G. himalayense* 'Plenum' and *G. pratense* 'Plenum Violaceum' are good double varieties.

Cultivation
Grow in full sun or light shade in free-draining soil.

In early summer, after the first flush of flowers, clip untidy plants back hard to encourage fresh, compact growth.

Gypsophila Caryophyllaceae
Baby's breath ③

* *Annual or perennial*
* *Tiny flowers in summer; good for cutting*
* *Thrives on chalky soil*
* *Hardy*

Gypsophila bears clouds of tiny, delicate white or pink flowers in panicles, making it a valuable texture plant and a fine addition to vases of cut flowers. The border perennial *Gypsophila paniculata*, with narrow leaves and heads of white flowers, grows to 1m (3ft); 'Bristol Fairy' is a double form, and 'Flamingo' has double, pale pink flowers. The annual *G. elegans* has larger flowers; 'Covent Garden White' reaches a height of about 45cm (18in).

G. repens is a semi-evergreen, trailing perennial, ideal for a rock garden or bank. Its white or pink flowers on wiry stems spring from spreading mats of grey-green leaves. 'Dorothy Teacher' is a reliable form.

Cultivation
Gypsophila likes well-drained soil and an open, sunny position. Alkaline soils do not present a problem, and plants in acid soils will benefit from the addition of a little lime. Although perennials cope well with poor, light soils, they tend to be short lived in these conditions.

Stake flowers with split canes or twiggy sticks where necessary, and cut down flowering stems as they fade.

Sow seed of annual species in early spring. Divide *G. repens* in spring; named varieties of *G. paniculata* cannot be propagated successfully by small-scale gardeners.

Hakonechloa Gramineae
Hakonechloa ② ③

* *Perennial grass*
* *Attractive foliage and architectural form*
* *Hardy*

This slow-growing grass produces a fountain of attractive foliage throughout summer and into autumn and winter, making it a good specimen plant for a container. The usual form is *Hakonechloa macra* 'Aureola', with boldly striped green and yellow leaves that become tinged with red as they age. They are accompanied in autumn by panicles of long-lasting red flower spikes. The plant grows to around 60cm (2ft). 'Alboaurea' is slightly more compact and has more golden foliage.

Cultivation
Fertile, moisture-retentive soil is required; keep the roots moist at all times throughout the growing season.

A position in full sun is preferred and will ensure the best-coloured foliage. Divide plants in spring.

About the plants

Hamamelis Hamamelidaceae
Witch hazel

* *Deciduous shrub*
* *Fragrant winter flowers*
* *Colourful autumn foliage*
* *Hardy*

The witch hazels make spreading shrubs or small trees, with oval leaves which generally turn rich shades of yellow and red in autumn. The flowers have strap-shaped petals, which gives them a spider-like appearance. They are carried on the bare branches in winter and early spring, and often have an intensely sweet scent.

Hamamelis x *intermedia* is a hybrid between *H. mollis* and *H. japonica*; the flowers, carried throughout the winter, have crinkled petals and are delicately scented. Many cultivars are available, including 'Jelena' ('Copper Beauty'), with large, rich orange-yellow flowers, and a rather vigorous, spreading habit, and 'Diane', with striking red-orange flowers and particularly good autumn colour.

H. japonica makes a large shrub about 3m (10ft) in height. The foliage is glossy and mid-green, turning yellow in autumn. In early spring, 'Sulphurea' has pale yellow, crinkle-petalled flowers which are not as strongly scented as those of some other varieties.

H. mollis grows to 2m (6ft) or more; the scented, golden yellow, flat-petalled flowers are carried in mid-winter. 'Pallida' has large, paler yellow flowers.

Cultivation
Witch hazels prefers lime-free soil, which should be moisture retentive, with well-rotted organic matter added before planting. Full sun or semi-shade are suitable, in a position sheltered from cold winds.

Straggly shoots can be cut back after flowering is over.

Propagation is not practical for the small-space gardener.

Hamamelis mollis

Hebe 'Midsummer Beauty'

Hebe Scrophulariaceae
Veronica, hebe

* *Evergreen shrub*
* *Spikes of summer flowers and attractive foliage*
* *Hardy or half-hardy*

Hebes are particularly suitable for mild coastal areas, since they stand up well to salty winds. There are many species and varieties, varying from prostrate rock plants to medium-sized shrubs. Dense spikes of bottlebrush-type flowers are carried in summer, often in shades of purple, but also in white, pink and red.

'Autumn Glory' grows to some 60cm (2ft); it forms a rounded bush, with dark green leaves and violet-blue flowers from late summer well into autumn. 'Youngii' ('Carl Teschner') is more or less prostrate, making a low, spreading shrub with small, dark green leaves on dark stems and short spikes of purple flowers in summer. It is a good variety for rockeries or the edge of a bed.

The flower spikes of 'Great Orme' are deep pink, becoming pale pink from the base as the flowers age. The dark stems are clothed with glossy, mid-green foliage; the bush grows to around 1m (3ft). 'Midsummer Beauty' is a little taller, with glossy, green leaves tinted red on their undersides. Flowers are pale lilac. 'La Séduisante' is a compact, round shrub about 60cm (2ft) tall, with densely packed spikes of purplish flowers from midsummer.

As valuable for its foliage as for its flowers is *H. pinguifolia* 'Pagei', a dwarf shrub with dense, blue-grey leaves and short spikes of white flowers in spring and early summer. This variety makes an excellent rock garden plant and can be grown as groundcover, as well as in containers.

Cultivation
Well-drained soil is essential; hebes are tolerant of chalk. Grow in full sun and in a warm, sheltered position.

Trim plants back hard in spring to keep growth neat and compact. Take semi-ripe cuttings in summer and in cold climates overwinter them under cover to be sure of replacements in case of winter losses.

Hedera Araliaceae
Ivy

* *Evergreen self-clinging climber*
* *Attractive foliage*
* *Shade tolerant*
* *Hardy*

Ivies are very adaptable and easy-to-grow plants, good for difficult places such as cold, shady walls. Once established, they grow quickly, their woody stems clinging to any rough surface with little fringes of adventitious roots.

Leaves are generally lobed or triangular and variable in shape and size; those of many cultivars are attractively variegated. Juvenile growth is trailing, but once ivy has reached the top of its support, a different, adult type of growth is produced, with short, stiff branches bearing round heads of yellow-green flowers in autumn, which are followed by black berries.

Hedera canariensis is a rather tender species but thrives in sheltered patio gardens. 'Gloire de Marengo' has large, unlobed leaves variegated with silver and white towards the margins. Somewhat similar but hardier is *H. colchica* 'Dentata Variegata', whose large, unlobed leaves have a creamy variegation.

There are dozens of cultivars of the common English ivy, *H. helix*. Leaves are generally small and deeply lobed; growth is vigorous and can be invasive. Reasonably restrained varieties include 'Buttercup', which needs a position in full sun to develop its rich yellow foliage; 'Ivalace', with glossy, deep green leaves which are curled and waved at the margins; and 'Little Diamond', dwarf and bushy, with green, grey and cream, diamond-shaped leaves.

Cultivation
Ivies thrive in most soils and situations, although variegated varieties need full sun to retain their colouring.

Plants can be pruned in spring to keep them within bounds; if required, they can be cut back hard to produce fresh young growth. Soft tip cuttings can be taken in early summer. If cuttings are taken of the flowering shoots, they will produce non-climbing, rounded shrubs.

Red spider mite can attack plants in dry conditions, causing mottled foliage which soon falls. Increase humidity around plants by spraying them regularly with plain water.

Plant directory

Helichrysum bracteatum nanum

Helichrysum — Asteraceae
Everlasting, paper daisy, strawflower ① ② ③

* Annuals, perennials and evergreen shrubs
* Colourful, papery summer flowers or attractive foliage
* Hardy or half-hardy

Helichrysums are well known for their brightly coloured papery textured flowers, which can easily be dried to give everlasting flowers for arrangements, but there are also valuable foliage types.

The annual *Helichrysum bracteatum* (*Bracteantha bracteata*) bears daisy flowers in a wide range of red, pink, yellow, orange and white shades. Plants can be rather straggly, growing to some 1m (3ft), but dwarf varieties such as the **Bright Bikini** series are suitable for smaller spaces.

H. italicum (*H. angustifolium*) is a low-growing evergreen shrub some 60cm (2ft) or more high, with long, silver leaves. The leaves have a strong, spicy aroma, which is given off not just when they are handled, but when they are in the sun. It is known as the curry plant, and its aroma is not universally popular.

H. petiolare, with its trailing, downy, silver-leaved shoots, is particularly valuable for hanging baskets. '**Variegatum**' has creamy variegated leaves and those of '**Limelight**' are pale yellow. Although this species is moderately hardy, it is usually grown as a bedding plant, since it quickly becomes leggy and untidy.

Cultivation
Helichrysums like a sunny, open position in well-drained soil. The evergreen species need shelter from excessive rain in winter.

Sow *H. bracteatum* where it is to flower, or in pots indoors to be planted out after any likelihood of frost has passed. Propagate *H. petiolare* and *H. italicum* from softwood cuttings in summer, keeping the young plants under cover the following winter, if needed. Prune *H. italicum* fairly hard in spring to prevent plants becoming straggly.

Helichrysums can be attacked by downy mildew, which causes mouldy white patches on the leaves. If the attack is bad, spray with a suitable fungicide.

Helleborus — Ranunculaceae
Hellebore, ② ③

* Herbaceous or evergreen perennials
* Showy flowers in winter and early spring
* Hardy

The lobed leaves of hellebores are often as attractive a feature as their flowers, and in reasonably mild areas the foliage is retained throughout the winter. The plants form hummocks 30–60cm (12–24in) high. The green, white, pink or purple flowers are cup-shaped, often nodding, with prominent golden stamens.

Helleborus argutifolius (*H. corsicus*) has deeply divided, spiny-edged, deep green leaves forming a spreading clump. The green, nodding flowers are carried in clusters in late winter. '**Pacific Mist**' has mottled leaves. *H. foetidus* has divided leaves and elegant panicles of nodding flowers – pale green with red margins – are produced in early spring. The best variety is the **Wester Flisk Group,** with striking red stems, which tolerates the dry ground under trees.

The Christmas rose, *H. niger,* has relatively broad, divided, deep green leaves and nodding, pure white flowers with golden stamens in late winter. '**Potter's Wheel**' has very large, showy flowers.

Slightly later flowering is *H. orientalis,* the lenten rose. Flowers may be cream, pink or purple, often with darker freckling inside the cup.

Cultivation
Light or moderate shade and free-draining but moisture-retentive, humus-rich soil is ideal for hellebores. Once established, they resent disturbance.

Do not let the soil dry out in spring and early summer. Mulch around *H. niger* with straw or chipped bark as the buds develop to prevent the blooms from being splashed with soil.

Faded flowers can be removed, but plants seed themselves freely if allowed. Species and varieties cross-breed readily, giving rise to interesting new hybrids.

Slugs and snails can damage plants in early spring and should be controlled with slug bait or an organic alternative. Black spots on the leaves are caused by fungal leaf spots. Destroy affected leaves and spray the plant with a suitable fungicide.

Hemerocallis — Liliaceae
Day lily ② ③

* Perennial
* Short-lived but plentiful lily-like flowers
* Hardy

The colourful, lily-like blooms of day lilies are carried on tall stems above clumps of arching, grassy foliage. Each flower lasts only a day, but the succession of blooms persists for several weeks in the summer.

Many garden hybrids have been bred, some up to 1m (3ft) or more, but others compact and suitable for small spaces. '**Beauty to Behold**', to 60cm (2ft) has lemon yellow trumpets with a green throat; '**Bertie Ferris**' has orange ruffled flowers 60cm (2ft) tall; and '**Children's Festival**', with ruffled petals in pale peach, grows to 60cm (2ft). '**Little Wine Cup**' has dainty, deep red and gold blooms on compact 45–50-cm (18–20-in) plants.

Cultivation
Grow in sun or light shade and rich, moisture-retentive soil. Don't let the soil dry out in the growing season. Once the plants are established, don't disturb them.

Cut down the flower stems when the flowers have faded. Slugs and snails can be very damaging to the young shoots in early spring, so use slug bait or an organic alternative to control them.

About the plants

Heuchera sanguinea

Heuchera   Saxifragaceae
Coral flower

* Evergreen perennial
* Attractive foliage and summer flowers
* Good groundcover
* Hardy

The round, lobed leaves of heuchera, in green, bronze, purple or silver, form a large, rounded clump. Dainty stems of small, bell-shaped flowers are carried well above the foliage in summer; the flowers may be rich red, pink or white.

Good garden hybrids include 'Firefly' with scarlet flowers; 'Red Spangles', bright crimson; and 'Pearl Drops', white. Bressingham Hybrids include a range of mixed colours. For foliage effect, 'Palace Purple' has deep purple-red leaves against which the small, white flowers are an effective contrast; 'Scintillation' has leaves marbled with silver and bell-shaped flowers tipped with deep pink; and 'Pewter Moon' has silver-veined leaves with red backs and pale pink flowers on a compact plant. The broad leaves of low-growing (30cm/12in) 'Rachel' are purplish and the flowers a soft coral colour.

Cultivation
Heuchera likes well-drained but moisture-retentive soil, preferably containing plenty of well-rotted organic matter, and a position in semi-shade.

If the plants are required for foliage effect alone, flower stems can be removed as they form; cut flowers last well in water.

Plants can be divided in autumn.

Hibiscus   Malvaceae
Hibiscus, mallow

* Evergreen or deciduous shrub
* Large trumpet-shaped flowers in summer
* Hardy or tender

This plant makes a rounded shrub to some 1.5m (5ft) tall. *Hibiscus rosa-sinensis* is a tender species with oval, mid-green leaves with toothed margins and funnel-shaped flowers with prominent anthers. Flowers may be red, pink, orange, white or yellow.

More popular for growing outside in cool climates is the hardy *H. syriacus*, with deep green, lobed leaves and large flowers from late summer into the autumn. 'Blue Bird' has violet-blue flowers with a deeper coloured centre; 'Lady Stanley' is white, semi-double, with a deep red eye; and 'Woodbridge' is rosy pink with a carmine centre. 'Coelistis' has single pale mauve flowers, rose at the base and 'Hamabo' is pale pink with a crimson centre. 'Ardens' has pale, reddish purple flowers.

Cultivation
Grow *H. syriacus* varieties in fertile, humus-rich, well-drained soil and a sunny, sheltered spot. In colder gardens they will benefit from the protection of a wall.

H. rosa-sinensis makes a good patio plant for the summer, but in cool climates must be moved under cover before the first frost, or treated as an annual and replaced.

Water plants in containers regularly; buds and flowers will fall if the roots dry out. Pinch prune young plants in spring. Take softwood cuttings in early summer, or semi-ripe cuttings later in the season.

Aphids and whitefly find hibiscus attractive and should be treated with a suitable insecticide.

Hosta   Hostaceae
Plantain lily

* Herbaceous perennial
* Bold, attractive foliage
* Shade tolerant
* Hardy

Plantain lilies form large clumps of striking leaves, which vary widely in form and size and are often attractively textured or variegated. Stems of pale, delicate, trumpet-shaped flowers in summer can be a bonus.

Many varieties are vigorous, large-leafed, spreading plants, so take care when selecting varieties for small spaces and containers. 'Ginko Craig' has deep green leaves with narrow white margins and grows to 30cm (12in); 'Ground Master' is a little larger, and with a much broader white edge to the leaves. 'Golden Prayers' has textured, yellow-green leaves and 'Golden Tiara' has heart-shaped, deep green leaves edged with lime green. Both reach about 15cm (6in) high. 'Shade Fanfare', growing to 45–60cm (18–24in), is a reliable variety with pale green, cream-edged, heart-shaped leaves and pale lavender flowers in summer.

Cultivation
Hosta thrives in shade and fertile, moisture-retentive soil, which must not be allowed to dry out. Add well-rotted organic matter to the soil before planting. Remove faded flowers and dead foliage at the end of the season. Plants can be divided in spring.

Slugs and snails, which destroy the foliage, are a major problem, but container-grown plants are less likely to be badly damaged by these pests.

Humulus   Cannabidaceae
Hop

* Perennial herbaceous climber
* Attractive lobed leaves
* Hardy

Humulus lupulus is the common hop, whose papery fruit clusters are used to flavour and preserve some types of beer. The plant produces vigorous twining, scrambling stems and has deeply lobed, toothed leaves. The golden-leafed 'Aureus' is most commonly grown in gardens.

Cultivation
Plant humulus in sun or light shade where it can scramble up a support such as a pergola. Free-draining soil is preferred.

Plants can be propagated from softwood cuttings in spring.

Aphids may attack young shoots and can be controlled with a non-persistent insecticide.

Humulus lupulus 'Aureus'

Plant directory

Hyacinthus Liliaceae
Dutch hyacinth ① ② ③

* Bulb
* *Fragrant flower spikes in spring*
* *Hardy*

The densely packed flower spikes of hyacinths are one of the familiar sights of spring. The rounded bulbs produce glossy, mid-green, strap-shaped leaves and, usually, a single, fleshy flower spike packed with many fragrant, open, bell-shaped flowers in a wide range of colours. Hyacinths are ideal for containers or as spring bedding.

The dozens of cultivars in existence arise from *Hyacinthus orientalis*. Reliable garden varieties include '**Amsterdam**', rosy red; '**Anna Marie**', pale pink; '**City of Haarlem**', light yellow; '**Delft Blue**', violet-blue; '**Jan Bos**', red, '**L'Innocence**', white; and '**Ostara**', deep blue.

Multiflora hyacinths have less formal, looser spikes of flowers and produce several spikes to each bulb; they are available in blue, white and pink.

Cultivation
Plant in autumn in well-drained soil, and in an open, sunny or lightly shaded position. Best results are obtained by lifting the bulbs as soon as the foliage has died down, drying them off, storing them over the summer, and replanting them the following autumn.

Overwet soil conditions will cause the bulbs to rot.

Hyacinthus 'Ostara'

Hydrangea Hydrangeaceae
Hydrangea ② ③

* *Deciduous shrubs and climbers*
* *Showy, rounded flowerheads in summer*
* *Hardy or slightly tender*

The most familiar hydrangea is *Hydrangea macrophylla*, a bushy shrub growing to some 1.2m (4ft), with light green, oval, toothed leaves and rounded heads of colourful flowers from mid- to late summer. Florets may be sterile or fertile, the sterile ones being largest and most colourful.

Mophead (hortensia) hydrangeas consist mainly of sterile florets; lacecaps have sterile florets around the outside of the flowerhead and smaller fertile florets in the middle, giving a lacy effect. Flower colour is affected by soil acidity, acid soils giving blue flowers and alkaline soils pink or red; white varieties are unchanged by the type of soil.

Mophead varieties that have good, clear colours in suitable soils include '**Générale Vicomtesse de Vibraye**', rosy pink or light blue; '**Hamburg**', deep pink or deep blue; '**Queen Elizabeth**', rosy pink or mid-blue. '**Ami Pasquier**' is a dwarf variety usually better in alkaline soils, where it has deep crimson flowers. '**Madame Emile Mouillère**' has white flowers, which become tinged pink as they age.

Good lacecaps include '**Blue Wave**', lilac pink or blue; '**Lanarth White**', with white sterile florets and pink or blue fertile florets; and '**Mariesii**', rosy pink or rich blue.

The hybrid *H.* '**Preziosa**' is similar in habit to a mophead, with round heads of deep rosy red flowers and neat foliage tinged with bronze-purple.

H. paniculata grows up to 3m (10ft) tall, and has arching shoots with dense, terminal panicles of white flowers. Those of '**Grandiflora**' are particularly large and turn pink as the flowers age.

The climbing hydrangea *H. anomala petiolaris*, with toothed, pointed leaves and flat, lacy heads of cream flowers in early summer, is a vigorous grower that will quickly cover a shady wall.

Cultivation
Hydrangeas like moisture-retentive soil containing plenty of organic matter, and a sheltered position in sun or light shade.

They make excellent container plants, when they should be watered freely during the growing season. For blue flowers, use ericaceous (lime-free) compost and apply aluminium sulphate.

Prune *H. macrophylla* back to fat buds in early spring, or after flowering in mild climates. *H. paniculata* should be cut back to within 5cm (2in) or so of the previous year's growth in early spring.

Plants may be propagated from softwood cuttings in early summer.

Hypericum Clusiaceae
St John's wort ③

* *Perennials and deciduous or evergreen sub-shrubs and shrubs*
* *Colourful summer flowers*
* *Some varieties suitable for groundcover*
* *Hardy or half-hardy*

The bright golden, cup-shaped flowers of St John's wort, with their prominent stamens, are an attractive sight in summer. Leaves are oval, mid- to deep green. Plants vary from prostrate creepers to upright shrubs, suitable for rock gardens, borders or banks.

The evergreen or semi-evergreen rose of Sharon, *Hypericum calycinum*, makes a spreading shrub some 30cm (12in) tall, which is spangled with large, golden flowers during summer and well into autumn. It is excellent for poor, dry soils and makes good groundcover, but it can be invasive, so take care to plant it where it can be contained.

H. '**Hidcote**' flowers profusely from midsummer to autumn, and forms a compact, semi-evergreen shrub about 1.2m (4ft) tall. The saucer-shaped flowers are larger than those of most hypericums. *H.* x *inodorum* '**Elstead**', with deep green leaves and little starry yellow flowers with long stamens, is slightly smaller. The flowers are followed by attractive salmon pink berries.

Cultivation
Any reasonably fertile, free-draining soil is suitable, preferably in an open, sunny spot.

Cut upright shrubs back by about one-third in spring. *H. calycinum* usually benefits from harder pruning and should be

About the plants

cut to within a few centimetres of the base. Plants can be propagated from softwood cuttings in summer.

Hypericums, particularly *H.* x *inodorum* 'Elstead' are prone to attack by rust disease; use fungicide sprays as a preventive.

Ilex   Aquifoliaceae
Holly   ② ③

* *Evergreen or deciduous shrub or tree*
* *Attractive berries in autumn and winter*
* *Hardy*

Hollies are generally grown for their colourful red (occasionally yellow) fruits, but many cultivars are worth growing for their attractive foliage alone. There are separate male and female plants, so if berries are required a female plant must be obtained and a male plant grown nearby to pollinate it. Do not be misled by the variety names – King or Queen in the name does not necessarily indicate the expected sex.

Ilex x *altaclerensis* is a vigorous hybrid, growing to more than 6m (20ft) where space allows; the dark green, glossy leaves are often almost spineless. '**Belgica Aurea**' has lightly spined, dark green and grey mottled leaves with a creamy yellow margin. Although it is a female, berries are not freely produced. '**Camelliifolia**' is upright, with purple-black stems, deep green, glossy, virtually spineless leaves and a good crop of large red berries. Despite its name, '**Golden King**' is a female, but berries are sparse. The large leaves have a few spines, and are glossy green with a broad yellow margin.

I. aquifolium, the common holly, has deep, green, wavy-edged leaves armed with sharp spines. '**Ferox**', the hedgehog holly, has prickles over the whole leaf surface as well as at the margins; '**Ferox Argentea**' has silver-edged leaves. Both plants are male and relatively slow growing.

'**J. C. van Tol**' or '**Pyramidalis**' are the varieties to grow if you have room for only one plant – they are self-pollinating, and produce reliable crops of bright red berries when grown alone. '**Silver Queen**' (a male) is a dense, fairly compact shrub with dark shoots and cream-edged leaves; young leaves are pink.

Cultivation
Hollies will grow in almost any soil, but prefer one that is well drained. Grow variegated types in full sun for the best leaf colour; green varieties will do well in shade.

Holly makes a good specimen plant in a tub, and can be clipped to shape in summer. Cut out plain green shoots on variegated types as soon as they are seen. Propagate plants from semi-ripe cuttings in summer.

Impatiens, New Guinea hybrid

Impatiens   Balsaminaceae
Busy lizzie   ① ② ③

* *Annual or perennial grown as annual*
* *Profuse summer flowers in a wide colour range*
* *Half-hardy*

These plants, growing to 15–45cm (6–18in) are popular for summer bedding and excellent in containers. They have succulent stems and soft, pointed leaves which may be coloured. The flowers are spurred, with open, flat faces in white, red, pink, lilac and salmon shades; the petals may be marked with white to give a star effect.

Most bedding impatiens are hybrids. Popular varieties are the **Accent Series**, in mixtures or single colours, including stars; the **Deco Series**, with bronzy leaves; the **Super Elfin Series**, compact plants in a good colour range; and the **Spectra Series**, a New Guinea impatiens with extra-large flowers and bronze or variegated foliage. '**Double Rosette Mixed**' has double or semi-double flowers like tiny rosebuds.

Cultivation
Busy lizzies grow well in sun or light shade, and in moist, fertile, but free-draining soil. Plant them out after the risk of frost has passed, and keep them well watered during summer, but never waterlogged. Liquid-feed with a high-potash fertiliser every 14–21 days.

Particularly good plants may be potted up and overwintered under cover. Cut them back hard in early spring to promote new growth for use as softwood cuttings. Plants may also be raised from seed.

Control aphids with a non-persistent contact insecticide. Slugs and snails can also be a problem when young plants are growing Use slug bait or an organic alternative.

Ipomoea   Convolvulaceae
Morning glory   ① ② ③

* *Perennial climber usually grown as an annual*
* *Showy, funnel-shaped summer flowers*
* *Half-hardy or tender*

The twining stems of morning glory will quickly trail from a hanging basket or cover a pillar. Most of these plants are short-lived perennials which are most satisfactory when grown as annuals. The leaves are heart shaped, and from midsummer to early autumn a succession of funnel-shaped flowers unfurl. These open out in the morning and fold up in the afternoon.

The most popular variety is *Ipomoea. (Convolvulus) tricolor* '**Heavenly Blue**', with abundant, sky-blue, white-throated flowers for a long season. It rapidly reaches 3m (10ft) or so. *I. nil* '**Early Call Mixed**' with heart-shaped or lobed leaves and flowers in scarlet, deep red, salmon, pink and white, flowers earlier than *I. tricolor*.

Cultivation
Free-draining, fertile soil containing plenty of well-rotted organic matter is required. Grow in a sheltered position in full sun. Provide a support for the stems to twine around, or let them trail from a basket or container. Don't let the soil dry out.

Raise plants from seed sown in spring.
Control aphids with a contact, non-persistent insecticide where necessary.

Ipmoea tricolor '**Heavenly Blue**'

Plant directory

Iris danfordiae

Iris Iridaceae
Iris ① ② ③

* *Rhizomes or bulbs*
* *Distinctive flowers in spring and summer*
* *Hardy*

Irises can be divided into the rhizomatous border types, which flower mainly in early summer, and bulbous varieties, which include the Reticulata group of dwarf irises. Rhizomatous irises have stiff, sword-shaped leaves and tall stems of flowers with three large, downward-curving petals, known as falls, and three smaller, upright ones, known as standards. Some have bristly beards of coloured hairs in the centre of the falls.

Among rhizomatous irises growing to 30–45cm (12–18in) are 'Banbury Ruffles', deep blue with ruffled petals, 'Eyebright', yellow flowers with purple-brown markings and 'Green Spot', which is creamy white with green markings.

Bulbous irises include the Dutch, Spanish and English irises, which grow to about 1m (3ft) and flower in succession from spring to late summer in a wide range of colours.

Particularly suitable for small spaces are Reticulata irises, no more than 20cm (8in) tall. *Iris danfordiae* produces lightly fragrant, bright yellow flowers in late winter or early spring, when the narrow leaves are only just appearing.

I. histrioides, with blue flowers marked with darker blue, white and yellow on the falls, flowers even earlier. 'Major' is a strong, deep blue.

The flowers of *I. reticulata* come a little later; they are fragrant, with a deep purple hue and yellow markings on the falls. 'Cantab' has light blue flowers and 'J. S. Dijt' is purple-red.

Other Reticulata hybrids include 'Joyce', blue with white and yellow markings; 'Harmony', pale blue with white and yellow markings; and 'Katharine Hodgkin', whose flowers are delicately marked with yellow, pale blue feathering and deeper violet-blue spots and streaks on the falls.

Cultivation
Rhizomatous irises like free-draining but moisture-retentive, fertile soil and an open, sunny position. Plant with the tops of the rhizomes just showing. Increase plants by dividing the rhizomes after flowering.

Bulbous and dwarf irises are ideal for shallow pans and containers, or the rock garden. They like light, free-draining soil, and tolerate chalk. Plant the bulbs in autumn; they can be lifted and divided after the foliage has died down.

Slugs and snails may attack the young foliage; use slug bait or an organic alternative if necessary.

Jasminum Oleaceae
Jasmine ② ③

* *Deciduous or semi-evergreen shrubs and climbers*
* *Starry flowers at various seasons, often scented*
* *Hardy or slightly tender*

Jasmines are scrambling twiners or wall-shrubs with delicate, trumpet-shaped flowers; many species are tender and are grown as houseplants in colder climates. Of the hardy species, two are especially popular.

Jasminum nudiflorum (winter-flowering jasmine) is a lax, arching, deciduous shrub best grown against a wall; it will need tying in to a support to keep it neat. The bright green, leafless stems carry starry yellow, unscented flowers throughout winter and early spring, even in severe weather.

The common jasmine, *J. officinale*, is a summer-flowering climber. The leaves are mid-green, divided into leaflets, and are semi-evergreen in mild locations. White, very sweetly scented flowers are carried in clusters throughout the summer.

Jasminum nudiflorum

Cultivation
Grow jasmine in free-draining soil in a sunny position. *J. officinale* needs a sheltered spot, but *J. nudiflorum* is hardier.

After flowering has finished, cut back the flowered shoots of *J. nudiflorum* almost to the base and trim back outwards-facing shoots. Thin out *J. officinale* after flowering as required.

Propagate by semi-ripe cuttings in summer.

Juniperus Cupressaceae
Juniper ① ② ③

* *Evergreen conifer*
* *Handsome foliage and architectural shapes*
* *Hardy*

Junipers are versatile plants suitable for a wide range of different situations. Although they can make tall forest trees, there are many dwarf and slow-growing forms suitable for small spaces. Some species are narrow and columnar, others wide-spreading and prostrate; foliage may be green, blue, silver or gold. Instead of cones, they carry round berries with a distinctive aroma, which are used for flavouring gin.

One of the most popular of all dwarf conifers, *Juniperus communis* 'Compressa' forms a neat column about 75cm (30in) tall. It is widely used in rock gardens and among heathers. On a larger scale, *J. scopulorum* 'Skyrocket' is exceptionally narrow and upright, with bluish foliage. Although it can eventually reach 6m (20ft), it is very slow growing and will remain suitable for a small space for many years.

J. virginiana is another slow-growing species, more or less conical in shape; 'Grey Owl' has silver-grey foliage and forms a spreading, low-growing specimen up to 3m (10ft) tall.

Among prostrate and spreading forms, *J. squamata* 'Blue Carpet' makes a low, silver-blue mat about 30cm (12in) high. *J. s.* 'Blue Star', which forms a low, rounded bush to 50cm (20in), has attractive, steely blue leaves, and *J. s.* 'Holger' is a low shrub to 1m (3ft), with silvery foliage which has creamy yellow tips when young.

Cultivation
Most well-drained soils are suitable. A position in full sun is preferred, particularly for the forms with coloured leaves, but junipers will tolerate shade well.

Prune out damaged branches in late spring.

Plants may be increased from semi-ripe heel cuttings in late summer.

About the plants

Kniphofia 'Little Elf'

Kniphofia   Liliaceae
Red hot poker, torch lily ③

* Herbaceous or evergreen perennial
* Bright, poker-like flowers in summer
* Hardy

Red hot pokers make a mound of grassy foliage from which arise tall flowering stems bearing dense spikes of overlapping, tubular flowers. Orange-red is the main colour, but yellow and cream varieties exist.

Most garden plants are hybrids growing to around 1m (3ft). 'Goldelse' flowers in early summer, with slender pale yellow spikes; 'Bees' Lemon' is taller, with rich yellow flowers in mid- to late summer; 'Little Maid', with creamy yellow flowers, grows to 60cm (2ft); and 'Samuel's Sensation' has tall scarlet flower spikes in mid- to late summer.

Cultivation
Light, free-draining soil is essential; grow red hot pokers in full sun. Do not let the soil dry out during the growing season.

Cut down faded flower stems and tidy the leaves in late autumn. Do not remove all the dead leaves, since they help to protect the crowns against excessive winter rain.

Laburnum   Leguminosae
Golden chain ③

* Deciduous tree
* Abundant flowers in spring and early summer
* All parts poisonous, especially the seeds
* Hardy

The pendent racemes of golden, pea-like flowers make golden chain a beautiful specimen in late spring and early summer. It forms a spreading tree up to 6m (20ft) tall, but is usually about half that height in gardens. Leaves consist of three light green leaflets with silky hairs on the undersides.

Most common is *Laburnum anagyroides*, which carries dense flower clusters in late spring. A golden-leafed form, 'Aureum', is prone to revert to plain green. 'Erect' has more upright branches, making it a good choice for small spaces. A weeping variety, 'Pendulum', is often grafted on to a stock to make a small, graceful tree.

The Scotch laburnum, *L. alpinum*, has slightly larger leaves and longer racemes of flowers than *L. anagyroides*, and flowers a few weeks later. *L. x watereri* is a hybrid between *L. anagyroides* and *L. alpinum*; 'Vossii' is the most popular variety, with very long racemes of flowers, freely carried.

Cultivation
Laburnums grow well in any soil except heavy, poorly drained types. The trees prefer full sun, but will tolerate light shade.

Pruning is not normally required, but where children may have access to the tree, the seed pods should be removed and destroyed safely as soon as they begin to form; fallen pods should be gathered up.

The species can be raised from seed sown in autumn; propagation of named varieties is not practical for small-space gardeners.

Lamium   Labiatae
Deadnettle ② ③

* Herbaceous or semi-evergreen perennial
* Attractive foliage
* Useful groundcover
* Hardy

Deadnettles are easily grown plants which tolerate poor soils and growing conditions. While they provide excellent groundcover, they can also become troublesome weeds if care is not taken to curb their spread.

The mid-green leaves are oval, with toothed edges, but most cultivated varieties have coloured or variegated foliage. Flowers are hooded and carried in whorls up the square stems in early summer. They may be purple-pink or yellow, but are usually of secondary interest to the foliage.

Lamium galeobdolon 'Variegatum' ('Florentinum') grows to 23cm (9in); the leaves are attractively silvered, with green veins, and yellow, rather straggly flowers appear in summer. This is an invasive plant which is suitable only for containers in small garden areas.

L. maculatum can also be invasive. Its leaves have a broad central stripe or splash of silver, and the flowers are deep purplish pink. 'Beacon Silver' has silver, heavily veined foliage with green margins and mauve-pink flowers; 'Pink Pewter' and 'White Nancy' have similar foliage and soft pink and white flowers respectively.

Cultivation
Deadnettles will grow in any well-drained soil and are good for poor, dry, sandy sites. They tolerate shade well.

When the plants are being grown for their foliage effect, the flowers can be cut off as they form. Divide plants in autumn or spring, or increase them by softwood cuttings in early summer.

Lathyrus   Leguminosae
Sweet pea ① ② ③

* Annual or perennial climbers or bedding plants
* Usually fragrant, colourful summer flowers
* Hardy or half-hardy

The annual climbing sweet pea, *Lathyrus odoratus*, with its tendril-tipped leaflets, is well loved for its large pea-type flowers in a wide range of colours and fancy forms. Many varieties have a strong, sweet scent, but some modern varieties, grown specifically for flower size, form and colour, have lost their fragrance.

A number of low-growing, bushy, non-climbing varieties have been bred and are particularly suitable for confined spaces and containers. They include varieties such as 'Knee Hi', 'Bijou', 'Snoopea' and 'Patio Mixed'. There are hundreds of climbing varieties in red, pink, salmon, cream, white, lilac and purple, as well as bicolours. Perennial species include *L. grandiflorus*, climbing to around 1.5m (5ft), with pink and purple-red flowers, and *L. latifolius*, a vigorous climber that reaches 2m (6ft) or more, with deep rosy pink flowers.

Cultivation
Sweet peas need well-drained but moisture-retentive soil with plenty of well-rotted organic matter. Give plenty of water while the buds are forming, and a high-potash liquid fertiliser every 10 days from the time flowering starts. Provide supports in the form of netting or wigwams of canes to which plants can cling.

Remove faded flowers regularly for a long flowering season. Cut down perennials almost to soil level in autumn.

Sow seed in early spring and in autumn, too, in mild climates; soaking the seed overnight or nicking the seed coat carefully with a sharp knife will speed germination, which can otherwise be slow.

Plant directory

Laurus Lauraceae
Sweet bay ② ③

* *Evergreen tree*
* *Aromatic deep green foliage*
* *Suitable for growing as a standard*
* *Hardy or slightly tender*

The bay tree, *Laurus nobilis*, has a long history of cultivation. The strongly aromatic leaves are lanceolate and glossy deep green; the tree grows to some 9m (30ft) or more where space allows, but can be kept neat and compact by pruning. It is popular as a clipped specimen in tubs.

In spring, clusters of fluffy, greenish yellow flowers wreathe the branches; they are most conspicuous on clipped plants in containers. The leaves can be used in cooking and form part of a classic *bouquet garni*. Tear the edges of the fresh leaf to bring out the flavour.

Cultivation
Well-drained, reasonably fertile soil is required. Even where plants are hardy, the foliage is damaged by cold winds and prolonged frosts, so a sheltered spot is necessary. Keep the soil moist but never waterlogged during the growing season.

Clip plants to shape in summer, and propagate by semi-ripe cuttings. Rub out any shoots growing from the stems of standards as soon as they are noticed.

Brown leaves with curled edges may be caused by cold winds or hard frosts; trim off affected shoots and move plants to a more protected position.

Scale insects are a common problem; inspect the reverse of the foliage frequently and scrape off any scales that are found there. Bad infestations usually need treating with white oil or a systemic insecticide; don't use the leaves of treated plants in cooking until the safe interval indicated on the packaging has elapsed. Black, sooty deposits on the foliage are caused by sooty mould, which forms on the secretions of scale insects; the mould can usually be wiped off, but you must deal with the scale insects to prevent the problem recurring.

Lavandula angustifolia 'Hidcote'

Lavandula Labiatae
Lavender ② ③

* *Evergreen shrub*
* *Fragrant summer flowers*
* *Aromatic grey foliage*
* *Hardy or slightly tender*

Lavender is well known for its strongly scented, lavender-blue, tubular flowers, which are carried in dense spikes on stiff stems. It is a valuable decorative shrub, with silver-grey foliage, sometimes divided, which is also aromatic when lightly crushed. Flowers dry well, retaining their strong scent. For the best results, pick them when they are in bud, just before they open.

Old English lavender is *Lavandula angustifolia*, but hybrids are most frequently available. 'Hidcote' is a reliable, compact variety with grey-green leaves and dense spikes of purple-blue flowers; it grows to 75cm (30in) and flowers in midsummer. Another compact grower is 'Munstead', with narrow leaves and intense blue flowers from mid- to late summer. 'Twickel Purple' has broader leaves and long flower spikes. For a change of colour, there are 'Loddon Pink', with early, pale pink flowers, and the white-flowered, dwarf 'Nana Alba' which grows to about 30cm (1ft).

French lavender, *L. stoechas*, is a small, early flowering, dense shrub with purple flowers, each spike being topped by a tuft of long-lasting, rosy purple bracts. These are particularly prominent on the butterfly lavender, *L. stoechas pedunculata*.

Cultivation
These Mediterranean natives like fertile, free-draining soil and a warm, open, sunny position.

Deadhead plants after flowering, and trim them lightly with secateurs to maintain a neat appearance. In spring, carry out further trimming to encourage bushy growth and prevent plants becoming leggy; plants often look bedraggled after a cold winter and will benefit from being cut back quite hard.

Propagate by taking semi-ripe cuttings in summer.

Leucojum Amaryllidaceae
Snowflake ① ② ③

* *Bulb*
* *Pendent white flowers in spring or autumn*
* *Hardy*

The flowers of snowflake bear a slight resemblance to those of snowdrops: they are pendent, bell shaped, and white with green markings on the petals. The spring snowflake, *Leucojum vernum*, grows to 15–20cm (6–8in) and flowers in late winter and early spring. The summer snowflake (*L. aestivum*) is confusingly named, since it flowers from early to late spring. The nodding heads of white and green blooms are carried on stems up to 1m (3ft) tall, amid clumps of spear-shaped, dark green foliage.

Much less common is the autumn snowflake, *L. autumnale*. Growing to around 15cm (6in), it has very fine, grassy leaves and slender, wiry stems bearing a dozen or more delicate, bell-shaped, white-flushed-pink flowers in early autumn.

Cultivation
Plant the bulbs in autumn. The spring and summer snowflakes both thrive in moisture-retentive soil in dappled shade; autumn snowflake prefers free-draining soil and full sun. Keep spring and summer snowflakes moist throughout the growing season. Divide the clumps after flowering.

Lewisia Portulacaceae
Lewisia ① ② ③

* *Herbaceous or evergreen perennial*
* *Showy flowers in late spring and early summer*
* *Ideal for rock gardens and walls*
* *Hardy*

Lewisias form rosettes of fleshy, mid-green, oblong leaves and produce a profusion of flowering stems carrying open-faced flowers. Colours range from pink, rose and salmon to yellow, orange, red, purple and white. Some species are rather difficult and need specialised conditions in an alpine house, but many of the hybrid strains are easy to grow in a rock garden or in containers.

The evergreen **Cotyledon Hybrids** are the most popular; there are various reliable selections, including the **Ashwood Strain** and the **Sunset Strain**.

Cultivation
Lewisias need moisture-retentive but free-draining, lime-free soil and sun or semi-shade. Mulch around the neck of the plants with chippings or small gravel to

About the plants

ensure good drainage around the crowns. They are often best planted on a slope or sideways in a rock crevice to ensure that water drains away from the centre of the rosettes. Excess moisture, especially in winter, causes the crowns to rot. Shallow pans, or stone or clay troughs, make suitable containers; lewisias do not usually do well in plastic pots.

The plants produce offsets which can be detached in summer and rooted in sandy compost. They can also be raised from seed sown in spring.

Slugs and snails may damage the foliage; use slug bait or an organic alternative.

Lilium   Liliaceae
Lily   ② ③

* *Bulb*
* *Fragrant summer flowers*
* *Hardy or half-hardy*

Many species and varieties of the stately lily are grown. The unusual bulbs consist of overlapping, fleshy scales with no tunic (papery covering), and are prone to damage and drying out before planting. Each bulb produces a single stem with lanceolate leaves, often in whorls, along almost its entire length. The flowers are carried in groups at the top of the stem, and are generally large and trumpet shaped, with six petals and prominent stamens. They may be white, pink, orange or yellow, sometimes striped or freckled, and are usually fragrant. In some species, the tips of the petals curl back to form a Turk's-cap shape.

Almost all lilies make excellent container plants. *Lilium auratum*, the golden-rayed lily of Japan, grows to 1.5m (5ft) and has wide, open flowers up to 25cm (10in) across. They are white, with a central golden band on each petal and a heavy sprinkling of purple-brown spots. This lily requires lime-free soil and is often short-lived. The Madonna lily, *L. candidum*, has pure white, funnel-shaped, strongly fragrant flowers on 1.2-m (4-ft) stems. It is good for containers, but likes a little lime added to the compost.

L. regale is easier to grow; the trumpet-shaped flowers are white, flushed gold in the throat, and with purple backs to the petals. Another popular white lily is *L. longiflorum*, the Easter lily (Christmas lily in the Southern Hemisphere), growing up to 1m (3ft), with strongly fragrant blooms. Flowers of the tiger lily, *L. lancifolium* (*L. tigrinum*), have strongly recurving petals giving a Turk's-cap effect. They are a glowing orange, freckled with purple spots.

There are many hybrid varieties. Well-established, reliable cultivars include: '**Enchantment**', orange, funnel-shaped

Lilium auratum

flowers with black speckled throats; '**Connecticut King**', star-like blooms with rich yellow petals ; '**Star Gazer**', rosy red with narrow white margins and darker spots in the throat; and '**Shuksan**', small, pendent, Turk's-cap flowers, orange-yellow petals spotted with brown.

Cultivation
Plant lilies in autumn in free-draining, fertile soil. Most like an open, sunny position, but with cool, moist roots. In containers, water sparingly until growth appears, then water more freely to keep the compost moist but never waterlogged. Liquid feed with a high-potash fertiliser every 10 days in the growing season.

Bulbs can be propagated from bulb scales or, in some species, from bulbils, which appear in the leaf axils.

Aphids and the larvae of lily beetle may attack the plants and should be controlled with insecticide. Slugs and snails can also cause damage. Wet soil conditions can lead to rotting of the bulbs.

Lithodora   Boraginaceae
Lithodora   ① ② ③

* *Evergreen sub-shrub*
* *Prostrate or trailing*
* *Showy, early summer flowers*
* *Hardy*

The most popular species is *Lithodora diffusa*, which is often known as *Lithospermum diffusum*. It forms a low mat of narrow, evergreen leaves; the stems trail over rocks and walls and in early summer bear clusters of intense blue, funnel-shaped flowers, which often cause the plant to be mistaken for a gentian. '**Heavenly Blue**' is a common variety; '**Grace Ward**' has slightly larger flowers.

Cultivation
L. diffusa requires ericaceous (lime-free) soil, which must be moisture retentive but well drained. Grow in full sun. Lithodora is excellent for rock gardens, and does well in containers and at the edge of raised beds. Trim the plants after flowering, and take semi-ripe cuttings in summer.

Lobelia   Campanulaceae
Lobelia   ① ② ③

* *Annual or herbaceous perennial*
* *Freely produced flowers in summer*
* *Trailing varieties ideal for hanging baskets*
* *Hardy or half-hardy*

Lobelia is an indispensible basket and container plant, flowering continually from spring and all through summer. The plants grown are usually hybrids of *Lobelia erinus*, a half-hardy perennial grown as an annual. Leaves are small, oval or lanceolate, mid-green or bronze, and flowers are small, lipped and, typically, blue. Plants grow to about 15cm (6in) high; some have a trailing habit, others are more upright and bushy.

Among trailing types are '**Sapphire**', deep blue with a white eye; **Cascade Series** in red, blue and white; and '**Regatta Blue Splash**', white flowers with light blue markings. Bedding lobelias include '**Cambridge Blue**', pale blue flowers; '**Crystal Palace**', deep blue flowers and bronzy foliage; and '**Rosamund**', rosy red with a white eye.

Slightly less well known is the perennial border lobelia, *L. cardinalis*. It grows to 75cm (30in), with mid-green or deep bronze-red, lanceolate leaves and brilliant scarlet, lobed flowers in midsummer.

Cultivation
Moisture-retentive soil and a sheltered position in full sun or semi-shade suit bedding lobelias best, but they will grow almost anywhere. Water regularly and liquid-feed with high-potash fertiliser every 7–10 days. Grow bedding lobelias from seed sown in spring (autumn in mild areas).

L. cardinalis likes fertile, moist soil. In cold areas, protect the roots with a heavy mulch of chipped bark, straw or similar material. This plant will also grow in shallow water at the edge of a pond. It can be raised from seed, or divided in spring.

Lobelia '**Rosamund**'

Plant directory

Lonicera Caprifoliaceae
Honeysuckle ② ③

* *Deciduous or evergreen climbers and shrubs*
* *Sweet-scented, tubular flowers at various seasons*
* *Hardy*

Although the climbing species are the best-known members of the family, there are several attractive shrubby honeysuckles, too. The flowers are long and tubular, with prominent stamens; they are mainly yellow or cream, sometimes flushed with red or purple. Most have a strong fragrance.

Climbing plants produce strong, twining, woody stems. *Lonicera periclymenum*, the common honeysuckle, is a vigorous scrambler, with creamy yellow, red-flushed flowers in summer. It has given rise to two popular deciduous varieties: 'Belgica' (early Dutch honeysuckle) which has yellow and red flowers in early summer, and 'Serotina' (late Dutch honeysuckle), which flowers from late summer into autumn with blooms that are deep red outside and white within.

L. japonica is evergreen or semi-evergreen, with oval, light green leaves and small, creamy white, fragrant flowers in summer and early autumn. 'Aureoreticulata' has leaves marked with an attractive network of gold, but it is less likely to hold on to its leaves during cold winters.

Of the non-climbing species, the winter-flowering honeysuckles are, perhaps, the most valuable. *L. fragrantissima* and *L. standishii* are similar. Both grow to around 2m (6ft), but *L. standishii* tends to be narrower; it is also more likely to be evergreen. Both bear creamy white, fragrant flowers from midwinter to early spring.

Cultivation
Grow honeysuckles in ordinary, free-draining soil that has had some well-rotted organic matter added. The climbers like a cool, moist root run and will grow well in sun or semi-shade. Provide some support for young stems; they will soon twine over posts, pergolas, sheds, arches and so on.

When climbers have finished flowering, prune out some or all of the flowering stems. Prune scrubby species to shape in mid-spring. Propagate plants by semi-ripe cuttings in summer.

Lysimachia Primulaceae
Loosestrife, creeping Jenny, moneywort ① ② ③

* *Herbaceous or evergreen perennial*
* *Attractive foliage and flowers*
* *Hardy*

Lysimachia nummularia 'Aurea'

The most useful loosestrife for small garden spaces and containers is the prostrate, spreading creeping Jenny, *Lysimachia nummularia*. The small, round, fresh green leaves are carried in pairs on long, trailing stems, and cheerful, bright yellow buttercup-type flowers appear in summer. The plant is easy to grow in most situations, and can be invasive. Golden-leafed 'Aurea' is slightly more restrained than the species, and is much more commonly grown.

Cultivation
This plant prefers, cool, moist, fertile soil, but adapts well to dry conditions. It can be grown in sun or shade and will thrive on a bank or tumbling over the top of a wall, but take care to plant it only where its spread can be restricted. It makes an excellent hanging basket plant, and should be watered freely when grown in containers. Plants are easily propagated by softwood cuttings in late spring and summer.

Magnolia Magnoliaceae
Magnolia ② ③

* *Deciduous or evergreen trees or shrubs*
* *Showy flowers, usually in spring*
* *Hardy or slightly tender*

Magnolias make stately, noble plants, often with spectacular, large, waxy blooms. Some species are fussy about soil and situation, and may take many years to flower; several make large trees that demand a large space.

But two in particular are good for small areas. *Magnolia liliiflora* makes a rounded bush up to 3m (10ft) high, with broad, oval, glossy green, deciduous leaves. From mid- to late spring into summer, it carries large, erect, chalice-shaped flowers, which are rosy purple on the outside and creamy white inside, and have a delicate perfume. 'Nigra', with deep wine-red flowers, is popular.

M. stellata, the star magnolia, is a wide, spreading shrub some 2m (6ft) high. In mid-spring it bears a profusion of starry,

Magnolia stellata

fragrant flowers with narrow white petals, which appear before the mid-green, lanceolate leaves. 'Waterlily' has larger flowers with more petals; 'Dawn', 'Rosea' and 'Rubra' have flowers tinged with varying degrees of pink.

Hybrids between *M. liliiflora* and *M. stellata* have been produced; they have a long flowering season and produce abundant, narrow-petalled flowers with strong, purple-pink colouring. 'Susan' is the most commonly available.

Cultivation
Magnolias require lime-free, fertile, free-draining but moisture-retentive soil, which should be enriched with plenty of well-rotted organic matter before planting. They will not grow well in light, dry soils. Keep the roots moist throughout the growing season, and mulch each autumn.

Plants can be propagated by semi-ripe cuttings in summer, or by layering.

Flowers may be damaged by frost, which causes the petals to turn brown.

Mahonia Berberidaceae
Mahonia, Oregon grape ③

* *Evergreen shrub*
* *Handsome foliage and architectural form*
* *Scented winter flowers followed by blue berries*
* *Hardy*

The leathery, glossy, dark green leaves of mahonia are composed of a number of leaflets with spiny tips, shaped rather like holly leaves. Small, bell-shaped, yellow flowers are borne from autumn to spring in dense clusters, or in drooping or upright racemes; they have a strong, sweet scent.

The Oregon grape, *Mahonia aquifolium*, grows to 1–2m (3–6ft) tall and blooms in early spring, producing large numbers of conical flower clusters. These are followed by blue-black berries in grape-like clusters. 'Apollo' is a vigorous, dense-growing form, and 'Atropurpurea' has foliage which is burnished purple-red in winter.

M. 'Heterophylla' is a small shrub growing to 1m (3ft) or so, with narrow, glossy green leaves composed of wavy-edged leaflets that turn reddish purple in winter. In spring, small clusters of yellow flowers are carried at the tips of the shoots.

M. japonica carries its flowers in long, slightly drooping racemes throughout the winter. Its growth is stiffly upright to about 2m (6ft). Plants of the Bealei Group (sometimes listed as *M. bealei*) have shorter, more upright racemes of flowers.

The vigorous hybrid *M. x media* grows to about 1.2m (4ft), with leaves in tiers, which gives it a strong, architectural shape. 'Charity' has shuttlecocks of flowers in long, spreading racemes at the tips of the stems in early winter; these are fragrant but less strongly scented than in some other species.

Cultivation
Grow mahonias in a lightly shaded spot in fertile, moisture-retentive soil. If necessary, prune to shape in mid-spring; *M. aquifolium* responds well to being cut back hard every few years. Propagate by semi-ripe cuttings in summer.

Powdery mildew can sometimes cause white, powdery patches on the foliage; spray affected plants with a suitable fungicide.

Malus Rosaceae
Crab apple

* *Deciduous tree*
* *Spring blossom and autumn fruits*
* *Hardy*

Crab apples are good-value trees for small gardens; they provide interest in spring, when the cup-shaped, apple blossom flowers appear, and again in autumn and into the winter, with their small, colourful fruits. The fruits are edible and can be used for making crab-apple jelly; if they are left on the tree they often attract wild birds. Many varieties of crab apple have the added bonus of attractive autumn foliage.

Of the species commonly grown, *Malus floribunda* makes a spreading tree up to 5m (15ft). In spring, it bears a profusion of blossom. The flowers are deep pink in bud, opening to pinkish white, and are followed by berry-like yellow fruits. *M. sargentii* is a small, shrubby, spreading tree, up to about 3m (9ft) tall. In mid-spring the branches are covered with white flowers, which are followed by long-lasting, bright red fruits. The leaves are sometimes three lobed.

M. tschonoskii has a narrowly conical habit; although it may ultimately reach more than 10m (30ft), it remains suitable for a small space for several years. Flowers are white, tinged with pink, and are sometimes followed by small green and red fruits; in autumn, the leaves take on shades of yellow, red, orange and purple.

Among the best named varieties are 'Golden Hornet', with white flowers followed by yellow fruit like large cherries; and 'John Downie', white flowers followed by relatively large yellow fruits, flushed red, and excellent for culinary use. 'Profusion' (*M. x moerlandsii* 'Profusion') lives up to its name, with many deep purple-pink single flowers in spring, coppery purple young foliage and small red fruits. 'Van Eseltine' is a compact, columnar tree, with semi-double pink flowers and round yellow fruits.

Cultivation
Crab apples thrive on nearly all soils except badly drained clays. Don't let the roots dry out while trees are flowering. Prune trees to shape when they are dormant, cutting out weak, damaged or crossing branches.

Crab apples are prone to the same diseases that affect ordinary apples, including scab and fireblight. Scab can be controlled by a preventive fungicide spraying programme; fireblight is difficult to control, but affected branches should be cut out well beyond the damaged area and burned if possible.

Aphids and caterpillars can be dealt with by spraying with a non-persistent pesticide.

Monarda Labiatae
Bergamot

* *Herbaceous perennial*
* *Aromatic foliage and summer flowers*
* *Hardy*

The oval, light green, hairy leaves of bergamot with their strong citrus scent are valuable in perfumery and for potpourri; an infusion of the leaves is known as Oswego tea. The plant forms a rounded mound up to 1m (3ft) high, and bears tiers of shaggy-headed flowers in pink or red in summer. The blooms are attractive to bees.

Monarda didyma 'Croftway Pink' has soft pink flowers; those of 'Cambridge Scarlet' are an intense, brilliant red.

Cultivation
Bergamot likes a fertile, moisture-retentive soil and an open, sunny position, although it will tolerate light shade. Plants can be invasive, so choose their position carefully. Cut down stems in autumn and mulch the roots with well-rotted compost or other organic matter.

Myosotis Boraginaceae
Forget-me-not

* *Annuals and short-lived perennials, usually grown as biennials*
* *Small, usually blue flowers in spring*
* *Hardy*

The small, bright blue, white-eyed flowers of forget-me-nots are carried in loose sprays in mid- to late spring. They are often teamed with tulips. Plants have pale green, lance-shaped leaves and branch freely.

Myosotis alpestris, the alpine forget-me-not, growing to 15cm (6in) high or less, is a short-lived perennial very much at home in a rock garden. The clusters of bright blue flowers with yellow eyes are borne just above the mound of hairy leaves in late spring and early summer.

This species is thought to be a parent of many of the hybrid varieties grown from seed as spring bedding, and treated as biennials. 'Blue Ball' is compact and bushy, reaching about 20cm (8in), with deep blue flowers; 'Rosylva' is a pale lilac-pink forming a neat mound about 15cm (6in) high; 'Royal Blue' is early and free flowering, and taller, at about 30cm (12in).

M. sylvatica reaches about the same height and makes vigorous, branching growth. The deep blue flowers are larger than those in other species.

Cultivation
Forget-me-nots are usually easy to grow and are not fussy about soil or position. They do best in free-draining but moisture-retentive soil in sun or semi-shade.

Sow seeds in summer and overwinter plants in their flowering positions, or buy in plants for bedding out in spring. Pull them up as soon as the flowers are past their best. If powdery mildew is a problem, use a suitable fungicide.

Monarda didyma

Plant directory

Narcissus Amaryllidaceae
Daffodil   ① ② ③

* Bulb
* Spring flowers in a range of forms
* Hardy

Narcissus is probably the most popular of all spring bulbs, and hundreds of cultivars exist. These cover an enormous variety of sizes and flower forms in a colour range of white, cream, yellow and orange.

The most familiar flower form is the trumpet daffodil, with six pointed, flat petals and a central trumpet at least as long as the petals. Among the rest of the 12 official divisions of the genus are large- and small-cupped varieties, which have a short central cup instead of a trumpet; double and semi-double varieties; and split-cupped types, often having flat, orchid-like blooms.

There are also several divisions of dwarf narcissus, which are particularly attractive for small gardens and containers, where they can be appreciated at close quarters. *Narcissus bulbocodium*, the hoop petticoat daffodil, grows to around 15cm (6in), with narrow, rush-like leaves. The 2.5-cm (1-in) long flower cup is cone shaped, with prominent curving stamens; the slender petals behind it are insignificant. Colours range from pale lemon to deep yellow.

The flowers appear in late winter and early spring, as do those of *N. cyclamineus*. This species has golden-yellow flowers with large trumpets around 5cm (2in) long and petals swept sharply back like those of a cylamen flower.

N. triandrus (angel's tears), with nodding, cream flowers which have cupped centres and reflexing petals, is very dainty; it grows to around 15cm (6in).

Among the named varieties, '**February Gold**' (all yellow); '**February Silver**' (yellow trumpet and white petals); '**Tête-à-Tête**' (yellow with deeper trumpet, several flowers per stem); and '**Dove Wings**' (cream petals and pale yellow cups), all growing to about 30cm (12in) high, have a typical trumpet daffodil shape in miniature. '**Hawera**' is a *triandrus* type with pale yellow, nodding flowers, while '**Minnow**' has clusters of four rounded flowers per stem, with cream petals and a yellow cup; these grow to 20cm (8in).

'**Pipit**', a jonquil with several flowers on a stem, usually reaches 10–15cm (4–6in), and has small-cupped flowers, whose pale yellow cups and petal centres turn white as they age. The 15-cm (6-in) '**Rip van Winkle**' is entirely different, with star-like, shaggy double flowerheads of lemon yellow.

Cultivation
Virtually all divisions and sizes of *Narcissus* make excellent container plants, or can be grown in beds or naturalised in turf. Small varieties are excellent for rock gardens. They like fertile, well-drained, moisture-retentive soil and a spot in sun or partial shade.

Plant the bulbs in autumn; in borders they may be left in place to flower for several years or they may be lifted annually and replanted. Plant to twice the depth of the bulb. Water container-grown plants regularly, and feed all bulbs with a high-potash fertiliser once or twice between flowering and the leaves dying down.

Cut down faded flowers before they set seed. If possible, allow the foliage to die down naturally, leaving it until at least six weeks from the time the flowers begin to fade in order to build up the bulbs for flowering the following year.

Increase plants by bulb offsets.

Narcissus fly larvae destroy the bulbs below ground; draw soil up round the necks of the growing bulbs in early summer to help prevent the fly laying its eggs. Failure to flower may be caused by overcrowding and poor soil fertility, bulbs planted too shallowly, or leaves being prematurely removed the preceding year.

Nicotiana Solanaceae
Ornamental tobacco   ① ② ③

* Annuals or perennials usually grown as annuals
* Scented summer flowers
* Hardy or half-hardy

Set ornamental tobacco where its sweet fragrance can be appreciated in the evening, when it is most intense. Plants may be tall and stately with white, trumpet-shaped flowers, or short and compact with flowers in a wide colour range. Nearly all are scented, but some of the more compact and colourful bedding varieties have lost some of their fragrance. Some species have flowers which open only in the evening, but modern hybrids have been bred to produce flowers that remain open all day long.

Among popular types are the **Domino Series**, growing to around 30cm (12in) high, which are available in red, green, pink, salmon, purple, and white, with some bicolours; and the **Nicki Series**, growing to 40cm (16in) with flowers in a similar colour range. The **Sensation Series** is taller, at up to 1m (3ft). Particularly suitable for containers is the compact **Starship Series** in burgundy, lime green, pink, red, rose and white.

Cultivation
Full sun and reasonably fertile, free-draining soil are required. Deadhead plants to encourage a long flowering season. Raise plants from seed sown in spring.

Aphids can be a nuisance, particularly on young plants; spray with a non-persistent insecticide where necessary.

Oenothera Onagraceae
Evening primrose   ② ③

* Annuals, biennials and perennials
* Summer flowers
* Hardy or slightly tender

The open, funnel-shaped, yellow flowers of evening primrose are short lived, but they are produced in profusion for a long period in summer. They tend to open only in the late afternoon and evening. Leaves are mid-green and lance shaped. Oil from the seeds is well known for its pharmaceutical use.

Oenothera fruticosa (*O. tetragona*) '**Fireworks**' forms a spreading clump some 40cm (16in) tall. Spikes of lightly fragrant, cup-shaped, glossy yellow flowers are carried from midsummer; buds and stems are tinged red.

O. macrocarpa (*O. missouriensis*) has open, lemon-yellow flowers, sometimes marked with red on the outside of the petals. The buds open in the evening, but

Narcissus 'Tête-à-Tête'

About the plants

the flowers last for several days; the seed pods are also decorative. Stems are lax and sprawling, and the plants generally reach only 10cm (4in) tall.

O. speciosa has white flowers which turn pink as they age; **'Pink Petticoats'** is pale pink with white and gold centres. The flowers are strongly scented, especially in the evening. The plant reaches 45cm (18in), and makes good groundcover, but it can be invasive. All three species are perennial.

Cultivation
Oenothera demands light, free-draining soil and full sun. Do not let the roots dry out once the buds have started to form. Cut the stems down to soil level in autumn.

Although perennial, the plants are often short lived; take softwood cuttings in early summer to guard against losses. Plants can also be divided in autumn, and they may be raised from seed sown in spring.

Ophiopogon Liliaceae
Lilyturf

* Evergreen perennial
* Showy foliage
* Hardy or slightly tender

Lilyturf is a grass-like plant with long, narrow, arching leaves. The white lilyturf is *Ophiopogon jaburan;* the variety **'Vittatus'** (also known as **'Variegatus'**) has green and white striped leaves, but is rather tender. Small, round, white flowers are carried in short spikes. More popular is *O. planiscapus* **'Nigrescens'**, with deep purple, almost black foliage in arching clumps. Lilac and white flowers are followed by purple-black fruits. This plant makes a particularly effective contrast with grey or silver-leafed subjects.

Cultivation
Grow lilyturf in sun or light shade, in fertile, free-draining soil containing plenty of organic matter. Choose a sheltered position; *O. j.* **'Vittatus'** particularly may be killed by cold winters, so move it under cover or mulch it for winter protection. Propagate plants by division in spring.

Osteospermum Asteraceae
Osteospermum

* Evergreen perennial
* Showy, daisy-like flowers in summer
* Hardy or half-hardy

Osteospermum is related to and sometimes confused with *Dimorphotheca*. The plants grow to 30–60cm (12–24in) high, have

Osteospermum 'Whirligig'

lance-shaped, grey-green leaves and daisy-like flowers in profusion in summer.

Many named plants have been raised. **'Buttermilk'** has creamy yellow flowers with purple-brown eyes; **'Cannington Roy'** has pink flowers on prostrate stems. **'Whirligig'** has petals that are crimped in the centre and open out to a spoon shape at the tips; flowers are white, tinged blue, with blue centres, and have a dazzling effect. **'Pink Whirls'** has lilac spoon petals. **'Silver Sparkler'** has white and blue flowers, and cream-variegated foliage.

O. jucundum (*Dimorphotheca barbersae*), with rosy pink flowers in summer, some of which have deeper coloured eyes, forms neat clumps up to 30cm (12in) high.

Cultivation
Osteospermums require a mild climate and a sheltered, sunny position. Soil must be well drained; very fertile soils will promote leaf production at the expense of flowers.

Propagate plants by softwood cuttings in early summer, using non-flowering shoots.

Paeonia Paeoniaceae
Peony

* Herbaceous perennial or deciduous shrub
* Large, fragrant early summer flowers
* Handsome foliage
* Hardy

Peonies produce some of the finest, most striking flowers of early summer. The blooms may be single, semi- or fully double, or anemone-flowered, where the centre is filled with fluffy, stamen-like petaloids. Herbaceous varieties are most popular; their burgundy-red shoots are among the earliest border plants to put in an appearance in spring. Most varieties grow to about 1m (3ft) and are derived from *Paeonia lactiflora*.

The fully double, strongly scented **'Duchesse de Nemours'** is one of the oldest named varieties but still one of the best whites. **'Dayspring'** is a compact variety growing to 75cm (30in); it has pale pink, single flowers and a good perfume. The reliable **'Sarah Bernhardt'** has large, globe-shaped, double flowers of a clear silvery pink. **'Kelway's Glorious'** has huge, mounded, double white flowers, sometimes tinted pink or red, with a strong perfume. **'Bowl of Beauty'** is a favourite anemone-flowered type, with rich pink petals and creamy white petaloids. **'Kelway's Majestic'** has rosy-red petals and lilac-pink petaloids with silver and gold highlights.

Tree peonies are deciduous shrubs and include *P. delavayi*, an upright plant to 2m (6ft), with deeply divided, rich green leaves and red, semi-double flowers with gold stamens, and varieties of *P. suffruticosa*. These usually grow to about 1.2m (4ft) and carry cup-shaped, single or semi-double flowers in late spring and early summer. They have a silky texture and fine perfume.

Many Japanese and Chinese varieties are listed, with suitably romantic names. **'Kaow'** (king of flowers) has large, semi-double, crimson flowers with gold stamens; **'Gessekai'** (kingdom of the moon), also called **'Hakuojisi'**, has huge white flowers with crimped petals, and **'Hana-kisoi'** (floral rivalry) cherry pink flowers and a strong perfume. Chinese varieties include **'Da jen fen'** (gold-dusted pink) and **'Fen dang bai'** (white phoenix).

'Souvenir de Maxime Cornu' is a large shrub, notable for its unusually coloured, peachy yellow, fully double flowers, each ruffled petal margined with red.

Cultivation
Herbaceous peonies like fertile, well-drained but moisture-retentive soil, in sun or partial shade. Shade them from early morning sun, which may damage the flowers after a cold night. Because they start into growth so early, a sheltered position helps to protect the new shoots. Tree peonies are more difficult to grow, and need more protection.

Plant the top of peony crowns no more than 5cm (2in) below the soil surface; plants will fail to flower if set too deeply. Peonies should not be disturbed once planted; they generally take a season or two to begin flowering, but once established are undemanding.

Deadhead the plants, and cut down the foliage of herbaceous types in autumn.

Paeonia suffruticosa

Plant directory

Parrotia persica

Parrotia   Hamamelidaceae
Iron tree, Persian ironwood   ③

* *Deciduous tree*
* *Good autumn colour*
* *Hardy*

There is only one species of iron tree grown, *Parotia persica*. While this can reach 8m (25ft) tall, in gardens it generally forms a spreading shrub or small tree. It has attractive flaking, grey bark, but it is for its brilliant red and gold autumn leaves that it is chiefly grown. The weeping variety '**Pendula**' is slow growing and forms a mound up to 2m (6ft) high.

Cultivation
Unlike most other members of the Hamamelidaceae family, iron tree tolerates alkaline soils well. It requires a fertile, free-draining but moisture-retentive soil and a position in full sun. Take softwood cuttings in summer.

Parthenocissus   Vitacaeae
Virginia creeper, Boston ivy   ② ③

* *Deciduous climber*
* *Spectacular autumn colour*
* *Hardy*

A strong-growing, self-clinging climber, Virginia creeper attaches itself to its support with sticky-tipped tendrils. Some species are rampant growers which need to be kept in check.

The true Virginia creeper is *Parthenocissus quinquefolia*. The leaves consist of five (sometimes three) oval leaflets with toothed margins; mid-green in summer, they turn spectacular shades of red and orange in autumn. The plant often incorrectly known as Virginia creeper is *P. tricuspidata* (Boston ivy). This usually has entire, three-lobed leaves, although they may be divided into leaflets on young plants. It, too, has excellent autumn colour; the foliage of '**Veitchii**' becomes a deep purple.

One of the best-value species for smaller areas is *P. henryana*. It is a vigorous grower, but not as rampant as Boston ivy or Virginia creeper. The leaves, with three or five lobes, are dark purplish green with beautiful silver veins, making them attractive throughout spring and summer as well as when they turn red in autumn.

Cultivation
Virginia creeper grows well against walls and fences, or up trees, pillars and pergolas in shade or semi-shade. Free-draining soil is required. *P. henryana* needs a sheltered position, but the attractive variegation tends to disappear in a sunny site. Provide support for the young shoots until the plants get established and start to cling on their own.

Prune plants in summer to keep their growth under control.

Parthenocissus can be propagated by softwood cuttings in early summer.

Passiflora   Passifloraceae
Passion flower   ② ③

* *Evergreen or semi-evergreen climber*
* *Spectacular summer flowers*
* *Hardy or half-hardy*

Most of the passion flower family are tender climbers that need warm, frost-free conditions, although one species, *Passiflora caerulea*, is unreliably hardy. It has mid- to dark green, lobed leaves on scrambling woody stems, which climb by means of tendrils. In summer, large, complex flowers are carried, which have white, petal-like sepals and a corona of slender filaments banded deep purple, white and blue. The stamens and stigmas are prominent.

The plant derives its common name from the flowers which some regard as a symbol of Christ's Passion: the sepals represent the 10 apostles (minus Peter and Judas); the five anthers the five wounds; the stigmas the nails; and the corona the crown of thorns. The leaves represent the hands of the persecutors, and the tendrils, whips and scourges.

Passiflora caerulea

In warm, sunny conditions, egg-shaped yellow fruits follow the flowers; they are attractive but of no value for eating. The variety '**Constance Elliott**' has large, pure white flowers. There are other warm climate passion flowers, including the edible one.

Cultivation
Plant passion flowers in free-draining but fertile and moisture-retentive soil, and provide a trellis or similar support for the tendrils to twine around. Water regularly during the spring and summer. In cold areas, provide winter protection for young plants; once established, *P. caerulea* is reasonably frost hardy.

Prune out frost-damaged growth in spring. Thin out and tip back branches to keep plants tidy. Propagate by semi-ripe cuttings in summer or from seed in spring.

Pelargonium   Geraniaceae
Geranium   ① ② ③

* *Evergreen perennial, often grown as an annual in cold climates*
* *Colourful summer and autumn flowers*
* *Aromatic foliage*
* *Half-hardy or tender*

Geraniums are among the most popular summer-flowering plants, ideal for growing in containers. There are hundreds of cultivars, split into several groups: Regals, with oval, toothed, rough-textured leaves and relatively large, more or less trumpet-shaped flowers; Zonals, with leaves marked by a distinct dark band, and uneven, five-petalled flowers; Ivy-leafed, with flowers like those of zonals but rather succulent leaves and trailing stems; and Scented-leafed, with notably aromatic foliage in a diverse range of forms and colours.

Pelargonium 'Ringo Scarlet'

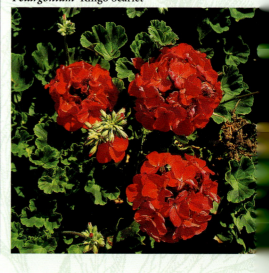

About the plants

In cool climates, Regal and Scented-leafed pelargoniums are grown more as houseplants than in gardens; Zonals and Ivy-leafed plants are popular for outdoor use.

Zonals generally grow to about 30–60cm (12–24in), though they can become taller; miniature varieties are under 30cm (12in). Flowers are carried in rounded heads on tall stems; they may be single, semi-double or double, in many shades of white, red, pink, salmon, orange and purple. Some varieties have flowers that fall readily (shatter) when the stems are knocked.

Reliable varieties include **'Apple Blossom Rosebud'**, with tightly packed, double, pink and white flowers; **'Mr Henry Cox'**, with red, green and yellow foliage and pink flowers; **'Dolly Varden'**, with scarlet flowers, maroon and green leaves edged white; and **'Irene'**, deep crimson-pink, semi-double flowers. Plants which can be raised from seed include the **Elite Series**, **Century Series**, **Multibloom Series** and **Video Series**.

Ivy-leafed varieties have less spectacular heads of flowers but are excellent trailing plants for baskets and containers. They are derived from *Pelargonium peltatum*. **'Rouletta'** has semi-double, striking red and white flowers; **'L'Élégante'** has pale lilac flowers and mid-green foliage with creamy white margins which turn pink in cool conditions; **'Evka'** flowers early, with scarlet blooms and variegated foliage. **'Summer Showers'** is one of the few ivy-leafed types that can be raised from seed.

Cultivation
Easy to grow in a wide range of conditions, but free-draining soil and an open, sunny position are preferred. Keep the plants moist at all times once the buds start to form, but do not overwater. Feed fortnightly with a high-potash liquid fertiliser.

Deadhead regularly to ensure a succession of blooms. At the end of the season, plants can be overwintered in pots under cover in cold climates. Prune in autumn (cold climates) or early spring, taking cuttings from the new growths that arise. Sow seed of suitable varieties under cover in early spring. Rust can be a troublesome fungus disease; pick off and burn affected leaves and spray plants with a suitable fungicide.

Penstemon Scrophulariaceae
Penstemon ②③

* *Semi-evergreen perennial*
* *Long season of summer flowers*
* *Hardy or slightly tender*

The elegant spikes of penstemon flowers resemble those of foxgloves. The blooms are trumpet shaped, in shades of pink, red,

Petunia 'Pampas Blue'

purple and white, sometimes with throats of a contrasting colour; they are carried from midsummer into the autumn. Leaves are lanceolate, mid- to light green, and the plants are evergreen in suitable conditions. They usually grow to some 60cm (2ft) tall.

Many named varieties exist. **'Andenken an Friedrich Hahn'**, commonly known as **'Garnet'**, has wine-red flowers. **'Apple Blossom'** is very pale pink, with a deeper pink margin to the petals; **'Mother of Pearl'** is lilac-shaded white, with purple speckling in the throat. **'Sour Grapes'** has flowers of a deep wine-purple, while **'Pershore Pink Necklace'** has large, rosy pink flowers with white throats with a deeper pink necklace.

Cultivation
A sunny position in moisture-retentive but well-drained soil suits penstemons. In cold areas, mulch the crowns in winter; plants tend to be short slived.

Cut down faded flower stems. Take softwood cuttings from non-flowering shoots in summer.

Petunia Solanaceae
Petunia ①②③

* *Perennial grown as an annual*
* *Fragrant, showy summer flowers*
* *Half-hardy*

Petunias have large, funnel-shaped flowers, usually strongly honey scented, which are carried on bushy or trailing plants through the summer. They are excellent for containers, including hanging baskets. Leaves are oval, mid-green and slightly sticky to the touch; stems are lax, growing 15–30cm (6–12in) tall. The flowers may be double or single, in shades of blue, pink, red, lavender, purple, yellow and white, including bicolours; star types have a bold white stripe down the centre of each petal.

The large flowers of **Grandiflora** petunias are prone to weather damage; **Multifloras** have smaller but more rain-resistant blooms. Of the many varieties available, good grandiflora selections include the **Express Series**, including 'Express Star'; the **Duo Series**, with double flowers; the **Ice Series**, with white margins to the petals; and the **Daddy Series**, with heavily veined single flowers. **'Prism Sunshine'** is a non-fading yellow, with deep yellow centres and creamy coloured margins.

Multiflora types include the **Frenzy** and **Primetime Series**, and the relatively new milliflora **Fantasy Series**, which produces compact, free-flowering plants with small, neat flowers in a wide range of colours.

Cultivation
Petunias are best grown in reasonably sheltered, sunny positions where the flowers will not be damaged by wind. They prefer free-draining soil. Water regularly and liquid feed with a high-potash fertiliser every 10–14 days. Deadhead plants frequently to prolong the flowering season.

Grow from seed sown under cover in early spring, or buy young bedding plants.

Petunias can be affected by various viral diseases, for which there is no cure; these are spread by aphids, so control aphid infestations promptly, using a non-persistent insecticide where necessary.

Plant directory

Philadelphus 'Belle Etoile'

Philadelphus   Hydrangeaceae
Mock orange   ③

* Deciduous shrub
* Fragrant spring to summer flowers
* Hardy

An easy-to-please plant, philadelphus makes an arching shrub up to some 2m (6ft) tall. The leaves are ovate, fresh green and deeply veined and the white, usually four-petalled, flowers have a central boss of golden stamens and are strongly scented. They are carried from spring or in early summer.

Philadelphus coronarius is a dense shrub with creamy white flowers; 'Aureus' has golden foliage which fades to pale green as it ages; 'Belle Etoile' is a compact plant, whose creamy white flowers are stained red at the base of the petals; 'Beauclerk' is similar, but the flowers are a little larger and whiter. The vigorous, prolific flowering 'Virginal' has semi-double or fully double blooms.

Cultivation
Philadelphus likes free-draining soil and full sun or partial shade; 'Aureus' retains the golden colour of its leaves best in a lightly shaded position.

Prune out some of the older branches after flowering, retaining strong new shoots which will start flowering the following year. Increase plants by softwood cuttings in early summer, or semi-ripe cuttings later in the season.

Aphids often infest the young shoots in spring; use a non-persistent contact insecticide to control them.

Phormium   Agavaceae
New Zealand flax   ③

* Evergreen perennial
* Striking, sword-shaped leaves
* Hardy or half-hardy

Phormiums are good 'architectural' plants, with their bold clumps of sharply pointed, strap-shaped leaves. They are reasonably hardy, but may be killed by prolonged cold spells. Their tall panicles of summer flowers are of secondary interest to the leaves.

The two species grown are *Phormium cookianum* and *P. tenax*: there are also several hybrids between these two species. *P. cookianum* is a smaller, more compact plant, growing to around 1.2m (4ft) with a spread of 30cm (1ft). *P. c.* 'Tricolor' has mid-green leaves edged with cream and red. *P. tenax* reaches 2–3m (6–9ft), and has stiff, leathery foliage, broader than that of *P. cookianum*. *P. t.* 'Purpureum' has bronzy purple leaves.

'Dazzler' has striking, purple and pink striped leaves, while 'Yellow Wave' has slightly drooping leaves striped with green and yellow. There are several variegated 'Maori' varieties, including 'Maori Chief' (scarlet, crimson and bronze), 'Maori Maiden' (bronzy-green and red) and 'Maori Sunrise' (pink edged with bronze).

Cultivation
Plant phormiums in fertile, moisture-retentive but free-draining soil in a sunny, position, sheltered from extreme cold. A covering of straw or similar material will protect the crowns from severe frost.

Plants can be divided in spring.

Phyllitis   Aspleniaceae
Hart's tongue fern   ② ③

* Evergreen or semi-evergreen fern
* Bright green fronds
* Hardy

Phyllitis scolopendrium, the hart's tongue fern, is also known as *Asplenium scolopendrium*. The shiny, bright green fronds are entire and strap shaped, with undulating margins; the plant grows to about 40cm (16in). There are several types with more strongly waved, crisped or frilled leaf margins, usually listed as Crispum, Cristatum, Marginatum and Undulatum Groups.

Easy to grow outdoors in warm climates are *A. australasicum*, *A. aethiopicum* and *A. bulbiferum*, known as mother spleenwort or hen and chickens fern.

Cultivation
A. scolopendrium grows well in a moisture-retentive alkaline soil which contains plenty of humus; peat can be added to light soils. Grow in a shady spot and keep the plants well watered throughout the growing season. Remove faded foliage regularly.

Divide established plants in spring.

Picea   Pinaceae
Spruce   ② ③

* Evergreen conifer
* Attractive foliage and tree shapes
* Hardy

While many species of spruce make large forest trees, there are also several excellent dwarf and slow-growing varieties, ranging from compact little buns to medium-sized shrubs. The branches are carried in whorls, with slender, needle-like leaves and pendulous cones.

Picea abies, the Norway spruce, has given rise to several good dwarf cultivars. 'Little Gem', which grows to about 45cm (18in) after many years, makes a small, dense, flat-topped globe suitable for a rock garden. 'Ohlendorffii' is rounded when young, extending slightly to become more conical as it grows. Eventually it may reach about 1.5m (5ft) The spreading 'Pumila' has branches in distinct layers, making a flat-topped bush no more than 60cm (2ft) tall, but up to twice that in width.

P. glauca makes a neat, conical conifer with blue-green leaves; one of the best-loved varieties is *P. g. albertiana* 'Conica', a dense, cone-shaped tree with small, soft needles of bright green. After many years' growth it may grow as tall as 2m (6ft). The variety 'Alberta Blue' has silver-blue foliage at its most intense in late spring and early summer.

Cultivation
Spruces like moist, fertile, preferably acid soil; they do not thrive on very alkaline soils. Grow them in sun or partial shade in a sheltered position.

Picea glauca albertiana 'Conica'

208

About the plants

Young shoots may be damaged by frosts; prune out the dead portions, retaining the tree's shape as far as possible, and provide protection or move the plant to a more sheltered position.

In hot, dry conditions, red spider mite can be troublesome. Spray plants regularly with plain water to increase humidity, and use a suitable insecticide when necessary.

Pieris   Ericaceae
Pieris   ② ③

* *Evergreen shrub*
* *Colourful young foliage and spring flowers*
* *Hardy or slightly tender*

Like most of the Ericaceae, pieris requires lime-free soil; in chalky areas, it can be grown successfully in a tub filled with ericaceous compost. The plants are very striking, making more or less rounded, compact shrubs with lanceolate or oblong leaves that are often brightly coloured when they are young. Panicles of waxy, white, pitcher-shaped flowers may be produced in profusion in late spring and early summer.

Pieris '**Bert Chandler**' has leaves which develop from bright salmon pink through cream and white to dark green as the season progresses; the best colours are produced on plants in an open, sunny position. This variety is grown solely for its foliage, as flowers are rarely produced. It is a compact plant, growing to about 1.5m (5ft).

The popular *P. floribunda* '**Forest Flame**' is larger, reaching 3m (9ft) or more, which makes it less suitable for small spaces. The foliage colours are similar to those of '**Bert Chandler**', but '**Forest Flame**' does have the advantage of bearing more large, spreading sprays of flowers.

P. formosa has also produced some good garden varieties, but again most of these are tall and vigorous.

Varieties of *P. japonica* are a better bet; these make dense, rounded, medium-sized shrubs with young leaves of a coppery shade becoming glossy green. '**Christmas Cheer**' has pink flowers, fading to white and is an early bloomer; '**Debutante**' is a low-growing, compact form with white flowers in upright panicles; '**Dorothy Wyckoff**' is an upright bush with small, white flowers, and '**Grayswood**' bears drooping heads of white flowers on a small, compact shrub.

'**Little Heath**' is a dwarf variety with very small, glossy leaves variegated silver and flushed pink when young; '**Little Heath Green**' is similar, but without the variegation.

Cultivation
Give pieris the same treatment as rhododendrons. They like rich, acid, moisture-retentive soil, preferably with added peat, and a sheltered position in light shade. Do not allow the roots to dry out during the summer.

Deadhead the plants when the flowers fade, and prune back frost-damaged young shoots in early spring. Take semi-ripe cuttings in summer.

Pinus   Pinaceae
Pine   ② ③

* *Evergreen conifer*
* *Attractive foliage and tree forms*
* *Hardy*

The pines range from dwarf, rock garden forms to tall trees, and often make attractively weatherbeaten shapes. The needle-like leaves are carried in bundles of two, three or five.

Pinus mugo, the mountain pine, has given rise to several dwarf varieties: '**Gnom**' grows slowly to 2m (6ft), forming a dense, deep green globe; '**Mops**' is a similar shape but not so tall, at around 1m (3ft); '**Humpy**' is perhaps the most dwarf form, slowly reaching 30cm (1ft); '**Ophir**' makes a spreading, rounded shrub some 60cm (2ft) high, with bright golden winter foliage which turns yellow-green in summer.

There are also some good dwarf forms of the Scots pine, *P. sylvestris*. '**Beuvronensis**' forms a domed shrub up to 1m (3ft); '**Watereri**' is larger, growing slowly to 2m (6ft) or more, although remaining small and compact for several years.

Cultivation
Pines generally grow well on light, rather poor soils. Acid soil is preferred, but some species tolerate chalk. Choose an open, sunny position.

Propagation is not practical for the small-space gardener.

Pinus mugo '**Mops**'

Potentilla fruticosa '**Elizabeth**'

Potentilla   Rosaceae
Cinquefoil   ② ③

* *Herbaceous perennial or deciduous shrub*
* *Summer flowers in a range of colours*
* *Hardy*

Potentillas have foliage and flowers rather similar to those of strawberry plants. The palmate leaves are covered with silvery hairs, and the flowers are open and cup shaped, with conspicuous stamens.

The herbaceous perennial types grown in gardens are usually hybrids derived mainly from *Potentilla atrosanguinea*. '**Gibson's Scarlet**' has bright red flowers; '**Gloire de Nancy**' has large, semi-double, orange-red flowers; and '**William Rollison**', semi-double, orange flowers with yellow centres. They all grow to 30–45cm (12–18in) high and flower from early or midsummer onwards.

Shrubby potentillas have deeply cut leaves and grow to around 1.2m (4ft), depending on variety. Most are varieties of *P. fruticosa*, which has bright yellow flowers like buttercups, but new varieties have flowers in a much wider range of colours, including red, pink, orange and white; however, these shades tend to fade in hot sun. '**Goldfinger**' has large yellow flowers; '**Maanelys**' ('**Moonlight**') has pale yellow petals that are lighter below. '**Princess**' has pale pink flowers, fading to white in hot, dry weather. The semi-double flowers of '**Snowbird**' are white; '**Sunset**' has deep orange blooms.

Cultivation
Potentillas need light, free-draining soil and an open, sunny position or partial shade.

The branches of shrubby species can be pruned back by one-third in spring to keep them compact.

Perennials can be divided in spring or autumn, and shrubs can be increased from softwood cuttings in early summer.

Plant directory

Primula Primulaceae
Primrose

* *Herbaceous perennial*
* *Showy flowers in spring and summer*
* *Hardy*

The primula family is wide and diverse, with plants suitable for many situations. Most are easy to grow and are suitable for containers, rock gardens, raised beds and borders. Some like the damp soil beside water features.

Primula auricula has rosettes of pale grey-green leaves which are often covered with a white meal (known as farina). The flat-faced, often strikingly coloured, flowers are carried in umbels on 23-cm (9-in) stems in spring; they have a sweet, honey scent. Some of the most spectacular are the so-called show auriculas, with flowers that have a brilliant white centre and petals of various colours with green, white or grey edges. These are good for containers where the flowers can be admired at close quarters, but they need to be protected from rain, which will spoil them. Other auriculas are less fussy and grow well on rock gardens or in containers in the open.

The drumstick primrose, *P. denticulata*, has globular heads of flowers on 30-cm (12-in) stems, in shades of rose, pink, lilac and mauve. *P. pulverulenta*, known as the candelabra primula because of the way its whorls of flowers are carried in tiers on the stems, grows to 60cm (2ft) and has flowers in shades of pink, red or orange-red. The flowers of *P. vialii*, carried in erect spikes; open from the bottom of the spike and are pale lilac, while the buds are red.

Among the most familiar primulas is the primrose, *P. vulgaris*, whose short-stalked, pale yellow flowers, nestling in their rosettes of crinkled leaves, are one of the first signs of spring. The cowslip, *P. veris*, has taller (20-cm/8-in) stems topped with clusters of tubular, yellow, fragrant flowers. Cross-breeding between these two species has given rise to the polyanthus, with large, primrose-type flowers carried in clusters on stout stems. There are many named selections of seed-raised polyanthus available, also primrose varieties with large, colourful flowers similar to polyanthus but carried singly on the stems; both types are valuable for bedding and for containers. Flowers are available in red, yellow, white, purple, orange and pink, usually with a pronounced yellow eye.

Among other good hybrid primulas are **'Guinevere'** ('Garryard Guinevere'), with pale purple-pink flowers and bronzy purple rosettes of foliage; **'Wanda'**, with early, purple-red flowers with a small, or no, eye; and the **Gold-laced Group**, where each brick red petal is margined and bisected with a fine gold line, making the five petals appear like ten.

Cultivation
Primulas like fertile, moisture-retentive soil and an open, sunny or lightly shaded position. Plants can be divided after flowering, or raised from seed.

If aphids are troublesome, treat them with a non-persistent insecticide. Plants are subject to various viral diseases which cause stunting and distortion of growth; there is no treatment, and affected plants must be destroyed. Controlling aphids will help to prevent the spread of viruses.

Prunus Rosaceae
Flowering cherry, cherry laurel

* *Deciduous or evergreen shrub or tree*
* *Spring blossom or handsome foliage*
* *Hardy*

The prunus family is large and includes plums, peaches, almonds, apricots and laurel, as well as cherry – but it is perhaps the flowering cherry that is most widely grown and admired. The plants vary in size size from medium shrubs to large trees; the foliage of deciduous types is generally lanceolate and light green, sometimes colouring attractively in autumn.

Among the flowering cherries are **'Amanogawa'**, a popular, narrow, columnar tree with bronzy leaves and soft pink flowers, growing up to 7m (23ft) and **'Cheal's Weeping'** (sometimes listed as **'Kiku-shidare-zakura'**), with arching branches and deep pink, double flowers, to 5m (16ft). *P. incisa* **'Kojo-no-mai'** is a dwarf Fuji cherry, growing to 1.5m (5ft), with pink flowers fading to white and good autumn foliage. **'Spire'** (*P. x hillieri* **'Spire'**), a narrow, vase-shaped tree, grows to 8m (26ft), with pale pink flowers and attractive autumn colour; and *P. subhirtella* **'Autumnalis'**, a winter-flowering cherry, with semi-double, pale pink flowers sporadically throughout the winter months, reaches 7m (23ft) or so.

The evergreen *P. laurocerasus* (cherry laurel) is a bushy shrub to 4.5m (15ft); it has glossy, oblong leaves and long racemes of small white flowers followed by cherry-like fruits ripening to black. **'Otto Luyken'** is a low-growing, compact form to around 1m (3ft) high, but spreading more widely: it has upright spikes of flowers in spring.

P. lusitanica (Portugal laurel) is similar to *P. laurocerasus* but is hardier and easier to grow on poor soils. **'Variegata'** has leaves narrowly margined with white and is slower growing than the species.

Cultivation
Grow prunus in an open, sunny position in free-draining, reasonably fertile soil; *P. laurocerasus* and *P. lusitanica* are shade tolerant.

Evergreens can be pruned hard in spring to keep them compact and shapely. Flowering cherries do not normally require any pruning. Evergreens can be increased by semi-ripe cuttings in summer; flowering cherries are usually grafted and it is not practical for the small-scale gardener to try to propagate them.

Caterpillars and aphids can be a problem on young growth and should be treated with a suitable insecticide. Flowering cherries are sometimes attacked by the bacterial disease fireblight; affected branches should be cut out and destroyed.

Pyracantha Rosaceae
Firethorn

* *Evergreen shrub*
* *Summer flowers and autumn and winter berries*
* *Hardy*

Firethorns are among the most valued garden shrubs, having such a long and varied season of interest. In early summer, small, creamy white flowers with prominent stamens are clustered thickly on the spiny branches among fresh green, oblong leaves. These are followed by long-lasting clusters of red, orange or yellow berries.

Firethorn can be grown as a free-standing shrub, when it may reach 3m (10ft) or so, although its prickly growth is generally too vigorous for small spaces. It is easier to keep

Pyracantha 'Mohave'

210

under control when trained as a wall shrub, and this is the way it is most often grown.

Pyracantha angustifolia has narrow, oblong leaves, which are dark green above and felted grey beneath; the berries are bright orange-yellow and last well into the winter.

'**Golden Dome**' is a smaller, spreading, arching shrub, very dense in habit, with plentiful orange-yellow berries.

The berries of '**Navaho**' are later than some others to ripen; they are carried in dense clusters, are slightly flattened and turn from orange to deep orange-red.

The compact and bushy hybrid *P. x watereri* grows to around 2m (6ft) and is free flowering and fruiting, with bright red berries.

Cultivation
Pyracantha will grow in most reasonably fertile, free-draining soils, in sun or partial shade. Make sure that the soil is kept moist at flowering time to encourage the berries to set.

Provide a trellis or similar support for wall shrubs, and train in young shoots as they grow.

Prune back wall-trained shrubs after flowering, cutting outwards-growing shoots right back to the main stem; free-standing plants can also be clipped at this time.

The plants can be propagated from semi-ripe cuttings in summer.

Firethorns are prone to several diseases, including fireblight and scab. Scab attacks in wet summers and can be treated with a suitable fungicide; fireblight cannot be chemically controlled and affected branches must be pruned out and destroyed.

Some varieties, such as '**Lalandei**', are particularly susceptible to disease; more modern varieties are claimed to be disease resistant, but opinion is often divided as to how resistant they really are.

Pyrus Rosaceae
Ornamental pear ③

* *Deciduous tree*
* *Attractive foliage and tree shape*
* *Hardy*

The only common ornamental species is *Pyrus salicifolia*, the willow-leafed pear, with silver-grey, lance-shaped leaves and creamy white flowers in spring. It is normally represented in cultivation by the variety '**Pendula**', a graceful weeping tree which grows to about 6m (20ft) eventually, but usually remains suitable for small spaces for many years.

Although it bears fruit, this not very attractive and is inedible.

Cultivation
The weeping pear does best in free-draining, fertile soil, in sun or light shade. Any strong, upright shoots emerging from the top of the crown should be pruned out, cutting back to the main stem.

Propagation is not practical for small-space gardeners.

Rhododendron Ericaceae
Azalea, rhododendron ② ③

* *Evergreen or deciduous shrub*
* *Colourful spring and early summer flowers*
* *Needs lime-free soil*
* *Hardy or slightly tender*

The rhododendron genus is vast, containing hundreds of species, to which can be added many more hundreds of varieties and cultivars. Some rhododendrons make towering shrubs with huge leaves, while others are dwarf, alpine plants. In between, there is a good range of small to medium-sized shrubs suitable for containers and small growing areas.

Rhododendrons have funnel-shaped flowers in a wide range of colours, including white, cream, pink, violet, lilac, salmon, yellow, orange and red. The flowers often have prominent stamens and may be sweetly scented. The leaves are usually dark green, lance shaped, sometimes leathery and frequently hairy.

There are many hybrids ideal for small-space growing, among them '**Alison Johnstone**' (bell-shaped, orange-pink flowers, 1.5m (5ft) high); '**Blue Diamond**' (lavender-blue, funnel-shaped flowers, slow growing to 1m (3ft) high); '**Curlew**' (open, pale yellow flowers, proportionately large, on a dwarf bush 30cm (1ft) high); '**Elizabeth Lockhart**' (deep rosy red, bell-shaped flowers and bronze leaves, 60cm (2ft) high); and '**Ptarmigan**' (pure white, funnel-shaped flowers on a spreading 30-cm (1-ft) shrub). All these are evergreen.

Rhododendron yakushimanum has given rise to a large number of varieties known as **Yakushimanum Hybrids**; all are compact shrubs with usually bell-shaped flowers in a wide colour range.

Azaleas are often regarded as a different group. They are small shrubs with proportionately smaller leaves and flowers and may be deciduous or evergreen. They tend to be very free flowering, and are most suitable for containers and small spaces.

Deciduous azaleas growing to 1.5m (5ft) or under include '**Freya**', salmon pink double; '**Homebush**', semi-double, rosy purple shaded pink; '**Narcissiflorum**', pale yellow, semi-double, scented flowers; and '**Strawberry Ice**', pale pink with deeper pink petal tips and yellow throats. Many deciduous azaleas also have good autumn foliage colour.

Among the evergreen azaleas are the beautiful, compact, small-flowered **Kurume** azaleas from Japan, such as '**Azuma-kagami**', deep pink hose-in-hose flowers, 1.2m (4ft); '**Hatsugiri**', numerous purple-red flowers, 60cm (2ft); '**Hinode-giri**', bright crimson, and '**Hinomayo**', clear pink, both 1.5m (5ft). '**Kirin**' is a dwarf type with silvery rose pink flowers.

Cultivation
Rhododendrons need lime-free soil, which is moisture retentive but free draining, and rich in organic matter. They grow well in light shade, in a sheltered position, where they will not be exposed to cold, drying winds.

Dryness at the roots will cause flower buds to fall, so keep the soil just moist, and give container-grown plants regular liquid feeds, preferably with fertilisers specifically for ericaceous plants.

Deadhead after flowering. Cut back straggly plants in spring.

Plants can be increased by layering or cuttings, but they may be hard to propagate.

Mottled yellow foliage is often caused by nutrient deficiency, which may be due to lime in the soil; feed affected plants with sequestered iron.

Rhododendron 'Blue Diamond'

Plant directory

Robinia Leguminosae
False acacia ③

* *Deciduous tree or shrub*
* *Attractive foliage and flowers*
* *Hardy*

False acacias have attractive, pinnate leaves composed of pairs of light to dark green leaflets, usually on spiny stems. Racemes of pea-like flowers are carried in early summer.

The most commonly planted form is *Robinia pseudoacacia* 'Frisia', with its golden yellow foliage, which gradually turns more green during summer. Flowers are creamy white and fragrant. This variety makes a graceful tree, which can be grown successfully as a shrub if it is cut back hard (stooled) annually. A less common variety is 'Pyramidalis' ('Fastigiata'), a narrow, columnar tree with spineless branches.

Also useful for small spaces is *R. x slavinii* 'Hillieri', which makes a small, round-headed tree with attractive ferny foliage and lilac-pink flowers.

The rose acacia, *R. hispida*, produces brittle, bristly, suckering stems, which can be trained successfully against a wall, and will grow to 2m (6ft) or more. The pinnate leaves are mid-green and racemes of rosy pink flowers are carried in late spring.

Cultivation
Robinias require a light, free-draining soil and are particularly suitable for dry areas. They prefer a sunny, reasonably sheltered position.

To grow *R. pseudoacacia* as a shrub, cut the branches back almost to the base in spring. Tie in the shoots of wall-trained shrubs to their supports in the growing season. Separate any suckers from parent plants during the dormant season and replant them.

Rosa Rosaceae
Rose ① ② ③

* *Deciduous shrub or climber*
* *Colourful, often fragrant flowers from spring to autumn*
* *Hardy*

Some of the most popular garden plants, roses have been cultivated for many hundreds of years. They are divided into a number of main groups.

Old roses (Old-fashioned roses) include groups such as Alba, Bourbon, China, Damask, Gallica and Moss roses. They usually make fairly large, open shrubs and have large, double blooms with a strong perfume. Most flower only once in a season.

Modern roses include modern shrubs; Large-flowered bush (Hybrid Tea); Cluster-flowered bush (Floribunda); groundcover, climbing and rambling roses. Most have been bred to give a long season of bloom.

Species roses often have simple, single flowers and include wild species and natural and cultivated species hybrids.

Old roses have been enjoying a revival in popularity for some years, but most are not really suitable for small spaces. Their growth tends to be lax and spreading, and their brief flowering season does not give good value. But *Rosa gallica* 'Versicolor' ('Rosa Mundi') is a neat-growing shrub to around 1.2m (4ft) and has striking crimson and white striped flowers; it is known to have been cultivated for at least 400 years.

Some old roses, such as China, Bourbon and Hybrid Perpetuals do have the ability to repeat flower. 'Irène Watts' has peach-pink flowers on neat 60-cm (2-ft) bushes; 'Comte de Chambord' has rich pink, full, quartered flowers and grows to 1.2m (4ft); 'Souvenir de la Malmaison' has large, pale pink flowers on a low, spreading bush to 1m (3ft); 'Reine des Violettes' is an almost thornless 1.2-m (4-ft) plant, with flat, full-petalled flowers in purple, red and lilac.

Modern shrub roses, including English roses, are often more suitable for small areas. Some of them combine the best attributes of old roses with more compact growth, disease resistance and repeat flowering. These include 'Mary Rose', with rose-pink, loose-petalled flowers, 1.2m (4ft); 'Cottage Rose', cupped blooms in deep pink, 1m (3ft); 'The Countryman', clear pink, rosette-shaped blooms, 1m (3ft), and 'Fair Bianca', pure white, 1m (3ft).

Patio and Miniature roses are perhaps the most suitable for small-space growing. Patio (dwarf cluster-flowered) roses grow to 45-60cm (18-24in), while miniatures are below 38cm (15in). Both are ideal for containers. Patio rose varieties include 'Anna Ford', orange-red; 'Bright Smile',

Rosa gallica 'Versicolor'

clear yellow; 'Cider Cup', deep apricot; 'Sweet Dream', apricot-peach and 'Sweet Magic', orange tinted with gold. Among the miniatures, ideal for window boxes, are 'Dresden Doll', shell-pink moss rose; 'Easter Morning', ivory white; 'Little Flirt', orange-red; and 'Yellow Doll', soft yellow.

Climbers and Ramblers are perfect for growing up walls and pillars and over pergolas and arches. Among those making reasonably restrained growth are 'Breath of Life', apricot pink; 'Golden Showers', freely produced, semi-double, creamy yellow flowers; 'New Dawn', silver-pink, fragrant flowers; and 'Zéphirine Drouhin', carmine-pink, freely produced, fragrant flowers on almost thornless stems.

Cultivation
Roses like a sunny position in fertile, free-draining but moisture-retentive soil. Water the plants well during dry spells, and feed with a special rose fertiliser.

Prune in spring, just as the buds are starting into growth. Remove all dead or dying stems. Then prune modern bush roses back by two-thirds, or slightly more, of the previous year's growth, cutting to an outwards-facing bud. Prune old roses, climbers, and ramblers more lightly.

Old roses can be grown from semi-ripe and hardwood cuttings, but modern roses are budded on to rootstocks and plants from cuttings tend to be less robust.

Pests and diseases attacking roses, include black spot, rust, mildew, aphids and caterpillars. Use combined insecticides and fungicides where necessary; otherwise use fungicides as a preventive spray, and non-persistent contact insecticides only where the attack by pests is apparent.

Rosmarinus Labiatae
Rosemary ② ③

* *Evergreen shrub*
* *Aromatic foliage and summer flowers*
* *Culinary herb*
* *Hardy*

One of the most useful and attractive herbs, rosemary is just as valuable as a decorative plant as it is for the kitchen. The slender, needle-like leaves are dark green on the upper side and silver beneath, and give off a strong scent when brushed against. Pale to mid-blue, hooded flowers appear towards the tips of the branches in summer.

Rosmarinus officinalis (common rosemary) is a dense, bushy shrub to about 1.5m (5ft); 'Miss Jessopp's Upright' has a more erect habit and forms a good hedge. 'Prostratus' makes dense mats of foliage sprinkled with blue summer flowers and

About the plants

Rosmarinus officinalis

needs a warm, sunny position; it is a good plant for a rock garden or the top of a stone wall in a sheltered garden. '**Severn Sea**' is a dwarf variety, with arching branches up to about 1m (3ft), and has intense blue flowers.

Cultivation
Rosemary is hardy, but does best in a reasonably sheltered, sunny position; it is not suitable for very cold, exposed gardens. Free-draining, light soil is necessary; in containers, use fertile potting compost mixed with a little sharp sand. Water when conditions are very dry, but make sure the soil is never waterlogged.

Prune back hard in spring when plants become straggly and ungainly. Propagate from semi-ripe cuttings in summer.

Salix Salicaceae
Willow ③

* Deciduous tree
* Attractive foliage and tree shape
* Hardy

Willows are plants to be wary of in small spaces; many species are fast-growing, large trees that quickly become an embarrassment. They are thirsty plants that take large quantities of water from the soil and can cause problems with drains and the subsidence of buildings on certain soils. Fortunately there are several types that do not pose a problem for small-space gardens.

Leaves are usually lance shaped and silvery grey, or oval and deep green. Male and female plants are separate; the males generally bear more striking catkins in late winter and early spring.

Salix alba is a large, fast-growing, spreading tree unsuitable for all but the largest gardens, but *S. a. vitellina* and *S. a.* '**Britzensis**' ('**Chermesina**') are different. When cut back hard (stooled), you can enjoy their shining, coloured winter stems – bright red for '**Britzensis**', and orange yellow for *S. a. vitellina*.

For a miniature weeping willow, plant *S. caprea* '**Kilmarnock**', a small tree growing to some 2m (6ft), with pendulous branches bearing attractive catkins in late winter.

S. matsudana '**Tortuosa**' is a curiosity, with its twisted, spiralling branches making a good winter feature, although for small spaces *Corylus avellana* '**Contorta**' (corkscrew witch hazel) gives much the same effect and is easier to keep under control and within bounds.

S. hastata '**Wehrhahnii**' is a slow-growing, branching shrub reaching just over 1m (3ft); in early spring the branches are thickly studded with upright, silver-white catkins which then expand into fluffy golden globes.

Cultivation
Willows like moisture-retentive soil and a position in full sun. Plants grown for their coloured winter stems should be cut back hard to within about 5cm (2in) of the base in early spring every other year.

Plants can be propagated by semi-ripe cuttings in summer or hardwood cuttings in winter; most are easy to root.

Anthracnose can be a serious disease, but it mainly affects the larger weeping willows; it causes reddish spotting and early fall of leaves and die-back of shoot tips. Regular fungicide sprays from early spring to summer may help to prevent it.

Salvia Labiatae
Sage ①②③

* Annuals, perennials and semi-evergreen or evergreen shrubs
* Attractive flowers; often aromatic foliage
* Culinary herb
* Hardy or slightly tender

Salvias have the square stems and hooded flowers that are typical of Labiatae, but they are otherwise very varied and versatile plants. They may be grown for their flowers, colourful bracts, or ornamental or fragrant foliage.

Salvia farinacea is a perennial usually grown as an annual. It has lance-shaped leaves and 45-cm (18-in) erect spikes of summer flowers. '**Victoria**' is an intense violet-blue shade, with dark purple stems. *S. viridis* (*S. horminum*), clary, is a half-hardy annual up to 45cm (18in). The leaves are oval, and veined blue; white or pink bracts towards the top of the stems make a colourful show in summer and are good for cutting.

There are several attractive, slightly tender perennial salvias that deserve a sheltered spot. They include *S. patens*, with whorls of deep or pale blue hooded flowers, and *S. microphylla* (*S. grahamii*) with bright crimson flowers. *S. splendens*, a perennial treated as annual, is a well-known bedding plant, with neat mounds of oval, toothed leaves. It produces large spikes of hooded, usually scarlet, flowers, around 30cm (12in) tall, throughout the summer. '**Blaze of Fire**' is a popular red variety; salmon, purple, white and lavender flowers are also available in mixtures such as **Phoenix Mixed** or as separate colours in the **Sizzler Series**.

Culinary sage (*S. officinalis*), with its strongly aromatic, oval, wrinkled and slightly furry leaves, is a useful plant for a herb garden and there are several ornamental varieties, too. '**Purpurescens**' has purple young foliage which becomes purple-green as it matures; the irregularly margined leaves of '**Icterina**' are mid-green and splashed with pale green and yellow.

Cultivation
Salvias like a sunny position in moderately fertile, free-draining soil. Plant out half-hardy types after all risk of frost is over. Slightly tender perennials need a sheltered position with some winter protection. Take cuttings and overwinter them under cover to guard against winter losses.

Plants can be raised from seed sown in spring, or from softwood cuttings in early summer. Perennials can be divided in autumn or spring.

Salvia farinacea '**Victoria**'

Plant directory

Sambucus   Caprifoliaceae
Elder   ② ③

* Deciduous shrubs or trees
* Decorative foliage, flowers and fruits
* Hardy

The flattened heads of white flowers carried by the common elder (*Sambucus nigra*) in early summer have a refreshing, sweet scent; both they and the round black berries that follow can be used to make cordials and wine. Leaves are composed of five to seven leaflets and may be attractively coloured.

S. canadensis (American elder) grows to around 4m (12ft) and has slightly domed heads of creamy flowers. **'Aurea'** has golden foliage and red berries. There is also a golden-leaved form of common elder, *S. nigra* **'Aurea'**, which is more vigorous and can reach 5m (15ft) although it is usually smaller. **'Guincho Purple'** has purplish green to purple-black leaves and soft pink flowers opening to white.

The red-berried elder, *S. racemosa*, grows to 3m (10ft). **'Plumosa Aurea'** has yellow leaflets with finely cut and serrated margins. The ferny, finely divided leaves of **'Tenuifolia'** give it a strong similarity to a cut-leafed Japanese maple. *S. nigra laciniata* also has finely divided foliage.

Cultivation
Elders are easy to grow, preferring an open position in moisture-retentive, fertile soil, but tolerating poor soils well.

Plants can be cut back hard each winter when they are being grown for their decorative foliage; this encourages the formation of strong young shoots. If flowers and fruits are required, cut young shoots back by half in winter and remove older branches entirely. Propagate plants by softwood cuttings in summer or hardwood cuttings in winter.

Aphids often attack the tips of the shoots; where necessary, spray with a non-persistent contact insecticide. Do not use insecticide when the flowers are open.

Saxifraga   Saxifragaceae
Saxifrage   ① ② ③

* Evergreen perennial
* Attractive leaves and spring flowers
* Alpine and rock garden plants
* Hardy

This extensive genus of low-growing plants includes many suitable subjects for small spaces and containers. Plants vary widely, although they usually have attractive silvery rosetted or mossy foliage and open, five-petalled flowers in white or pink.

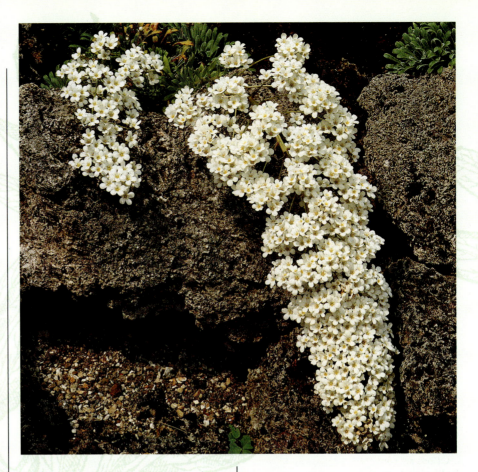

Saxifraga longifolia 'Tumbling Waters'

Saxifraga cochlearis has rosettes of oblong, silver leaves with white encrustations on the leaf margins. Loose sprays of white, yellow-centred blooms on dainty, dark stems 20cm (8in) high are produced in early summer.

S. **'Elizabethae'** is sometimes listed as **'Carmen'**; it forms a cushion only 2.5cm (1in) high, with rosettes of spiny leaves. In spring the foliage is almost hidden by pale primrose, saucer-shaped flowers. The foliage mats of *S. x irvingii* **'Jenkinsiae'** are a little larger and silvery green; this plant carries soft lilac-pink flowers in spring.

S. longifolia **'Tumbling Waters'** is among the showiest saxifrages when flowering. The white-encrusted foliage forms grey rosettes, from which arise long, arching panicles densely packed with small white flowers – very effective cascading over rocks or walls. The rosette dies after flowering but is replaced by offsets.

Cultivation
Generally the mossy-foliaged saxifrages like moisture-retentive but well-drained soil and a partially shaded position; the silver-rosetted types like full sun and can withstand dryer conditions. Those with encrusted leaves like some lime in the soil. All saxifrages are good for planting in rock gardens and troughs.

Mulch the necks of the plants with chippings and protect them from excessive winter rain.

Plants can be divided after flowering. If the small rosettes do not yet possess their own roots, insert them in pots of sandy compost, which should be kept only just moist until roots have formed.

Scaevola   Goodeniaceae
Scaevola, fan flower   ① ② ③

* Perennial grown as an annual in colder climates
* Fan-shaped summer flowers
* Trailer
* Half-hardy

This plant has become increasingly popular as a trailer for the edges of containers and for hanging baskets. The lopsided and fan-shaped flowers, carried in profusion on lax stems, are usually purple-blue. Most plants available are varieties of *Scaevola aemula*; **'Blue Fan'** and **'Blue Wonder'** are the ones usually offered. **'Sapphire'** is a fairly new compact variety in deep purple-blue; **'White Charm'** has yellow-eyed white flowers.

Cultivation
Plant in moisture-retentive but free-draining soil. Once flowering starts, liquid-feed every 10–14 days with a high-potash fertiliser. Softwood cuttings can be taken in early summer.

About the plants

Scilla Hyacinthaceae
Squill ① ② ③

* Bulb
* Early spring flowers
* Hardy

These generally dwarf bulbs are easy to grow in containers, beds and rock gardens. They have glossy, strap-shaped leaves and nodding, or starry, usually blue flowers.

Scilla bifolia produces one pair of leaves per bulb, which appear before the flowers in early spring. The 15-cm (6-in) flower spike carries a dozen or more light blue, pink or white flowers. The flowers of *S. siberica* 'Atrocoerulea' ('Spring Beauty'), the Siberian squill are a more intense, rich blue. These nodding, bell-shaped flowers are carried in groups of two to four on 15-cm (6-in) stems; several flower stems may be produced per bulb. The wide, strap-shaped, glossy green leaves precede the flowers.

Cultivation
Plant the bulbs to twice their depth in well-drained but moisture-retentive soil in autumn. They will grow in full sun or partial shade.

Offsets are sometimes produced and can be lifted and separated from the parent bulbs as the foliage dies down.

Sedum Crassulaceae
Stonecrop, ice plant ① ② ③

* Evergreen or semi-evergreen perennial
* Attractive foliage and flowers
* Hardy

Stonecrops are succulent plants, well adapted to dry conditions. Some species can be grown on walls or in rock gardens, others as border plants; all those described will do well in containers.

Sedum acre (wallpepper) is a spreading, mat-forming plant that grows happily on bare rocks and walls. The fleshy leaves are tiny, and the shoots are densely covered in brilliant yellow flowers in summer. The variety 'Aureum' has yellow foliage. Plants spread widely but are easily restrained.

S. spathulifolium 'Cape Blanco' has clustered rosettes of thick, fleshy, blue-grey leaves tinged with red. They form a spreading mat, and in early summer bear heads of small yellow flowers on short stems.

A larger plant for borders, or as a specimen in a container, is the ice plant, *S. spectabile*. This grows to about 45cm (18in) and has broad, grey-green, fleshy leaves and lax, succulent stems. Wide, flat flowerheads of small, starry flowers with prominent stamens appear in mid- to late summer and persist into the autumn; they are rosy pink and very attractive to butterflies. 'Brilliant' has a deep, rich colour.

Cultivation
Free-draining soil and a position in full sun suit most stonecrops. Cut back the spread of mat-forming varieties as necessary.

Plants are easily propagated by division or softwood cuttings in summer. Plants that have been overwatered, or are growing in poorly drained soil, may rot at the base.

Sempervivum Crassulaceae
Houseleek ① ② ③

* Evergreen perennial
* Attractive rosettes of leaves; starry flowers
* Hardy

Sempervivum belongs to the same family as *Sedum* and, like those plants, have fleshy, succulent leaves which form tight rosettes and are sometimes tipped with red. They are suitable for rock gardens, walls and troughs.

Sempervivum arachnoideum, the cobweb houseleek, forms crowded clusters of red-tipped, fleshy leaves covered in fine white webbing, which makes them look as though spiders have been busy among its leaf tips. In summer, rose pink flowers are carried in clusters on 15-cm (6-in) stems. *S. tectorum*, the common houseleek, has similar rosettes without the webbing; the leaves are touched with purple or deep red. Deep red flowers appear in summer on 30-cm (12-in) stems. It is sometimes seen growing on tiled roofs.

S. 'Commander Hay' has large, dull red rosettes with green tips.

Cultivation
Plant sempervivums in full sun and very free-draining soil; they need little aftercare.

They are easy to propagate by offsets; break off a rosette and replant it at once if it already has roots, or pot it up in gritty compost if roots have not yet formed.

Sedum spathulifolium 'Cape Blanco'

Senecio 'Sunshine'

Senecio Compositae
Senecio ① ② ③

* Annuals, herbaceous perennials and evergreen shrubs
* Attractive foliage and summer flowers
* Hardy or slightly tender

Senecios have the familiar daisy flowers of the *Compositae* family, but they tend to be grown more for their silver foliage.

Senecio cineraria (*S. maritima*) is an evergreen shrub nearly always treated as an annual. It has deeply lobed leaves covered in dense, fine hairs which give them a bright silver-grey colour; they make a mound about 30cm (12in) tall. The most popular variety is 'Silver Dust', with very finely cut, lacy, silver-white foliage; 'White Diamond' has silver-green leaves which are not so finely divided.

S. 'Sunshine' (*Brachyglottis* Dunedin Hybrids 'Sunshine') is an evergreen shrub growing to around 1m (3ft). The oval leaves are felted and silver when young, becoming mid- to dark green as they age. Loose clusters of bright yellow flowers are carried from early summer.

Cultivation
Like all grey-leafed plants, these senecios can cope well with dry soil and like full sun. 'Sunshine' prefers a sheltered position and grows well in coastal areas.

S. cineraria can be raised from seed, and the young plants set out after the risk of frost has passed. The flowers detract from the foliage and are generally removed.

S. 'Sunshine' can be increased by taking semi-ripe cuttings in summer. Remove flowers when they fade, and cut back straggly shoots in autumn.

Plant directory

Sorbus Rosaceae
Rowan, mountain ash ③

* *Deciduous tree*
* *Attractive foliage, flowers and berries*
* *Hardy*

The rowan or mountain ash, **Sorbus aucuparia**, is an elegant, medium-sized tree with ferny, pinnate leaves. Heads of hawthorn-like flowers in spring are followed by bunches of red berries. 'Beissneri' has glowing orange-red bark, red stems and finely divided leaves; it may eventually grow to 7m (22ft). 'Fastigiata', with dark green leaves and brilliant red fruits, is slow growing and columnar in habit, reaching about 5m (15ft) after several years. 'Sheerwater Seedling' is another upright, compact tree which grows to 4m (12ft). *S. commixta* 'Embley' is noted for its autumn foliage colour: the notable purpled-red leaves remain on the tree until late in the season.

Less commonly seen is the dwarf shrub *S. reducta*, which has upright stems around 45cm (18in) tall, with pinnate leaves that turn bronzy red in autumn. The small, round berries are rosy pink or pinkish white. This shrub usually produces many suckers, but non-suckering selections are sometimes available.

Cultivation
Well-drained, reasonably fertile soils are suitable, preferably lime free, since many sorbus are not long-lived on alkaline soils. Most sorbus are grown as specimen trees, but *S. reducta* can be grown in a rock garden or as a border plant.

Plants can be propagated by softwood cuttings in summer.

Sorbus may be attacked by fireblight, which causes flowers and foliage to wither, turn brown, and hang on the tree with a scorched appearance; prune out and destroy affected branches immediately.

Taxus Taxaceae
Yew ② ③

* *Evergreen conifer*
* *Attractive foliage and tree shapes*
* *Hardy*
* *Poisonous*

Although the dark green, needle-like leaves of yew make it a useful foil for brighter-leafed plants, among the many varieties of common yew (**Taxus baccata**) are several with golden foliage. Yew trees are tough and hardy, and will put up with poor growing conditions; they are notoriously slow growing but can survive to a great age.

Taxus baccata 'Standishii'

They are amenable to hard pruning, and very useful for topiary.

Male and female forms exist; the females bear fleshy, red, berry-like arils. The flesh of the aril is harmless, but the single seed it encloses, and all other parts of the tree, are extremely poisonous.

T. b. 'Elegantissima' is a dense shrub, with golden young foliage that becomes green margined with gold as it ages. 'Fastigiata' is a popular upright, columnar yew; 'Fastigiata Aurea' has golden variegated leaves. The semi-prostrate 'Repandens', a spreading plant growing to some 60cm (2ft), is good for groundcover. 'Standishii', with rusty gold foliage, has a compact, columnar shape very suitable for containers. The pale yellow summer foliage of 'Ivory Tower' turns to rich creamy shades in autumn and winter.

Cultivation
Yews will grow on virtually any soil except a heavy, waterlogged one and are happy on chalk. They will grow in sun or shade, but varieties with coloured foliage are usually better in full sun.

Pruning can be carried out to shape the plants at any time of year. Cuttings with a heel can be taken in autumn.

Thymus Labiatae
Thyme ① ② ③

* *Evergreen shrub or perennial*
* *Aromatic foliage, spring and summer flowers*
* *Culinary herb*
* *Hardy*

The small, oval or lanceolate leaves of thyme have a warm, sweet fragrance and are widely used in cooking, but the plants are of great decorative as well as culinary value. They are low-growing, creeping or upright plants, with clusters of lipped, pink or white summer flowers, attractive to bees.

Garden thyme, **Thymus vulgaris**, has narrow, dark green leaves and grows to about 20cm (8in). Upright heads of mauve flowers are carried in summer. *T. v.* 'Silver Posie' is a compact, silver-margined variety. *T. x citriodorus*, with its sharp citrus scent, is lemon thyme; the golden-foliaged 'Aureus' forms a spreading shrub up to 25cm (10in) tall with pale lilac flowers. The dense mats of *T. pseudolanuginosus* have hairy stems and furry grey-green leaves; *T. herba-barona* has deep green leaves that smell of caraway.

T. serpyllum, wild thyme, makes spreading mats of tough stems with tiny green leaves. 'Annie Hall' has pale pink flowers while those of 'Coccineus' are rich crimson.

Cultivation
Thymes may be planted in containers, rock gardens, raised beds and borders; they need free-draining soil and a position in full sun. They will also grow well when planted in cracks in paving, releasing their full aroma when lightly trodden on.

Cut off the faded flowers with secateurs and trim straggly plants in autumn. Take heel cuttings in late summer.

Thymus serpyllum 'Coccineus' *(left) and* Thymus *'Winter Beauty'*

Trachycarpus Arecaceae
Chusan palm, windmill palm ② ③

* *Evergreen palm*
* *Attractive foliage and architectural shape*
* *Hardy or slightly tender*

Warm climate gardeners have a wide range of palms to choose from, but *Trachycarpus fortunei* gives an exotic appearance to a garden. It is comparatively hardy but needs shelter from cold winds, so provide winter protection for young plants in cold areas.

The leaves are pleated like a fan, and may be up to 1m (3ft) wide. They are carried on long, toothed stalks arising from a stout, hairy trunk. In early summer, panicles of small, cream flowers may appear.

Cultivation
Grow in moderately fertile, free-draining soil in full sun in a sheltered position.

Remove dead leaves when necessary.

Propagation is not practical for small-space gardeners.

Tulipa Liliaceae
Tulip   ② ③

* *Spring-flowering bulb*
* *Colourful flowers; some types have attractive foliage*
* *Hardy*

Along with daffodils, tulips are perhaps the best known spring bulbs, valued for their typically goblet-shaped flowers carried on long stems. There are many different types of tulip, flowering from early spring to early summer, and ranging in height from 10cm (4in) or less to over 1m (3ft). The flowers may be open and flat, cup shaped, double, frilled, or waisted, in a range of colours including bicolours and feathered or streaked varieties. Botanically, they are split into 15 divisions, each division containing a large number of varieties.

Among the most useful for containers and small spaces are the shorter-growing types such as **Kaufmanniana**, **Fosteriana** and **Greigii** hybrids. **Kaufmannianas** flower from early spring, with blooms that are generally bicoloured and open out flat in full sun. The foliage is usually attractively mottled with purple-brown streaks. Varieties include '**Ancilla**', pink outside, white inside with a red and gold throat; and '**Heart's Delight**', deep pink outside, pale pink inside, with a red and yellow throat.

Fosterianas have large, single flowers from early to mid-spring and include '**Juan**', bright orange-red, waisted flowers with a yellow-splashed base; and '**Rockery Beauty**', brilliant red.

Tulipa 'Estelle Rijnveld'

The foliage of all **Greigii** hybrids is striped and variegated with reddish brown, and the leaf margins are usually undulating. '**Red Riding Hood**' has particularly attractive foliage and bright red flowers with a black base to the petals; '**Toronto**' produces up to three flowers on a stem, with rosy-red, pointed petals.

Among the species tulips, one of the most rewarding is *Tulipa tarda*, which produces four or five flowers on short stems in early spring; they have pointed petals, which are white with a large, central gold blotch.

Cultivation
Plant tulips in late autumn in well-drained soil in a sunny position. When the leaves have died down, the bulbs may be lifted and stored in a cool, dry place until it is time to replant them. In light, free-draining soils they may be left in the ground. Young bulbs can be separated from the parent and replanted at lifting time.

Remove dead blooms during the flowering season.

Aphids may sometimes attack the young shoots and can be controlled with a non-persistent insecticide where necessary. Slugs may also damage shoots and foliage; use slug bait or an organic alternative.

Viburnum Caprifoliaceae
Viburnum

* *Deciduous and evergreen shrubs*
* *Attractive foliage and flowers; sometimes fruits*
* *Hardy*

The viburnum genus is wide and diverse, but contains some excellent winter-flowering shrubs. Among the best known is *Viburnum* x *bodnantense* '**Dawn**', an upright, deciduous shrub to 2.5m (8ft), with clusters of very fragrant, pink flowers, deep pink in bud, carried on the bare stems during mild spells throughout the late autumn and winter. The leaves are oval, and bronzy green. *V. farreri*, one of its parents, is similar, but with white flowers.

V. davidii is an evergreen with dark green, strongly veined foliage, which forms a compact mound about 1m (3ft) high. Clusters of small white flowers are carried on red stems from spring to midsummer; these are sometimes followed by pointed, brilliant turquoise berries. Male and female plants must be grown together in order for the females to berry; sexed plants are available from some suppliers.

V. tinus (laurustinus) is also evergreen, with glossy, dark green foliage. In winter it bears plentiful flat heads of small, starry white flowers, which are tinged pink in bud and are followed by blue-black berries. '**Eve Price**' and '**Gwenllian**' are both small-leafed, compact forms; '**Variegatum**' is slower growing than the species and has mid-green leaves attractively variegated with yellow, but the white winter flowers do not stand out against the foliage as effectively as on the plain-leafed types.

Cultivation
Viburnums prefer fertile, moisture-retentive soil, although many will cope well with dry soils. A position in full sun is best, but light shade is tolerated.

After flowering, prune out some older shoots from deciduous species to keep the plants compact; when necessary, evergreens may be thinned out in early summer.

Propagate viburnums by taking semi-ripe cuttings in summer.

Viburnum bodnantense 'Dawn'

Plant directory

Vinca Apocynaceae
Periwinkle ① ② ③

* *Evergreen shrub*
* *Trailing or prostrate habit*
* *Summer flowers*
* *Hardy*

The glossy, dark green leaves of periwinkle make excellent groundcover, with starry, bright blue flowers peeping out from the mat of foliage from late spring through to autumn. Like most effective groundcover plants, they can be invasive and must be positioned with care.

Vinca major (greater periwinkle) is a vigorous plant growing to 45cm (18in) tall, with large blue flowers throughout the summer; it is a strong-growing and invasive plant. 'Variegata' has leaves edged with creamy white; the leaves of 'Maculata' have a central golden splash.

Less rampant is the lesser periwinkle, *V. minor*. Its appearance is similar to that of *V. major* but it is smaller in all its parts, growing to only about 15cm (6in) high but still spreading widely. 'Alba' and 'Gertrude Jekyll' have white flowers; 'Argenteovariegata' has creamy white variegated leaves. The azure blue flowers of 'La Grave' are particularly large; those of 'Azurea Flore Pleno' and 'Multiplex' are double.

Cultivation
Vincas can be grown in most well-drained soils in sun or shade, but flower better in sun. They are good plants for containers, where their spread can be controlled.

The spreading stems root at the nodes as they go, and plants are easily propagated by division, or by pegging sections of the stems into moist soil.

Vinca major

Viola 'Ardross Gem'

Viola Violaceae
Violet, pansy ① ② ③

* *Annuals and perennials, deciduous or semi-evergreen*
* *Summer or winter flowers*
* *Hardy or half-hardy*

Violets have oval or heart-shaped leaves and usually distinctively flat-faced, five-petalled flowers. They are suitable for growing in a large number of situations, including containers of all sorts, rock gardens, beds and borders.

Viola odorata, the sweet violet, flowers during the winter, producing small, sweetly fragrant flowers amid mounds of heart-shaped, light green leaves 10cm (4in) high. The plants spread by means of runners and form dense clumps. Flowers are violet-blue, pink or white; named varieties include 'Princesse de Galles', deep blue; 'Marie-Louise', double mauve; and 'Coeur d'Alsace', which is pink.

Pansies (*V.* x *wittrockiana*) are perennials usually grown as annuals. They have oval leaves and relatively large, flat-faced flowers in a wide range of colours and bicolours; they may flower in summer or late winter. Summer-flowering **Majestic Giants** have large blooms in many colours. **Universal Plus**, with orange, red, pink, violet, blue, white and yellow blotched or plain flowers, is one of the best winter-flowering strains.

Cultivation
These plants can be grown in sun or light shade in any fertile, reasonably moisture-retentive soil. Deadheading plants will give a longer succession of bloom.

Perennials may be propagated by division, those grown as annuals by seed.

Violas are subject to viral diseases, which cause deformed, stunted growth, sometimes with mottled foliage. Destroy badly affected plants and control aphids to help curb the spread of viruses.

Violets are often attacked by red spider mite; infestations show as dry, flecked foliage and failure of the plants to thrive. Infestations usually occur in dry, hot conditions; spray the plants with water to increase humidity and move them into a shady position.

Vitis Vitaceae
Vine ③

* *Deciduous climber*
* *Attractive foliage and fruits; autumn colour*
* *Hardy or slightly tender*

These climbers with lobed or heart-shaped leaves can be grown up walls or over pergolas; they climb by means of tendrils. The grape vine, *Vitis vinifera*, is widely cultivated for its fruits, both for eating and for wine making. There are also several varieties grown for their decorative value.

V. coignetiae, the crimson glory vine, has large, slightly hairy, heart-shaped leaves, which turn rich crimson in autumn; it is a vigorous grower which will quickly cover a large wall. *V.* 'Brant' is a fruiting variety with lobed leaves, which in autumn turn deep red or brownish purple, with prominent, lighter-coloured veins; the grapes are black and are freely produced in small bunches.

There are many varieties of *V. vinifera* that will produce edible fruits in a warm, sheltered situation; two grown for their foliage are 'Incana' ('Dusty Miller'), with leaves thickly covered in a white meal, and 'Purpurea', with deep red or purple leaves and insignificant fruits.

Cultivation
Plant in moisture-retentive but free-draining, fertile soil in an open, sunny, warm and sheltered position. Provide support for the shoots to twine around.

Prune by shortening young shoots and thinning out some of the older branches in early autumn. Hardwood cuttings can be taken during the dormant season, or semi-ripe cuttings in summer.

Aphids may be a problem on young shoots and can be treated with a non-persistent insecticide. If mildew occurs, use a suitable fungicide.

About the plants

Weigela Caprifoliaceae
Weigela

* Deciduous shrub
* Late spring to early summer flowers
* Hardy

Weigela forms a medium-sized, rounded bush with trumpet-shaped flowers in early summer. These are sometimes followed by another flush of bloom later in the season. The mid-green, oval leaves are deeply veined.

Weigela florida is the most popular species grown; it has slightly arching branches up to 2m (6ft), and pink flowers in late spring. *W. f.* 'Variegata' is slower growing and more compact, reaching some 1.2m (4ft). Its leaves have a broad, creamy white margin and the flowers are pale pink. *W. f.* 'Foliis Purpureis' is even more compact, and its deep purple-green foliage contrasts well with the flowers, which are deep pink on the outside, offset by the pale pink within.

There are many hybrid varieties of weigela, among them 'Evita', a dwarf, spreading shrub with bright red flowers, and 'Victoria', with very dark purple-flushed leaves and deep rosy red flowers on a bush about 1m (3ft) tall.

Cultivation
Grow in well-drained, moderately fertile soil, preferably in full sun, although weigelas will tolerate partial shade.

Prune out a proportion of the older branches each year, cutting them back to the ground; this encourages the formation of strong, new shoots that will flower in their second year. Varieties grown for their foliage can be pruned back hard in spring but will not then bear flowers.

Plants can be propagated by semi-ripe cuttings in summer.

Yucca Agavaceae
Adam's needle

* Evergreen shrub
* Bold foliage and architectural shapes
* Hardy or half-hardy

Exotic-looking *Yuccas* have rosettes of narrow, sword-shaped foliage, which is often sharply spiny. Tall stems of showy, bell-shaped, creamy flowers are carried on established plants in summer.

Yucca filamentosa, with stemless rosettes of stiff, blue-green leaves margined with fibrous threads, grows to 1–2m (3–6ft). Creamy white, bell-shaped flowers are carried on tall stems in summer when the plants are a few years old. 'Bright Edge' has leaves with a fine yellow margin. *Y. flaccida* is a smaller plant with narrow, deep green leaves that tend to bend down at the tips; creamy white flowers on 1-m (3-ft) tall stems appear from mid- to late summer. 'Golden Sword' has leaves with a central yellow stripe.

Y. gloriosa has a short, stout stem, and forms a small tree about 2m (6ft) tall. On top of the stem is a tuft of stiff, spiky, blue-green leaves. Panicles of flowers are carried from midsummer through to early autumn; they are creamy white, sometimes tinged red on the outside.

Y. recurvifolia also has a short stem which, unlike that of *Y. gloriosa*, tends to branch; the leaves are blue-green and curve backwards. The white, late-summer flowers are produced only after several years.

Cultivation
Yuccas like free-draining soils and full sun; plant them in a reasonably sheltered position. They grow very well in containers. Some species, particularly *Y. gloriosa*, need to be positioned carefully in small spaces because of the dangerously sharp, spiky foliage. Take care that the plants are not overwatered in the dormant season, or the roots will rot. Remove the flowering stems once the flowers have faded.

Plants can be increased by the suckers that form naturally; remove them from the parent plant in spring.

Large, grey, brown-edged spots on the leaves are caused by leaf spot fungus.

Yucca gloriosa

Remove any badly damaged leaves and spray the plants with a suitable fungicide.

Zantedeschia Araceae
Arum lily, calla lily

* Deciduous or evergreen, tuberous-rooted perennial
* Bold foliage and showy flower spathes from spring to midsummer
* Hardy, half-hardy or tender

The exotic flowers of the arum are formed from a club-shaped spadix (flower spike) surrounded by a large spathe (bract), which may be white, green, pink or yellow. Plants are inclined to be on the tender side, and even the hardy varieties prefer a sheltered position and a warm climate.

Zantedeschia aethiopica has glossy, deep green, arrow-shaped leaves with distinct veins. The plant forms a mound up to 1m (3ft) high, and in early to midsummer produces long stems topped by a large, showy, funnel-shaped white spathe surrounding a fleshy yellow spadix. 'Crowborough' is one of the hardier forms; 'Green Goddess' is also relatively hardy, and has a green spathe with a white throat.

The golden arum, *Z. elliottiana*, grows to about 60cm (2ft). The heart-shaped leaves are marked with white spots and streaks; the spathe is a rich golden yellow.

The pink arum, *Z. rehmannii*, reaches about 45cm (18in); it has plain green leaves and a narrow, funnel-shaped, pale pink to deep maroon spathe. Both these species are frost tender.

Cultivation
Plant arum lilies in fertile, moisture-retentive soil in a warm, protected position in sun or partial shade. Water plants regularly during the growing season to keep the soil moist at all times. *Z. aethiopica* can be grown as a marginal plant in a water garden, with the roots covered by 15cm (6in) of water.

Container-grown plants should be gradually dried off after flowering and the tender species overwintered under cover at a minimum temperature of 7°C (45°F). If *Z. aethiopica* is to be overwintered outside in cool areas, cover the planting area with straw or similar material for extra protection.

Plants can be increased by offsets in the dormant season.

Round, dark grey blotches may form on the leaves, spathes and leaf stalks, sometimes causing leaves to fall. This most frequently occurs in cool, moist climates, and is caused by a fungal leaf spot disease. Destroy any affected foliage and spray the plants with a suitable fungicide.

219

Index

Page numbers in *italic* refer to captions to pictures or to text in boxes

A

Abies 158, 168
Acanthus 168
acclimatization 38–9
Acer 54, 104, 158, 162, 164, 165, 168
Achillea 163, 169
Aconitum napellus 47
Actinidia 166, 169, *169*
Adam's needle *see Yucca*
adelgids 168
Adiantum 162, 169
African daisy 163, 185
African lily *see Agapanthus*
Agapanthus 169
Agave 89, 163, 170
air 96
air pollution, plants tolerant of 162
Ajuga 160, 162, 170, *170*
 layering 147
Alchemilla 87, 89, 162, 170
algae in ponds 69, 71
algicides 71
alleys 20, *20*
Allium 170
Aloe 163, *163*, 171
alpine gardens 58–9, *58–9*
alpines 58–9, 63, *119*, *120-1*
Anemone 105, 160, 163, 171
angel's trumpet *see Brugmansia*
annuals 102
anthers 97
anthracnose 213
antirrhinum 135
anti-theft devices 43
aphids 152, *152*, 155, 171, 172, 184, 195
apple 76,
 scab 155
Aquilegia 171, *171*
arbor-vitae *see Thuja*
arbours 64
arches 64
architectural plants 90
Argyranthemum 132, 172
Armeria 163, 172, *172*
Artemisia 172
arum lily 15, *see also Zantedeschia*
Arundinaria 165, 173, *173*
aspect 36
Asplenium scolopendrium see Phyllitis scolopendrium
assessing the situation 34–40
Aster 135, 155, 173, *173*
aubergine 74
Aubrieta 160, 173
Aucuba japonica 88, 162, 167, 174
auricula 210
autumn colour plants 164
autumn crocus *see Colchicum*
azalea 79, 81, 211
 see also Rhododendron
Azolla caroliniana (*A. filiculoides*) 69

B

baby's breath *see Gypsophila*
Bacillus thuringiensis 152
Bacopa 'Snowflake' *91*
balconies 24–5, *24*, 25, 39
 climbing plants on 25, 63
 microclimate 39
bamboo 165, 173, *173*
barberry *see Berberis*
basements 30–1, *30*, *31*, 39
 microclimate 39
basil 73
bay *see Laurus nobilis*
bear's breeches *see Acanthus*
bedding plants 102
beetroot 74
Begonia 16, 91, 105, 174, *174*
 propagation 107
bellflower *see Campanula*
Bellis perennis 174, *174*
Berberis 162, 164, 165, 174-5
bergamot *see Monarda*
Bergenia 102, 160, 162, 167, 175
Bidens ferulifolia 91
biennials 102
biological control 150, 153
birch 104
bird of paradise flower *32*
black currant 77
black-eyed Susan 60
bleeding heart 185
blind gardeners 46
blossom end rot 99, 154, *154*
blue fescue *see Festuca glauca*
blueberry 77
Boston ivy *see Parthenocissus*
botrytis (grey mould) 96, 154, *154*, 185, 199
Bougainvillea 166, 175
boundaries 42
box *see Buxus*
box-leafed honeysuckle 132
brachyglottis 86
brackets 18
Brassica oleracea 54, 86, 175, *175*
brick raised beds 78, 80-1
Briza 176, *176*
broom *see Cytisus; Genista*
Brugmansia 161, 176
buckler fern *see Dryopteris*
Buddleja 161, 162, 163, 176
 pruning 134
bugle *see Ajuga*
bulbils 149
bulbs 105
 division 148, *149*
bupririmate 155
busy lizzie *see Impatiens*
butterfly bush *see Buddleja*
butyl pond liners 67–8
Buxus (box) 119, *140*, 162, 163, 176 *176*
 topiary 132, *133*

C

cabbage, ornamental *see Brassica oleracea*
cabbage palm/tree *see Cordyline*
cabbage white butterfly 152
calamondin *see* x *Citrofortunella microcarpa*
calcifuges 99, *101*
calcium 99, 154
Californian lilac *see Ceanothus*
Californian poppy *see Eschscholzia*
calla lily *see Zantedeschia*
Calluna vulgaris 165, 177, *177*
Camellia 54, 81, 99, 113, 162, 177
Campanula 160, 177
Campsis 166, 178, *178*
candelabra primula 210
canes 128, 129
Canna 178
Canterbury bell *see Campanula*
capsicum 74
carbaryl 152, 153
carbendazim 154, 155
carbon dioxide 96
carnation *see Dianthus*
carrot 74
cascades 70
caterpillars 152, *152*
Ceanothus 160, 166, 178–9, *178*
century plant *see Agave americana*
Cercidiphyllum japonicum 164, 179
Chaenomeles 39, 162, 166, 179, *179*
Chamaecyparis 158, 179
chamomile 73
chard 75
Cheiranthus see Erysimum
cherry *see Prunus*
cherry laurel *see Prunus laurocerasus*
Chilean glory flower 166, 186
Chimonanthus praecox 165, 179
Chinese gooseberry 169, *see also Actinidia*
Chionodoxa 160, 180, *180*
chives 73
chlorosis 99
Choisya 161, *161*, 165, 180
Christmas lily *see Lilium*
Christmas rose *see Helleborus*
chrysanthemum *see Argyranthemum; Dendranthema*
Chusan palm *see Trachycarpus*
cider gum *158*, 189
cinquefoil *see Potentilla*
Cistus 163, 180
Citrus 158, *158*, 180, *180*
x *Citrofortunella microcarpa* 15, 180
Clematis 60, 64, 181, *181*
 layering 147
clematis wilt 181
climate 38–9
climbers 20, 60–4
 on balconies 25, 63
 cold shaded walls 167
 in containers 60
 controlling 62-3
 planting 114
 scented 62
 self-clinging 60
 and shade 60
 warm, sunny walls 166
clipping 135

clubroot 175
Colchicum 47, 181
colour 34
 depth 51
 hot/cool 51, 53, 90, *91*
 pastel 90, *91*
 use of 53
colour wheel 51
columbine *see Aquilegia*
communal gardens 30
compost 79, *100–1*
 in containers 118
 ericaceous *101*, 118
 hanging-basket 118
 peat-substitute *101*, 118
 soil-based (loam-based) *100*, 118, *118*
 soilless 24
 soilless (peat-based) 24, 100, 118, 136
 sterile 150
concrete block raised beds 80
conservatories 32
containers 15, 16, 18-19, 82-5
 climbers in 60
 cold, exposed sites *88*
 conifers for 158
 drainage 116, 118, 136
 foliage plants 92
 fruit and vegetables in 15, 72, 74–7
 grouping 56, *57*
 growing in 116–25
 painting 50–1
 planting up *116*, 119
 self-watering 40
 shady positions 89
 sunny positions 89
 supports in 128–9
 trees for 158
 watering 119
 in winter 141
Convallaria majalis 47
copper 99, 155
coral flower *see Heuchera*
cordons 130
 pruning 131, *131*
Cordyline 54, 90, 165, 182, *182*
corkscrew hazel *see Corylus avellana* 'Contorta'
corms 105
Cornus 54, 148, 160, 162, 165
 layering 146
 propagation 148
 pruning *134*
Corylus 182
 C. avellana 'Contorta' 54, 165, 182, 213
Cotinus coggygria 164, *164*, 182–3
Cotoneaster 60, 160, 162, 164, *164*, 183
courgette 75
courtyard gardens 29, *29*, 64
cowslip *see Primula*
crab apple *see Malus*
crane flower 32
cranesbill *see Geranium*
creeping dogwood 160
creeping Jenny *see Lysimachia*
crimson glory vine *see Vitis*
Crocus 105, 160, 183, *183*
crown imperial 46, *see also Fritillaria*
cuckoospit 177

220

Index

currants 77
curry plant 46 *see also Helichrysum*
cuttings 107, 144
    semi-ripe 144–5, *145*
    softwood 144–5, *144*
Cyclamen 105, 183
Cytisus 161, 162, 163, 184

D

daffodil *see Narcissus*
Dahlia 105, *156*, 164, 184
daisy 40, 54, 102
    double *see Bellis perennis*
damping off 96, 154, *154*
Daphne 47, 161, 184, *184*
Datura see Brugmansia
day lily *see Hemerocallis*
deadheading 134
deadnettle *see Lamium*
delphinium 126
Dendranthema 164, 184–5, *185*
    division *149*
    pinching out *135*
derris 152
design 48–93
Dianthus 161, *161*, 185
Dicentra 185, *185*
Dimorphotheca 163, 185
disabled gardeners 44–6, 78
disease control 150–1, 154–5
division 148, *148–9*
dog's-tooth violet *see Erythronium*
dogwood *see Cornus*
Dorotheanthus 163, 186, *186*
downy mildew 154, *154*, 194
drainage 40
    balconies 24
    basements 31
    containers 116, 118, 136
    raised beds 79
    roof gardens 27
drainpipe pots 125, *125*
drainpipes 18
drumstick primula 210
dry conditions, plants adapted to 163
dry-stone wall 80, *115*
Dryopteris 162, 186
Dutch hyacinth *see Hyacinthus*
dwarf French beans 75
dwarf reed mace *see Typha minima*

E

early-flowering plants 160
earwigs 184
Easter lily *see Lilium*
Eccremocarpus 166, 186
echeveria 40, *149*
Echinops ritro 46
eggplant 74
Elaeagnus 162, 186
elder *see Sambucus*
elderly gardeners 44–6
elephant's ears *see Bergenia*
enclosed gardens 28–31
entrances 22
equipment 110
Eranthis 160, 187
Erica 160, 165, 187, *187*
Erysimum 87, *102*, 187
Erythronium 160, 188, *188*
Escallonia 162, 188

Eschscholzia 163, 188 *188*
espaliers 130
Eucalyptus 104, 158, *158*, 162, 165, 188-9
    pruning *134*
Euonymus 54, 88, 160, 162, 164, 167, *167*, 189 *189*
Euphorbia 87, *92*, 165, *165*, 189
evapotranspiration 98
evening primrose *see Oenothera*
evergreen framework 54
everlasting flower *see Helichrysum*
exposed sites 88
eye-catching garden style *51*
eye-catching plants 90-1

F

fairy moss 69
false acacia *see Robinia*
false cypress *see Chamaecyparis*
family trees 76
fan flower *see Scaevola*
fan-trained trees 131, *131*
Fatsia japonica 38, 162, 166, 189, *189*
Felicia amelloides 91
fences 20
    growing plants up 62–3
fenitrothion 152
fertiliser 118, *136*, 137, 141
    slow-release 118
Festuca 190
    F. glauca 46, 165, 190, *190*
fibreglass pond moulds 67
Ficus carica (fig) 166, *166*, 190
fireblight disease 179, 183, 203, 216
firethorn *see Pyracantha*
fish 67
flea beetles 152, *152*
flooding 31
flooring in conservatories 32
flowering quince *see Chaenomeles*
foliage 34, 92
foliar feeds 137
forget-me-not *see Myosotis*
formal garden style *51*
fountains 70, *70*, 141
frames, growing over 132, *132*, 133
Fritillaria (fritillary) 162, 190, *190*
froghoppers 177
frogs 67
frost 99
frost pockets 39
fruit 15, 72, 76-7
fruit trees, training 130-1
Fuchsia 18, *91*, 190-1
    buying *107*
    propagation 107
    standard 132, *132-3*
full-brick wall 80
fungal disease 96, 154, 155
fungicides 154, 155

G

Galanthus 160, 191, *191*
gamma-HCH 153
garden centres 108
garden rooms 32
garden styles 51
Garrya elliptica 167, *167*, 191
Genista 163, 191, *191*
Gentiana (gentian)192, *192*

Geranium 40, 160, 192, *192*
    see also Pelargonium
gladiolus 105
gladwyn iris 47
Glechoma hederacea 'Variegata' *93*
globe thistle *see Echinops ritro*
Gloriosa superba (glory lily) 60
glory-of-the-snow *see Chionodoxa*
glyphosate 139
golden chain *see Laburnum*
golden hop 166, 195, *195*
granny's bonnet *see Aquilegia*
grape hyacinth 86
grey mould (botrytis) 96, 154, **154**, 185, 199
ground space 34
    complete lack 16, 18
groundcover plants 160
growing bags 72, 124
    planting *124-5*
gum tree *see Eucalyptus*
Gypsophila 192

H

Hakonechloa 92, 163, 192
half-brick wall 80
half-hardy annuals 102
half-standard plants 132
Hamamelis 161, 164, 165, 193, *193*
hand tools 110, *110*
hanging baskets 18-19, *18*, 84-5
    compost 118
    lining 122-3
    pastel colours *91*
    planting up 122-3, 123
    self-watering 85
    solid-wall 84
    types 122-3
    year-round interest 54
hard landscaping for year-round interest 54
hardening-off 38-9
hardy annuals 102
hardy plants 38
Harry Lauder's walking stick *see Corylus avellana* 'Contorta'
hart's tongue fern *see Phyllitis*
hay rack 85, *123*
hazel *see Corylus*
heath *see Erica*
heather 54, *81*
    see also Calluna; Erica
Hebe 163, 166, 193, *193*
Hedera 60, 86, 88,160, *160*, 162, 165, 167, 193
    growing over a frame 132, *132,* 133
    on outbuildings 64
    supports for 129
Helichrysum 46, *91*, 163, 194, *194*
Heliotropium (heliotrope) *93*
Helleborus (hellebore) 102, 160, *160*, 194
Hemerocallis 194
herbs 46, 73, 93
Heuchera 92, 195, *195*
Hibiscus 162, 166, 195
holly *see Ilex*
hollyhock *102*
honeysuckle *see Lonicera*
hop *see Humulus lupulus*
hose lance 18

hosepipes 40
Hosta 87, 89, 162, 195
houseleek *see Sempervivum*
humidity 40
Humulus lupulus 166, 195, *195*
humus 100
Hyacinthus (Dutch hyacinth) 39, 161, 196, *196*
Hydrangea 20, *104*, 167, 196
Hypericum 160, 162, 196-7

I

ice plant *see Dorotheanthus; Sedum*
Ilex 47, 158, 162, 165, 197
Impatiens 18, 91, 197, *197*
    supporting *127*
Indian shot *see Canna*
informal garden style *51*
insecticides see pesticides
insurance 24, 26, 42, 43
Ipomoea 60, 163, 165, 197, *197*
Iris 47, *105*, 165, 198
    propagation 148
iron 99
iron tree 164, *see also Parrotia persica*
ivy *see Hedera*

J, K

Japanese aralia *see Fatsia japonica*
japonica *see Chaenomeles*
Jasminum (jasmine) 161, 166, 167, 198, *198*
Juniperus (juniper) 46, 88, 158, 198
kale, ornamental *see Brassica oleracea*
Katsura tree *see Cercidiphyllum japonicum*
Kerria japonica 148
kiwi fruit 169
Kniphofia 163, 199, *199*
knives 110
kohlrabi 74
Kolomikta vine *see Actinidia*

L

Laburnum 47, 162, 199
lady's mantle *see Alchemilla*
lamb's ears *see Stachys byzantina*
Lamium 160, 162, *162*, 199
lapageria 60
Lathyrus 60, 166, 199
    supports for 128
Laurus nobilis (laurel, sweet bay) 54, 73, *104*, 132, 200
    pests on 153
Lavandula (lavender) 73, 161, 163, 200, *200*
layering 146-7, *146*
    runners 147, *147*
    serpentine 147, *147*
leaf blotch 154
leaf miners 152, *152*
leaf scorch 40
leaf spot 154
learning difficulties, gardeners with 47
leaves 97
lemon *158*, 180
lemon verbena 46
lenten rose *see Helleborus*
lettuce 75
Leucojum 160, 200
Lewisia 115, 200-1

221

Index

light 36, 37, 96
lighting
  artificial 96
  security 43
Ligustrum vulgare 47
Lilium (lily) 93, 161, 201, *201*
  division 149
lily of the valley *see Convallaria majalis*
lilyturf *see Ophiopogon*
lime-hating plants 99
ling *see Calluna*
liquid feeds 118
Lithodora diffusa (*Lithospermum diffusa*) 201
Livingstone daisy *see Dorotheanthus*
Lobelia 16, *18*, 91, 100, 201
log raised beds 80, *81*
Lonicera 60, 132, 161, 162, 165, 202
loosestrife *see Lysimachia*
Lotus berthelottii 90
Lupinus (lupin) 47, 102, 126
Lysimachia 60, 91, 202, *202*

M

macroclimate 38-9
Madonna lily *see Lilium*
magnesium 99
Magnolia 38, 162, 166, 202, *202*
Mahonia 161, 165, 167, 202-3
maidenhair fern *see Adiantum*
Malcomia maritima 35, 46
male fern *see Dryopteris*
mallow *see Hibiscus*
Malus 76, 162, 164, 203
mancozeb 154, 155
manganese 99
manger 85, *123*
maple *see Acer*
marguerite *see Argyranthemum*
marigold 135
marjoram 73, *93*
mealy bugs 171
mesclun 75
mesembryanthemum *see Dorotheanthus*
mesh supports 129
metaldehyde 153
methiocarb 153
Mexican orange blossom *see Choisya*
mezereon *see Daphne*
Michaelmas daisy *see Aster*
microclimate 39
millstone ponds 70
mini-ponds 68-9, 69, 141
mint 73
mirrors 53, *53*
mister 110
mock orange *see Philadelphus*
molybdenum 99
Monarda 203, *203*
moneywort *see Lysimachia*
monkshood 17
Monstera deliciosa 38
morning glory *see Ipomoea*
Moroccan broom 46, *see also Cytisus*
mosaic virus 155

mountain ash *see Sorbus*
Myosotis 54, *87*, 102, 155, 203

N, O

naked ladies *see Colchicum*
Narcissus 86, 105, 160, 204, *204*
  division 149
nasturtium *see Tropaeolum*
Nephrolepis 99
Nerium oleander 47
New Zealand flax *see Phormium*
Nicotiana 35, 46, 93, 161, 204
nigella 87
night-scented stock (Virginian stock) *see Malcomia maritima*
nitrogen 99, 113, 137
Norway spruce *see Picea abies*
nurseries 108
nutrients 99, 137
Oenothera 204-5
offsets 148, 149
oleander *see Nerium oleander*
onion, ornamental 170
Ophiopogon 92, 205
orange 158, 180, *180*
orange ball tree 176
oregano (marjoram) 73, *93*
Oregon grape *see Mahonia*
Origanum vulgare (marjoram) 73, *93*
ornamental onion *see Allium*
ornamental tobacco *see Nicotiana*
ornaments 54
Osteospermum 205, *205*
Oswego tea 203
outbuildings 64
outside rooms 51
overwintering 140
oxygen 96
oxygenating plants 69

P

Paeonia 205, *205*
pansy *see Viola*
paper daisy *see Helichrysum*
paperbark maple 165
Parrotia persica 164, 206, *206*
parsley *see Petroselinum crispum*
Parthenocissus 19, 60, 63, 129, 164, 167, 206
partially sighted gardeners 46
Passiflora (passion flower) 206, *206*
paths 22
patio gardens 28, *28*
  microclimate 39
pea-sticks 129
peach 77
peach leaf curl 77
pear 76
  ornamental 162, 211
  scab 155, *155*
pearl grass *see Briza*
Pelargonium 18, *19*, 91, 206-7
  buying 107
  lemon-scented 46
  propagation 107
  taking cuttings 144
  tying in 127
Penstemon 207
peony *see Paeonia*

pepper 74
perennials 102
  shrubby 104
  supporting 127
pergolas 28, 64, *64*
periwinkle *see Vinca*
Perlite 100, *101*
permethrin 153
Persian ironwood *see Parrotia persica*
perspective 52
pest control 139, 152-3
  chemical 151
  without chemicals 150
pesticides 151
  concentrates 151
  natural 150
  ready-to-use 151
  safe use 151
Petroselinum crispum 73, *93*
Petunia 16, *18*, *19*, 91, 93, 207
Philadelphus 161, 162, 208, *208*
phloem 97
phlox 154
Phormium 208
phosphorus 99, 113, 137
photosynthesis 96
Phyllitis scolopendrium 208
Phytolacca americana 47
Picea 158, 208-9, *208*
Pieris 79, 99, 209
pill bugs 153, *153*
pillars 64
pinching out 135
pine *see Pinus*
pink *see Dianthus*
Pinus 158, 209, *209*
pirimicarb 152
pirimiphos-methyl 152, 153
planning 48-93
plant pots 120, 141
  plastic 24
plant trolley 119
plantain lily *see Hosta*
planting 114-15
  among bricks *114-15*
  in containers *116*
planting plans 86-93
plants
  bare-root 108, *108*
  buying 109
  buying in 107
  categories of 102-5
  container-grown 109
  growth 96-101
  healthy 109, *109*, 150-1
  mail-order 107, 108
  parts of 97
  plug plants 107, *107*
  raising 106-7
  ready-to-use 107
  root-balled 108
  unhealthy *109*
plastic tube pots *124*, 125
Pleioblastus see Arundinaria
plug plants 107, 107
plum 76, 77
poisonous plants 47
pokeweed *see Phytolacca americana*
polyanthus 54, 154, 210, *see also Primula*
Polygonum baldschuanicum 64

ponds 13, 67-8, *67*
  raised 68
  sunken 68-9
  in winter 141, *141*
porches 22, 64
Portugal laurel *see Prunus*
potager 72, *72*
potassium 99, 113, 137
potato 74, 155
Potentilla 209, *209*
potting bench 45
potting on 121, 138, *138*
powdery mildew 155, *155*, 174, 203
primrose *see Primula*
Primula 87, 160, 210
privet *see Ligustrum vulgare*
productive garden 51, 72-7
propagation 107, 142-9
propagator 142-3
propiconazole 155
pruning 131, *131*, 134-5, *135*
  climbers 62
  hard *134*
  rules *134*
Prunus 47, 72, 77, 158, 160, 162, 164, 165, 210
  fan-trained 131, *131*
pulleys 18
PVC pond liners 67-8
Pyracantha 54, 60, 162, 164, 165, 210-11, *210*
pyrethrins 152
Pyrus salicifolia 162, 211

Q, R

quaking grass *see Briza*
quarter-standard plants 132
radish 75
raised beds 27, 44, 45, 72, 78-81, *78*
rake 110
red currant 77
red hot poker *see Kniphofia*
red spider mites 152-3, *152*, 176, 182, 193, 209
repotting 139, *139*
respiration 96
rhizomes 105, 148
Rhododendron 79, *81*, 99, 113, 211, *211*
  layering *146*
Robinia 162, 212
rock gardens 59
rock plants 58
rock rose *see Cistus*
roof gardens 26-7, *26*, *27*, 62
  climbing plants on 63
  microclimate 39
rooting powder/gel 144
roots 97, 100
rootstock 76
Rosa 161, 164, 166, 212, *212*
  blackspot 154
  standard 132
rose of Sharon *see Hypericum calycinum*
Rosmarinus officinalis (rosemary) 73, 163, 212-13, *213*
rowan *see Sorbus*
Rudbeckia 'Toto' 91
rue 46
runner beans 60, 75

Index

supports *128*
runners, layering 147, *147*
Russian vine 64
rust 155, *155*

S

safety 44
sage *see Salvia officinalis*
St John's wort *see Hypericum*
salad mixture 75
salad onions 75
Salix 158, 162, 165, 213
    standard 132
Salvia 46, 73, *93*, 163, *163*, 213, *213*
Sambucus 214
Satureja hortensis (summer savory) *93*
sawflies 153, *153*
Saxifraga (saxifrage) 212, 214, *214*
    layering *147*
scab 155, *155*, 203
Scaevola 214
scale insects 153, *153*, 200
scent 34-5, 46, 62, 93
scented plants 161
Scilla 215
scree compost 58
scree gardens 58-9
screen houses 32
screening 13, 35
sculpture 54
seasonal interest 35
secateurs 110
Sedum 89, 163, 215, *215*
seed sticks 106
seed tapes 106
seedlings 107, *107*, 108
seeds 142-3
    fine *142*
    large *143*
    mail-order 106
    pelleted 106
    saving 106
    sowing 106, *142-3*
seep-hose 40
Sempervivum 89, 163, 215
    offsets *149*
Senecio 163, 215, *215*
shade 96
    climbers in 60
    conservatories 32
    container planting 89
    density 36-7
    plants tolerant of 162
shade houses 32
shared gardens *30*
shoots 97
shrubs 104
silk tassel bush *see Garrya elliptica*
silver beet 75
silver fir *see Abies*
skimmia 38, *86*
slugs 153, *153*, 177, 178, 194
smoke bush/tree *see Cotinus coggygria*
snails 153, *153*, 177, 178, 194
snow gum 189
snowdrop *see Galanthus*
snowflake *see Leucojum*
soil 100
    acid/alkaline 113
    chemical content 113
    clay 112-13, *112*
    pH *112-13*
    sandy 112-13, *113*
    testing 112-13
sooty mould 200
Sorbus 164, 216
sound 46, 47
southernwood *see Artemisia*
sowbread *see Cyclamen*
space, creating illusion of 52-3
special needs gardening 44-7
spindle bush *see Euonymus*
split canes 128
spotted laurel *see Aucuba*
sprayer 110
sprinklers 40
spruce *see Picea*
spurge *see Euphorbia*
squill *see Scilla*
Stachys byzantina 34, 46
stakes 129
staking 126, *126*, 139
stamens 97
standard plants 126, 132, *132-3*
Star-of-the-Veldt *see Dimorphotheca*
statues 54
stem 97
stepovers *131*
steps 22, *22*, *50*
stigma *97*
stone
    raised beds 80-1
    reconstituted *83*
stonecrop *see Sedum*
stopping 135
storage 52
strawberry 38, 77
    layering 147
strawflower *see Helichrysum*
strelitzia 32
style, unity of 53
subshrubs 104
subsidence 40
suckers 148
sulphur 99, 155
summer savory *see Satureja hortensis*
sun-loving plants 89, 163
sun traps 37
supports 110, 126-9, 139
sweet bay *see Laurus nobilis*
sweet pea *see Lathyrus*
Swiss cheese plant *see Monstera deliciosa*

T

Taxus baccata 47, 104, 158, 216, *216*
    topiary 132
temperature 99
    optimal 38-9
tender plants 38-9
terracotta pots *82-3*, 141
theft 42-3
thiophanate methyl 154
thrift *see Armeria*
Thuja occidentalis 104
Thunbergia alata 60
Thymus 73, *93*, 160, 216, *216*
tiger lily *see Lilium*
time 34
tomato 74, *74*
tools 110
    adaptations 44, 46
topdressing 121, 139, *139*
topiary 132, *132*, 133
topsoil 79
torch lily *see Kniphofia*
tower pots *124*, 125
trace elements 99
Trachycarpus 217
trailing plants 60-4
training plants 130-3
transpiration 98
tree ties 129
trees 104
    for containers 158
    staking 129
trellis *27*, 42, 43, 52, 129
    fixing to walls 129
triforine 155
tripods 64
trompe l'oeil 53, *53*
Tropaeolum 60
troughs 16, 18, *19*, *84*, *91*, 93, 120
    alpine *119*, *120-1*
trowel 110
trumpet vine *see Campsis*
tubers 105, 148, *149*
tubs *84*, 120
tufa rock garden *59*
Tulipa (tulip) *87*, 105, 160, 217, *217*
two-spotted mite *see* red spider mite
tying in 127
Typha minima 69

U, V

urban situations 42-3
vandalism 43
variegated plants 96
vascular bundles 97
vegetables *13*, *15*, *72*, 74-5
ventilation in conservatories 32
veronica *see Hebe*
vertical gardening 60-4
Viburnum 162, 165, *165*, 217, *217*
Vinca 89, 160, 162, 218, *218*
vine *see Vitis*
vine weevil 153, *153*
Viola 54, 100, 154, 160, 218, *218*
    layering 147
violet *see Viola*
Virginia creeper *see Parthenocissus*
Virginian stock *see Malcomia maritima*
virus diseases 155, *155*
Vitis (vine) 42, 77, 164, 218

W

walkways 20, *20*
wall anchor *19*
wall plants 60
wall pots 16, 18, *84*
wallflower *see Erysimum*
walls 20
    fixing to *19*
    fixing trellis to *129*
    fixing wires to *128*
    growing up 62-3
    planting against 114
    planting in 63
warmth 99
water 98
    supply 40
water gardens and features 46, 47, 67-71
    in winter 141
waterlily 69, 141
water pumps 70
water-retaining granules *40*
waterfalls 70
watering 40, 136-7, *137*
    containers 119
    special needs gardening 46
watering can 40, 110
weeding 139
weedkiller 139, *139*
Weigela 219
weight
    on balconies 24
    distribution on roof gardens 27
wheelchair gardening 44, 78
white cedar 104
white currant 77
whitefly 175, 176, 195
wildlife 15
willow *see Salix*
wilting 98
wind chimes 47
wind-rock 126
windbreaks on roof gardens 27
windflower *see Anemone*
windmill palm *see Trachycarpus*
window boxes 16, 18-19, *85*, 120
    fixing 121-2
    preparation 122
    safety 121-2
winter aconite *see Eranthis*
winter care and protection 140-1, *140*, *141*
winter interest 165
winter iris *see Iris unguicularis*
wintersweet *see Chimonanthus praecox*
witchhazel *see Hamamelis*
woodlice 153, *153*
wormwood *see Artemisia*

X, Y, Z

xylem 97, *97*, 98
yards 31
    microclimate 39
yarrow *see Achillea*
year-round interest 54, 165
yew *see Taxus*
Yucca 46, 54, 163, 219, *219*
Zantedeschia 15, 219
zinc 99
zinnia *102*
zucchini 75

Acknowledgements

Picture credits

t = top; b = bottom; l = left; c = centre; r = right

2 Clive Nichols, 5t Steven Wooster/The Garden Picture Library, 5b Photos Horticultural, 6t Friedrich Strauss/The Garden Picture Library, 6b Elizabeth Whiting & Associates, 6-7t Garden Matters, 6-7b Harry Smith Collection; 8t Jerry Harpur, 8b Elizabeth Whiting & Associates; 10 Lynne Brotchie/The Garden Picture Library, 10-11 Friedrich Strauss/The Garden Picture Library; 12l Niall McDiarmid/Robert Harding Syndication, 12r Clive Nichols/Designer: Jill Billington; 13 Amateur Gardening/Your Garden; 14 Elizabeth Whiting & Associates; 15 Ron Sutherland/The Garden Picture Library; 16 John Glover/The Garden Picture Library; 17 Lynne Brotchie/The Garden Picture Library; 18t & c Chas Wilder, 18b Amateur Gardening/Your Garden; 19l Chas Wilder, 19r Garden Matters; 20 Garden Matters; 21 Steven Wooster/The Garden Picture Library; 22 Garden Matters; 23 Jerry Harpur; 24t Linda Burgess/The Garden Picture Library, 24b Chas Wilder; 25 Ron Sutherland/The Garden Picture Library; 26t Elizabeth Whiting & Associates, 26b Clive Nichols/Designer: Victor Shanley; 27 Clive Nichols/Designer: Randle Siddeley; 28t John Glover/The Garden Picture Library, 28b Elizabeth Whiting & Associates; 29t Ron Sutherland/The Garden Picture Library, 29b Garden Matters; 30-31 Elizabeth Whiting & Associates; 32 Spike Powell; 33 Elizabeth Whiting & Associates; 34l Andrew Sydenham, 34r Peter McHoy; 35t Elizabeth Whiting & Associates, 35b Harry Smith Collection; 36-37 Elizabeth Whiting & Associates; 38t Photos Horticultural, 38b Elizabeth Whiting & Associates, 38-39 Elizabeth Whiting & Associates, 39 Andrew Lawson; 40 Chas Wilder; 41 Amateur Gardening/Your Garden; 42t Simon Butcher/Houses & Interiors, 42b Clive Nichols; 43 Jerry Harpur; 44 Amateur Gardening/Your Garden; 45 Help the Aged/Designer: Andrea Parsons; 46t Amateur Gardening/Your Garden, 46b Chas Wilder; 47t Tim Shepherd/Oxford Scientific Films, 47b Harry Smith Collection; 48 Chas Wilder, 48-49 Garden Matters; 50 Elizabeth Whiting & Associates; 51t Jerry Harpur, 51b Clive Nichols/Designer: Louise Hampden; 52tl Clive Nichols/Designer: Sue Guerney, 52tr Andrew Lawson, courtesy: Mirabel Oster, 52b & 53 Harry Smith Collection; 54 Chas Wilder; 55 Harry Smith Collection; 56 Clive Nichols/Mrs Dymock; 57t Clive Nichols, 57b Jane Legate/The Garden Picture Library; 58 Chas Wilder, 58-59 Chas Wilder, 59 Garden Matters; 60 Andrew Lawson; 61 Steven Wooster/The Garden Picture Library; 62-65 Elizabeth Whiting & Associates; 66 Photos Horticultural; 67 & 68t Harry Smith Collection, 68b & 69 Chas Wilder; 70 Zooid Pictures/Garden Matters; 71 Clive Nichols/Designer: Mrs Preston; 72 Amateur Gardening/Your Garden; 73 Chas Wilder, 73tr Clive Nichols; 74 Chas Wilder; 75tl Harry Smith Collection, 75tr & b Chas Wilder; 76l Ken Muir, 76r & 77 Chas Wilder; 78 Amateur Gardening/Your Garden, 78-79 Elizabeth Whiting & Associates; 80 Chas Wilder; 81t Clive Nichols/Home Farm Trust-Chelsea 94, 81b-85 Chas Wilder; 86l Clive Nichols/Designer: C. Cordy, 86r Andrew Lawson, 86-87 Andrew Lawson, 87 Harry Smith Collection; 94 Chas Wilder; 94-95 Elizabeth Whiting & Associates; 96 Chas Wilder; 99 Charles Krebs/Tony Stone Images; 100tl & tr Chas Wilder, 100bl Garden Matters, 100br Harry Smith Collection; 101t Peter McHoy, 101c Chas Wilder, 101bl & cb Garden Matters, 101br Chas Matters, 101br Chas Wilder; 102tl Garden Matters, 102bl & r A-Z Botanical Collection; 103 A-Z Botanical Collection; 104t Harry Smith Collection, 104b Garden Matters; 105tl Harry Smith Collection; 105tr Peter McHoy, 105bl A-Z Botanical Collection, 105br Martin P. Land/Garden Matters; 106-108t Chas Wilder, 108b Photos Horticultural; 110-114 Chas Wilder; 115t Harry Smith Collection, 115b Chas Wilder; 117 Clive Nichols/Daniel Pearson, Chelsea 93; 118 Clive Nichols/Designer: Claus Scheinert; 119t Clive Nichols/Designer: Anthony Noel, 119b Clive Nichols/Designer: Anne Dexter; 120-122 Chas Wilder; 123t Elizabeth Whiting & Associates, 123b Chas Wilder; 124-139 Chas Wilder; 140 Clive Nichols/Designer: Anthony Noel; 156 Chas Wilder, 156-157 Harry Smith Collection; 158l A-Z Botanical Collection, 158r Harry Smith Collection; 159 Bjorn Svensson/A-Z Botanical Collection; 160l Bjorn Svensson/A-Z Botanical Collection, 160r Harry Smith Collection; 161t & bl Garden Matters; 161br-163l Harry Smith Collection; 163r Garden Matters; 164 Garden Matters; 165t Harry Smith Collection; 165b Geoff Kidd/A-Z Botanical Collection; 166l David Henderson/A-Z Botanical Collection, 166r & 167 Harry Smith Collection; 168 Geoff Kidd/A-Z Botanical Collection; 169t Harry Smith Collection, 169 Sandra Ireland/Houses & Interiors; 170 & 171l Harry Smith Collection, 171r A-Z Botanical Collection; 172t Harry Smith Collection, 172b Steffie Shields/Garden Matters; 173t Geoff Kidd/A-Z Botanical Collection, 173b Geoff Kidd/A-Z Botanical Collection; 174 Garden Matters; 174-175 Garden Matters, 175 Chas Wilder; 176 Harry Smith Collection; 177t Garden Matters, 177b Harry Smith Collection; 178l Geoff Kidd/A-Z Botanical Collection, 178r Garden Matters; 179l Harry Smith Collection, 179r Terence Exley/A-Z Botanical Collection; 180t Steffie Shields/Garden Matters, 180b Bjorn Svensson/A-Z Botanical Collection; 181-182 Harry Smith Collection; 183 A-Z Botanical Collection; 184 Harry Smith Collection; 185l Garden Matters, 185r M.P. Land/A-Z Botanical Collection; 186 Jeremy Hoare/Garden Matters; 187l Terence Exley/A-Z Botanical Collection, 187r Sheila Orme/A-Z Botanical Collection; 188 Harry Smith Collection; 189l Garden Matters, 189r Harry Smith Collection; 190 Harry Smith Collection; 191l Sheila Orme/A-Z Botanical Collection, 191r Garden Matters; 192-193 Harry Smith Collection; 194 A-Z Botanical Collection; 195 Garden Matters; 196 Harry Smith Collection; 197t Garden Matters, 197b A-Z Botanical Collection; 198 Harry Smith Collection; 199 Garden Matters; 200 Geoff Kidd/A-Z Botanical Collection; 201l Harry Smith Collection, 201r J. Brunsden Rapkins/A-Z Botanical Collection; 202l Geoff Kidd/A-Z Botanical Collection, 202r & 203 Garden Matters; 204 Harry Smith Collection; 205l Harry Smith Collection, 205r A-Z Botanical Collection; 206t Garden Matters, 206bl Harry Smith Collection, 206br Garden Matters; 207 Harry Smith Collection; 208l Michael R. Chandler/A-Z Botanical Collection, 208r Harry Smith Collection; 209l Adrian Thomas/A-Z Botanical Collection, 209r Harry Smith Collection; 210 Geoff Kidd/A-Z Botanical Collection; 211 Martin P. Land/Garden Matters; 212 Steffie Shields/Garden Matters; 213l Geoff Kidd/A-Z Botanical Collection, 213r Anthony Cooper/A-Z Botanical Collection; 214-218l Harry Smith Collection, 218r Garden Matters; 219 David Henderson/A-Z Botanical Collection

If the publishers have unwittingly infringed copyright in any illustration reproduced, they will pay an appropriate fee on being satisfied of the owner's title.